Bombardier John Harris

AND THE
RIVERS OF THE
REVOLUTION

William W. Betts, Jr.

HERITAGE BOOKS
2007

HERITAGE BOOKS
AN IMPRINT OF HERITAGE BOOKS, INC.

Books, CDs, and more—Worldwide

For our listing of thousands of titles see our website
at
www.HeritageBooks.com

Published 2007 by
HERITAGE BOOKS, INC.
Publishing Division
65 East Main Street
Westminster, Maryland 21157-5026

Copyright © 2006 William W. Betts, Jr.

All rights reserved. No part of this book may be reproduced or transmitted in any form or by any means, electronic or mechanical, including photocopying, recording or by any information storage and retrieval system without written permission from the author, except for the inclusion of brief quotations in a review.

International Standard Book Number: 978-0-7884-3379-5

For
Maddie, Stephie, and Will,
and for all of those
whose sacrifices
gave birth to the nation

CONTENTS

A Prefatory Note ix

A Word about the Rivers of the Revolution xi

Acknowledgments xv

Order of Events xvii

Chapter I: The St. Lawrence 1

Chapter II: The Hudson 23

Chapter III: The Brandywine 35

Chapter IV: The Schuylkill 87

Chapter V: The Passaic 115

Chapter VI: The Susquehanna 139

Chapter VII: The Ohio 207

Chapter VIII: The Delaware 277

Appendix A: The Truth about Molly Pitcher 321

Appendix B: Lafayette Returns 327

Image Credits 333

Works Consulted 337

Notes 349

Index 385

A Prefatory Note

This is the story of John Harris, a Salem, New Jersey, farmer who devoted eight years of his early life to the cause of the American Revolution. He served throughout the entire war (except for four months of sickness), participating in six major battles, countless "skirmishes," two river expeditions, and the recovery of Philadelphia.

He served under Generals George Washington, John Sullivan, George Rogers Clark, Henry Knox, and William Irvine, as well as Colonel Thomas Proctor, Colonel Daniel Brodhead, and Major Isaac Craig. And he enjoyed associations with such prominent Revolutionary War figures as the Marquis de Lafayette, Baron von Steuben, Anthony Wayne, Baron Johann De Kalb, Nathanael Greene, and Alexander Hamilton. Thus his story becomes a chronicle of the American Revolution and testifies dramatically to the inspired devotion and willing sacrifice that characterized the patriot.

The War of the Revolution was a long war, a very long war. Its duration was more than twice that of the tragically long War Between the States, and more than twice also that of the United States' involvement in World War II. From its beginning, with "the shot heard round the world" until the signing of the Treaty of Paris, the war lasted eight and one-half years. It was a war for independence; it was fought by a small band of ill-equipped volunteer tradesmen and farmers against the powerful British Empire and its army of professional soldiers. It was a war fought by boys against men, for during most of the rebellion the average age of the Continental Army soldiers was nineteen, and the militia forces were surely younger still. It was

A Prefatory Note

not a universally popular war, for at least one in every five of the two and one-half million people living in the thirteen English colonies remained loyal to the Crown, and many of these were vigorously active in their opposition to the rebellion.

Surely very few of the 260,000,000 Americans who live today as citizens of the fifty states are equipped by history to measure the sacrifice that was paid for the freedoms they presently enjoy. Possibly not one can appreciate *fully* the quality of life that was gained for him or for her. Most appropriate for the Revolution are the stirring words of Winston Churchill, who was saluting the Royal Air Force in its heroic defense of England during the darkest hours of World War II, "Never in the field of human conflict was so much owed by so many to so few."

It isn't only that the British surrender at Yorktown gave birth to a new nation. What is most important is that the War of Revolution brought forth upon this continent an entirely new way of life, governed by a spirited reverence for freedom, which was guaranteed by a production of documents so revolutionary in their principles that their acceptance by the people must have seemed a miracle to the Old World.

Now, more than two centuries removed from the Treaty of Paris which brought an official end to the War, we may experience great difficulty in bringing the Revolution to life. A torrent of recent books, like Jeff Shaara's *Rise to Rebellion* and *The Glorious Cause*, Allan Eckert's *That Dark and Bloody River*, David Hackett Fischer's *Paul Revere's Ride* and *Washington's Crossing*, and David McCullough's *1776,* and biographies of our founding fathers John Adams, Thomas Jefferson, Alexander Hamilton, Benjamin Franklin, and His Excellency George Washington, as well as films like *The Patriot,* have doubtless helped a lot. To read of the life of one who served the cause of the Revolution as a soldier for almost the entire eight and one-half years of the war can be a big help too. Here follows, in all of its available details, the exciting, and typical, life of a Revolutionary War soldier, bombardier John Harris, of Salem, New Jersey.

A Word about the Rivers of the Revolution

In very large measure the War of the Revolution was fought on the rivers and lesser waterways of the British colonies. It was fought on the St. Lawrence, home to the firmly British strongholds of Montreal and Quebec; it was fought on the East River of New York, and on the Hudson, which featured Fort Washington and Fort Lee. It was fought on the Mohawk, on the Susquehanna, and on those twin rivers of New Jersey, the Raritan and the Passaic; it was fought on the Allegheny, on the Chemung, on the James and York Rivers of Virginia, on the Brandywine, on the Schuylkill, the Delaware, the Monongahela, the Ohio, and some forty streams of Pennsylvania's Northumberland County and neighboring counties.

The two principal wintertime encampments for the Continental Army were established on the Passaic River in New Jersey and on the Schuylkill in Pennsylvania.

The most strategic of the frontier forts were built upon the rivers: Forts Henry and Nelson and McIntosh on the Ohio; Fort Armstrong on the Allegheny; Fort Freeland on Warrior's Run and the West Branch of the Susquehanna; Fort Wintermoot and Forty Fort on the North Branch of the Susquehanna; Fort Cumberland at the junction of Wills Creek and the Potomac; Fort Island (Mud Island) and Billingsport Fort on the Delaware River; Fort Stanwix on the Mohawk. From these forts, and from a number of others so situated, garrisoned forces would mount their assaults or stage their defense of the settlers. The rivers provided routes for large expeditions and for small war parties, and a means of defense and refuge as well.

The Indian trails, which for hundreds of years had followed the rivers and streams closely, made for a convenient network of passages through the river valleys. These of course became the fur-trade routes for the early settlers, and served as pathways for settlement itself.

And when the war came, these Indian trails and the waterways became extremely strategic, just as they had for the French and Indian Wars earlier and the age-old tribal conflicts. And when the war ended it was most fitting that Pennsylvania, which had come to terms with her fierce adversary the Seneca war-chief Cornplanter, would provide a home for him and his people on the Allegheny; and it was fitting too that Mother England would accommodate her most powerful Indian ally, the Iroquois leader Joseph Brant with a vast grant of land on the Grand River in Ontario for his Mohawk warriors and their families.

And throughout the long war, any farm boy or tradesman who signed up for much service as a soldier in the ranks of the Continental Army could expect to find himself for a substantial amount of that time on a river somewhere.

John Harris was a farm boy. He was born on the Delaware River. Through the glad days of his happy South Jersey boyhood he delighted in the big river, and in the lesser Salem River (called a "crick"), and in Alloway's Creek and in Stowe Creek. He grew up with the muskrats and the blue heron, with the turtles and the terns. But, like so many, he had this happy life of the farmer and the excitements of his childhood abruptly terminated by Lexington and Concord.

John Harris was to serve the cause of the Revolution for virtually the entire war. For most of that time he found himself actually on a river, or very close. He was ten months on the Schuylkill, with Valley Forge and the subsequent restoration of Philadelphia; he was six months on the North Branch of the Susquehanna, marching all the way from Easton, Pennsylvania, to the river and up the river into New York State and almost to Lake Ontario. And back again. In the spring and summer of 1780, with fifty fellow artillerymen, he marched west along the Potomac through Maryland to Fort Pitt. He was for three and one-half years, during some of the most trying times of the Revolution, stationed at Fort Pitt, which presided over the junction of the Monongahela and Allegheny Rivers to form the great river that the Indians called "the beautiful river" and the settlers called "that dark and bloody river."

Bombardier John Harris was during the long war of the Revolution engaged in some of the most intense and fierce fighting–at Long Island, at White Plains, at the Brandywine, at Germantown. And he survived the miseries of Valley Forge and Morristown. But of all his wartime experiences, he considered the most arduous, the most exhausting, the most nervous, to be the disastrous and fruitless expedition of George Rogers Clark down the Ohio River from Fort Pitt past Wheeling and Cincinnati to the Great Falls at Louisville. And back upriver.

And when the war was ended, John Harris was "promptly" discharged from the Continental Army. The news that the *final* version of the Treaty had been signed in Paris required twenty-seven days to make its way across the Atlantic and out to Fort Pitt. But when he finally held in his hand the certificate of discharge, adorned by the signature of Brigadier General William Irvine, Harris declared to his friend and constant companion Samuel Blackwood that he was going straight home to "my river." And so he did. The river was the Delaware of course, and for the broad water that he knew so well his love had grown only stronger. He bought one island, then another. And these islands he farmed (in his fashion), and on them he cared tenderly for his wife and brought up his children. And here still–after eight long years–he found the muskrats and the great blue heron.

Acknowledgments

John and his wife Lydia Smith Harris had eleven children; their grandchildren numbered twenty; their great-grandchildren numbered fifty-one. Besides, together they could claim seventy-six nieces and nephews. Today those who can count themselves descendants of this marriage are legion. Happily, many are sufficiently interested in their ancestry as to make connections; and, most fortunately, not a few of the John Harris family have worked very hard to preserve letters and diaries and journals and family bibles and all kinds of documents and heirlooms in which the history is written. This little book is what it is only because of the dedication to family that from a time long before the Revolution has inspired such of its members as Benjamin Harris, of Salem, New Jersey; Harrison Smith Morris and Mabel Jackson Ohl of Germantown, Pennsylvania; Amos Harris and his daughter Catherine ("Kate") of Salem, New Jersey; Robert Butcher and his cousins William B. Vanneman and Mildred Ogbin, also of Salem; Lois Seeligsohn of Collingswood, New Jersey, of the Blackwood family; Jane Buckley Jackson, of Indiana, Pennsylvania; and Marjorie Hoopes Mitchell and U. S. Army Colonel John Mitchell of Cataula, Georgia. For graphics and formatting the book owes much to Thomas Betts, the great, great, great, great, great grandson of John Harris.

Grateful appreciation is also here expressed for the generous and vigorous research help provided by Librarian Alice Boggs and the Salem (N.J.) Historical Society, by Librarian David Smith and the

Acknowledgments

Cumberland County Historical Society; by Ms. Michele Corcoran, Head of Inter-Library Services at the Stapleton Library of Indiana University of Pennsylvania; by Phillip Zorich, Head of the Pennsylvania Collection at Indiana University of Pennsylvania; and by the indefatigable James Gerencser, archivist at Dickinson College in Carlisle, Pa. The U. S. Army Military History Institute of the Carlisle Army Barracks in Carlisle, Pa., has been very helpful; and so too have been battlefield tour guide Westley Butler Davis of Downingtown, Pa., and Wayne Bodle, Professor of History at Indiana University of Pennsylvania, and Donna Bluemink, who was born and raised in Bucks County, Pennsylvania, and is a devoted descendant of Colonel Thomas Proctor, who for seven years headed up John Harris's artillery regiment. And to my *very* helpful editor at Heritage Books, Debbie Riley. And of course to all of the dedicated historians whose research and writings have preserved the record of the War for Independence and have made vivid the story of the birth of the nation an incalculable debt is acknowledged.

Order of Events

September 10, 1753	Birth of John Harris
February 8 or 9, 1764	Birth of Lydia Lucette Smith
March 22, 1765	The Stamp Act
June 29, 1767	The Townshend Acts
March 5, 1770	The Boston Massacre on King Street
December 16, 1773	The Boston Tea Party
March 7, 1774	Boston Tea Party # 2
September 5 - October 26, 1774	The First Continental Congress
October 10, 1774	Battle of Point Pleasant, Virginia
April 19, 1775	Battles of Lexington and Concord
May 10, 1775	Capture of Fort Ticonderoga (Ethan Allen and Benedict Arnold)
May 10, 1775	Second Continental Congress declares war on Great Britain
June 15, 1775	Washington named Commander-in-Chief of the Continental Army
June 17, 1775	Battle of Bunker Hill (fought in part on Breed's Hill)
July 3, 1775	Washington assumes command of the Continental Army in Cambridge, Massachusetts
October 1, 1775 - March 17, 1776	Siege of Boston
October 27, 1775	Thomas Proctor appointed Captain of Artillery (Pa.)
November 13, 1775	Richard Montgomery captures Montreal
December 30 - 31, 1775	Americans defeated at Quebec City. Death of Montgomery; Benedict Arnold wounded

Order of Events

March 17, 1776	British under General William Howe forced from Boston
May 17 - 19, 1776	"Battle" of The Cedars, Quebec
June 7 - 8, 1776	Battle of Three Rivers, Quebec. British capture General William Thompson and Colonel William Irvine
June 7, 1776	Richard Henry Lee calls for a resolution of independence
July 4, 1776	Declaration of Independence adopted
August 2, 1776	Declaration of Independence signed
August 27 - 30, 1776	Battle of Long Island (Brooklyn)
September 16, 1776	Battle of Harlem Heights
October 26 - 28, 1776	Battle of White Plains, N. Y.
November 16, 1776	Fall of Fort Washington
November 20, 1776	Fall of Fort Lee
December 26, 1776	Battle of Trenton
January 3, 1777	Battle of Princeton (death of General Hugh Mercer)
January 6 - May 28, 1777	Continental Army at Morristown, N. J.
March 1, 1777	Samuel Blackwood of Salem, N. J., enlists in the Continental Army
April 10, 1777	John Harris of Salem, N. J., enlists in the Continental Army
April 13, 1777	Battle of Bound Brook, N. J.
June 14, 1777	"Betsy Ross" flag adopted
July 5, 1777	British re-capture Fort Ticonderoga
July, 1777	Indian Council at Oswego. Iroquois ally with the British

Order of Events

August 6, 1777	General Nicholas Herkimer defeated by British and their Indian allies at Oriskany, N. Y.
August 22, 1777	General John Sullivan assaults Staten Island
September 11, 1777	Battle of the Brandywine (Lafayette wounded)
September 20-21, 1777	The Paoli Massacre
September 26, 1777	British begin occupation of Philadelphia
October 4, 1777	Battle of Germantown (death of General Francis Nash)
October 7, 1777	Battle of Bemis Heights (Arnold wounded–again)
October 17, 1777	General Burgoyne surrenders to General Gates at Saratoga, N. Y.
December 4-8, 1777	Battle of Whitemarsh, Pa.
December 19, 1777 - June 19, 1778	Valley Forge winter encampment
February 6, 1778	The French Alliance
March 7, 1778	General William Howe recalled to England, replaced by Sir Henry Clinton in Philadelphia
March 15, 1778	The British, under Colonel Mawhood invade Salem County, New Jersey
March 17, 1778	Battle of Quinton's Bridge
March 21, 1778	Massacre at the Hancock House, Salem, N. J.
May 1, 1778	Battle of Crooked Billet, Pa.
June 18, 1778	Clinton evacuates Philadelphia
June 28, 1778	Battle of Monmouth
July 1, 1778	Massacre at Wyoming, Pa.
September 27, 1778	Massacre at Tappan
November 11, 1778	Massacre at Cherry Valley, N. Y.

Order of Events

December 29, 1778	British capture and occupy Savannah, Georgia
July 15 - 16, 1779	General Anthony Wayne seizes Stony Point, N. Y.
July 29, 1779	Battle of Fort Freeland
July 31 - October 7, 1779	General John Sullivan Campaign against the Iroquois
August 11 - September 14, 1779	Colonel Daniel Brodhead Expedition against the Iroquois
August 28, 1779	Sullivan routs Indians and British at Newtown
April 7, 1780	Battle of Coshocton
May 12, 1780	British capture Charleston, S.C.
May 23 - June 25, 1780	Isaac Craig artillery company marches from Carlisle, Pa., to Fort Pitt
July 11, 1780	French troops arrive at Newport, R. I.
August 2, 1780	Indian-British Schoharie Expedition, N. Y.
August 16, 1780	Battle of Camden, S. C. Death of Major General Johann De Kalb (August 19)
September 25, 1780	Benedict Arnold's treasonous plot discovered
October 14, 1780	Nathanael Greene named Commander, Southern Army
January, 1781	Mutiny staged by 1300 soldiers of the Pennsylvania Line
March 2, 1781	Articles of Confederation adopted
May 15, 1781	Battle of Guilford Courthouse, N. C.
July 29 - November 26, 1781	George Rogers Clark Ohio River anti-Indian Expedition, Fort Pitt to the Great Falls (Louisville)
October 19, 1781	Cornwallis surrenders to Washington at Yorktown
March 6 - 8, 1782	Gnadenhuetten massacre of the Moravian Indians

Order of Events

May 25, 1782	Sandusky Expedition against the Ohio Indians, led by Colonel William Crawford
June 6, 1782	Torture death of Colonel William Crawford
July 13, 1782	The burning of Hannastown, Pa.
November 30, 1782	British sign Articles of Peace
April 19, 1783	Congress ratifies preliminary peace treaty
August 19, 1783	The Battle of Blue Licks
September 3, 1783	The Treaty of Paris
September 30, 1783	Bombardier John Harris and Sergeant Samuel Blackwood discharged from the Continental Army at Fort Pitt
November 25, 1783	British troops leave New York City
December 23, 1783	Washington resigns as Commander-in-Chief
January 12, 1785	John Harris marries Lydia Smith
April 14, 1789	Washington, reluctantly, accepts Presidency
October 20 - 22, 1790	General Josiah Harmar defeated by the Miami war-chief Little Turtle and the Ohio Indians in the Maumee Valley
November 4, 1791	General Arthur St. Clair defeated by Little Turtle on the Wabash River
August 20, 1794	Anthony Wayne defeats the Shawnee war-chief Blue Jacket and the Ohio Indians at Fallen Timbers
August 3, 1795	Treaty of Greenville (Anthony Wayne)
September 17, 1796	Washington's Farewell Address (not delivered orally, first printed September 19)
December 14, 1799	Death of George Washington ("the debt which we all must pay")
November 24, 1802	Death of Mohawk war-chief Joseph Brant

Order of Events

March 29, 1814 — Death of Bombardier John Harris

August, 1824 - October, 1825 — Lafayette tours the United States

February 18, 1836 — Death of the Seneca war-chief Cornplanter

I

THE ST. LAWRENCE

By the rude bridge that arched the flood,
Their flag to April's breeze unfurled;
Here once the embattled farmers stood;
And fired the shot heard round the world.

— **Ralph Waldo Emerson**

It was already well into April, and the vibrant green and the gold of the always welcome spring were everywhere. It had been a warm and gentle spring, and farmers were well into their plowing. The rich brown of the turned soil lay glistening in the morning sun, and the plover raced along the furrows. Young John Harris, who had been mending fences in the lower pasture, was just coming in from the fields when his sister Sophia came running toward him with stunning news from two far away villages of New England.

Her given name was Zerviah, and they called her Sophia. She was a very pretty girl, and was impelled by a vitality that was foreign to her brothers. She was now in her thirteenth year. She was very fond of all of her brothers, but she was closest to John. She doted on John. "What does it all mean?" she asked.

"Well, Sophie, it's bad. I think it means war, war with King George. We've lost some of our people, you see. There's trouble ahead."

"What'll you do, John?"

"Oh, don't fret about it, Sophie. Plenty time to figure on it. We'll see."

Though he was still a very young man, he had promptly understood from her excited and somewhat garbled report exactly what the affair at Lexington and Concord surely meant. He knew that the war, so long expected, had finally begun. In the village of Salem, New Jersey, as well as in the larger cities of Philadelphia and Boston and New York, for many weeks now, young men and middle-aged had been getting ready for what they knew was coming. Talk of militia was everywhere and plans to form additional units had been drawn up in Delaware, New Jersey, Maryland, and Pennsylvania, and young men were readying themselves for drill and for the military discipline that was so foreign to the farm or the mill.

John wondered about his five brothers. He wondered how they would react to the eruption that had occurred so dramatically north of Boston. For himself he was decided. He knew that it would take him some time, but he meant to be in the action just as soon as he could manage it. As Sophie disappeared into the house, he turned to his chores. He prayed for the warming sun. It had been, so far, a very good spring, but today he felt a chill in the air. As he strode toward the ramshackle shed, there was a spring in his step, but he felt just the suggestion of a chill in the air.

Like so many of the colonial families to whom the war had come, the Harrises were new to America. John's grandfather, Samuel, with his brother Thomas had come from southern Wales, landing first in Long Island, and after a short time moving south to the region of Cohansey in Cumberland County, New Jersey. They brought to the new world an impressive ancestry, for in their line can be found such illustrious names as the Princess of Wales, and her father King John of England, as well as Henry I of England and Charlemagne and

Malcolm, King of Scots, the elder son of King Duncan, murdered by Macbeth.[1]

Royalty was far from Samuel Harris's mind, however, when he arrived in the Cumberland County region of New Jersey. He married a lady of his own age, Sarah Johnson, the daughter of Nicholas Johnson of Cumberland County, and settled down happily to life in the New World. He assumed property from Nicholas Johnson and permitted his son Abraham to live on a "plantation," which he had purchased from John Chandler of Alloway's Creek. Upon the death of his wife Sarah, in 1761, he married Rachel Hood, the widow of Robert Hood of Hopewell Township.

In his will, composed just twelve days before his death on January 16, 1773, Samuel Harris turned over to his son Abraham "the plantation where he lives in Alloways Creek Township."

On this land, some 150 acres of open ground and wood lots, Abraham of course was already comfortably settled, and his seven children had been born. It is the property that has come to be known as the Johnson Harris place. To the west lay the enormous, 10,000-acre tract of land owned by Annie Salter; and adjacent to the Harris property was Wood's Upper Mill and the road that runs from Quinton's Bridge to the Mill. Here Abraham had built, or restored, a log house into which he had settled with his new wife, Esther Langley (or Langly), and here were born six sons and a daughter. John Harris, the fourth-born, came into this world on September 10, 1753.

So John was not yet twenty-two years old when the news came to him from Lexington and Concord.

But the war in a formal way was still a long way off. The affair at Lexington and Concord had occurred on April 19, 1775. Not until two months later, the middle of June, would the colonies name a Commander for their military forces.

Certainly in New Jersey, the war still seemed far away, and in fact it was. But the people of Salem County had held a meeting as early as October 3, 1774, to express their sympathy for the citizens of Boston and to declare their outrage at the treatment their fellow colonials were receiving at the hands of General Thomas Gage, the Commander of the British forces. And the people who had assembled for the sympathy meeting actually raised 700 dollars and promptly dispatched it to Boston. Not to be outdone, the farmers and townspeople of neighboring Cumberland County held a tea party of their own. Great quantities of tea had recently been delivered to the New Jersey region by the British frigate *Greyhound*, the same ship that would later figure in the invasion of Long Island. On November 22, 1774, a band of "Indians," under cover of darkness lifted this tea from the storehouse in which it had been lodged, and produced a "beautiful" conflagration.[2]

One wonders whether the young John Harris (he would have been twenty-one) was in on the Salem meeting. Was he present for the Cumberland County tea party? Was his childhood friend Samuel Blackwood a party to these affairs? Such expressions of indignation would have been much to their liking, for both had always been very partial to the rebel cause. Both would one day soon be off to the militia, or the Flying Camp, as it was called in those days.

During the latter part of March, 1775, just before the trouble at Lexington would occur, the people of Salem County sent relief to the people of Boston. To these "victims of the vengeance of the Crown of England," they dispatched $420 in Spanish coin.[3] And at some time after the Battle of Lexington-Concord, the Associates of Upper Alloways Creek in the County of Salem, who included two of John Harris's older brothers, Jacob and Abraham, signed a pledge of allegiance to the colonies. The document read in part: "Solemnly Associate and Resolve, under the Sacred ties of virtue, honour and love to our Country that we will personally and as far as in our influence extends endeavor to support and carry into execution whatever measures may be recommended by the Continental and Provincial Congress for defending our Constitution and preserving the same inviolate."[4]

But actual fighting was yet to occur in New Jersey, and doubtless for most of the people the thought of a real, all-out war was distant from their minds.

The war came on slowly, but the sense of the inevitability of war had grown steadily more real through a long succession of dramatic events resulting in great unrest and agitation. That the war would surely come was announced to the colonies very early, with the Stamp Act of 1765. The Stamp Act, passed by the British Parliament, which did not include the voice of the colonies, made it very plain that the cost to England for the defense and administration of its colonies was to be borne by the colonies themselves. The Stamp Act was particularly offensive, for it required a stamp on all publications and legal documents printed in the colonies. It seemed to the colonists a further infringement upon their freedoms. It was vehemently condemned by the Sons of Liberty, a group of prominent citizens organized to protect the freedoms of the settlers of the thirteen colonies. Such persuasive voices as those of Samuel Adams, Patrick Henry, John Dickinson, and Paul Revere were raised in vehement protest.

The Stamp Act was almost promptly repealed, thanks to Benjamin Franklin, who addressed the Parliament with indignation, but within the year, on May 13, 1767, three similar measures (called the Townshend Acts) were introduced to the Parliament and ushered through by Charles Townshend (called "Champagne Charlie"). These bills were intended to and were expected to mollify the colonists, because Townshend had labeled the tax portion of the measures as *external* rather than *internal*, a term offensive to the colonists. In fact, though merchants and landowners were prospering, the whole idea of taxes was abhorrent to most people.

But, ironically, the bills only more inflamed the indignation that had been boiling. All three measures were repugnant; it even seemed to some that they were calculated to inspire antagonism: (1) the appointment of a board of commissioners with power to regulate the laws governing trade; (2) the suspension of the functions of the legislature of New York; and (3), probably most offensive, the imposition of a duty upon certain products, namely paper, glass, paint, red and white lead, and tea.

Even though these acts, too, chiefly because of the indignant opposition expressed by John Dickinson, in his *Letters from a Farmer in Pennsylvania,* were repealed, in 1770 (except for the tax on tea!), the colonists were not appeased. They had gotten a message, and had found it distasteful. They raised anew their rallying cry, "No taxation without representation."

The conviction that war was inevitable, that it could be the only solution to their problems, grew stronger. The certainty was made more strident by the Boston Massacre of March 5, 1770, in which five of the citizens who had assembled to protest the Townshend Acts were killed by the Redcoats.[5] It grew ever closer with the

Boston Tea Party, December 16,1773, and with a second Boston Tea Party on March 7, 1774, and with the passage of the Intolerable Acts by the British Parliament and the consequent meeting called for the First Continental Congress in Philadelphia that September.

The war for real finally arrived at Lexington, Massachusetts, on April 19, 1775.[6] Every schoolchild knows the story, made vivid by Longfellow's thrilling, though somewhat inaccurate, account of the midnight ride of Paul Revere to warn the people of the countryside. Called a "skirmish" by historians, the clash resulted in the deaths of eight of the seventy militiamen (called "minutemen" because of the speed with which they could assemble). The Redcoats, 700 dispatched by General Thomas Gage, who were met here were en route from Boston to Concord, their mission to destroy the powder and the guns which they understood had been stored there. At Concord, later that day, the forces clashed again. Now the minutemen numbered some 200. Rudely repulsed, the British hastened back to Boston, where before many months were passed, they would find themselves completely surrounded and under siege by a force now numbering a really formidable army of colonial militia.

Within three weeks from the time of Lexington-Concord, the Second Continental Congress assembled at Philadelphia, and promptly declared war upon the Great Britain of George III, at the same time considering whom to appoint to the command of the Continental forces. The rebellion, which for the time was only that, was in motion.

In the early going the fighting took place in the north. On May 10, the very day that the Second Continental Congress had been called into session in Philadelphia, Colonel Ethan Allen and his Green Mountain Boys of Vermont, together with troops commanded by Captain Benedict Arnold (eighty-three men in all), seized Fort Ticonderoga, on the shore of Lake Champlain. "Storming" the fort just at dawn while the British troops (only forty-four in number) were yet sleeping, the Rebels took over the fort without the firing of a single shot! Most gratifying was the capture of seventy-eight pieces of heavy artillery, including fifty-nine cannons.

And two days later the rebellious colonists under the gallant Seth Warner,[7] at the head of a detachment of the Green Mountain Boys, overran the British fortification at Fort Crown Point, just north of Ticonderoga, acquiring thereby 114 more of the sorely needed cannons and heavy ordnance.

The colonies were still looking for a Commander for their military forces. Due in large measure to the energetic efforts of John Adams, who nominated him on June 15, George Washington was chosen by the Continental Congress and accepted. The Continental forces, such as they were, had a Commander-in-Chief.

But before Washington could start to organize his army, two days after his appointment, the most significant battle of the early revolution took place in Boston. It was the battle fought at Breed's Hill (near Bunker Hill)[8] in the region of Charlestown, a little north of Boston proper.

Through the night of June 16, some 1200 farmers and tradesmen (now militiamen) worked tirelessly, with rude farm implements, to produce fortifications. By dawn's early light very respectable earthworks appeared at the crown of Breed's Hill.

Because of the fortifications and because the militiamen resolutely followed the orders of their inspiring commander Israel Putnam, who rode along the lines bellowing, "Don't fire until you see the whites of their eyes,"[9] it was a fierce battle. The British were commanded by Generals William Howe and the veteran Thomas Gage, at whose side the young George Washington had fought during the Braddock disaster twenty years earlier.

Israel Putnam

Only on the third assault (and then only because the militiamen had seen their ammunition expended) were Gage and Howe with their greatly superior force able to dislodge the colonials from their fortified positions. Lost in the last moments was the very valiant Joseph Warren, who only three days before had been commissioned a major general in the Massachusetts forces. The thirty-four-year-old physician, a good friend of Benedict Arnold, was shot in the head, reputedly by a British officer who recognized him and knew his worth. Warren, who had declined to assume the command from William Prescott and Putnam, and had insisted on fighting as an ordinary soldier, had been attempting to rally the militia near the redoubt commanded by Colonel Prescott when he was killed. It was reported that General Gage, when he had the news of Warren's death, declared, "It is well; that one man was equal to five hundred ordinary soldiers."

So this battle must go down as a British victory, but the cost to Gage's army was so terrific (226 killed and 828 wounded) that, some suppose, it resulted in undue or excessive caution on the part of Redcoats in battles to come. Certainly General Howe, who had assumed personal command of the British right flank throughout the action, was shocked by the tally.

Thomas Gage

Howe had served in the French and Indian Wars and had been in command of the light infantry under Major General James Wolfe on the Plains of Abraham in the memorable Battle of Quebec, September 13, 1759, where he fought most courageously. He enjoyed a very well deserved reputation for being very caring and protective of his troops. He did not like to lose men. Even though his forces were victorious at Breed's and Bunker Hill, the cost (more than 1000 casualties) was appalling to him. Besides, he could read from the battle that the victory did not win Boston for the British. He knew that at best the occupation of the city was on borrowed time.

Two weeks later, on July 3, Washington, only forty-three years old, but with lots of military experience (although never the command of a real army), now assumed, in Cambridge, Massachusetts, responsibility for all the Continental forces. At the time he was already in headquarters at the Wadsworth House, the home of Samuel Langdon, President of Harvard College. He found himself at the head of a rag-tag army. It could hardly even be regarded as an army. The soldiers were militia men who had enlisted for very short terms only. They were the products of incredibly poor discipline, and were inclined to be unhappy and even insubordinate. Their officers were themselves often indifferent to orders and were conspicuously inept in drilling and in the mechanics of warfare.

In mid-summer, Washington and the Congress, apparently persuaded that the people of Canada, given a chance, would rise up to support the rebellion, approved a plan to invade Quebec. Washington was particularly insistent, and felt the conquest of Canada should be accorded top priority.

On September 6, the order was given to draft the necessary 1000 men, Washington and the Congress not supposing that a massive force would be required. Owing to the indisposition of General Philip Schuyler, whom Congress had selected for command of the mission, the leadership was before long turned over to General Richard Montgomery, who was only thirty-nine years old at the time. Montgomery knew Quebec, in the same way that Howe knew Quebec. Sixteen years ago, at age twenty-three, he had been one of the 5000 men who under British General James Wolfe journeyed in boats down the St. Lawrence at night to force a battle with the French next day on the Plains of Abraham. Now appointed to command of the invasion force, with Quebec City the principal target, Montgomery was remembering that his General Wolfe had perished in the moment of victory in that dramatic battle so long ago.

Another arm of the army, a much larger force, composed of some 1000 volunteers, was placed under the command of Benedict Arnold, whom Washington had just promoted to Colonel.

Montgomery's command, composed of sharp-shooting rifle companies from Pennsylvania and Virginia, set out from Fort Ticonderoga. As they marched through Canada they experienced one success after another. Although the French and English Canadians were not rising up in support of

Benedict Arnold in Maine

the rebel troops, as Congress had hoped, on October 8 they took

Chamblee without difficulty; St. John's fell on November 3; and in just a little over a week after that Montgomery's very small but very confident army occupied Montreal.[10] However, during the siege of Montreal, because of some confusion in the crossing of the river, the impulsive Ethan Allen and his men, who rashly had not waited for the main force, were captured by General Robert Prescott, in command of the city. When Prescott discovered that he had just made a prisoner of the man who had overrun Ticonderoga in the spring, he became "greatly enraged," and ordered the intrepid Allen to be "bound hand and foot with irons." Determined to ship him to England, where he could be tried for treason, Prescott directed that Allen, who was a huge and very powerful man, absolutely fearless, be shackled to a heavy iron bar some eight feet long. In that condition Allen was confined in the hold of a war-vessel, "where he was kept five weeks without a seat, or a bed to lie upon." In England he received somewhat better treatment, but even there he was continued under very close guard, in Halifax, and on the prison ships in New York Harbor until the spring of 1778, when he was finally returned by way of prisoner exchange.[11]

Arnold, whose forces had been assembled at Cambridge, set out for Quebec on September 11, confident that he could reach Quebec City within the month. As it turned out, his journey through the wilderness of present-day Maine by way of birch bark canoes on the Kennebec River, turned out to be a most arduous one, and required two months. And instead of showing up with 1000 men for Montgomery, he arrived with a much decimated force, nearly half of his troops abandoning the enterprise.[12] By the time the armies came together (Arnold with 600 men and Montgomery with 300), winter had set in with the characteristic Canadian vengeance. Their force was bolstered some by Canadians (150-200) under Captain James Livingston, and a company of 50-100 under Captain Jacob Brown, in all an army of a little more than 1000. After a general council of war, December 16, they joined ranks and marched on toward Quebec City together.

The assault on the heavily manned garrison was prepared on December 30, the action continuing, much of the time through a fierce snowstorm, on the last day of the year. The fighting on the 31st was intense, and continued for three hours; but it turned to the British with the sudden death of General Montgomery, who was mortally wounded while leading his men in an attempt to pierce the second barricade inside the garrison. Killed at the same time were his aide-de-camp, Captain J. McPherson, and a number of other soldiers. Another of Montgomery's aides, Aaron Burr, who had come to Quebec with Arnold, and who was only twenty years old when he joined the expedition, was not harmed. In fact, Burr made a valiant attempt to evacuate the body of the fallen Montgomery.

Just a few moments after Montgomery fell, Arnold had his leg shattered by a musket ball fired from inside the garrison and, though protesting, had to be removed from the scene. The American forces, despite the courageous leadership of Arnold's replacement, Captain Daniel Morgan, were forced to withdraw. Casualties were heavy. Thirty of the rebel forces, including Montgomery, had been killed in the three hours of fighting; forty-two, including Arnold, had been wounded; and 389 (!) were captured, including Captain Morgan (so many that the Canadian officers did not know what to do with them). Arnold himself doubtless would have been made a prisoner, except for the fact that General Guy Carleton stopped the pursuing Redcoats short of the hospital to which the Colonel had been carried. In addition to all of these losses, which were devastating, during the campaign the American forces lost a number of men to the terrible typhus fever, and to smallpox, which was rampant.

British losses were incredibly light, only seven or eight killed, and fifteen, perhaps twenty, wounded.

The Battle at Quebec City thus became the second major defeat, if Breed's and Bunker Hill is counted the first, suffered by the amateur patriot forces. Those of Montgomery's force who survived the battle fell back all the way to the captured Fort Crown Point on Lake Champlain.

Richard Montgomery

But the conquest of Canada could not be counted a failure – not yet. In fact, Washington on January 18, fearing that an even stronger garrison would be installed, declared to General Schuyler that Quebec must be reduced before the end of winter.[13]

Printed as a part of the "Journal of a Physician on the Expedition Against Canada" was Montgomery's intimation of just how impossible was the "capture of Canada." Just five days before his tragic death, General Montgomery had dispatched a message to Schuyler: "It is of the utmost importance we should be possessed of Quebec before succors can arrive; and I must give it to you as my opinion . . . that we are not to expect a union with Canada till we have a force in the country sufficient to insure it against any attempt that may be made for its recovery."[14] To replace the fallen Montgomery, Congress offered the command of the Continental forces in Canada to General Charles Lee. But when Lee, complaining of gout, declined the appointment, Major General John Thomas was offered and accepted the post. Thomas, a surgeon and an officer of great character and incomparable ability, had commanded at Dorchester Heights in Boston the night they were fortified.

In the spring of 1776, the Congress appointed Benjamin Franklin and two of its Maryland members, Charles Carroll and Samuel Chase, who had vigorously opposed the Stamp Act, to a commission charged with winning over the people of Canada to the rebel cause. Although all three (and Carroll's brother, who went along) were ardent patriots and on their mission worked most strenuously to secure the support of the French Canadians, the effort failed miserably. Carroll, a very wealthy man who had lots to lose in the Revolution and who would one day be the last surviving signer of the Declaration of Independence, kept a journal of the enterprise. It is clear from his account that the sympathies of the French Canadians were firmly with King George; and it can be assumed that this was the case largely because of the privileges they enjoyed through the Quebec Act of 1774, which not only installed a permanent administration but accorded the French Canadians (most of whom were Roman Catholic) complete religious freedom.

And the military campaign to win Canada continued to go badly, very badly. At the Cedars, May 17-19, the Americans put up no fight at all. In fact, the "battle" has to go down in the annals of

American military history as one of the most ignominious moments of all.

Late in April, Colonel Benedict Arnold had ordered Colonel Timothy Bedel, with 390 men and two pieces of artillery to take post at the Cedars, a point of land forty-three miles upriver from Montreal on the St. Lawrence, "to prevent any goods being sent to the upper country, and to guard against a surprise from the enemy or their Indians."[15]

At the middle of May, Colonel Bedel, alarmed by what he had been told by a friendly Indian about the enemy strength, turned over his command to Major Isaac Butterfield and went back to Montreal. Butterfield simply surrendered to the British General Guy Carleton and the Indians–without conditions.[16]

Back in Philadelphia the Continental Congress got the report on the Cedars on top of "the doleful, the dismal, and the horrible" news they had had steadily from Canada ever since Quebec. In a letter to General John Sullivan, dated four days after the surrender, May 23, 1776, John Adams expressed the bitter disappointment of the Congress:

The surrender of the Cedars appears to have been a most infamous piece of cowardice. The officer [Major Butterfield], *if he has nothing to say for himself more than I can think of, deserves the most infamous death. It is the first stain upon American arms. May immortal disgrace attend his name and character! I wish, however, that he alone had been worthy of blame. We have thrown away Canada in a most scandalous manner.*[17]

In the diary kept by Dr. Lewis Beebe, who served the Canada campaign as a physician, appears this entry for Tuesday, July 9: "Col. Beadle [Bedel] & Maj^r. Butterfield, remain under an arrest; pray that they may be soon try'd & hanged."[18] It may be supposed that this feeling was very nearly universal among the troops.

Naturally this conduct was condemned by Washington, and both men were promptly scheduled for court martial. The trial, which was held at Ticonderoga, did not take place until some ten weeks later, August 1. But by the court both officers were cashiered, and forbidden ever to hold a commission again in the service of the

Continental Army.[19]

The fiasco at The Cedars is memorable also for the participation in it of some 600 Iroquois warriors, mostly Mohawks, who would be allied with the King throughout the long war.

Coming hard on the heels of this embarrassment was the dark news, two days later, that General Thomas had been struck down by the dreaded smallpox. He had barely time to turn over his command, to Brigadier General William Thompson,[20] before he died. The date was June 2. The death of Thomas, an exceptionally able officer, was, like the death of Montgomery just a few months earlier, a very costly blow to the hopes of the patriots.

General Thompson had not been in the saddle long before the Canada Expedition suffered a third humiliating defeat, in much confused action. This was the battle of Three Rivers (Trois Rivieres), the fighting taking place on June 7-8.

For the Battle of Three Rivers, General John Sullivan,[21] in command of the reinforcements for the Quebec campaign, and dispatched from the preparations for the defense of New York City, would arrive very late, because of bad weather. The assault on this British bastion, located on the St. Lawrence River midway between Montreal and Quebec, and named Trois Rivieres because of the three channels by which the St. Maurice here enters the St. Lawrence, thus had little chance of success.

The American forces were for the most part Pennsylvania volunteers (a very few from New Jersey), recruits assembled by Colonel Anthony Wayne (202 from his native Chester County) and by Colonel William Irvine, a physician from Carlisle, Pennsylvania (1450 recruits).[22] Now under the command of General William Thompson, the force proceeded, without artillery, at the direction of Canadian guides, who proved to be treacherous. Eventually they found themselves totally lost and in great disorder.

In the terribly confused fighting that followed, Irvine's force was cut off from the main body and reduced to seven (!) men. These soldiers wandered the swamps for twenty-four hours, before, finding themselves surrounded, they finally surrendered to General Nesbitt.[23]

Because Colonel William Irvine is one of the most conspicuous officers in the eventful history of bombardier John Harris, whose fortunes are being followed here, and because what happened at Three Rivers is, with the treachery and the disorder and confusion, not unlike what happened many times during the course of the Revolution, the pages of his eye-witness report should prove interesting, if not indeed fascinating.

It should be remembered that Colonel William Irvine is a physician. Although as a very young man he saw some service as a surgeon with the British in the Seven Years' War, he is not really a military man. In the scattered settlement of Carlisle he has been delivering babies and ministering to those afflicted by pneumonia, cholera, smallpox, and the terrible fevers. Because he has composed a fighting force out of Pennsylvania farmers and tradesmen, and because he is, at thirty-three, older by far than almost all of the men he has assembled, he has been given officer rank and command. All of a sudden he finds himself snatched by fate from his medical practice and deposited deep in the wilderness of Quebec, at the head of a company of soldiers whose musket experience can be measured by the number of squirrels brought down from the oaks in the Pennsylvania wood lots. He is an officer member of the modest expeditionary force whose object is to capture Canada! Here in his own words, from the journal he kept as commander of the Sixth Pennsylvania Regiment, is Colonel Irvine's account of the end of his first, short-lived, ill-fated, ignominious, and somewhat bewildering military experience:

June 7th, 1776–Col. Irvine's regiment, and three companies of Col. Wayne's embarked in batteaus at Sorrell [Sorel, twenty-five miles to the south of Trois Rivieres], *under the command of Gen. Thompson, and proceeded to Nicollet* [Nicolet, on the south bank of the St. Lawrence], *where we found and were joined by Col.* [Arthur] *St. Clair, who had almost seven hundred men under his command.*

June 8th–Crossed the river to Point de Lac [Pointe du Lac];*the pilot deceived us, for his orders were to steer to within four miles of Trois Riviere. Point de Lac is nine miles. Notwithstanding this disappointment we marched with all possible expedition for Trois Riviere; but here our misfortune began. Our guide led us quite out of the way into a swamp, which was sufficient to engulf a thousand men. Before we got disentangled from this dreadful place daylight appeared, so that instead of attacking the town of Trois Riviere before day (as was designed) we found ourselves three or four miles from it.*

Here we were at a loss what to do; had no intelligence of the strength of the garrison; to attack was hazardous, and to retreat without knowing the enemy's strength we could not think of, therefore marched on.

The river now on our right about fifty yards, we were soon discovered, and were saluted by the men-of-war. They fired incessantly while we marched about three-quarters of a mile; here we inclined to a wood on our left, in order to avoid the fire from the shipping, but avoiding one evil we fell into a greater; for we now entered into a swamp, which I suppose to be four miles over. Nature, perhaps, never formed a place better calculated for the destruction of an army. It was impossible to preserve any order of march, nay, it became at last so difficult, and the men so fatigued, that their only aim was how to get extricated; many of the men had lost their shoes, and some their boots.

At length, about seven o'clock, some officers reached one extreme of the swamp, a few went forward to reconnoiter, brought account back that they saw clear ground and horses at a little more than a quarter of a mile. Then Col. St. Clair, Lieut. Col. Allen, and myself, with a few other officers, strove to draw the men up in some order, which we found impracticable. The General [Thompson] *then got up with us, and ordered as many as could . . . be collected, to move forward to the cleared ground, there to form, which was accordingly done with as much expedition as could be expected from men worn down with fatigue, and who were exquisitely thirsty and faint. A few moments after we were formed, the General ordered the whole body to move on, in order to join Col.* [William] *Maxwell's division of whom we had no account of from our first entry into the swamp, but from a soldier, who said he saw some men about a half mile in front.*

A brisk firing then began, which we took to be Maxwell's party. Gen. Thompson then ran towards the front, the firing increased, and seemed very hot. The General sent word to me to send forward the riflemen of my regiment, but they being chiefly in the rear could not get up as soon as he or I wished. Those of them belonging to the companies then in front, I ordered to turn out and march in Indian file, passing the word for the rear to follow in the same order. I then advanced in front and joined the General, but by this time

The St. Lawrence

Maxwell's division was entirely broken and retreating in such disorder, that there was no possibility of rallying them.

Gen. Thompson then ordered us to retreat fifty paces into the woods, where he and I used every argument we were masters of to collect and engage the men to make a stand, but our utmost efforts were in vain; not more than about forty men could be got together, and before this was done a minute, the communication between us and our main body was entirely cut off. The General, Lieut. Bird, and Myself were the only officers now together.

When we were consulting what was best to be done with our small party, we were fired on from all quarters by the Canadians, who were in ambush and skulking in the bushes. We then retreated, in hopes to fall in with some of our people; but the farther we marched, instead of our numbers increasing, they decreased, for in less than ten minutes we mustered but seven in all. The whole day we marched through swamps and thickets alternately without any kind of refreshments, except stagnant water, of which we drank freely.

We heard a great deal of firing all day, both great guns and small arms; the latter were sometimes very near us. In the evening we hoped we were nearly opposite where we expected our boats to be. We halted, to rest and consult what was best to be done, when we suddenly were alarmed by a brisk firing where we expected our boats to be, and by which we hoped to escape. The firing we supposed to be on the party with the boats. This nearly destroyed every hope of getting off; we then concluded to lie by till after dark and push a few miles up a river, where there appeared a possibility of finding a canoe, in which we might cross.

About eleven P.M. we marched again four miles, when we discovered a sentry. Knowing then there must be a party of soldiers near, we took a road to our left, in hopes to get past; but now we got into another swamp, which caused our entire overthrow. In short, we waded and wandering here until near daylight; our strength and spirits being now nearly exhausted, we made a fire, lay down and slept about an hour. In the meantime a soldier of our party was dispatched to endeavor to discover the strength and situation of the enemy. At daylight he returned with the disagreeable intelligence that we were quite surrounded, and no way left to get out; to confirm what he stated, we soon saw small parties of soldiers and Canadians *dispatched on all sides, who began to fire on stragglers.*

Gen. Thompson, Bird and I then concluded it would be better to deliver ourselves up to British officers, than to run the risk of being murdered in the woods by Canadians. Indeed we were so exhausted as to be unable to march further; accordingly we went up to a house where we saw a guard, and surrendered ourselves prisoners at discretion.

Col. Nesbit commanded here, by whom we were cruelly treated. His party marched hence for Trois Riviere; a strong guard marched with the whole of the prisoners. Gen. Thompson and I had the honor of being marched for six miles in the common crowd, without further distinction than being placed near the front. The commanding officer would neither allow us horses or a carriage, though we requested it, and represented to him our miserable condition. Notwithstanding, we were hurried off in a few minutes, and pushed exceedingly fast for six miles, when we arrived at headquarters.

Generals Carlton and Burgoyne were both here, who treated us very politely. They ordered us refreshments immediately; indeed Gen. Burgoyne served us himself. We were then ordered in a boat, and put under the conduct of one officer only, Lieut. Wilkinson of the Sixty-second, an exceedingly genteel young man . . . . Now went aboard a transport ship in the river.[24]

Altogether, the Americans lost twenty-five men killed, and 236 (!) captured. Anthony Wayne was wounded[25] and, besides Thompson and Irvine, a number of other officers, were notable among the captured. Although a great many of the prisoners were promptly paroled home, having promised not to fight again against the Crown, Colonel Irvine was not released from the Dauphin Jail until the first week of August. On August 6, a number of prisoners released by the British at this time were placed on five transport vessels convoyed by the frigate *Pearl* and shipped south. Colonel Irvine was among those conveyed by the *Prince of Wales*. These ships, after a month-long voyage, stood in to Sandy Hook on September 11 and 12, "in plain view of the British encampment on Staten Island and the fleet of about four hundred vessels and transports in the harbor."[26] For almost two years Irvine continued on parole, a freedom that required his pledge to stay out of the Revolutionary military service until May of 1778.[27] The Colonel returned to the Army too late for the action at New York City, at Trenton and Princeton, at the Brandywine and Germantown, and the encampment at Valley Forge, but in time to assume command of the Seventh Pennsylvania Regiment in the Battle of Monmouth, in which also his former house servant, Molly Ludwig Hays (Molly Pitcher) figured conspicuously.

In the Battle of Three Rivers, the British, commanded by General Guy Carleton, lost only eight men killed.[28]

The Canada campaign had begun in September of 1775. It ended, for all intents and purposes, with the Battle of Three Rivers, June 8 of 1776. Arnold, on June 18, was the last to leave the sinking ship, embarking by canoe, as he had come, for Lake Champlain.

The rout at Three Rivers, together with the disappointments suffered at the city of Quebec, and at The Cedars, had put an end to any hope the Americans may have had for the conquest of Canada. The campaign into Quebec and on the St. Lawrence River had proved disastrous, and the news when it reached Washington and the Congress was devastating. By the end of June all of Canada had been completely evacuated by the Americans; and Canada from that time on (except for the promptly aborted invasion prepared at Albany by Generals Lafayette and De Kalb in March of 1778, at the time of Valley Forge), is dismissed from the Patriot cause.

Because the conquest of Canada had been extremely important to Washington, and because he had not received the hoped-for active support of the people of Canada, and because he had lost Generals John Thomas and Richard Montgomery[29] and had seen General William Thompson and Colonel William Irvine captured and Benedict Arnold wounded, and because two of the defeats that were suffered by the colonial forces bordered on the humiliating, he had to be sorely hurt. It was not a death blow to the revolution, but it was a deep wound. All that could be hoped for now was that Canada would remain neutral. The failure of the combined forces to succeed on the St. Lawrence had dampened a great deal the initial exhilaration evoked by victories at Ticonderoga and at Crown Point.

Meanwhile Washington, while following closely the fortunes of his regiments in Quebec, was not idle at home. He was building a disciplined fighting force. Even as early as the end of the year 1775, Washington and his officers were beginning to take some genuine pride in the army that was developing. While this newly organized army was laying siege to Boston, General Washington, on New Year's Day, 1776, ordered the Grand Union Flag (which had been urged though never actually officially approved by the Second Continental Congress) with its thirteen vividly red and white stripes hoisted on the liberty pole above his headquarters at Prospect Hill, in Cambridge, "in compliment of the United Colonies."[30] And soon, thanks to Betsy Ross, he would have a new flag.

By the end of the winter Washington and his officers had molded out of their militiamen and the new volunteers a very effective fighting machine. And the Continental Congress had resolved to provide him, as soon as it could, a force of 30,000 (!) men. In March, less than a year from the engagement at Lexington, Washington found himself already at the head of a well disciplined and well trained force of 18,000 men, most of them volunteers from the New England colonies. With this army, Washington forced the British altogether out of Boston. Fortifying the Dorchester Heights, which look out over the city from the south, Washington so entrenched his troops and so well established his position as to make an assault upon them unthinkable.

Besides, it could be said that at this moment the American artillery was born-- with the arrival of the British guns that the young patriot soldier Henry Knox had delivered from the captured Fort Ticonderoga and Fort Crown Point. The captured guns had rested idle for seven months before Knox had the happy idea that they might prove "useful" to the Boston problem. Over a period of six weeks, from December 5 until the middle of January, by sledges and by boats, over incredibly torturous, frozen roads, through a bitter cold, Knox, with his brother William and whatever men he could enlist, wrestled twenty-nine of the Ticonderoga artillery pieces and that many more of those seized at Crown Point, all the way to Boston. With these guns installed at the heights of Dorchester, the British positions in the city, even the fleet in the harbor, were now vulnerable. Because Knox's success in this enterprise led to his appointment at the head of the

American artillery, which thus meant the steady development of this arm of the Continental Army, and the steadily increasing effectiveness of the cannon, at Sullivan Island, in the mouth of the harbor at Charleston, S.C. (where in June of 1776 the gallant Colonel William Moultrie repulsed a British assault with a spectacular employment of garrison artillery), at Trenton, at the Brandywine, at Monmouth, and finally at Yorktown, his expedition, from Lake Champlain to Boston, has to be counted a truly momentous episode of the war.

Knox had twenty cannon in place on the Heights by the end of February, and the bombardment of the British positions was underway the first week of March. Howe, who by this time had replaced Gage (who had been called back to England) at the head of the British forces, contemplated an assault on the Heights, but the cost of Breed's-Bunker Hill was giving him pause. When a most ferocious winter storm arrived, his decision was made easy. Within two weeks his preparations to withdraw from the city were complete. On St. Patrick's Day, the Redcoats, taking with them a large Loyalist population of Boston, set sail for Nova Scotia, to the resounding cheers of the rebels.[31]

The date was March 17, 1776. The war was now begun in earnest. And it was clearly a war for all of the thirteen colonies. That was plain enough. Washington had proclaimed it emphatically, on the first day of the new year, 1776, with that dramatic unfurling of the Grand Union Flag over the army encampment at Cambridge. It had been a thrilling sight, those thirteen stripes in their alternating vivid red and white.

But of course nobody in the colonies, not a single soul (excepting John Adams), nor anybody in the England of King George III, had any idea, not any idea in the world, just how very long a war it would be.

With the great news trickling down from Boston, but not really because of it, young John Harris of Salem, New Jersey, joined the flood of volunteer farmers and tradesmen who were swelling the ranks of the militia. At about the time the Redcoats were ushered out of Boston, Harris enlisted in some company of militia, possibly a detachment of Pennsylvania militia, and almost certainly an artillery unit, for a period of six months. His father, Abraham, had died in February, at age fifty-three, and had left his land, 150 acres, to his six sons.[32] But John, now twenty-two years old, put his farming on hold. The land his father had given him he placed in the charge of his older brother Abraham, and sometime that spring he enrolled in the Flying Camp, as militia units were sometimes called, just in time to get in on one of the most important battles of the now fully fledged rebellion.

But in the first week of July the Second Continental Congress, meeting in Philadelphia, adopted the Declaration of Independence, which meant a totally new declaration of War. The conflict that would rage from now on could no longer be considered a rebellion or a civil war or even a revolution; it was now a war between two sovereign nations, one arguably the most powerful empire in the world, and the other an infant nation composed of disparate and very sparsely populated states.

And so ended the War for Independence. It had lasted a little over fourteen months. It ended in the birth of a new nation. Independence is proclaimed, and assumed, if not permanently assured. And now begins the War between that new nation, with its flag of thirteen stripes, and an empire fortified and emboldened by the tumult and turmoil of eight centuries.

Until this time, the action had been carried on in the north, in New England, in upper New York State, and in Canada. And so far, except for Quebec, almost all had gone remarkably well for the Patriots. Everything was about to change.

II

THE HUDSON

In a chariot of light from the region of day
  The Goddess of Liberty came.
Ten thousand celestials directed the way
  And hither conducted the dame.
A fair budding branch from the gardens above,
  Where millions with millions agree,
She brought in her hand as a pledge of her love,
  And the plant she named Liberty Tree.

— **Thomas Paine**

General George Washington and General William Howe, who with Gage had commanded the British forces at Breed's Hill and who had in October succeeded Gage as Commander-in-Chief, were now locked-in adversaries. Both appreciated that the war, which had so far been fought in Boston and north of Boston, and in Canada, would be moving south. Both understood that New York City, strategically, and for a host of other reasons as well, was critical, was absolutely vital. John Adams in January had referred to the city as "the key to the continent." And clearly both Washington and Howe felt the same way. Both knew how *very* crucial was control of the city. And certainly both could appreciate the urgency.

And neither was shy about the mission. Howe actually welcomed the prospect of a battle for the city. After all, he was in a superior position in terms of numbers of troops; and, besides, maybe even more important, he commanded the water. The British Navy, with a huge number of frigates and gunboats, could bring a devastating artillery to the battle. But Washington, though without this confidence and certainly a very long, long way from arrogance, simply knew that he *must* control the city. Consequently, shortly after the British exodus from Boston, he moved his army south. The British had evacuated on March 17; Washington removed from his headquarters at Cambridge on April 4, headed for Providence, Rhode Island. By the middle of April he was fortifying the city of New York.

William Howe

Hoping to establish an effective defensive posture, Washington placed a large portion of his troops on Brooklyn Heights, across the Bay from Manhattan. General Howe, on July 8, arrived at Staten Island with a force of 9,000 troops. Here he awaited the arrival of his older brother, Admiral Richard Howe, with his frigates and his gun boats and supply ships, as well as the additional forces of British infantry and Germans.[1] Figures vary among historians, but certainly the British forces were overwhelmingly superior in numbers, and may have included (after the Admiral's appearance on July 12) as many as 32,000 men (some say 45,000!). Washington's forces at this time could hardly have exceeded 11,000. Besides, the British had, after

Admiral Howe showed up, some seventy warships in the harbor. Naturally, the British were very, very confident. Admiral Howe had predicted at the time of his setting out from Nova Scotia that "Peace will be made within ten days after my arrival."

After invitations to Benjamin Franklin and to George Washington to sue for clemency were rebuffed (not even really acknowledged), the brothers Howe launched their assault. The battle, sometimes called the Battle of Brooklyn, or the Battle of Long Island, was joined on August 27.

Richard Howe

Actually the Battle of Long Island is but the first stage of the five-part struggle for possession of New York City. The Battle of New York City was a long and much involved, scattered affair. It can be said to include the engagements on Long Island-Brooklyn, the siege of Manhattan, the watch-and-wait period of the Harlem Heights, the battle of White Plains, and the surrender of Forts Washington and Lee. As such, it lasted for a period of three months, from Howe's invasion of Long Island on August 22 to the abandonment of Fort Lee on November 20.

Washington had placed General Charles Lee in command of the defense of New York, including Fort Washington and Fort Lee, but in time Major General Israel Putnam, in a somewhat confused chain of command, had taken over. Except for Washington himself, Putnam was the highest ranking officer in the Continental Army. He had been the first to be commissioned at the rank of Major General. He had to his credit a good deal of military experience, serving with the British during the French and Indian Wars.

And he had suffered some close calls. In 1758 he had been captured by the Indians and condemned to their favorite execution. Putnam was tied to the stake, and was about to be roasted alive, when, only at the last instant, he was spared because of the intervention of a French officer.[2]

He had been plowing in the field on his Connecticut farm when he first heard the news of Lexington-Concord, and he promptly rode to Cambridge to assist in the raising of an army.

He had been one of the two principal commanders of the rebel forces at Breed's-Bunker Hill, and is sometimes credited with the command, normally attributed to Colonel Prescott, "Don't fire until you see the whites of their eyes."

At the time of the Battle of New York he was, however, some fourteen years older than Washington. He was not a young man. He did have among his aides, however, a very young man, in the person of Aaron Burr.

Artillery was going to be a problem for the rebels. On June 10, 1776, Colonel Henry Knox reported to Washington that there were "mounted and fit for action in the city and neighboring posts, 121 heavy and light cannon." The problem was that these cannon required the service of 1210 men, and Knox at that time had for his gun crews only 520 officers and men. He urged Washington to draft at least that many more from other battalions.[3]

The British fleet had reached the entrance to the Hudson River on June 29. With his rude army of tradesmen and farm boys able to view the awesome flotilla of British warships, and tempted to count the guns, Washington now delivered one of those inspirational speeches he was to become famous for: "The time is now near at hand which most probably determines whether Americans are to be free men or slaves. The fate of unborn millions will now depend upon the courage and conduct of this army .... Let us therefore rely

Forcing the Hudson River Passage – 1776

upon the goodness of the cause . . . . to animate and encourage us to great and noble actions."[4]

General William Howe landed on Staten Island July 3; and, after mighty preparations, transported his troops to Long Island, landing them on the beaches to the south of the American positions. The date was August 22. The battle would be joined four days later, when the British began their march northeast to assault the American positions.

By this time the British forces included at least 8000, and perhaps as many as 17,000 (!) German mercenaries, and they were supported by 400 ships and transports, including ten ships-of-the-line, and a great many frigates, which had arrived from Nova Scotia, from Great Britain, and from the Carolinas.

Fortunately for the rebels, though Washington's forces were short in numbers, and were largely militiamen, not well trained, and inadequately armed, an appeal to the country had resulted in an additional six or seven thousand volunteers. The army had swelled considerably. But of course it was still far inferior to that of the British and their German mercenaries.

Washington's forces included only one regiment of artillery, described by Knox as without skilled gunners and equipped with old iron field-pieces, "honey-combed, broken and defective."[5] It may be thought probable that it was made up largely of militiamen. And it is very likely that John Harris, who was an artilleryman throughout his army career, was a member of this regiment. It is clear from family documents that he was with the militia forces under Washington when in the summer of 1776 the Continental Army marched from Boston southward to occupy New York City and to establish a defense of the city. And his personal recollections report that he was "in the Battle of Long Island." And it is known that at this time he was still a militiaman. What is not known is just what company of militia he was enrolled in, or even whether it was a Pennsylvania detachment or a New Jersey one.[6]

He definitely was not with the Flying Camp that was stationed at Fort Washington during this fall. And he was not a member of the gun crew that was positioned on Laurel Hill, over the Harlem River a little north of Fort Washington, manning the battery that came under bombardment from the British frigate *Pearl.*[7]

That engagement was made most memorable by the heroism of the wife of a matross member of the crew who replaced her fallen husband at the guns. She served until she was wounded by three bursts of grapeshot to her shoulder. This courageous woman was the very Irish Margaret (Molly) Corbin (sometimes rendered Cockran), who had accompanied her husband John to war. The date was November 16, 1776. After the war she became the first of her sex to be awarded a pension by any government for service in the Revolution.[8] She was eventually awarded a private's half pay for life.[9]

But there were other artillery stations as well, and though it is thought likely that Harris was with the section attached to Lord Stirling (General William Alexander, of New Jersey), it is futile to try to figure out exactly where the young artilleryman was during this action.

In any case, the artillery of the Continental Army played but a modest role in the defense of New York City. General Nathanael Greene, who had been at Breed's Hill and who had been placed in charge of fortifications on Long Island, and who had himself presided through the summer over the health of the military community, had been felled by the fever in the midst of his organizing, and had turned over the leadership of his 800 men to General John Sullivan, who had recently arrived from Lake Champlain, and had just been promoted (August 9) to Major General.

At strategic spots along that range of hills on the Island which extends from the Narrows to Jamaica, Sullivan placed twenty cannon, and at Brooklyn Heights he positioned a redoubt of seven guns. Brigadier General Lord Stirling[10] had only two cannon. These he located at the edge of a group of trees on Battle Hill, as it is now known, in order to command the road which ran along the left of his line. All guns were overrun, and both Sullivan and Stirling were eventually captured. General Sullivan had hoped to escape by secreting himself in a cornfield, but he was surprised there by a company of German grenadiers and made a prisoner of war. Many of Sullivan's men, including the artillerymen, one of whom may have been John Harris, escaped by hiding in the woods or by fighting their way through the advancing Redcoat lines.

The fighting was fierce in many quarters, the forces of Stirling behaving with extraordinary valor before capitulating, and seeing their commander captured, Stirling surrendering to the Hessian General Leopold Philipp von Heister. Also lost in the early fighting was the militia General Nathaniel Woodhull, who, captured by British dragoons, was consigned to a prison ship and there died of wounds received either before his capture or, as some insist, perhaps from wounds suffered *after* his capture.

All in all, the action did not go well for the rebels. Because General Howe had so skillfully maneuvered the British forces into a position at Washington's rear, he was able to force the Continental Army steadily to retreat, and great confusion, total disarray, was the consequence.

Colonel Henry Knox, keen about the artillery of course, has left an account of the fighting in an August 27 letter to his wife Lucy: "About two o'clock in the morning (yesterday) the enemy attacked the woods in front of our works on Long Island, where our riflemen lay. They attacked with a chosen part of the Hessians, and all the light infantry and grenadiers of the army, and after about six or seven hours' smart skirmishing our people fell back in front of our works. The enemy lost nearly one thousand killed [!]. We lost about the same number killed, wounded, and taken prisoners, among whom are General Sullivan and Lord Stirling . . . . I met with some loss in my regiment: they behaved like heroes, and are gone to glory."[11]

During the evening hours of August 29, one week into the fighting, Washington made a critical decision, electing to abandon Brooklyn! This would require, of course, the crossing of the East River into New York, a perilous enterprise at the very best.

In a miraculous evacuation[12] General John Glover and his Marblehead, Massachusetts, fishermen, under cover of darkness, clouds and fog, were able to ferry nine thousand surviving Continental Army soldiers, together with their baggage and the light artillery (but no heavy artillery), across the East River at Brooklyn Ferry and into Manhattan. The withdrawal was accomplished without detection by the British, beginning as it did in the late evening of August 29 and reaching completion by dawn on the 30th. And not one man lost.

John Harris was almost certainly one of the artillerymen so dramatically evacuated.

Howe was shocked when he discovered that the Continental Army had totally disappeared. But he promptly assembled his forces and organized a siege of Manhattan. By September 16 Washington had formed a new line at Harlem Heights, and here resolved to rest his troops and to determine just what Howe might be planning next.

Meanwhile momentous events were occurring in Philadelphia. On September 17, though bombardier John Harris and his fellow militiamen would not know anything of it for some weeks to come, the Continental Congress took another giant step forward. Mother England had been chastising her wayward children and urging them rudely back to the nest. Now she would have to regard the colonies in an altogether new light. Two months and two weeks after the colonies had been declared by Congress to be free and independent, they were established in a wholly new identity by an all-inclusive name. Thanks in large measure to the inspirational pamphleteer Thomas Paine, who had urged the phrase, the colonies from this time forward were to be known as The United States of America. There were thirteen of them. Each would one day have its own star in the flag of Betsy Ross. And, who could know, perhaps one day another star or two might appear in that brilliant field of blue. Already folks in the wilderness known as Kentucky were beginning to think that way.

At Harlem Heights little real fighting occurred. The rebels did enjoy something of a victory over the Redcoats in one "sharp skirmish." In another action, at Kips Bay, their forces were routed in a shameful panic. After almost a month in this position, Washington, on October 12, led his army, which had been rejoined by General Stirling (via a prompt prisoner exchange) and by a recovered Nathanael Greene, to White Plains, leaving Fort Washington, garrisoned by more than 2000 men, under the command of Colonel Robert Magaw,[13] a very feisty Bedford County, Pa., attorney.

The march from Harlem Heights to White Plains was a most difficult one, as the patriot army was left now with but a very few horses, and the field guns had to be transported by the artillerymen heaving at drag ropes.

Howe, having pursued Washington to White Plains, finally, on October 26-28, engaged the Continental Army, the most significant fighting occurring on Chatterton's Hill on October 28. When the patriot forces were at length dislodged from their entrenchments, Howe in organized pursuit may have won a decisive victory here, but he chose, instead, to await reinforcements. By the time he was ready to renew the assault against Washington's troops, which had regrouped near North Castle, torrential rains made attack unthinkable. An astounded Washington awoke November 4 to find that the Redcoats had thrown in the bag and had marched back to Manhattan. Without claiming victory, Washington withdrew his forces from the region five days later.

Bombardier John Harris left no account of White Plains in his recollections, but one of his many fellow Salem Countians who were serving there, Ensign John Blaire, did. In writing to Captain Jacob Du Bois, who at that time, October 26, was in Pilesgrove in Salem County, Blaire delivered this report:

We are now encamped in this plain with the main body of our Army, which now appears very numerous; and really is so. This is the place our General means to make the main stand, I think, as the whole Army is now employed in heaving up breastworks and entrenching; only what is daily on guard; which is doubled since we left New York Island; the reason is they have to go out to relieve the Sentinels on our outer lines six or seven miles, and to place Sentinels on all the Heights between us and the Enemy. They keep daily advancing. We have been alarmed every day for days past and marched out to meet the enemy; but they have as yet thought it prudent to keep their distance, but it is generally believed that their main attack will ensue in a little time for many circumstances. One of the main ones is, the season being so well spent, and it has always been a rule with the British Army to go into Winter quarters this month. There is scarcely a night passes, but some of our scouting parties have a skirmish with their outer sentinels, which consist chiefly of Tories. A few nights ago a party of ours fell in with a party of theirs consisting of about fifty; with which a short skirmish ensued and our party came off victorious and brought off thirty of those Deluded Animals; and left a number of dead on the ground. We lost two and four wounded, one of whom is since dead, and one belonging to Captain Kelly's Company named Reed Bennet—we yet keep our lines good on York Island; there are two brigades there still. We lie on marching orders with four days provisions ready cooked, and strict orders that no soldier be out of hearing of the Drum by day or night, on pain of Death.

The letter was continued the next day, and ended with a reference to Fort Washington: "This morning a heavy cannonading began and still continues, which is three hours; it appears from this to be at Mount Washington; but the occasion of which we do not as yet know."[14]

Not long after Blaire had heard this artillery fire, Washington received the devastating news about Fort Washington. Although he had not really nurtured much hope, he had understood all along what a stunning blow it would be to suffer the loss of the two principal forts of the entire region, Fort Washington and Fort Lee.

Fort Washington, now in the charge of Colonel Robert Magaw, was a five-sided earthenworks fortification at the crest of Mount Washington overlooking the Hudson River in northern Manhattan. It had been built in the previous summer by Washington's troops.

Magaw, never short on spunk, had spurned British invitations to surrender, and continued for some time to feel confident he could hold the fort. But by early November, having suffered many casualties, it became plain to him that he could not. On a very cold and blustery afternoon, with a light snow contributing to the gloom, he turned over Fort Washington, with all of his troops (nearly 3000 men) and 161 cannon, to the British General Charles Cornwallis and the Hessians. General Wilhelm Knyphausen accepted his sword. The date was November 16. Among the losses were 100 artillerymen.

Magaw was made a prisoner of war and delivered to the notorious British prison ships, probably to the *Jersey,* the most awful of all and popularly known as "Hell." It was generally believed that the morning salutation of the officer of the guard was: "Rebels, turn out your dead."[15]

Washington, who had been following closely the fortunes of

The Hudson

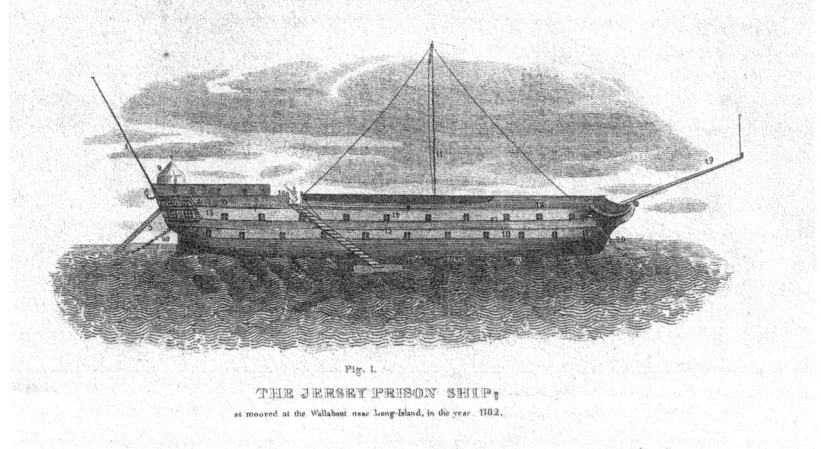

THE JERSEY PRISON SHIP,
as moored at the Wallabout near Long-Island, in the year 1782.

The Jersey

Fort Washington, now had to consider Fort Lee, which was on the opposite side of the Hudson River from Fort Washington, on the Palisades on the New Jersey shore. Fort Lee, which had been built expressly to command the Hudson River, had, like Fort Washington, a certain symbolic value. It had been known first as Fort Constitution and was now named in honor of Washington's top lieutenant, the British-trained General Charles Lee. But by now it had become very clear to the Commander-in-Chief that it would be futile to continue the defense of Fort Lee. On November 20, he ordered General Greene, who had been inclined to defend the fort, to abandon it. Greene promptly withdrew the garrison and with that action brought an end to the Battle of New York.[16]

Victory was clearly and totally to the British. The defending Continental Army had been forced to surrender New York City (including Fort Lee and Fort Washington), lost an inestimable quantity of munitions and supplies, suffered more than 1500 casualties, saw two high-ranking generals captured, as well as Colonel Magaw, and a large number of lesser officers, and experienced such a terrible blow to morale that new volunteers could hardly be expected. In fact desertions began immediately to occur wholesale, complete companies abandoning the army en masse. Some insist that if General Howe had more promptly followed up his victory in pursuit of Washington's withdrawing forces that the war would have ended in the fall of that year, just five or six months after the new nation had declared its independence. But Howe in fact apparently thought that the war was over. And he could hardly be blamed for that. From every means of measurement it must have seemed so.

Except for Yorktown, the Battle of New York was the most significant battle of the entire Revolution. In no other battle was the final outcome of the war so close to being determined. The King's men here came within a hair's breadth of bringing the rebellion to a very early end. For this magnificent victory, which had apparently squelched the rebellion, General Howe, who was a cousin to King George III, was made a baronet. From this time forward he would be known as *Sir* William Howe, and although he would not be present in the city, or even in the country, after the spring of 1778, New York would continue to be occupied by the British until 1784!

And though the war had not ended, for the Continental Army it was certainly a dark hour. It trudged south through New Jersey at the lowest point of its fortunes. Many felt that all hope was gone, that there could be no recovery for the Patriots; many thought that success would be possible only if the Commander-in-Chief were replaced. Everybody was experiencing dire forebodings. Except General Washington!

III

THE BRANDYWINE

Once upon a time, an eagle soaring around a farmer's barn and espying a hare, darted down upon him like a sunbeam, seized him in his claws, and remounted with him into the air. He soon found that he had a creature of more courage and strength than a hare, for which notwithstanding the keenness of his eyesight, he had mistaken a cat. The snarling and scrambling of the prey was most inconvenient, and, what was worse, she had disengaged herself from his talons, grasped his body with her fore limbs, so as to stop his breath, and seized fast hold of his throat with her teeth. "Pray," said the eagle, "let go your hold and I will release you." "Very fine," said the cat, "I have no fancy to fall from this height, and be crushed to death. You have taken me up, and you shall stoop and let me down." The eagle thought it necessary to stoop accordingly.

— **Benjamin Franklin**

The Continental Army continued in its doldrums following its evacuation of New York City. Together with 3000 Continental troops Washington had been forced to flee southward through New Jersey and then across the

Delaware River into Pennsylvania. As the Army lumbered south it continued to lose men, perhaps as many as one out of three! Some of these simply deserted, some noted that their enlistment had expired, one at least, a common soldier named John Harris, withdrew, not because his enlistment term in the militia was expired, which it was, but because of a severe illness. He was taken sick, suffering spasms of chills and fever which suggested the typhus, as the troops retreated southward through Somerset County, and it would be almost five months before the young man recovered sufficiently to return to the war.

Howe, as noted earlier, was quite certain there was no fight left in the Continental Army. As far as he was concerned the war was over. Of course there would be some mopping up to do and there may be discovered some pockets of resistance, but for him the handwriting was plain on the wall. During the fighting in New York, he had even dispatched the captured Major General John Sullivan to Philadelphia with overtures of peace in the name of Lord Howe. Then he settled back to await a communication from the Continental Congress and considered how the peace might be negotiated. Rather than pursue the remnants of Washington's army, he simply solidified some of the positions he now held in New Jersey.

When the captured General Sullivan appeared before Congress on September 3 as Lord Howe's envoy, with a request for a conference, he was met rudely, especially by John Adams. The General, whom Adams' biographer has described as "a swarthy, arrogant man," had hardly begun to speak when Adams whispered to his neighbor Dr. Benjamin Rush the opinion that he would have preferred that there on Long Island a musket ball had passed through Sullivan's head.[1] The good doctor, though possessed of marvelous powers, could not have known at that time how vital General John Sullivan would prove to be to the Patriot cause, else he might have whispered a mollifying remark of his own.

When he had himself a chance to speak, Adams registered a vehement protest in which he expressed his opposition to any meeting with the Howe brothers. But after four days of intense debate, during which the term "independence" was heard a thousand times, the Congress elected to dispatch a committee for "talks." Ironically, for he had been the most fervently opposed to a meeting, but significantly too, because his voice was strongest for staying the course, John Adams found himself a unanimous choice for the delegation. Joining him were Benjamin Franklin, not likely to concede much, and the twenty-seven-year-old Edward Rutledge, who had studied law at Oxford University in England, and who had signed the Declaration of Independence. On September 9 the trio got underway for Staten Island.

It was not until September 11 that the meeting with Lord Howe occurred, on the island, at the Billopp House, which was owned by a Tory. The meeting, as it turned out, consisted of little more than some absurd pleasantries and some ill-disguised snide remarks. As Lord Howe did most of the talking, it took him a while to appreciate that the matter of independence was not, and really never had been, on the table. When after some three hours he finally perceived that fact, he abruptly terminated the "discussion." Surviving is the nutshell report of a member of the Admiral's staff. It reeks of the contempt that regularly characterized the attitude of British officers toward those who were urging independence: "They met, they talked, they parted, and now nothing remains but to fight it out against a set of the most determined hypocrites and demagogues, compiled of the refuse of the colonies, that ever were permitted by Providence to be the scourge of the country."[2]

At least General Sullivan had won his release from the British. And he would figure conspicuously in the action at Trenton and Princeton. Within a year, somewhat ironically, he would lead an assault on Staten Island that would take his troops right past the Billopp House. And for six more years Sullivan would be out front in the rebellion, only the success of which could keep John Adams from swinging from a yardarm.

But the Howe brothers had read it right. They did right to urge a cessation of the hostility and to propose the surrender of the idea of independence. Without feeling any great necessity for it, the British command ordered a pursuit of Washington's beleaguered troops, and indeed eventually launched a rather vigorous attempt to catch up with his retreating forces, pressuring the much fragmented patriot army southwest through Newark, Brunswick, and Princeton, into the region of Trenton. In a little over two weeks' time, the troops of George Washington, having suffered the fall of New York, were now compelled to vacate New Jersey, totally. At this point the British pursuit became half-hearted, the Hessians and the Redcoats now content with pillaging. Howe and Cornwallis, who by this time had received the news of the surrender of Rhode Island to General Henry Clinton without resistance, saw no need to lose more men to a war that had ended. They were as much aware as Washington himself of the conditions. The Continental Army was decimated, demoralized, and destitute. By the end of the year in which the Declaration of Independence had been authored and signed it had been reduced to impotence. Its troops numbered now a mere 2000 (!), and these, to a man, were so badly clothed and equipped, and so poorly fed as to count for little. Washington and Congress had been feverishly trying to raise new troops, but in vain. So little hope seemed to attach to the cause and so little was left of the army, only an insignificant few "joined up." To anyone who might be appraising the situation, the end of the war must have seemed close at hand. But no reading of the state of affairs should fail to take into account the character of the man in charge. This is where the brothers Howe made their mistake, and this is why any soldier taken by despair should have felt ashamed. Washington, who had even admitted in one communication that "the game was about up," was keenly aware that only with a responsive victory for the Patriot forces could the young nation be saved. And he knew that this victory would have to come soon, very soon. And he knew that the victory would have to be complete; it had to be something that no one could fail to see as a victory for the Continental Army. It had to be made plain that the Army was not prostrate after all. Incredibly, General George Washington was able to snatch just such a victory from the cavernous jaws of despair. And he did not even wait for the end of the year.

John Harris, languishing at home in Salem, fighting his own fight against a stubborn fever, and cared for by an adoring sister, was going to miss out on one of the most glorious moments of the war. But Harris, like thousands of others close to the Army, must have been thrilled by the news when it finally came to him.

The Brandywine

Washington had chosen Christmas night, a time which, as he probably calculated, would not find the Hessian hirelings all that alert. He knew that surprise would be important, probably necessary, if he was to bring this business off. Close to 1,000 German soldiers (three regiments), trained and experienced, with six light guns, were billeted in Trenton. Most of these were the same men who had fought through the battle of New York, who, though treating prisoners cruelly, had shown an impressive soldier savvy. This force was under the command of the very able Colonel Johann Gottlieb Rall (often Rahl), who had fought valiantly for the British at the Battle of White Plains, and had led the Hessian assault on Fort Washington. Rall, who had established his headquarters at the Stacy Potts house on Warren Street, was twelve years older than Washington, a professional soldier with thirty-six years of service, and a veteran of the Seven Years' War. His troops, although they had earned a well deserved reputation for plundering and rape, were battle hardened and severely disciplined. Washington was not expecting a walk in the park.

The Commander-in-Chief, during the week before, had made a plea to New Jersey and to Pennsylvania for militiamen. Very few showed up from New Jersey, but there did appear at Trenton a very substantial force, perhaps as many as 2000, from southeastern Pennsylvania, just in time to help out. Washington's soldiers were chiefly from seven of the thirteen colonies, from General Sullivan's New Hampshire, from Massachusetts and Connecticut, from New York and Pennsylvania, from Delaware and Virginia.

In spite of the prospect of a heavy snow storm and a subsequent freezing rain, Washington was determined to effect a crossing of the broad and formidable Delaware River. He spent most of Christmas Day and the early evening at the McConkey's Ferry Inn, organizing with his officers the plan of attack. After some discouragement at considered crossing points, he ordered the mission. It was to be a three-pronged crossing. Besides the principal force, under Washington, Colonel John Cadwalader (a Philadelphia merchant and a cousin to John Dickinson) was to cross, with Colonel Joseph Reed, at Bristol; and General James Ewing was to cross at Trenton Ferry.

With the Commander-in-Chief in the van, the ferrying of the main body of troops across the river finally got underway. The conditions could hardly have been more wretched, but the soldiers, many of whom had no footwear of any kind, were uncomplaining. Colonel John Glover and his 400 Marblehead fishermen, who were accustomed to this sort of thing, manned the boats. And they had lots of help from the local boatmen from the Philadelphia and New Jersey regions, who rounded up what craft they could, including a number of the commodious Durham boats designed for the transport of iron ore on the river. In all, they carried across 2400 men (eight to ten per boat), eighteen cannon, the necessary horses, and the officers, including General John Sullivan,[3] who had returned to the harness with his characteristic energy, and the very able and resourceful General Nathanael Greene.

Because of the terrible weather, the crossing to the east bank required very nearly ten hours, and the force found itself way behind schedule. The guns of Henry Knox were the big problem, and caused delay not only in the crossing but in the march to follow. The troops did not all reach the other side of the river until three o'clock in the morning (Washington had hoped for midnight), and by the time they were assembled and organized into columns and made ready to move, it was already four o'clock in the morning. Besides, there was the incessant pelting sleet and cold rain to contend with. But the march to Trenton was conducted expeditiously, the force after five miles splitting into two separate armies, one under the command of General Sullivan, and one under the command of General Nathanael Greene, Washington riding with Greene. Washington at this time had no way of knowing that the crossings planned for the other two forces had been so much delayed by the river conditions (whole fields of floating ice) that Cadwalader and Ewing would not be in time for the surprise assault.

At eight o'clock a.m. (Washington had hoped for five o'clock), now in broad daylight, December 26, Washington launched the attack. He had the American guns stationed in such a way, at the top of a little rise which commanded a view of the community's two principal roads, as to ensure confusion among the startled Hessians. And, in fact, the artillery (One of the sections, a company of New York State artillery, was commanded by Captain Alexander Hamilton, who had organized and outfitted the unit himself) played a big part in discouraging any organized resistance. As it turned out, the surprise

Washington had been counting on proved sufficient, and the resulting confusion ensured a complete victory. In the fighting, which lasted at most an hour and a half, nearly 900 Hessians were captured, twenty were killed, including Colonel Rall, who may have neglected warnings and who was indeed surprised,[4] and almost 100 additional were wounded. Although a great many of King George's hirelings were able to escape, the entire garrison was overrun by the patriots.

The Hessians surrendered all of their artillery, six brass pieces, three-pounders.

In the general action at Trenton, the American force suffered, incredibly, only four men wounded, including Captain William Washington (obliquely related to General George) and his subordinate, Virginia-born, eighteen-year-old Lieutenant James Monroe,[5] who was a veteran of Harlem Heights and White Plains, and who here took a very nearly fatal musket ball to the chest (The bullet remained in his shoulder until his dying day.); and two (perhaps as many as five) soldiers frozen to death in the marching.

Also contributing to the marvelous success were the twenty-year-old Aaron Burr; the later-to-be fourth President of the United States, twenty-five-year-old James Madison; and the later-to-be Chief Justice of the Supreme Court, John Marshall, who was just a little beyond his twenty-first birthday at the time of the action. The Battle of Trenton has been called the "first American Christmas." For Washington, it was the victory that he needed.

The Battle of Trenton is a most significant one for Thomas Proctor's Pennsylvania Artillery (in which bombardier John Harris would serve throughout the remainder of the war), which had been formed in October of 1775, as it marks the first real action for this regiment. Major Proctor had been directed to send part of his battalion to join the main army in time for the assault on the Trenton garrison. To meet this request, Proctor detached fifty men from the Company of Captain Thomas Forrest, and placed Forrest in command with officers Third Lieutenant Patrick Duffy of his own company and First Lieutenant Worley Emes of the Company commanded by

Lieutenant Colonel John Martin Strobagh. The detachment was equipped with two brass six-pounders and two 5.5" howitzers.[6]

Forrest's troops took part in the December 26 attack on the Hessian garrison, and, for a first action, conducted themselves admirably.[7] On December 28, Lieutenant Duffy, who had been born in County Longford, Ireland, and had enlisted on March 14, provided, and not a little proudly, Major Proctor some account of their experience. He reported that the artillerymen had returned to McKonkey's Ferry the day before (the 27th), "after a very fataguing (though very successfull) engagement, in which [I] can assure you, the artillery got applause." He was pleased to be able to add that "I had the Honour of being detach'd up the Main Street in front of the Savages [Hessians--called "savages" ever since their extreme brutality (the bayoneting of prisoners) in the fighting at Long Island became well known], without any other piece, and sustained the fire of Several gunns from the Houses on each side, without the least loss . . . ." And then he closed out his report with a lament: "The men are very much Nonplus'd for Shoes and Watch Coats." He very much hoped that Major Proctor could produce these articles for the detachment.[8]

From Captain Forrest, Major Proctor heard pretty much the same story the very next day. Forrest wrote that " . . . we have return'd from Trenton after defeating the Brass Caps and Crous coups." And then, like Lieutenant Duffy, he complained of the condition of the men. "Am now under marching orders on an other Expedition over the river [action of Assunpink], but the men are not able to move for want of Shoes and Watch Coats, which I expect you'll forward [by] bearer immediately with Gunn Screws and the Regimental Coats . . . ."[9] It is not known just how much equipment Proctor showed up with, but he did arrive in person from Fort Island, and with additional men and two more guns.[10]

The Battle of Trenton spilled over into what is sometimes considered The Second Battle of Trenton, often called the Battle of Assunpink, which occurred a week after the opening action. Lord Cornwallis, appalled by what he had heard of the Hessian surrender, set out for Trenton from Princeton on January 2. He was following the Post Road, a distance of some sixteen miles. Most fortunately for the American forces (now much swollen in number), which were now assembled on the farther side (the south side) of the creek known as

Assunpink, Cornwallis met a very stubborn resistance in the person of Colonel Edward Hand[11] and his Pennsylvania riflemen, who had fought so valiantly at Long Island. Hand, who while in command of the Western Department had not proved an enthusiastic or effective Indian fighter, here deployed his soldiers Indian style, and while steadily falling back to the south, had them fire with their squirrel guns from behind trees and from well scattered positions. He was able to keep the skirmishing going throughout the afternoon, and so much delayed the British that they did not arrive in Trenton until dusk, failing three times to cross the Assunpink Creek. But Henry Knox, with characteristic pride, insisted that it was the American artillery, composed of 30-40 pieces (some of them captured Hessian guns), which "saved the day." And indeed it was his infant artillery which thrice turned back the Redcoats at the bridge.

Rudely repulsed, Cornwallis now considered a night-time attack, but at last rejected that proposal and determined to wait for morning. Washington, who had been persuaded to continued action by the late but welcome arrival of Cadwalader in New Jersey, now, reputedly at the suggestion and insistence of General Arthur St. Clair, who was still smarting from the embarrassment experienced at Three Rivers, determined on Princeton! At midnight he moved his army out, stealing away quite undetected. He was marching back the road Cornwallis had come.

Now flushed with the novel sensations of success, Washington moved quickly to Princeton. Through this clever maneuvering at Assunpink he had been able not only to sidestep the troops of Lord Cornwallis but to put him out of his intended action. Now he would engage whatever British regulars were left at Princeton.

With his two strong arms, Sullivan on the right and Greene on the left, he marched his Continental troops with an impressive number of militia toward the British garrison. The battle was joined at the farm of Thomas Clarke, whose fields lay just outside the tiny village of Princeton.

Although the advance party, under the command of General Hugh Mercer (whose valor in the battle of New York had been conspicuous), suffered extremely heavy casualties, the Americans carried the action into the community of Princeton itself, and finally drove the British in disarray from Nassau Hall[12] (principal building of the College of New Jersey, the campus home of James Madison), which during the action was occupied alternately by the British and Americans.

Perhaps even more miraculously than at Trenton, the remnants of the Continental Army now won, at Princeton, a complete victory, in effect defeating the formidable force commanded by Lord Cornwallis. The date was January 3, 1777.

And again, Proctor's artillerymen, inexperienced as they were, figured impressively in the action. Now attached to the brigade of Colonel John Cadwalader,[13] who had been too late in crossing the river for the battle of Trenton (but whom Washington much respected), they advanced briskly into the community of Princeton itself, and there promptly, and happily, discovered three brass six-pounders which had been abandoned by the fleeing Redcoats. As the resourceful Proctor did not have with him enough horses to tow away all three of the guns, he unharnessed the horses from one of his old guns, a very inferior iron piece, and hitched them to one of the brass guns. A second captured gun was hurled into a well, but, as they feared the appearance of Cornwallis at any moment, the third was left on the field for the British to return to.[14] Lost in the battle was the valiant and very popular General Hugh Mercer,[15] who was mortally wounded on the farm fields of Thomas Clarke by the foot soldiers of His Majesty's 17th and 55th Regiments. The General, although terribly hurt and surrounded on the field, refused to surrender, and was bayoneted more than a dozen times. He was carried to the Clarke House, which was being used as a hospital by both the Redcoats and the Americans, and there lingered for some nine days. He finally succumbed to his wounds on January 12.

Hugh Mercer

The victories at Trenton and Princeton were in consequence

Thomas Clarke House

of (1) the surprise Washington had counted on, which was insured by the timely arrival of the fierce winter weather; (2) the strategic skills of Washington and his officers, perhaps especially in the deployment of the infant artillery; (3) the inspiring figure of Washington himself, who was regularly in the heat of the action; and (4) the dogged determination of the patriot soldier, who, amazingly, transformed the fatigue of the river crossings and the marches through the storm into the spirited momentum that carries the day.

The effect of the Trenton-Princeton victories, especially after Washington established solid positions on the high ground at Morristown, in north-central New Jersey, was to occasion a British withdrawal from all of New Jersey. As the Redcoats holed up in New York City, some observers were even tempted to call their leaving a "retreat."

And of course another, most considerable, effect was to cement General George Washington in his post as Commander-in-Chief. But it should be noted that even *before* these engagements Congress had not only formally expressed its confidence in its Commander-in-Chief but had most significantly extended his authority over the military operation.

It was also recognized that as the war proceeded, the artillery of Henry Knox was becoming ever more consequential. At the three battles of Trenton, Assunpink, and Princeton, the American artillery not only outnumbered the British and Hessians in field guns (more than two to one), but made them more effective.

The time beginning with Christmas night and including the Battle of Princeton is sometimes referred to as the Ten Crucial Days. Although these victories came, as most do, at the painful cost of good men, including General Hugh Mercer, it was an auspicious beginning to the new year. Washington and his devoted soldiers had, for the time, saved the new nation.

At the close of the action at Princeton, while the army was in camp at Somerset, Washington's chief artillery officer, now a Brigadier General, Henry Knox, had a recommendation to make to his Commander-in-Chief. "Let us get on to Morristown!" he declared. And Washington was ready.

Washington at Princeton

As the armies regrouped in the early part of 1777, the British High Command devised a plan, which, they were confident, would put an end to the rebellion (They continued to call it a "rebellion.") by year's end. The plan was elaborate, as it involved three large armies, one force under General John Burgoyne, another under General Barry St. Leger, and a third under General Howe. The idea was to separate, with scissors movements, the northern colonies from the southern. As it happened, the plan was destined to fail.

During the late winter and early spring of the year, because of the American successes at Trenton and Princeton and the British evacuation of New Jersey, militiamen, both old and new, were coming into the Continental Army in ever-increasing numbers. Some preferred the militiaman status, but others were joining the regular army. John Harris, of Salem, New Jersey, his recovery perhaps speeded by the news of victories close to home, was determined to become a member of the "real" army under Washington.

Even though Harris, with his own land now, must have been considering the life of the farmer as he recovered from his illness, nothing could dissuade him from his determination to participate in the Revolution. On April 10, 1777, he enlisted, probably at Philadelphia, in the regular army "for the duration." Because of his experience, he was promptly ranked as a bombardier and assigned to the 4th Continental Artillery Regiment under the command of Colonel Thomas Proctor.[16] Harris's friend Samuel Blackwood, who had joined up on March 1, was already with Proctor's artillery.[17]

The 4th Continental Artillery had grown out of a company that had been formed as a Pennsylvania unit in October of 1775, chiefly for the defense of Philadelphia and the Delaware River. In the beginning the " regiment" was to be composed of a captain, a lieutenant, and twenty-seven enlisted men. It was to afford protection to Philadelphia from its post on Fort Island (Mud Island) in the Delaware River, at that point where the Schuylkill enters the larger stream.[18]

On October 27, the very day that he had made application to the Pennsylvania Council of Safety, Thomas Proctor was appointed Captain of Artillery, "with authority to raise a company," and his father, Francis Proctor, Sr., was commissioned lieutenant. The Proctors, father and son, had emigrated from Ireland, and Thomas had established himself as a carpenter in Philadelphia. Neither had had any miliary experience to speak of.

By December, stationed still at Fort Island and "presiding" over the Delaware River, the company was composed of ninety men and by July had increased to 114 men. Eventually it was enlarged to a two-company battalion, finally becoming the Pennsylvania Artillery Regiment (known later as the 4th Continental Artillery Regiment). In its larger size, the Regiment was composed of as many foreign-born as native-born. Most of the foreign born had come to this country from Ireland and England, some from Germany. One of the originals was John Hays, a Carlisle, Pa., barber, best known as the husband of "Molly Pitcher," whose heroics helped to distinguish the Battle of Monmouth.[19]

During the Revolution the primary weapons of war were the muzzleloading flintlock musket (which in able hands could be fired four times a minute), with its attached bayonet, and the various types of cannon. The secondary weapons were the Pennsylvania rifle, affectionately called the "squirrel gun" (which had a greater range and was more accurate than the musket), the pistol, and the cutlass. But at the beginning of the war there was really very little in the way of cannon available to the Continental Army. As time went on, it became steadily more apparent that artillery was not only an important cog in the war machine, it was absolutely vital. Washington, appreciating that effective artillery was a condition of success, charged Henry Knox early on with the building of this segment of the army. Knox was a good choice.

By the middle years of the war the Continental Army included four full-scale regiments of artillery, with detachments dispatched hither and yon. The commander of each regiment held the rank of Colonel. For most of the time during the war, Charles Harrison commanded the First Regiment; John Lamb had the Second Regiment, which was originally a New York State regiment, and would distinguish itself at Yorktown; John Crane had charge of the Third; and of course Proctor the Fourth. The Third Continental Artillery, though called the "Third," was actually the oldest of the four regiments. It had been organized originally by Colonel Richard Gridley of Massachusetts in 1775, shortly before Proctor's regiment was formed that fall. Command of the Third Regiment passed first to Henry Knox and finally to Colonel John Crane, who throughout the war would outrank all other artillery colonels.

By the time the war heated up, the Artillery had become a big part of the American forces; and it had become steadily more and more respected. By some it was even regarded the elite of the army.

The artillerymen are of course responsible for the transport, positioning, and firing of the muzzle-loading field cannon and siege howitzers. The function of the field cannon, firing in a flat trajectory, is to propel solid balls against barricaded troops and enemy cannon.

The Brandywine

To produce a kind of shotgun effect, the cannon would fire grapeshot and canister shot (made up of chains and all sorts of nasty stuff). Grapeshot was employed against advancing enemy troops, and it could be deadly. Howitzers, which, like the field cannon, were on wheels and mobile, fired in a higher trajectory, launching "bombs" into forts.

For a standard field cannon the gun crew was composed of at least seven men and sometimes of as many as fourteen. The sergeant, under the command of a captain or lieutenant, would oversee, and each member of his crew had his own very specific job to do, and each knew all of the roles. And all, desirably, would be so well trained that every move, with its critical timing, had become second nature. It was a practiced art, and required great skill. This skill of course was acquired through rigid training and through experience.

The artillerymen were responsible for quite an inventory, and their ammunition wagons carried, besides the cannon balls and canisters of grape shot, so many items that a check-off list was essential to the supply sergeant. They needed adequate quantities of everything necessary to the firing of the guns. They needed ramrods, and wormers, and sponges. They needed bags of powder and priming horns. They needed the linstock, which accommodates the slow match.

The procedure for firing required, above everything else, perfect timing. John Harris and every member of his crew would have the timing down pat. All the members of his crew were well trained in all of the functions, and if a member were to fall, anyone else could replace him.

First, of course, the field piece is hauled into position with drag ropes. Four or five men could be required, or, especially if a slope is involved, even horses. As the barrel of the cannon moves freely in its carriage it can be elevated or lowered easily. This is done by means of an elevating screw, the proper angle being determined by the gunner's quadrant. It is the job of the wormer to make certain that any sparks which may remain from the previous firing are extinguished and that all residues are removed from the barrel. With a sponge he cleaned the bore. Debris that may have built up in the bore was constantly being removed with an instrument called, affectionately, by the gunners, a wad hook.

The powder was generally pre-measured and contained in a

bag, cloth or paper. After the bag of powder is forced to the rear of the barrel, the rammer with his rod drives the cannon ball, or whatever is to be fired, snug against the powder. With a "pick" the bag of powder is pierced, and the tiny "touch-hole" at the breech end is primed with the ignition powder. All is ready for the command to "Fire." And a smoldering wick supplies the spark.

Of course the occupation of the artilleryman was a dangerous one, for a cannon, because of mismanagement or carelessness, or because of ancient or defective material, could explode on the spot. And it very often did so.

Cannon are known by the weight of the ball being fired. Hence there are the "four-pounder" and the "six-pounder" and the "12-pounder," which would have a range, for solid shot, of 800 or 900 yards, for grape shot not so far. Guns were as large as the 32-pounder, but nothing bigger than the 12-pounder was practical in the field. Washington rarely had anything larger than the six-pounder.

The cannon were on wheels, so they were mobile; but they were extremely heavy, often reaching a weight of 3200 pounds. Such great strength is required to move the field pieces that for any distance horses (as many as twelve) must be used. In the Continental Army, civilian drivers, the owners of the horses, were often employed to transport the cannon. Guns were towed by horses; the cannoneers marched on foot.

Generally the artillerymen are in advance of the infantry, in order to "soften up" the enemy, or, in the case of Indians, to frighten them, four guns to each brigade. The horses have pulled the cannon to approximately the firing site. Now the animals are unharnessed and taken to safer ground. It is up to the gun crew now. The matrosses, through brute strength, wrestle the firing piece into its place in the battlefield. The crew maneuvers the cannon up to the firing line, and fixes it in position. A major problem is the recoil. The explosion is so terrific that the gun carriage is driven back violently at the time of the firing, sometimes a good distance. Now of course the gun has to be "run up" and repositioned.

Generally an elevated piece of ground is sought for the artillery. Getting the cannon up a slope, especially when the ground is rugged, can be a chore, and requires time. But that is only half the battle, and the easier half at that. The artillerymen are responsible for the field pieces. When a retreat is sounded, the artillerymen do not simply fall back from the front. They withdraw *with* their cannon. And that means, for the heavy pieces, bringing up the horses and hitching them up. Many artillerymen who have survived two or three hours of shelling are lost in the effort to salvage their gun.

But the guns must be saved, if at all possible. When casualties after a battle are tallied, it is so many officers killed, wounded, captured and missing; so many men killed, wounded, captured and missing; so many field pieces destroyed or captured.

So time is important. If the artillery is to conduct an orderly retreat it needs time. And often there is no time. Time then needs to be bought for the artillery. Generally it is provided by the infantry, by means of a covering fire. Some officers during the Revolution, Anthony Wayne notable among them, developed quite a knack for doing just that.

Bombardier John Harris, when it was available, for the last four years of the war, wore the distinctive artillery uniform that was prescribed by the edict of 1779. Consequently he was attired in a bright blue coat, faced and lined with scarlet. The button holes were bound with a narrow lace, and the buttons themselves were yellow.[20] But for long periods of time, especially in the early going, the artillerymen, like the infantrymen themselves, had no uniforms at all, and often even, as at Valley Forge, had no shoes or adequate clothing.

Most members of the gun crew were known as matrosses. "Matross" is a term that is not used any more. During the Revolution it was the term employed for the gunner's mate, who assisted in the loading and firing and sponging of the guns.

John Harris was a bombardier in the gun crew. The term "bombardier" is British in origin and designates rank rather than duty. The term probably derives from the habit of calling a launched shell a "bomb." A bombardier was, in the opinion of his superiors, a skilled artilleryman and held rank as a non-commissioned officer equivalent to that of a corporal in the infantry, or something a little less. Toward the end of the war, the artillerymen having been granted a raise, bombardier John Harris was paid $9 a month, when pay came at all. His friend Samuel Blackwood, who served with the rank of sergeant, was paid a little more, $10 a month.

It should be noted, that the artillery had still another, and completely different function. That was to supply the ceremonial music. This, with its fifers and drummers, it regularly did, with gusto.

Of course neither Harris, nor his friend Blackwood, was with Proctor's artillery during its first real action, the fighting at Trenton and Princeton, but extraordinarily good service, as described earlier, was provided by the company commanded by Captain Thomas Forrest. His company was composed of fifty privates and the necessary officers, including the Irish Lieutenant Patrick Duffy, with two six-pounder brass field pieces.

After the successes of Trenton and Princeton, in which the artillery played not a major role but a significant role, Washington moved his army into winter quarters at Morristown, in the sprawling Passaic River watershed, in the northern part of New Jersey, and extending south about fifteen miles to the little village known as Pluckemin. Washington was at Pluckemin on January 4th and 5th. His headquarters, from January 6 until May 28, was at Arnold's Tavern. Proctor and Forrest had gone north to Morristown with the army, and on January 16 were joined there by Captain Strobagh's company. Some members of Proctor's regiment, doing duty especially for Pennsylvania, remained on the Delaware under the command of Captain-Lieutenant Hercules Courteney. At the encampment at Pluckemin, the artillery portion of the army was confined to its own location, the Artlllery Park, which surrounded the Van der Meer House.

A strategic location, between New York City and the new nation's capital at Philadelphia, the camp afforded a good opportunity to monitor the activity of the British Army, now quartered in New York City. Besides, the terrain appeared to Washington to be very defensible; and Morristown was at the center of a kind of spider web of communications. But most important to the Commander-in-Chief were the people of the region. Washington felt very confident that he would have here at Morristown the enthusiastic and generous support of the community.

But Washington had not snuggled up in this encampment to

nurse his wounds. He was feeling pretty good about his young army, and he had been made most happy to receive the flood of enlistments which promptly followed the dramatic victories at Trenton and at Princeton. Now he could continue with renewed confidence the building of the Continental Army into the fighting force he knew would be ultimately necessary.

He was close enough to Howe, garrisoned in New York City, to keep an eye on him, but he was also close enough to be vulnerable. And he actually expected that a major strike would be forthcoming, perhaps soon. Accordingly, from his headquarters, he directed the installation of fortifications, and established a surveillance system that could report regularly on Howe. He supposed that Howe had designs on Philadelphia, and that he could at almost any time make a move in that direction.

One of Washington's first official duties, upon arriving at Pluckemin, indeed the day after, was hardly what he had expected it would be. He was asked by his close friend, the Army's surgeon, Dr. Benjamin Rush,[21] who had tended the wounded at Assunpink, to attend a funeral. Although this was to be the funeral of a British officer, Washington, in his characteristically gracious manner, was most happy to oblige. No one knew better than Washington the terrible cost of war, and in the case of his own army the price to be paid for freedom. And no one could feel more deeply the pain of casualties. Besides the grief, there was with Washington the agony of responsibility. Those who had any sort of conscience had to feel passionately about what they were doing.

Rush, Washington had heard, had been reduced to tears by the news of the death of his good friend Captain William Leslie of the 17th British Regiment. Rush had gotten to know the Leslie family while he was a medical student at the university in Edinburgh, Scotland. "Willie," as he was always popularly known, belonged to the nobility. He was the second son of the Earl of Leven. And he had a sister, Jean, of whom the young Benjamin Rush had grown very fond.

The circumstances which brought about the burial of a British officer at the encampment of the American Army are truly amazing. The young captain (he was twenty-six) had been killed at Princeton, on January 3, struck down by two musket balls. He had been a member of a very small British detachment which at Clarke's Orchard, near where General Mercer fell, just outside Princeton, had run into the main force of the Rebel army. But as he died, he collapsed into the arms of his servant, Peter Macdonald, who then tenderly placed the body in a British supply wagon. This wagon, however, was abandoned by the Redcoats in the confused aftermath of the fighting and was confiscated and taken by the patriots to Morristown. Next day, the astonished soldiers discovered the body of Captain Leslie in the wagon. In one of his pockets they found a letter, which had been addressed to him by Dr. Rush. In this letter Rush was urging Leslie, if ever he was taken prisoner, to try to get paroled to the Rush family home in Philadelphia. Because of this letter of course Rush was notified of the death of the officer, and the doctor, deeply moved, arranged for his burial in Pluckemin.

Thomas Mifflin

It was a ceremonious affair. Under the supervision of General Thomas Mifflin,[22] Leslie was buried with full military honors. Besides Washington and Mifflin, there were in attendance Generals Henry Knox and John Sullivan. Dr. Rush, in the year following the end of the war paid for and had erected a gravestone memorial to his young friend. The inscription upon the stone reads: "In Memory of the Honorable Captain William Leslie of the 17th British Regiment–Son of the Earl of Leven in Scotland. He fell on Jan. 3, 1777, Aged 26 years at the battle of Princeton–His friend Benjamin Rush M. D. of Philadelphia hath caused this Stone to be erected as a mark of his esteem for his worth and of respect for his noble family."

During the winter months of 1777, while encamped in the Morristown region, Washington kept up a constant stream of correspondence with his officers, who were hither, thither, and yon, and with the Congress and with the Pennsylvania Department of Safety. One of his officers who was with him through this time was

John Sullivan, but as he was day and night skirmishing with the British outposts, all across the northern section of New Jersey, he was not in camp much. General Henry Knox, in charge of all artillery, was in camp only the first two weeks, as he took leave on January 17.

From the time Proctor's artillery was in camp, the soldiers were busy. The General Orders from Washington's Headquarters on January 23, directed Major Proctor "to inspect and arrange the artillery in such manner as he shall think best, for the defence of this place, taking care to have such repairs immediately made, as may be wanting, with horses allotted to each piece [of artillery], and all necessary harness ready."[23]

A week later, January 31, Washington notes, in a letter to the Pennsylvania Council of Safety, that he has learned from Proctor that some 140 artillerymen of his Corps are now doing duty at the forts upon the Delaware River. Very eager to beef up the artillery of the main army, he requests the Council, which still has authority over Proctor's artillery, to detach "about 100 of these men to be put under the command of Major Proctor," presently here at Morristown.[24]

On February 5, while still at the Morristown Headquarters, Major Thomas Proctor of the Pennsylvania Artillery was given Continental Army rank. He was commissioned Colonel of the Regiment and given command of the Fourth Continental Artillery. On the same date, Thomas Forrest, having served in Proctor's Pennsylvania artillery battalion as Captain of the Second Company, and later with Proctor as the first major, was promoted to Lieutenant Colonel.[25]

For Proctor this was a big promotion. The Fourth Continental Artillery, at the time of its organization, had been authorized eight companies, but at this time was composed of only seven. It would swell at the middle of July to the prescribed eight and continue in force until the summer of 1779, when it would be reduced again to seven.[26]

On March 1, Proctor's artillery was helped out some by new enlistments. One of these was Samuel Blackwood of Salem, New Jersey, a good friend to John Harris, who would become in five weeks his comrade until the end of the war. Blackwood was promptly commissioned Sergeant and assigned to Proctor's artillery. It is not known whether Blackwood was assigned to the forts on the Delaware or to Proctor's encamped artillery at Morristown.

General Henry Knox, in command of all artillery, had taken leave shortly after the main army made camp for the winter at Morristown. In the absence of General Knox, Washington had, on January 17, turned over temporary command of the artillery of the Continental Army to Colonel Proctor. Actually, the only artillery force that remained with the main army from January through April were Proctor's men (not his whole regiment) and two companies of New Jersey artillery.[27]

On March 7, the Pennsylvania Council of Safety, having honored Washington's request for more of Proctor's men, now requested Washington for Proctor's presence in Philadelphia. Washington begged off, noting that until General Knox returned to the encampment he needed Proctor at the head of the artillery forces.[28] And one week later, with still no Knox, he dispatches a letter to the General, in which he urges him to get back to Morristown, as he is going to have to send Proctor to Philadelphia.[29]

On May 29, Washington moved his headquarters a little south to Middlebrook.

When on April 10, John Harris, determined to be in the service of Washington, enlists in the Continental Army, he is, like Blackwood, assigned to the 4th Continental Artillery, under the command of Colonel Proctor and Lieutenant Colonel Thomas Forrest. He is designated a bombardier and is made a member of Company B, which at that time was under the leadership of Captain Hercules Courteney and still in its position on the Delaware River protecting Philadelphia.[30]

Very shortly thereafter, on April 13, Proctor's regiment of artillery lost the services of two of its bravest officers and twenty members of the gun crews.

This costly action is called the Battle of Bound Brook, and it is an episode of war that was a part of the "skirmishing" that was occurring during the time Washington was encamped close to New York City. It involves General Benjamin Lincoln,[31] who at Assunpink and Princeton had assumed command of the corps of the captured General Charles Lee. Lincoln had been charged by Washington with the protection of the region surrounding Bound Brook, on the Raritan River, just south of present-day Plainfield and five or six miles north of Brunswick (now New Brunswick), where General Lord Cornwallis was billeted. Cornwallis, in command of some 17,000 troops had been conducting frequent foraging raids, but had lost a lot of men in the region around Plainfield.

Much of what is now known of the Battle of Bound Brook comes from the diary of Johann Ewald, a Hessian in the services of the British. It was he who drew up the battle plan.

Benjamin Lincoln

Lincoln here had at his command only a small detachment, some 500 members of the 21st Pennsylvania Regiment, a portion of Proctor's artillery regiment, and some militia. Lincoln was doing his best to protect the region, but these men were insufficient in number to provide a guard for six square miles, or even to patrol it effectively. Well aware of Lincoln's inadequacies, Cornwallis asked Ewald for a strategy of attack, and on the early morning of April 13, Palm Sunday, put it into execution. Passing in the pre-dawn darkness through the sparse patrols Lincoln had posted along the river, Cornwallis' best troops, led by Cornwallis himself and General Grant, arrived undetected within 200 yards (!) of Lincoln's quarters. The surprise was so great that Lincoln's forces were routed, and Lincoln himself, who was headquartered in the Van Horne House, escaped by a hair's breadth. The British, having had their way in the limited action, now contented themselves with destroying such stores of ammunition and provisions as they could locate. The whole operation required but an hour and a half, before Cornwallis crossed back over the river and began his return to Brunswick. That evening General Lincoln, now bolstered by reinforcements returned to his post.[32]

Lord Howe in his account of the battle reported the British losses as three killed and four wounded. On the day after the battle,

Washington reported to the Board of War that the army's chief losses were two pieces of artillery and Lieutenants Ferguson and Turnbull with "about twenty men of Colo. Proctor's regiment." Explained Washington, "A party of horse was pushed so suddenly upon them that they could not possibly get off." It is not clear from his language whether Washington considered the lost soldiers killed or captured. Actually, both of the officers and most of the men were taken prisoner. Turnbull was kept a prisoner for almost three years. He is listed on the general return of the Pennsylvania Regiment of Artillery for March 29, 1780. Ferguson was held by the British even longer, finally being exchanged on Dec. 1, 1780.[33] As Harris was surely with Courteney on the Delaware River at this time, he could not have participated in the skirmish.[34]

Washington, as noted, had established his campsite at the Middlebrook Heights near Bound Brook on the Raritan River. He felt the need for a closer observation of the British troops in Perth Amboy and Brunswick. But on June 22, the British moved out of Brunswick altogether, assembling first at Amboy, and then withdrawing to Staten Island. It was at just about this time (actually June 14) that the Continental Congress officially adopted the "Betsy Ross" flag as the National banner. It is thought by some that the flag was first flown from Washington's headquarters at Middlebrook.[35]

Good news came to Washington on July 16. He was very pleased to hear that Congress had, at last, taken Colonel Proctor's Corps of Artillery into the Continental Service (Heretofore it had been a Pennsylvania unit at the whim of the Pennsylvania Council of Safety.). This accommodation was largely owing to the influence and lobbying of General Knox, whom Washington had been prodding. The Commander-in-Chief responded that very day, urging the Congress to order Proctor's Artillery to "join the Army immediately," which meant bringing it to Smith's Clove, on the west bank of the Hudson, where Washington would be by July 20. Then later that same day he dispatches a correction, suggesting that Proctor be told to stop at Trenton, where he is to join with Brigadier General Francis Nash.[36]

At this time there was a lot of activity in the north, but of course Proctor's artillery was not involved in the action there, which had British General John Burgoyne marching south from Montreal and had General Barry St. Leger, with his Indian allies, coming from Lake

The Brandywine

Ontario in the west, hoping to hook up with Burgoyne at Albany. All of this action of course was a part of the British general plan to divide the colonies. But St. Leger did not last long.

Oriskany Monument

Nicholas Herkimer

As Burgoyne moved south from Fort Ticonderoga toward Albany, General St. Leger was marching east, down the Mohawk River, also headed for Albany. But St. Leger, whose forces were composed not only of British Regulars but of large numbers of the fierce Iroquois, resolved on an attempt on the American garrison at Fort Stanwix.

Learning of an American force led by General Nicholas Herkimer,[37] which included a handful of Oneida warriors, who had not joined those Iroquois who were allied with the British, St. Leger prepared an ambush. In the fierce fighting which followed, at Oriskany, near Utica, New York, the British with their Indian allies routed the rebel forces and wounded Herkimer, the General taking a musket ball in the leg. Herkimer, having been propped up against the base of a beech tree, continued to direct the battle for a time, feverishly trying to restore order. But all was in vain and the General was carried back to his home by his withdrawing militia. Ten days later, after his leg had been amputated, the courageous Herkimer died.

Often described as "the bloodiest battle of the war" (Herkimer lost almost everybody, over 500 killed, or wounded, or taken prisoner), the engagement at Oriskany turned out to be the only real victory for the British in this northern half of their complex campaign.[38]

And the King's Men had little time to relish it.

St. Leger's forces marched on to Fort Stanwix and promptly placed the American garrison under siege. But eventually, chiefly because of the arrival of reinforcements under Benedict Arnold, they were compelled to abandon the siege, and ignominiously returned all the way to Montreal. Victory for the British had been turned into defeat and discouragement; and "the great plan" had been delivered a major setback. Now the rebel forces under Horatio Gates and Arnold could fix their attention entirely on the Burgoyne threat to Albany.

Proctor's artillery had not been in on the second action at Fort Ticonderoga, which saw the fort recaptured by Burgoyne; nor was it anywhere close when Burgoyne suffered two very damaging defeats in the battles of Saratoga Springs. But two months before Burgoyne would finally surrender his entire army to General Horatio Gates (October 17), the focal point of the war had become Philadelphia, as Washington had known it would. For a long time now, it had been almost certain that General Howe, still in New York City at midsummer, would determine on the capital city of the new nation.

It was for this reason that on July 16 Colonel Proctor had received orders from Washington to move the 4th Continental Artillery to Trenton. Proctor was able to get the regiment, with all of its cannon, to Trenton in eight days, and promptly dispatched orders to Captain Hercules Courteney, who was at Fort Island on the Delaware, to join the regiment there. The arrival of Courteney's company at Trenton, on August 22, marked the first time that the 4th Continental Artillery had ever been all together in one place![39] Now fully assembled, it stood in with General Francis Nash, awaiting further orders. It was ready for action.

The Brandywine

Meantime, while Washington was headquartered in Bucks County, Pa., the ever-restless General John Sullivan was making plans of his own. The British had been all summer sending out foraging parties, from the New York City region, many of them launched from Staten Island. They were constantly harassing the people of New Jersey and Connecticut, plundering cattle and seizing provisions for their garrisons. Sullivan, always imaginative and always inclined toward action, was determined with his 1000 troops to raid the principal source of the trouble, that is, Staten Island.

According to his information, which he carefully reviewed with his officers, while some 1600 British and Hessian regulars were stationed at the northeast end of the island, only about 1000 men were available to defend the shores he would be assaulting, and most of these were Tory militiamen, well scattered. He felt confident that from his encampment in the Hanover region, some twenty miles from his intended crossing, he could carry out a very successful hit-and-run expedition.

John Sullivan

Accordingly, on August 21 he set out for Elizabethtown (present-day Elizabeth) at the head of detachments from the brigades of William Smallwood and Prudhomme de Borre, with some few troops under the very able command of Colonel Matthias Ogden. The raid was launched on a fleet of small boats in the morning of August 22.

In the early action Sullivan's troops enjoyed considerable success, but after seizing some cattle and taking some prisoners, the officers experienced the same confusion and disorder that had attended General William Thompson and Colonel William Irvine at the ill-fated battle of Three Rivers. Here the troops did not find their way back to the point on which they had arrived, and as they searched in vain for the necessary boats, Sullivan lost close to 200 men and a good portion of his plunder. In the end the raid had to be counted a failure, and by some was even considered a fiasco. In the final tally (by the General's own estimate), the patriots lost ten killed, fifteen wounded, and 140 captured. So embarrassing was the outcome that the expedition was promptly made the object of an official investigation, and Sullivan himself was scheduled for trial before a Court of Inquiry.

The Court, presided over by Lord Stirling, and composed of Generals MacDougall and Knox, and Colonels Spencer and Clark, was not convened until later that fall, indeed not until a whole month after the battle at the Brandywine would be fought. By the time it finally did meet, on October 10, the dust had settled, and the officers had available to them some very reliable accounts of the action. By the 12th it had reached a verdict. The judges were unanimous in their opinion that the expedition was "eligible, and promised great advantage to the cause of America." Having considered all of the evidence available (much of it in the testimony of Sullivan's officers, particularly Ogden), they concluded that "General Sullivan's conduct in planning and executing the expedition was such that . . . he deserves the approbation of the country, and not its censure."[40] In short, he was exonerated, acquitted of all charges, and declared blameless. Washington's General Orders for October 16 published the findings of the court. Sullivan was pleased, of course, with the decision, but he could never feel all that good about any action which occasioned a Court of Inquiry.

On the very same day that Sullivan launched his raid on Staten Island, August 22, Washington was sending out orders in all directions. Now with his presumptions confirmed, and with the knowledge that Howe was in fact preparing to launch from Head of Elk in Maryland an assault on the nation's capital at Philadelphia, he dispatched imperatives to his officers. From his headquarters at Neshaminy Camp, near Hartsville, in Bucks County, Pennsylvania, he ordered General Sullivan to join the main army at once. In three weeks from the time he received the order Sullivan had his troops with the Commander-in-Chief at Wilmington.

On that same day, August 22, Washington issued orders which involved Proctor and his artillery regiment. The directive, addressed to Brigadier General Francis Nash, was throbbing with urgency:

> *Sir: You will immediately proceed with your Brigade and Colo. Proctor's Corps of Artillery to Chester. If you can readily procure Craft to transport the troops by Water you will. If you cannot, you will march by Land and send your Baggage by Water if there be Vessels Sufficient to carry it. Shou'd you be disappointed in this also, it must go by land in such Waggons as you can get for the purpose. I have this Minute received advice by express, that General Howe's fleet is high up in the North East part of Chesapeak Bay.*
>
> *P.S. Should you be obliged to march by land, I wish you to order your march so, as not to go thro' Philadelphia and to pass by it without halting your troops near it.*[41]

Proctor made it to Chester in good time, floating down the Delaware River by flatboat, but there immediately had still another order from Washington, who was now in Chester himself, urging the artillery not to delay in Chester ('this town") but to "proceed with all convenient dispatch to Wilmington."[42] There, while continuing with Nash, he was to unite with the division commanded by General Anthony Wayne. Proctor in a very short march was able to join forces with Wayne at Wilmington. The soldiers learned then that they would be marching north to some place called Chadds Ford.[43]

General Henry Knox was already at Wilmington. In a letter to his wife Lucy, composed September 1, he let her know what he knew about Howe's movements: "The enemy have landed at the Head of Elk, in Maryland, about twenty miles from this. Whether they intend to advance or not is not at present certain. We shall remain here a few days; and if they will not come to us, we shall go to them. It is supposed the enemy intend for Philadelphia; if so, they will meet with a stout opposition."[44] But Knox apparently had little idea about the size of Howe's force. The British army that had been transported to Maryland was huge. Some 260 vessels of all descriptions were required to ferry the Redcoats south to Head of Elk.

In the middle of all of this movement some desertions naturally occurred, a few from Proctor's force. According to the General Orders issued September 3, "Daniel Fennel of Col. Proctor's regt., charged with 'Deserting from the said regiment,' found guilty, and sentenced to receive one hundred lashes on his bare back, and to forfeit one month's pay for the use of the sick."[45] Bombardier John

Harris was an unwilling witness to this punishment.

The Brandywine[46] is a very small stream. It can hardly even be counted a river. Most call it a creek. It rises from the marshes north of the tiny community of Lyndell, and is bolstered some by the Indian Run Branch, Beaver Creek, Valley Run, and Taylor Run. Just north of the settlement known as Lenape, its West Branch joins the East. It is an idyllic, meandering creek, which only infrequently becomes enraged. With its quiet, mist-enshrouded waters it delivers a charm to that lovely valley of southeastern Pennsylvania in the region of Downingtown and West Chester, before flowing into the Christina River at Wilmington, and hurrying on to the Chesapeake. On September 11, 1777, it would assume a big place in American history.

On July 23, General William Howe, with Cornwallis, marched his troops (15,000 strong) aboard a fleet of British vessels, and by sea sailed south for the Chesapeake Bay. He might have elected to go up the Delaware River to Philadelphia; but he had chosen this route as safest and most expeditious. Proceeding north through the Bay, he landed, August 25, at what was then known as Head of Elk (present-day Elkton, Maryland), fifty miles south of Philadelphia and just a day's march from Chadds Ford.

Washington, monitoring the British movement, elected, with the 11,000 troops he had assembled, to intercept the army at the Brandywine. It was not enough of a stream to pose any difficulty to fording, but Washington thought it a good place to engage Howe, and he had chosen the Chadds Ford section at which to make a stand. It was Chadds Ford that provided the normal crossing for those traveling from Baltimore to Philadelphia, and Washington naturally assumed that Howe would be crossing here.

On the morning of September 9th the American army arrived in the region of the ford. Washington established headquarters at the farmhouse of the Quaker miller Benjamin Ring the next day. The very young Marquis de Lafayette, who would here be baptized a Patriot, was quartered very close by, at another Quaker farmhouse, that owned by Gideon Gilpin.

There was high ground at Chadds Ford, and Washington had pieces of Proctor's artillery stationed strategically. As a part of General Wayne's division, Proctor's guns were posted "upon the brow of a hill a little above Chadd's Ford," close enough to command a crossing of the stream at this point, and very close the center of the positions assumed by the Continental Army.[47] It was a redoubt of

Washington's Headquarters

sorts, with some protective light earthworks erected. Here, with support from General William Maxwell's light infantry, the Pennsylvanians of Anthony Wayne and the Pennsylvanians of Colonel Proctor were to hold this position.

It was early morning of a rather foggy September 11 when Howe arrived at the Brandywine. Yesterday had been John Harris's birthday, but he had not even known it. He rarely knew what day of the week it was, let alone what day of the month. He was now twenty-four years old, but he could not have been too sure of his age.

He did not even know just who it was who commanded the artillery just across the stream (It was the Hessian General Wilhelm Knyphausen, who had been instrumental in the British occupation of

New York, exhibiting great courage at White Plains and at Fort Washington), but he could see the guns being moved into place, and he knew that an artillery exchange would be the first order of business. And so it was.

But what the Americans did not understand was that Knyphausen here was simply "amusing" the rebels. He was to provide a distraction while a flanking march was performed by Howe and Cornwallis. He was obliging of course, and firing enough cannon to give the impression that Chadds Ford was a focal point. Proctor's artillery, including the gun manned by Harris's crew, returned the fire "with spirit."[48] However, Major Baurmeister, of the Hessian Regiment von Mirbach, was not impressed. Of the artillery firing from its position on the east side of the stream he had this appraisal: "Though the balls and the grapeshot were well aimed and fell right among us, the cannonade had but little effect – partly because the battery was placed too low."[49]

When in the afternoon the astonished Washington was informed by a friendly farmer of the actual position of Howe and Cornwallis, he promptly reorganized his divisions, sending the most unwelcome news to Chadds Ford that no relief troops would be

Lafayette's Headquarters

coming. The Ford must be held by Maxwell, Wayne, and Proctor, period.

Shortly after Washington had received the surprising report, Knyphausen heard the unmistakable gunfire of Cornwallis. By that, he knew that the flanking march had been completed, and that now the real battle would begin.

He now began to form his troops, at the same time ordering a barrage from all of his batteries, six 12-pounders, four howitzers, and all of the lighter artillery. When he had his troops fully organized, and had bombarded the positions of Wayne and Proctor relentlessly for the better part of an hour, he launched his attack. Proctor's guns were still active, and were able for a time to discourage the crossing that Knyphausen clearly seemed determined to make; but Maxwell with his muskets had been forced to retreat to the other side of the stream, and as Knyphausen had taken his troops downstream to the southernmost ford, he was able to accomplish a crossing. General Knyphausen himself was wading with the soldiers. At the head of the force were the General's highly touted Highlanders, a battalion of the 71st regiment; following were the Riflemen and the dreaded Queen's Rangers and the British 4th Regiment. General Johann Stirn's Hessians were last.[50] In all, though the main army had gone beyond, it was a potent force, and when it had crossed, its members quickly assembled into their units, reformed and attacked the American positions "furiously."

The American artillery had kept up a steady fire during all of this time, but the British cannon in the end proved the more effective, and troops came pouring into the hole made on the right flank, approaching to within some thirty yards before they were detected.[51] As one historian reported the scene: "No infantry had been deployed to cover the American cannon, and the crews on the extreme right of the artillery position had to flee, abandoning three of their guns. The rest of Proctor's force took up a position about two hundred yards to the rear; but before long General Wayne ordered the artillery to retreat, sending orders at the same time to Colonel James Chambers, commanding the 1st Pennsylvania Regiment, to cover the artillery's withdrawal."[52]

The British pursued the Americans to the Chester Road, and despite's Wayne's skillful handling of the retreating forces, the withdrawal, at least as far as the artillery was concerned, was not conducted in a very orderly way, and in fact the artillery very nearly lost its commanding officer. Just as the retreat was sounded Proctor had his horse, a beautiful black steed, shot out from under him.[53] Fortunately, Proctor and his men were able to escape, joining the infantry of General Wayne along the road to Chester, but the gun crews were in such disarray that they simply left their cannon where they were. "To my surprise," Colonel Chambers wrote, "the artillerymen had run and left the howitzer behind." Chambers was able, however, with sixty men from the 1st Pennsylvania, to salvage two cannon and then, while his regiment produced a covering fire, he dispatched a party to recover the howitzer as well.[54]

Even though the Redcoats, who had advanced very close, were producing a withering barrage, Chambers, as he later reported, was pretty sure that he had salvaged all of the artillery.[55] And a Negro driver named Edward Hector, who belonged to Harris's company, refused to obey orders to abandon the field and instead gathered up as many as he could of the muskets discarded by the fleeing infantrymen.[56]

While the action involving Knyphausen and Wayne was so heated that it almost seemed the principal action, one of the ironies of the battle is the fact that Knyphausen's forces were never intended to be more than diversionary. Howe, on coming to Chadds Ford, had quickly sensed the situation, and had employed General Knyphausen and his artillery in a maneuver meant only as a ploy, a kind of pseudo-assault directed at Chadds Ford so as to disguise the movement of the body of his army. He meant to take the forces of Cornwallis together with his own against the right flank of the Continental forces, which he did not expect could offer resistance. This was the element of the army, the right wing, commanded by General John Sullivan, the 3rd Division (1st and 2nd Maryland Brigade), which Washington had positioned at Brinton's Ford, about a mile upstream from Chadds Ford. The plan worked even better than General Howe had expected. He was able to get out around the patriot forces by edging off to the northwest and was actually able to move into a position between General Washington and Philadelphia.

The principal action was to the British. Sullivan's forces were completely routed by the Redcoats and were in full flight by the time the troops of Nathanael Greene came up for support. Only the heroic stand of Greene's men, who held firm once they arrived, and the equally valiant resistance provided by the troops under the immediate command of Washington, saved the rebel forces from total disaster. Darkness ended all. But Washington was forced to withdraw his entire force to the community of Chester.

Fortunately, Howe's Redcoats were much too exhausted to press the retreating patriots any farther. One young captain, some two years older than John Harris, an officer named John André, who had been captured by General Richard Montgomery in the Quebec campaign and later exchanged, explained to his journal: "Night and the fatigue the soldiers had undergone prevented any pursuit."

The battle involving the infantry of Wayne and Maxwell, and the artillery of Proctor, is sometimes called The Fight at the Ford. And it is generally dismissed as a skirmish action, not a big deal. But in fact what happened at Chadds Ford was extremely heated and long lasting, the chief action taking place from four o'clock in the afternoon until virtual darkness. The account sent by Major Baurmeister to his superior officer in Hesse-Kassel makes it very clear that *he* regarded the fighting at Chadd's Ford to be a battle of considerable moment. He noted that the American forces defended the crossing with great vigor, and that they put up "a stiff and prolonged defense" of the stream.[57]

The entire Battle of the Brandywine, of which Chadds Ford is a significant part, is generally regarded as one of the major battles of the Revolution, for in fact large forces were participating. Howe's army numbered some 18,000 , and Washington's forces were at least 11,000 strong, almost as many as he had when he undertook the defense of New York. Besides, there were heavy casualties. The British lost 600 men, and the Americans, even though they enjoyed the advantage of defensive positions, more than twice that many (900 killed and wounded, and 400 prisoners). The Marquis de Lafayette, not yet twenty years old and in his first military action in the Patriot cause, was so seriously wounded in the left thigh, while attempting to rally his troops, that he was lost to the army for some time.[58] And Colonel Proctor had had a narrow escape. And one of his artillery companies, that captained by Isaac Craig, suffered severe losses.[59]

The story is told that Washington himself had a very narrow

escape. According to some students of the battle, at the height of the action, the British officer John Graves Simcoe, who would head up the Queen's Rangers during the war, gave a "Hold your fire!" order to his men who were about to discharge their weapons at three fleeing Americans. One of these was reputed to be the Commander-in-Chief.

Two days after the battle, in a letter to his wife, Knox describes the action in great detail. He commends General William Maxwell, who "entirely dispersed a body of 300 Hessians," and assesses the losses: "It is difficult to ascertain our loss; but from the most particular inquiry I have been able to make, it will not exceed seven hundred or eight hundred killed, wounded and missing, and ten field pieces."[60]

All in all, it was a very bad day for the Continental Army. The only benefit that could be allowed the Americans was that the engagement at Brandywine did delay, if only for a little, the eventual British occupation of Philadelphia. In fact, the British did not reach the American capital until September 26, and by that time the patriot population and the Congress had had time to evacuate. In the time that he had gained, Washington had ordered removed from the city the materials most useful to the military. Whatever food and clothing could be transported out, as well as munitions and essential military supplies, was loaded into wagons and placed out of reach of the British. And, besides, Philadelphia was no longer the capital of the country. Howe never did capture the capital. It was very easy to move the capital. It required only that meetings of the Continental Congress be scheduled for another place. And the capital had thus been moved. Before Howe was able to reach the city, the Congress, which in the pre-Trenton days (December 20, 1776) had removed from Philadelphia to the safer Baltimore for almost three months, now was transferred again, this time some sixty-five miles west to Lancaster, a principal munitions center, and one day thereafter on south to the community of York, which made York, Pennsylvania, the capital of the United States. In the course of the War the seat of Congress (the capital) was moved eight times! Even the Liberty Bell, with no crack in it yet,[61] had been preserved. It had been carried off to Allentown, by way of Bethlehem, and hidden safely away in the cellar of the Zion Reformed Church,[62] there to await confidently its triumphant return to Philadelphia.

The Brandywine

John Harris saw lots of action in the Battle of Brandywine, but he was a survivor, and Colonel James Chambers had saved Harris's cannon for the work of another day.

That day was not long off.

As the British army continued its march on Philadelphia, Washington seemed content to retire "to the northern section of Chester County, where he apparently wandered without purpose along the Schuylkill for days."[63] But Wayne, feeling that the British, now camped at the Tredyffrin in the Chester Valley (a region that the General knew very well) were extremely vulnerable, urged an assault. When Washington did not take kindly to that idea, Wayne resorted to harassment and asked for support.

On September 20, nine days after the Brandywine, with his 1500 troops of the Pennsylvania Line, and hopeful of help from General William Maxwell coming from the north, but not waiting for it, Wayne moved into a position only three miles from the British encampment (18,000 Redcoats!) at Paoli. He had assumed all along that he was undetected, that the British were not aware of his presence. But, as a matter of fact, Wayne's movements had been monitored very closely.

That night the British Major General Charles Grey, under orders from Howe, launched "a well-planned, perfectly coordinated, surprise attack on Wayne's encampment."[64] Grey, in command of the 2nd Battalion of Light Infantry, a troop of Light Dragoons, and the 42nd and 44th Regiments, had insisted that no muskets be fired, and, in fact, had had all guns unloaded. This was to be strictly a bayonet operation. What ensued has been called the Paoli Massacre, and although that term for some seems improper,[65] certainly for the Patriot forces it was one

Charles Grey

of the most tragic episodes of the entire war.

It was an excessively dark night, the night of September 20-21, rainy and "wretched." The British were led to Wayne's encampment by Tory spies, who were, apparently, also able to provide the password. A letter by an unnamed British officer, which is with the Historical Society of Pennsylvania, provides an account of what ensued. He is writing on October 2, "at midnight in my tent," from the British encampment at Bebberstown (a portion of Germantown), seven miles from Philadelphia. He has been at the Brandywine, and having begun the letter with a description of that "bloody affair," he closes with his remembrance of Paoli. He recalls how he was relieved from sentry duty at sunset, and how he "was waked at Nine at Night to go on the bloody business." He describes the beginning of the attack, at one o'clock, the bayoneting of all of the sentries, and then the assault on the astonished soldiers at their campfires and in their tents, and "then followed a dreadful scene of Havock – The Light Dragoons came on Sword in Hand The Shrieks Groans Shouting, imprecations deprecations the clashing of Swords & Bayonets &c &c &c &c – (no firing from us – and little from them except now & then a few as I said before Scattering Shots) was more expressive of Horror than all the Thunder of the Artillery &c on the Day of action."[66]

The survivors of the initial surprise were driven two miles, the

The assault on Paoli

"scattered remnants" of Wayne's ravaged force finally arriving at White Horse in the early hours of the morning.[67]

It was a total rout of Wayne's soldiers. In his journal account of the attack, Thomas Sullivan, of the British Forty-Ninth Regiment of Foot, reports that the Redcoats "rushed in upon their Encampment, directed by the light of their fires, killed and wounded not less than 300 in their Huts and about their fires." He reports that the 42nd Regiment set fires to the tents, and remembers that many of the rebels would not even then come out, preferring death in the flames to the bayonet.

According to Sullivan, between seventy and eighty prisoners were taken, including several officers. "Darkness only saved the rest." The British carried off as well "the greater part of their Arms, and eight waggons loaded with Baggage and Stores."[68] John Harris and his fellows had the news the next day. They heard that "hundreds" had been slain, and they were informed that the four cannon Wayne had had with him had been captured and removed to the British encampment. In fact, the final tally when it was in showed that "only" fifty-three soldiers had been killed, and upwards of 100 wounded. And somehow, miraculously, Wayne, in rallying his troops after the initial surprise, had been able to salvage the four cannon. And indeed Wayne, though he may be faulted for jeopardizing his troops in the ill-advised encampment, exhibited his characteristic skill in managing the withdrawal. Out of the terrible confusion he was able to secure sufficient order to direct his soldiers to the west toward White Horse Tavern and the region in which General William Smallwood was camped with his Maryland militia forces.

The British in this surprise attack lost no more than twenty, and perhaps as few as one officer and three men killed. Four Redcoats were wounded.

In all, it was a disaster of great magnitude. The question was now, who is to be blamed. Wayne, of course, was immediately and naturally considered responsible, and suggestions of negligence and incompetence, and even cowardice, were leveled at him. And lots of rumors not flattering to Wayne began instantly to circulate. The formal review that was occasioned was most displeasing to him, and he insisted upon a full court martial. He was exonerated of the principal charges, and was particularly relieved to have the suggestion that he had behaved in a cowardly fashion completely and officially removed. Some were inclined to blame Washington himself, pointing out that in permitting himself to be dominated by officers who were jealous of Wayne, he did not oversee this operation as he should have. One historian puts it this way: "The conclusion that the careful student of the American Revolution must reach in appraising the conflicting accounts of the Paoli battle is that Wayne was caught napping."[69]

Despite the debacle, and tragic as it was, it was most fortunate for the revolution that Wayne was not stripped of his command or cashiered out of the Continental Army. It is difficult to conceive for the Patriots a successful end to the war without General Anthony Wayne.

Shortly after the rout at Paoli, Washington's main army was on the move again. On September 26 the troops marched from their encampment at Pott's Grove to Pennypacker's Mill (present-day Schwenksville) on the Perkiomen. The British were on the move too, or at least some of them. September 26 was in fact a big day for King George the Third. The command of General Cornwallis, which included two British Regular battalions and two Hessian grenadier battalions, and two squadrons of the 16th Dragoons, together with ten artillery field pieces, marched triumphantly into Philadelphia, "amidst the acclamation of some thousands of inhabitants, mostly women and children."[70]

Of course Philadelphia was no longer the capital of the new United States. All members of The Continental Congress had fled to the new capital, Lancaster, Pennsylvania, eight days before. The major part of the British army, under General Howe, who had been proceeding very cautiously, halted outside the city, at Germantown.

Washington, who by this time had seen his army much bolstered by a flood of enlistments, and now fully recovered from Brandywine, began to advance more rapidly, and by October 2 he was very close to Howe's encampment.

The British appeared to be now quite ready to settle in Benjamin Franklin's City of Brotherly Love for the winter. Washington studied the possibility that Cornwallis and Howe might be driven out. It was the fall of the year, and soon the Continental Army would be moving into winter quarters. At the moment it did not have a lot to take into winter quarters. As on that Christmas night of nine months ago, the Army needed a victory. A victory would mean a lot to morale, and would improve the chances for the troops to survive the winter.

When he considered how much his force had been bolstered by volunteers (He now had, besides 8000 regular troops, 3000 additional in militiamen.), Washington resolved on a strike against the forces commanded by Howe. These were now occupying the region close to the small community some five miles north of Philadelphia known as Germantown. Washington had the informed impression that Howe's troops could not number more than 9000 men (Actually he had a great many more men than that.), and he felt confident that with his slightly superior force and possibly artillery advantages he could launch an effective assault. But success could come, as he very well understood, only through a very strategically designed plan of attack. Accordingly, in consultation with his generals, Washington drew up a very complex battle plan.

The assault, to be made by four separate forces, required almost perfect coordination and was designed not only for surprise but also for a total envelopment of the British forces. General Sullivan, with one body of the regular army, would strike from the west at the very center of the British positions; at the same time forces under General Nathanael Greene, also regulars, would come from their positions in the north to assail the British right flank; detachments of militia from Maryland and New Jersey would be attacking from positions still farther north than those assumed by Greene and would hit the British in the right rear; very important was the assignment given to "the hero of Kittanning," General John Armstrong of the Pennsylvania militia, as it was the job of this unit somehow to get past the British on the left side and assume such positions as would block any retreat by the British toward Philadelphia.[71] It was a good plan, but it did not work.

In the first place, this four-pronged assault was scheduled for five o'clock in the morning of October 4. Naturally, it was still dark at this time. Besides that, it was very cold, the temperature hardly above freezing; and, to make matters even worse, there had settled into the area a very heavy fog. The American march was underway at 7:00 in the evening of October 3. It was a long, tough march, over very difficult, rough roads, from Metuchen Hill on the Skippack Road all the way to Chestnut Hill. The order of march as dictated by Washington had General Thomas Conway at the head of the column with his advance brigade, followed by Sullivan, Maxwell, and Nash. The Commander-in-Chief accompanied these troops. Just as the sun produced its faint, rosy glow in the east ahead of them, the troops reached Chestnut Hill.

The first fighting (at Mount Airy) was extremely hot and spirited. The engagement featured the troops of Conway and Sullivan, who of course were in the van, against those of Colonel Thomas Musgrave, by all accounts a most resourceful and courageous officer.

Thomas Musgrave

It was Musgrave who had been put in command of the forces which at Paoli had been employed by Grey to prevent the escape of Wayne's men to the north, and though this detachment saw no action at Paoli, it did its job. Musgrave was a hardened veteran. He had accompanied General William Howe to the colonies, and he had been wounded in the battle of Pelham Manor on the King's Highway, just about a year ago, on October 18.

Now Sullivan, in trouble, called for support from Wayne, and as these troops came forward Sullivan launched a bayonet charge against Musgrave. At this point there occurred one of those inglorious moments that all wars include.

Wayne's division was composed, in part, of the survivors of the Paoli surprise nighttime attack by the Redcoats under Major General Charles Grey. These men, who were remembering the bayoneting of the sleeping soldiers and the burning of the occupied tents, fought with fury in the back-and-forth bayonet charges, and when the British fell back they "took ample Vengeance for that Night's work,"cruelly doing their bloody business on the Redcoats who were surrendering, bayoneting "many of the poor wretches who were Crying for Mercy, in spite of their officers' exertions to restrain them."[72]   At last a British bugle sounded a retreat.

The British, still offering some resistance, had to fall back toward the little village of Germantown itself, and a number of the Redcoats, six companies of the 40th British Regiment (some 125 men) under the very able Colonel Musgrave, took positions inside the mansion of Judge Benjamin Chew,[73] a Loyalist.

Washington might have elected to bypass this "fortress," but he decided instead, with a portion of his force, to storm it.[74] The 4th Continental Artillery was here pressed into action, but apparently had been advised to employ only two guns. One of these guns was under

Assault on the Chew House

the command of 2nd Lieutenant Joseph Barker; and the second was under the command of 1st Lieutenant William Ritter.[75] Bombardier in the gun crew under Barker was young John Harris of Salem, New Jersey.

The gun, a six-pounder, had been wheeled into position immediately in front of the Chew House. William McMullen, an Irish-born matross member of the gun crew remembered that "the blast of its firing was so sharp that it caused blood to run from my ears."[76]

John Harris, who on at least one occasion after the war must have returned to the scene, long years afterwards, recollected it all vividly: "At the battle of Germantown we planted our cannon at the gate before Chew's house,–by the stone gate-posts which are there now. Just inside the gate lay six British grenadiers dead. We were ordered to fire grape-shot. After we fired a while it seemed as if we were not making as much impression as we ought; and as the fog was so thick we could not see very much. One of our officers rode up to the house where the British were, and when he came back he said, 'Boys, use cannon ball; it is a stone house.' But the fog lifted pretty soon, and as there were but a few of us we had to retreat. If we had known it was a stone house when we first commenced we would have knocked it to pieces, likely. The old shot shows to this day. The shutters are patched, and one shot went through it to the kitchen."

Clearly the artillery was quite ineffective, and the Redcoats were not dislodged; and though in the course of the fighting at the Chew Mansion, Colonel John Laurens, son of the President of the Continental Congress, constantly risking his life, made a number of valiant efforts to burn the building down, these too were totally unsuccessful.[77]

Confusion reigned over the last hours of the battle. For a while it looked as though Washington's ingenious plan was going to work, because those troops under the command of Washington, who had not been left at the Chew House, were threatening to cut their way through the British main position[78] and Greene, though late to the fray, was doing well. What caused the assault to fail was what in later years would be called "friendly fire." Soldiers in Greene's unit were misdirected by General Adam Stephen (later found to be drunk at the time) and wound up mistaking the infantry of General Anthony Wayne, who were a part of the Sullivan forces, for the enemy. Wayne's men of course fired back. In the chaos that followed somehow the forces of Greene got the impression that they were being hemmed in (General Armstrong later heard that "some officer" had called out, "We are surrounded!"), and because ammunition supplies were now almost exhausted, Greene ordered his troops to disengage.[79]

And that turned out to be the end of the battle. Armstrong, with his Pennsylvania militia, had had only a slight scrape with the enemy. In a letter composed almost a week after the battle he reported to General Horatio Gates that because he was under the strong impression that the British were in retreat, that the Patriots were victorious, he "fell in with the rear of the enemy . . . supposing them vanquished . . . and gave them a brush." But, as he reported to Gates, he was himself forced to withdraw because of the effects of the British artillery. In all, Armstrong suffered "but thirty-nine wounded."

With Greene's forces withdrawing, and Armstrong not in the main action, a general retreat was ordered. The British, now regrouped and buoyed by success, were quick to pursue, and did so, for a distance of some nine miles, all the way to Pennypacker's Mill. But General Wayne, with the Brandywine experience still fresh in his mind, had organized the artillery, doubtless including the cannon that had done so little damage to the Chew House, and was able to provide a rear guard sufficient to suppress the counter-attack.

The whole battle had lasted but four hours. What made it all so disappointing was that the American forces were so close to success (A battle can be turned by a little thing.). And it was a costly battle. The British, Washington learned long afterwards, lost 537 men, killed and wounded. Four officers were slain, and thirty were wounded. The Continental Army, as reported by the Board of War, lost even more, 673 men killed and wounded and 400 more captured. Among those lost in the action were fifty-three patriot soldiers "dead on the lawn" of the Chew House, "and four on its very doorstep."[80] Among the fallen were four officers, including the courageous Brigadier General Francis Nash, of Stirling's Division, one of Washington's most gallant and trusted officers. General Knox reported that Nash was "mortally wounded by a cannon ball taking off his thigh."[81]

The retreating forces carried off what wounded they could. Those who finally succumbed to their wounds were buried in the Mennonite cemetery in the region known as Towamencin.

One of Colonel Proctor's artillery companies, not Harris's, was almost completely wiped out. This was the company commanded by Captain Andrew Porter. Porter, who had left the marines for the artillery, had been personally engaged in the cannonading at Trenton, Princeton, and at the Brandywine. At Trenton, for his conduct under fire, for his tactical skills and his daring, he had received on the field and in person the commendation of General Washington.[82] Here at Germantown he lost nearly every man of his company.

The disappointment at Germantown can be blamed on the decision to assault the Chew mansion (Armstrong, for example, thought it "an ill-judged delay."), or on the Wayne-Greene confusion, but General Knox, while acknowledging the value to the British of possession of "some stone buildings in Germantown," blamed the failure to achieve victory on the terrible fog, "which had arisen about daybreak [and] become so excessively thick from the continued firing that it was impossible to discover an object at twenty yards."[83]

General Armstrong thought it all very sad. In his letter to Gates he declared it very much too bad that "a victory, a glorious victory, fought for and eight tenths won, was shamefully and mysteriously lost."

But whatever it was blamed on, it was indeed a lost battle and a costly one. There now stood nothing between the British and the occupation of Philadelphia, which a few weeks ago had been the young nation's capital city. Only the wise Ben Franklin could find any consolation. When he was advised of the American defeats at the Brandywine and at Germantown, and told that now Howe had Philadelphia, he is supposed to have replied, "Does General Howe have Philadelphia, or does Philadelphia have him?"

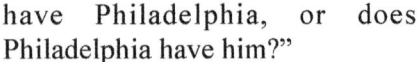

Johann De Kalb

Lafayette's good friend and mentor, the newly arrived Baron Johann De Kalb, shortly after the battle, on October 7, and with the pain of Brandywine still ever so acute, had formed a quick, and not altogether flattering, impression of General Washington. To his friend and patron, the Comte de Broghie, with whom he had served in the European wars, De Kalb delivered his view of his Commander-in-Chief:

> *I have not yet told you anything of the character of General Washington. He is the most amiable, kind-hearted and upright of men; but as a General he is too slow, too indolent, and far too weak; besides, he has a tinge of vanity in his composition, and overestimates himself. In my opinion whatever success he may have will be owing to good luck and to blunders of his adversaries. I may even say that he does not know how to improve upon the great blunders of the enemy. He has not yet overcome his old prejudices against the French.*[84]

Horatio Gates

The Battle of Germantown was the last major battle of the year, and it gave Washington and his men very little to take into winter quarters. Happily, as Knox had noted in a letter to his wife immediately after the close of the battle, "Our men are in the highest spirits, and ardently desire another trial."[85] And very happily too, the news that would arrive two weeks later, of Burgoyne's surrender to Gates in faraway Saratoga, New York, would provide a great lift to their morale.

Fourteen days after the battle, on October 18, while encamped on the Skippack Road, at the site on which they had tented just a short time ago, Washington's

John Burgoyne

army, weary from incessant camping and moving and with nothing much to feel good about, had some very special General Orders read to them. It was Washington's announcement to them that General Burgoyne had surrendered to General Horatio Gates at Saratoga. Said Washington: "Let every face brighten and every heart expand with grateful Joy and praise to the supreme disposer of all events who has granted us this signal success." He then ordered a salute by "Thirteen pieces of cannon" (including that of bombardier John Harris) to be followed by a "feu-de-joy with blank cartridges or powder by every brigade and corps of the army." And he directed his chaplains to top off the celebration by delivering to their several corps or brigades "short discourses suited to the joyful occasion."[86]

On October 19, Howe withdrew his troops from the region of Germantown, and entered the City of Brotherly Love with his entire force. For the next two months Washington camped here and there, always close to the city, harassing the Redcoats at every opportunity, but not succeeding in luring them into any major engagement. Although the British had parties out on the roads leading to Germantown almost constantly, and although nearly every day some contact occurred, Washington could do hardly more than to keep the British in a continuing state of alarm.[87] He had to settle for harassment, ambushes and nuisance assaults. Bombardier John Harris remembered a lot of them:

I was in a great many skirmishes around Philadelphia while the British had it in possession. As they would send out foraging parties around, the Americans would send out parties to capture them. It was late in the fall and we often had the Schuylkill River to wade. The officers would order us to hold up our ammunition to keep it dry. As I belonged to the artillery I usually rode over on my gun. One of those nights I thought my time was about to come. The English heard of our being after them and threw up intrenchments across a road in the wood; and as they had cannon it was expected, of course, that they would plant some to sweep the road; and as my gun came in the road as we marched up in order of battle expecting them to fire, I could see their camp fires blazing high. But the Americans kept marching up, marching up; but they [the British] *did not open their batteries. At last an officer rode up and looked over the breast-works. When he came back he said, 'Damn them! They have given up the bag; have left everything there to deceive us,–even their supper cooking!' But the officer would not let us eat it, hungry as we were, for fear of poison."*

As the bad weather drew ever closer, the impatient General Wayne once again proposed an attack on Philadelphia. And, as was his wont when he took hold of something, he put all the force of his personality behind it. Confidence and morale were fairly high at this time, what with the near-success of Germantown, and the great news from Saratoga. But when Washington on November 24 put the plan before his assembled officers, only four (including Stirling, and, naturally, the impetuous Wayne, and presumably the restless Sullivan) favored an assault. Eleven generals, and Baron De Kalb was one, voted against the proposal.[88] In a long letter written from the Artillery Park in Whitemarsh, November 25, Henry Knox responded to Washington's query by voicing strong opposition.

Washington put off a decision, partly because he wanted the opinion of General Nathanael Greene, who had been absent from the council, and partly because, even though he had lots of information about the fortifications of the city, he wanted to see for himself. The very next day, in the company of John Laurens, who had fought so valiantly at the Chew mansion, he set out on a reconnoitering mission to determine the extent and the quality of the British defenses. What he discovered was unsettling. He reported to his officers that he had achieved a very comprehensive view, and that he had found the works much, much stronger than he had been given reason to believe. Consequently, he concluded that an attack on the city was simply out of the question, and he persevered in his hope that the British might come out.

So for three more weeks the army, 11,000 strong, continued in its encampment at Whitemarsh, thirteen miles northwest of the city. Washington's informers have assured him that a British attack is coming. Washington hopes so. He is pretty well dug in high on the heavily wooded hills, and he has fifty-two pieces of heavy artillery, including that of Harris's company and that of Captain Andrew Porter. But the troops are suffering some from the weather, have not been well-provisioned, and have not been paid lately. Their anger Washington hopes will be taken out on the British, who, he believes, are on their way.

In fact, they are coming. They are marching in stealth, undetected they think. But Washington has taken his information seriously, and he is prepared. His army has been bolstered by the arrival of Captain Daniel Morgan's riflemen, who have been detached from the victorious army of Horatio Gates. Washington now can boast a force of nearly 13,000 men.

At midnight on December 4, General William Howe gives the command to march. With almost his entire army,12,000 troops (including the Queen's Rangers of Major John Simcoe, who are specialists in this kind of action), he emerges – he marches out of Philadelphia. Each man has drawn six days' rations. They march in secret, so they think.

Unbeknownst to Howe, he is being observed by one of Washington's most reliable and vigilant scouts, Captain Allen McLane. McLane is keeping Washington informed. The British are advancing along the Skippack and Manatawney (Ridge) Roads. McLane, who has the command of 100 very select horsemen, attacks the heads of both columns, and puts Howe's troops into such disorder that they change their course.[89] But despite McLane's harassment, the Redcoats proceed, and by 3:00 in the morning, long before the first gleams of light over Philadelphia, find themselves at Chestnut Hill, three miles short of the Rebel encampment. Here they camp until the battle can be joined.

Washington, alerted and prepared, has ordered the building of hundreds of campfires, to give the illusion that his force is stronger even than it is. This is a somewhat curious action, as the Commander-in-Chief of the Continental Army has been itching for a full-scale fight from his established position. The action begins with Washington's order to the Pennsylvania militia, six hundred troops under Brigadier General James Irvine,[90] to feel out the enemy. That mission results in an engagement with the British 2nd Battalion of light infantry and some advanced parties in the region of Chestnut Hill. The action is short, but very fierce, with extremely heavy fire and casualties on both sides. It ends with the capture of the wounded General Irvine (who lost three fingers from his left hand and suffered damage to his shoulders and neck), and the routing of the Pennsylvania forces.

From this time on the battle resembles that of two boxers

moving about the ring feinting for advantage. The British simply maneuver up and down the line of American positions, rarely approaching closer than one mile, searching for a weakness to exploit. The patriot forces respond of course by shifting their troops to match the heavier British forces. This kind of action continues for three days. Howe's soldiers accomplish little beyond the outrages committed against the civilian population of the region. They burn every house they come close to, despoiling property wherever they find it, and creating as much a sense of desolation as they can.

On the fourth day, December 8, Howe, disdaining an all-out assault on the American positions, withdraws from the field (but only after the wanton destruction of private property) and marches his army back to Philadelphia. Washington is, of course, much disappointed, because he had had every confidence that his force could win a major engagement.

Distinguishing the battle was the service of Morgan's riflemen, who proved very effective; and of course the action of McLane and his men, who were everywhere over the field. When Colonel Joseph Reed of Washington's staff[91] and Colonel John Cadwalader, who were at this time the best of friends but who in six months' time would not be, were sent out to observe the action, Reed had his horse shot out from under him. As he lay quite helpless on the field, Cadwalader drew his sword and was preparing to defend him against the Hessians of "No Flint" Grey, who were advancing with fixed bayonets, when McLane and his mounted men came riding up, just in time to panic the would-be murderers. It was a miraculous escape for two of Washington's most counted on

Daniel Morgan

officers.[92]

Casualties, considering that the fighting continued through three days, were not heavy. Of course, as usual, figures vary widely in reports. The British lost one officer and one of Simcoe's Rangers, and, according to Howe's own tally, 112 rank and file killed, wounded and missing[93] (Some accounts have the figure as low as sixty.). The Americans had one officer of Morgan's corps killed, and Brigadier General James Irvine wounded and captured.[94] Besides, 27-50 rank and file, many of them Irvine's militiamen, were killed or wounded (Some accounts have the figure as high as 90.). Major Simcoe, generally regarded as boastful, claimed "near 100" patriot casualties.[95]

So the Battle of Whitemarsh, like so many of the battles of the Revolution, did not advance the cause for either party significantly. What *could* have been a major, major battle, perhaps even accomplishing the end of the war, never became a decisive action. Here were the two main bodies of both armies, almost all of the men under the command of Generals William Howe and Washington, met on a battlefield just outside the city which had proclaimed the independence of the colonies. And here it could have ended.

Howe, by this time was beginning to understand that the destruction of Washington's army was the only way to bring the war to an end. Indeed, that is what he had hoped for when at midnight he marched out of Philadelphia. But Howe was ever reluctant to attack established positions, and certainly he was not going to assault troops that he had good reason to believe were superior in numbers to his own.

Washington, of course, was once again disheartened. He had drawn Howe out, and he had hoped for a major battle here. But it was not to be. Only once more would the two main armies meet in the field like this, and that battle, too, would prove inconclusive. The war had six long years yet to go!

Now it is time to hole up for the winter.

IV

THE SCHUYLKILL

Hungry and foot-sore on these cheerless slopes,
With wasted vesture and with shattered hopes;
Where wintry winds blew keen across the snows,
They watched and waited for their distant foes;
But no winds chilled their bosoms to despair,
For Freedom's fires still warmed the freezing air;
And Freedom's leader, with his cheering words,
Still nerved the trembling Continental swords;--
Renowned, revered, illustrious Washington!
The Nation's sire and the Nation's son.

— Reverend J. G. Walker

Valley Forge. No military engagement occurred at Valley Forge. The battle that was fought was waged against hunger, against cold, against despair. The gallant soldiers who closed out this battle in triumph have etched into the history books a chapter forever glorious and inspiring. In years long after, grizzled veterans of the War, in New Jersey, in Massachusetts, in Pennsylvania, with grandchildren snuggled in their laps, would declare, proudly, and not without a quaver in the voice, "I was at Valley Forge, you know."

Valley Forge has become a symbol for sacrifice. It is referred to as "hallowed ground," as "the birthplace of an army," as a "sacred shrine," and as the "crucible of victory." Some say that what happened there was a miracle. Today, the National Park established there in 1976 on the 200th anniversary of the Declaration of Independence[1] is a monument to the spirit which ignited and fueled the Revolution. It is not too much to say that the nation known today as the United States of America was born there. To be sure, it was an agonizing birth suffered over a period of more than five months and fraught with excruciating labor pains. But it was a good birth.

Someone has declared that every American schoolgirl and every American schoolboy should be required to read an account of the winter at Valley Forge. Even better, of course, would be the creation of a climate in which every schoolchild would *determine* for himself or herself to read about the encampment there. It is some story.

It begins on December 17, 1777. Washington had been harassing the British occupation of Philadelphia ever since the Battle of Germantown, which was fought on October 4. All through October and November he had made himself a nuisance, but not any of these skirmishes, nor even the battle at Whitemarsh, had done much to advance the war one way or another. By mid-December, while the army was encamped in tents at the Gulph Mill, which was about fourteen miles from Philadelphia, he knew that the decision on winter quarters must be made quickly.[2]

A council of his officers produced a number of nominations, but little agreement. Wilmington had been proposed, and was a popular recommendation, urged by Joseph Reed, Nathanael Greene, Lafayette, and John Cadwalader. When a site at Valley Forge was put forward, General De Kalb passionately expressed his opposition, declaring, "The idea of wintering in this desert can only have been put into the head of the commanding general by an interested speculator or a disaffected man."[3] But Wayne was very strongly for it and argued persuasively. And of course the Pennsylvania Council of Safety, whose chief concern at this time was Philadelphia, favored the site. At length Washington, noting that the Valley Forge site would be partially protected by the Schuylkill River, reached a decision, and

Valley Forge it was.

On Wednesday, the 17th day of December he prepared the soldiers to march the four to six miles from Gulph Mill, where the main army had been encamped since the 13th, to the new encampment. The decision to ride out the winter at Valley Forge has been made memorable by Washington's address to the troops, dated "Headquarters on the Schuylkill, Dec. 17, 1777."

As one historian described it, Washington congratulated his soldiers upon the campaign just concluded, noting the accomplishments, and then proceeded to praise the officers for their heroism and the soldiers for their endurance, counseling all to continue in both fortitude and patience. Then he acknowledged that he had made some mistakes and that some failures had occurred. And then he made it plain what it was they were fighting for, noting that "upon the whole, heaven had smiled upon their army and crowned them with success; that the end of their warfare was Independence, Liberty, and Peace, and that the hope of securing these blessings for themselves and their posterity demanded a continuance of the struggle at every hazard."[4]

But the day of the march, Friday, December 19, was a cheerless day, and it would take even more than the ringing rhetoric of the Commander-in-Chief to dispel the gloom registered in the heavy skies and the frozen ground. One impression of the scene follows: "The pitiless winter winds swept the hills and valley with unceasing fury, as the December sun sank into banks of snow-clouds, presaging the coming storm. The poverty of supplies in food and raiment was bitterly and profanely bewailed by shivering and unpaid officers and half-naked men as they crowded around the comfortless camp-fire of the bivouac, when suddenly the appearance of the Horse Guard announced the approach of the Commander-in-Chief."

And then this record of the scene moves into the language of Washington's adopted son, George Washington Parke Custis: "The officer commanding the detachment, choosing the most favorable ground, paraded his men to pay their General the honor of a passing salute. As Washington rode slowly up, he was observed to be eying very earnestly something that attracted his attention on the frozen surface of the road. Having returned the salute with that native grace and dignified manner that won the admiration of the soldiers of the

Revolution, the Chief reined in his charger, and ordering the commanding officer of the detachment to his side, addressed him as follows: 'How comes it, sir, that I have tracked the march of your troops by the blood-stains of their feet upon the frozen ground? Were there no shoes in the commissary's stores that this sad spectacle is to be seen along the public highway?' The officer replied: 'Your Excellency may rest assured that this sight is as painful to my feelings as it can be to yours, but there is no remedy within our reach. When shoes were issued the different regiments were served in turn; it was our misfortune to be among the last to be served, and the stores became exhausted before we could obtain even the smallest supply.'

"The General was observed to be deeply affected by his officer's description of the soldiers' privations and sufferings. His compressed lips, the heaving of his manly chest betokened the powerful emotions that were struggling in his bosom, when, turning towards the troops, with a voice tremulous, yet kindly, he exclaimed, 'poor fellows!' Then giving rein to his horse he rode rapidly away."[5]

Eleven or twelve thousand men, three-fourths of the entire rebel force, arrived at Valley Forge on the 19th day of December. It has been estimated that almost 3000 (more than one in every four) were unfit for duty, because of lack of shoes or lack of clothing.[6] Did John Harris have shoes? Possibly, as the Regiment of Artillery was often favored over the infantry.

Seventy-three regiments of infantry were stationed at Valley Forge. All of the colonies (now states), excepting Delaware, South Carolina, and Georgia, were represented by infantry regiments, and there were soldiers from every state, some no more than twelve years old! There were also an impressive number of the artillery (including elements of the 1st and 2nd Continental Artillery, and all of the 3rd and 4th, a corps of engineers, and Washington's 46-man Life Guard.[7]

Responsible for these men, in the most difficult of circumstances, was, of course, General Washington. Baron De Kalb, who had not been happy with the choice for winter quarters, and who had delivered guarded opinions of Washington throughout his early association, on Christmas Day, shortly after the men were settled, registered with his confidant the Comte de Broglie an impression much more positive than that communicated before. De Kalb, while acknowledging in Washington a hurtful fault, has come to appreciate

(1) how very difficult is Washington's position, and (2) how able he really is:

It is unfortunate that Washington is so easily led. He is the bravest and truest of men, has the best intentions, and a sound judgment. I am convinced that he would accomplish substantial results if he would only act more upon his own responsibility; but it is a pity he is so weak, and has the worst of advisors in the men who enjoy his confidence. If they are not traitors, they are certainly ignoramuses.[8]

Another letter composed by General De Kalb, only two weeks later, is certainly, because of the extremely trying conditions in which the Continental Army found itself, because of the British occupation of Philadelphia, and because of increasing political pressure upon the Congress, one of the most important letters of the entire war. De Kalb, with his enormous military reputation to speak from, apparently felt compelled to inform the Congress on its Commander-in-Chief. On January 7, from the darkness of Valley Forge, he penned these words to Henry Laurens,[9] President of Congress:

I cannot but observe, in justice to General Washington, that he must be a very modest man, and the greatest friend of the cause, for forbearing public complaints on that account, that the enemy may not be apprised of our situation and take advantage of it. He will rather suffer in the opinion of the world than to hurt his country, in making appear how far he is from having so considerable an army as all Europe and a great part of America believe he has. This would show, at the same time, he did and does more every day than could be expected from any general in the world, in the same circumstances, and that I think him the only proper person (nobody actually being or serving in America excepted) by his natural and acquired capacity, his bravery, good sense, uprightness and honesty, to keep up the spirits of the army and the people, and that I look upon him as the sole defender of his country's cause. Thus much I thought myself obliged to say on that head. I only could wish in my private opinion he would take more upon himself, and trust more to his own excellent judgment than to councils, but this leads me out of my way.[10]

Of course Washington knew nothing of this letter, but he must have sensed that he had won the respect and devotion, without even securing a real victory, of one of the most accomplished military men of the time. Before long he would dispatch De Kalb and Lafayette to Albany, commissioned "to win Canada."

But first he would welcome to the encampment another German officer. On January 8, Washington received a letter from Portsmouth, New Hampshire. It expressed the happy news that the Baron Friedrich Wilhelm Augustus von Steuben had reached America. Washington, aware that any officer who had served under Frederick the Great of Prussia might just possibly make a contribution to his young army, promptly invited the Baron to the Valley Forge winter quarters.[11]

In the meanwhile it was work against the winter.

Once the various brigades were established in their positions, Washington ordered the men to build log huts (They had been sheltered in the first days only by the tents they had brought with them.). Accordingly, the forests were hewn down and 12-man squads

Huts at Valley Forge

began to build the little houses which would protect them from the winter. The pamphleteer Thomas Paine was an interested observer. He wrote to Franklin: "I was there when the army first began to build huts. They appeared to me like a family of beavers, everyone busy, some carrying logs, others putting them together." Someone had had the bright idea to make a contest of the construction, with a prize going to the squad first to achieve completion. By December 29 there were 900 huts under construction,[12] and in three days the prize had been won, one dollar per man. By Feb. 8 most of the men were "hutted."

The huts, fairly uniform, naturally were not large, and measured only fourteen feet by sixteen, with a height barely over six feet. They could not accommodate twelve men all that comfortably. Lafayette, in a letter to his wife, composed early in the encampment, January 6, lamented the conditions. The huts he described as "little shanties that are scarcely gayer than dungeon cells."[13] But each had a fireplace and chimney, and all had their doors facing the company streets.[14]

The Army's field officers and the members of Washington's staff had quarters to the rear of the huts built for the troops. And the major officers were lodged in the homes that adorned the area. General Henry Knox lived at first in the home of John Brown, Sr., but, like some of the other officers, eventually moved into a hut, "in order to be closer to the men." Lafayette lived in the home of Samuel Havard, a rubble stone house perched on a little knoll on the south bank and about thirty-five feet above Valley Creek. And Washington had established his headquarters in the Isaac Potts House, today possibly the best known house in the country.

A soldier could hope for his prescribed daily ration, which would mean a pound of bread and a pound of some kind of fish or some kind of meat, together with a pint of milk, a quart of beer, some peas, beans, and a tab of butter.[15] But he could not expect it. Rations were in such short supply that starvation for many was not only possible, but quite likely. General Nathanael Greene,[16] who was Quartermaster for the Army, was a good man to have in charge of supplies. Ten years younger than Washington, he had been placed in charge of Boston after the British evacuation, and he had fought admirably at Trenton, the Brandywine, and Germantown. But clothing and subsistence for the army dug in at Valley Forge! It was an impossible job that he had. And then there were the horses, too. The horses, so necessary for the transport of the field artillery and the supply wagons and as mounts for officers, were in a bad way from the beginning. There was simply no food for the horses. On the 26th of February, General Greene advised his very close friend Henry Knox, who had been away from the encampment for a time, that "Hundreds of horses have already starved to death."[17]

Nathanael Greene

And for clothing the story was the same. There were no shoes at all for some, and for most there was but one shirt. The officers were no better off than the enlisted men. Perhaps they were worse off, as they had larger responsibilities, like patrol and supervision, and serving as "officer of the day." And officers were expected to pay for their own clothing too. General von Steuben, who could speak but a paltry English, described, long afterwards, in his own language the situation (here rendered into English): "The men were literally naked. . . . The officers who had coats had them of every color and make. I saw officers at a grand parade at Valley Forge mounting guard in a sort of dressing gown made of old blankets and woolen bed cover."[18] In fact, there was a shortage of *everything*. And the consequence was disease, all of the diseases occasioned by malnutrition, or by the lack of protection from freezing rain and bitter winds, like pneumonia. Few had been inoculated against smallpox, a constant threat. It has been estimated that during that winter at Valley Forge, which was uncommonly severe, some 3000 soldiers died from disease.[19] Some perished directly from the cold. Lafayette recollected that "feet and legs froze till they became black, and it was often necessary to amputate them."[20]

Even as late as June 17, as the Army was preparing to vacate the encampment, Washington reported to his officers that more than 2300 troops were sick in camp! Almost one in five. And the 2300 figure did not include those who had been hospitalized outside the encampment, another 1200 at least.[21]

As if material conditions were not bad enough, there was no real social life to be enjoyed. Washington had outlawed gaming, that is, any kind of gambling. But he did permit, and in fact encouraged, games that could be entered into for exercise and amusement.[22] The officers even played cricket, Washington himself participating at least once. And, remarkably, the Commander-in-Chief was okay with dueling, which was gambling at the highest level.

Under these conditions, trouble could be expected. And there was plenty of it. Desertions were occurring almost daily, and little could be done to discourage them. As the army had lost so many men from the gun crews in the battles of the Brandywine and Germantown, desertions from the artillery were particularly alarming. On February 27, Washington reported: "Our loss of matrosses in the last campaign in killed and wounded was considerable, and it has not been a little increased this winter by desertions from Col. Proctor's corps."[23] Five soldiers who had deserted and had been brought back were sentenced to execution, and in two cases the sentence was carried out. But desertions continued.

One of Proctor's officers, Lieutenant William Ritter, the officer who had commanded one of the two guns firing at the Chew House in the Battle of Germantown, was brought before a General Court Martial on April 14. The General Orders for April 15 included the notice that he "was tried for ungentlemanlike behavior and for going into the City of Philadelphia since the Enemy have taken Possession of it, acquitted of the charge of ungentlemanlike behavior but found guilty of going into Philadelphia since the Enemy have taken possession of it, being a breach of Article 5th. Section 18th. of the Articles of War, but on account of circumstances do only sentence him to be reprimanded in Brigade orders."[24] What the "circumstances" were is not known, but possibly Ritter was able to supply some good information about the British occupation of the city.

For lesser crimes, like theft and physical violence, flogging was the order of the day. Many soldiers were sentenced to 100 lashes

(!), and some to even more.²⁵ It was customary for corporal punishment to be carried out by members of the artillery unit, by the drummers and the fifers, who would be supervised by the ever-present drum major. For deserters who were not executed but assigned the lesser punishment of flogging, seventy-eight lashes were considered proper. A thief could expect thirty-nine. These figures are, apparently, a throwback to the old Mosaic number; but of course they varied considerably.²⁶ Washington's officers, as well as Washington himself, were capable of severe punishment, but were normally fair and even-minded.

Officers were not receiving their pay (It might be noted that Washington served throughout the war without pay.), and some simply resigned their commissions and went home. Even Lafayette, who could perceive silver linings in every cloud, became so sorely disappointed in the failure of Congress to honor some of his particular requests (although he too was serving without pay), that he threatened to go home! Only the persuasive skills of his influential mentor, the Baron De Kalb, tempered his resolve.

By the middle of the winter conditions were so bad that even mutiny seemed a real possibility. Washington himself noted the prospect. Brigadier General James Mitchell Varnum, who was in command of the Rhode Island troops, and who had been in the action at Harlem Heights and White Plains, had advised General Greene on the 14th of February that "in all human probability the army must dissolve." Two days later, just a week before his birthday, Washington wrote to his good friend George Clinton, who had just been elected in June the first Governor of New York State, an ominous appraisal of the situation: "For some days past there has been little less than a famine in camp. A part of the army has been a week without any kind of flesh, and the rest three or four days. Naked and starved as they are, we cannot enough admire the incomparable patience and fidelity of the soldiery that they have not been ere this excited by their sufferings to general mutiny and desertions."²⁷

But to John Harris, who is being followed here, there never occurred the slightest thought of desertion, let alone mutiny. He would have followed General Washington "to Hell itself." And Harris seems not to have been a party to the disorders in any way at all. In his remembrances of Valley Forge, he never expresses any complaint about his fellows, or about the officers. His name has not been discovered in any account of crime and punishment. Naturally, he did lament the conditions: "During the winter of 1777-78 we were so badly off for clothing one could track the soldiers over the frozen ground from the blood from their bare feet! And no blankets! We would lie down around our camp fire to sleep and our hair would freeze fast to the ground." And again, " I wintered at Valley Forge, 1777-78, with Washington; was starved and frozen. A soldier's life was worse than a dog's. The saying is, 'A dog's life is hunger and ease'; a Soldier's was hunger and hardships."

But there were some happy moments too, even joyous. One was occasioned by the date of February 22, which most of the officers and some of the soldiers knew to be the birthday of their General-in-Chief. On this date in 1778 he would arrive at the age of forty-six. It was one of those days so common to the Pennsylvania February, raw and dark, with rain off and on throughout. But the weather did little to dampen the spirit of the well-wishers. By all accounts Martha Washington immensely enjoyed the festivities, which were highlighted by a band formed from John Harris's artillery battalion. It must be supposed that the musicians were competent only with the fife and the drum, but all reports of the celebration insist that Lady Washington was thrilled by the music. And the General could only have been pleased.[28]

Many heart-warming incidents occurred. One of these is particularly amusing. Lady Elizabeth Porter, wife to Captain Andrew Porter of Proctor's Artillery, was in the habit of visiting her husband during the long winter's encampment.[29] She was a very handsome young lady, much accomplished in needlework. She regularly brought to her husband, besides small delicacies he was fond of, garments that she had made for him. One evening, as she was approaching the camp on horseback, she met a gentleman, apparently a soldier, but out of uniform. When he inquired whether he might be of help, she explained that she was the wife of Captain Porter and that she was on her way to his quarters.

Upon learning her name, the gentleman continued walking slowly beside her horse. As he adjusted its trappings, he exclaimed, "This is a fine animal."

"Thank you," said Lady Porter. "We raise our own horses,

and I can assure you that they receive the best of care."

As they continued on the way to the captain's quarters, the gentleman asked her a number of questions, most having to do with the soldiers of the encampment, their feelings about the war and so on. Lady Porter lamented that she could answer only for her husband, who, she insisted, was passionate about the cause and devoted to General Washington.

Just as they reached the intended portion of the encampment, the gentleman, who was smiling strangely, remarked, "There, I think I see your husband." Then he bowed most pleasantly, and started to turn away.

"Sir, " she said, "may I ask, to whom do I owe the honor of this courtesy?"

"Well, my good lady," said he, "you come into camp highly escorted."

"But by whom, I say?"

"By the Commander-in-Chief" was the reply

"Not by Washington!" exclaimed the startled wife. But when she shifted on her horse to achieve a better look, she found her escort vanished.[30]

Baron Friedrich von Steuben

Relief from the miseries of weather and inadequate food and clothing and boredom came, paradoxically, in the form of drills. All drills for the infantry were conducted by the regimental officers, and all under the watchful supervision of Baron von Steuben. Harris did not know whether it was true or not, but he had heard that von Steuben had a habit of venting his impatience in a most profane language, cursing out the soldiers in a thunderous German, or in a rather unpleasant sounding French, and ordering his aide to relay it all in plain English. Thus the poor, bewildered infantryman, for misunderstanding a command delivered in strange German or strange French, or tardy English, was now being dressed down in three languages. Artilleryman John Harris thought that was funny.

But it would be difficult to over-value what this German officer, who had served under the Prussian Frederick the Great, meant to the Continental Army during this trying time. And one day long after the war's end it was disclosed that he had delivered his entire personal fortune to the cause of the American Revolution. Like Lafayette, he was at Valley Forge a great inspiration to the infantry of the Continental Army.

Henry Knox

Perhaps the portly General Henry Knox can not be considered an "inspiration," at least not in the same way as von Steuben, but he was a powerful force for molding the good soldier. In the first place, he was a soldier's soldier. His artillerymen knew the role he had already played in the war of the Revolution. They knew about the part he had taken at Princeton and Brandywine, and at Germantown. Almost all of them knew that it was Henry Knox who had salvaged the cannon from the captured Fort of Ticonderoga, transporting fifty-nine cannons in twenty days 300 miles over "impassable," frozen roads to Boston, and bringing the guns to the Dorchester Heights, and positioning them, in time to force the British to evacuate the city. The gun crews, in drill day after day, had been trained into precision units by the father of the artillery.

And Knox, who with his equally stout wife Lucy, loved to dine with Washington and Martha, never changed the opinion of Washington he had expressed at the time of the appointment of the Commander-in-Chief, when he observed of him that he "fills his place with vast ease and dignity, and dispenses happiness around him."[31]

Washington had charged Knox with the building of a formidable artillery to serve the Continental Army. This he had done, in a remarkably short time. And he was a young man. At Valley Forge he was yet only twenty-seven, scarcely older than John Harris. And now, at Valley Forge, he continued to fashion an artillery that could help to win the war. The gun crews, when they were not in the employ of the engineers in constructing fortifications, were in drill, day after day after day. John Harris did not complain. He liked Henry Knox, liked him a lot.

Most of Knox's artillery was located in a central position of the encampment, so that the guns could be hurried to any threatened position on the perimeter. But a few of the field cannon were established in fixed positions, at sites considered very sensitive.[32] Although General Henry Knox was in over-all command of the artillery, it was Colonel Thomas Proctor and his captains to whom of course John Harris and his friend Samuel Blackwood answered.

Proctor could be a difficult man. As an officer he was extremely authoritative and officious. He was stubborn as a mule and highly opinionated, sometimes tough to reason with and subject to fits of temper. Like so many men of the artillery regiment, Proctor had been born in Ireland. Unlike the most of them, however, he had been a carpenter by trade, and was thirty-six years old when the war came. His character had been impugned once, but he had been completely cleared of those insinuations. Harris had seen enough of him at Chadds Ford and at Germantown to know that he did not want for courage. And he knew the artillery. And he was *very* proud of his Pennsylvania Artillery, so proud in fact that he would later resist the change of uniform required by the incorporation of his artillery into the Continental Army. Harris had never had any trouble with him, and neither had Sergeant Sam Blackwood.

One of Proctor's officers, however, found himself in big trouble early in the Valley Forge confinement. Captain Hercules Courteney, who had command of Company B in the 4th Continental Artillery (Harris's company), was tried by court martial on December 28. He was charged with dereliction of duty, specifically with "leaving his howitzer [the famous howitzer] in the field in the action at Brandywine [Sept. 11, 1777] in a cowardly, unofficerlike manner." He was found guilty by the court (It is not known whether Harris was asked to testify.), but, because of his good record, was sentenced to a reprimand only. Inasmuch as he was ever known to "support the character of a brave man," Brigadier General Henry Knox was asked to read the reprimand "in the presence of all the Artillery officers." However, even this sentence was disapproved. Because of what Washington declared to be "the state of the evidence," it was directed that Courteney be "discharged from arrest without censure."

But it was not long before Captain Courteney was standing in court again. This time, February 27, the charges were again neglect of duty, and, specifically, for leaving camp while serving as Officer of the Day, and for "lodging out of camp without permission." And this time, having entered a plea of "guilty," he was summarily dismissed from the service of the Continental Army.[33] Company B would have a new captain.

In the encampment at Valley Forge during that winter were an incredible number of officers. General Johann De Kalb was constantly complaining that there were "too many." In the Christmas Day letter De Kalb had written to the Comte de Broglie there was contained this passage: "In addition to this there is a series of officers very expensive and totally superfluous. Every brigade has its commissary of subsistence, its quartermaster, its wagonmaster, its commissary of forage, and each of these again has his deputies. Each general, again, is entitled to a special commissary of subsistence, and three commissaries of forage. All these men rank as officers, and really have nothing to do. My blacksmith is a captain! . . . It is safe to accost every man as a colonel who talks to me with familiarity; the officers of a lower rank are invariably more modest. In a word the army teems with colonels."[34] But all of these officers, quite without exception (although a very few were not all that devoted to Washington), had either already distinguished themselves on the field of battle, or would shortly do so.

Because the officers had quarters of their own, rather "off-campus," ordinary infantrymen and artillerymen, like John Harris, did not get to know them well on a personal level. But here were Alexander Hamilton, who served Washington as Aide-de-Camp; and General John Sullivan, of New Hampshire, who had had important commands at the Brandywine and at Germantown, and who had directed the assault on Staten Island, and whom Harris would shortly get to know much, much better.

Sullivan, who from the war's beginning until its very end had to be considered an extremely controversial officer, was never so close to his Commander-in-Chief as were Lafayette, say, or Henry Knox, or General Greene. And actually, here at Valley Forge, General Sullivan, although Harris could not of course perceive it, was a most unhappy camper. He had two real problems. In the first place, he was still smarting from the Inquiry brought against him because of the disappointment at Staten Island last August. And he was aware that certain members of the Congress had been out to get him, urging his removal from Washington's staff, not only because of the failed assault on Staten Island but also for their impression of his conduct at Brinton's Ford on the Brandywine, when his soldiers were routed. In the second place, he was by temperament not capable of idleness, and was offended when accused of inaction. While at Valley Forge, he was constantly proposing attack on Howe's Philadelphia army. At one point he vented his discontent by complaining about the people of the Philadelphia and Valley Forge region who were urging the army to engage in battle, declaring, "I am so weary of the infernal clamor of the Pennsylvanians that I am for satisfying them at all events, and risking every consequence in an action."[35]

But Washington, while not perhaps so eager to have the General as a dinner guest, understood how very resourceful the New Hampsherite could be. He regularly depended upon him for the necessary attention to "problems." And he was rarely disappointed.

Here at Valley Forge, at about mid-winter, Sullivan did finally complete a job that Washington had been long urging. Although he complained that he had too few tools and not nearly enough skilled carpenters, and though he insisted that the brigades who were supposed to be furnishing carpenters were keeping such men to build and repair the huts and sending him tailors instead, men who had never even seen an axe, let alone handle one, he did the job. He built a bridge across the Schuylkill to provide Washington the escape route he would need in the event of a massive British assault. He stood back from that with great satisfaction.

Sullivan's soldiers may have figured big in another way too. It is a fish story. For it was apparently they chiefly who captured the great numbers of shad which came up the Schuylkill during the

The Schuylkill

"famous" run of 1778. Historians are not at all agreed on the dimensions of this event, and surely it is much too much to say, as some do, that these shad actually saved the starving army, saved the Revolution, but of course the shad, ever how many there were, would prove a welcome relief to the diet of Washington's troops.

The river had been frozen over from time to time that winter, notably on March 5 and again on March 22; but by early April it had opened up, and during the last three weeks of May and early June, according to some accounts, the waters were teeming with spawning shad:

> Then, dramatically, the famine completely ended. Countless thousands of fat shad, swimming up the Schuylkill to spawn filled the river. Sullivan's men, accustomed to treading out fresh-water mussels in the stream, were astonished to see the water almost boiling with the struggling fish. Soldiers thronged the river bank. Then, at the advice of Pennsylvanians accustomed to the yearly fishing, the cavalry was ordered into the river bed. Carrying huge bushes, broken tree boughs, and long sticks, the horsemen rode upstream, noisily shouting and beating the water, driving the shad before them into nets spread across the Schuylkill at Pawling's ford, where the Perkiomen flows into the river. So thick were the shad that, when the fish were cornered in the nets, a pole could not be thrust into the water without striking fish. Thousands of the tasty, rich shad were netted at each haul. The netting was continued day after day, with more than a hundred horsemen continually beating the water, until the army was thoroughly stuffed with fish and in addition hundreds of barrels of shad were salted down for future use. The lavish fish feast was a dramatic close to a long period of privation.[36]

And from another record, a strikingly similar impression:

> The river ran shallow, and it was possible for cavalrymen to ride right up the middle of it, almost knee-to-knee. Each carried a cut bush with which he beat the water. At the narrowest point, Pawling's Ford, just outside of camp a little north of headquarters, where the Perkiomen's Creek emptied into the Schuylkill, nets had been spread. The fish swam in, got caught by the gills, and couldn't get back.

There were thousands of them, more and more coming all day, every day, all night too, for weeks . . . . For almost a month the whole camp stank, and men's fingers were oily. In addition, barrels had been held in readiness, and hundreds of these were filled with salted shad for future consumption.[37]

And of course these fish would be only those which had escaped the nets placed by the hungry Redcoats fourteen miles down river.

That the shad were a big deal for the encampment has been disputed, and there seems not to be a lot of hard evidence that the fish were anything like a life-saving boon to the troops. Washington, whose headquarters for three weeks would have looked out over this frantic scene, and who had been himself an ardent sport fisherman and even a commercial fisherman, and a shad merchant (netting 8000 shad in one season!),[38] seems never to have mentioned this bonanza in his war-time communications. It *may* have been the godsend that saved the Revolution, but the Commander-in-Chief was not giving it a lot of credit. Perhaps it was because this bounty arrived so late in the ordeal, at a time when the encampment was beginning to do a lot better. And then, too, just at the height of the river action, on the first day of May, arrived a bigger fish than any shad, the glorious news of the Alliance with France.

Besides John Sullivan, there were the stout General William Alexander, who, though he liked to be thought a Lord, could fight like a wildcat; and the ferryman, Brigadier General John Glover, of Long Island and Trenton fame; and Anthony Wayne, a Pennsylvania farmer of extraordinary military skill who had during this winter made a number of daring raids on British supply trains, and who had also led foraging expeditions all over eastern Pennsylvania and throughout Delaware and South Jersey (even into Salem and Cumberland Counties, John Harris's homeland); and Brigadier General Peter Muhlenberg, "the fighting parson,"[39] and Major General Nathanael Greene, perhaps Washington's most able field general, but here serving as Quartermaster. Greene was a New Hampshire foundryman, a Quaker. He had always had a bum leg, and he limped a little. He was a most resourceful officer and a shrewd strategist. He had disappointed Washington only once. He was a fairly young man yet, at thirty-five.

Of course one of the most important officers in the camp was the Marquis de Lafayette, who was something of an inspiration to the soldiers. He was an awkward walker too, with good reason. He had come limping into camp, leaning for support on a stick, still suffering from the wound inflicted at Brandywine, which had kept him in bed for several weeks. Fortunately the shot had not touched the bone, but the leg continued in a ghastly red and purple, constantly swollen as it was and extremely painful.

And his great regard and affection for the army's Commander-in-Chief, never disguised, certainly carried over to the common soldier, whose devotion to Washington steadily solidified. In a letter to his wife, the young Lafayette wrote, "This honourable man, whose talents and virtues I admire and whom I venerate the more the better I become acquainted with him, has done me the honour to be my intimate friend. When he learned that I had been wounded he sent me his own medical attendant, urging him to treat me with as much care as if I were not only the commander-in-chief's friend but his son."[40]

Marquis de Lafayette

Washington had given Lafayette at Valley Forge the command of a division, the Virginia Light Infantry, with instructions to drill and drill and drill. And for the most part he felt an important part of the Patriot army. But he was constantly appraising his role and earnestly trying to justify, to himself, and to his wife, his absence from his home and his country. Early in the life of the encampment at Valley Forge he penned one of those tender billets-doux his wife loved to receive. To the lonely Marquise Adrienne Lafayette, in faraway Paris, he wrote:

Camp near Valley Forge,
January 6, 1778
   Dear Heart:
      What a date! And what a place to write from in the month of January! I am in camp, in the middle of woods, fifteen hundred leagues from you, imprisoned in the middle of winter. A short while ago we were only separated from the enemy by a little river; at present we are twenty miles away, and it is here that the American army will pass the winter in little huts that are almost as gay as a prison cell.... The bearer of this letter will tell you of the agreeable spot that I choose instead of being with you and all my friends, in the midst of all possible pleasures. On my word, dear Heart, don't you believe that I must have good reasons to decide upon this sacrifice. Everything bids me go, but Honor says stay, and really when you shall know all the circumstances in detail concerning me and the army and my friend the Commander-in-Chief, and the whole American Cause, you will forgive me, dear Heart, you will excuse me, and I almost dare say that you will approve of me.... [41]

   Certainly Lafayette was a vitally important figure in the Cause, most insisting that the war would have come to a very different end without him and the support and participation of his country. Even here, at Valley Forge, the war swirled about him. He was invited to join in a conspiracy, headed up by one of Washington's most industrious detractors, the ambitious General Thomas Conway, an able and courageous officer who had been in the van at Germantown and in the midst of the first fighting.
   On the evening of the day he was nominated as Commander-in-Chief of the Continental Army, Washington had confided sorrowfully to Patrick Henry: "Remember, Mr. Henry, what I now tell you. From the day I enter upon the command of the American armies, I date the fall and the ruin of my reputation." And now it was beginning to seem a prophetic understanding.
   The plan had as its object the removal of Washington as Commander-in-Chief, and was supported by a number of very powerful voices, including those of Dr. Benjamin Rush and Thomas Mifflin, Washington's longtime good friends. Happily, though not

surprisingly, the young French officer declined any part in the plot, and of course was very glad to see it fail.[42] And in fact, the influential Lafayette practically insured its failure when he offered a moving and spirited toast to "our great general."

Besides all that, the young Frenchman even survived a kidnaping attempt organized by Howe. Through great good fortune, he simply was not at home at the time for which the scheme was scheduled.

Lafayette, however, was absent from the encampment for quite a long time in mid-winter. Washington, apparently half expecting the plan would never be executed, had put him in command of an expedition to invade Canada (again). This operation had been organized by General Horatio Gates, and "seemed," to Gates at least, to have the approval of the Congress. It got so far as to require Lafayette to depart the encampment for York and then on to Albany. But when he found himself at the head of a most inadequate number of soldiers, not well provisioned, and when it was learned that Canada "was quite ready for the invasion," the expedition was aborted.

He had left Valley Forge in February. He returned early in April, to more of the hard winter, and, yes, to more excitement. On May 18, Lafayette, under orders from General Washington was dispatched on an "intelligence" mission to Philadelphia at the head of a large company of soldiers (perhaps as many as 2100). No one knows what would have come of this endeavor had the British not learned of it. But Lafayette was betrayed by one of Colonel Proctor's artillerymen (not John Harris), who revealed the plan to Howe. The British organized an ambush, with a far superior number of troops, and when Lafayette marched into this he was able to escape only by feigning a counter-attack and taking advantage of the resulting confusion. It was skillfully done, and though the expedition went down as another failure, Washington was much relieved that it had not concluded in calamity.

There was very little of a military nature to be happy about that winter. But survival, and with much improved morale, was more than the army might have hoped for in December. And, after all, the British had registered no real gains against the rebellion. The Redcoats had been bottled up.

And, contrary to popular belief, the King's Men were not

enjoying all that great a winter in Philadelphia either, not the common foot soldier. The city was a garrison city, without much in the way of tentacles. With his patrols and his own foraging parties Washington had managed to keep a fairly tight cordon around the city. The British foraging expeditions, while rounding up some foodstuffs and supplies, were far from providing sufficient food or fuel. Shortages were real. Many of the Loyalists who had welcomed Howe to the city could not believe that the magnificent British army was not preparing an assault on the Valley Forge encampment. Certainly, they felt, at least in the spring the King's Men will destroy the impoverished rebel army. Only as the winter dragged its slow length along did these Loyalists begin to appreciate how really hopeless was the British position in Philadelphia.

It is also customary to suppose that during the long winter months of 1778, while Washington's main army was encamped at Valley Forge, and the British were occupying Philadelphia, just a few miles away, nothing much happened. In fact, a great deal happened. Both armies were constantly sending out foraging expeditions (generally headed up by Wayne in the case of the patriots); both were constantly patrolling the roads in the neighborhood of the city. Both were looking to harass the enemy as much as possible, just as they were in the days immediately preceding Valley Forge. Washington desired to keep the British "nervous." Consequently there was experienced a great deal of skirmishing, although *skirmishing* is a term which belittles much of the action which occurred. One instance may make the point.

A particularly big nuisance to the British during all of this time was Brigadier General John Lacy, Jr., who commanded troops of militia which varied in size from 300 to 500 men. Washington was depending upon Lacy to patrol the area immediately north of Philadelphia, between the Delaware and Schuylkill Rivers. He hoped that Lacy's patrols could provide him sufficient warning in the event of a British assault on Valley Forge. Besides that, knowing that Howe's garrison was ill provisioned, he expected the militia force to harass the British and make difficult their foraging expeditions. He also was aware that some trading with the locals was being accomplished. He desired to limit that.

On April 30, Loyalist sympathizers who had been observing

militia activity in their neighborhood got word through to Howe that General Lacy would be encamped "this night" (April 30) at the Crooked Billet Tavern (Hatboro). The British command seized on this information with delight. And in no time at all a force was assembled. As Major John Simcoe, who had been active in this countryside with his Rangers, knew the area well, he was ordered to round up his men and to report to Lt. Colonel Robert Abercrombie[43] at once. Abercrombie's command, when it was mustered that evening in the city, included, besides Simcoe's Queen's Rangers (430 strong), fourteen companies of light infantry (grenadiers), two troops (120 men) of Major Crewe's 16th and 17th dragoons, Captain Richard Hovendon's Philadelphia light dragoons, and Captain James's Chester County dragoons.[44]

This potent force marched out of the city at about 11:00 on the night of the last day of April, by way of Second Street. In the darkness the column proceeded stealthily to Huntingdon Valley, where Abercrombie elected to section off one body of his command. With the main force he marched west on to the Old York Road, meaning to assault Lacy's camp head-on. Simcoe he dispatched to the north so that he could cross to the other side of the encampment and complete an envelopment of the militia.[45]

As it turned out, the British arrival came as a complete surprise. On the morning of May 1, Lacy's soldiers at the camp near the Tavern awoke to find themselves effectively surrounded by Redcoats.

As the engagement was described a few days later by the Tory newspaper *The Royal Pennsylvania Gazette* of Philadelphia, "On Thursday night last a small [!] party of the British infantry, dragoons and Queen's Rangers . . . left this city about eleven o'clock and proceeded to the Old York Road. About a mile beyond the Billet they fell in with Lacy's brigade of militia, consisting of about 500 [300 is a more accurate figure] men and immediately attacked them." The article notes that the retreating troops were pursued for four miles and concludes with statistics.[46] There is no mention of atrocities.

But one historian puts it this way: "Of all the engagements fought during the winter, the Battle of Crooked Billet witnessed the most shocking blot on the honor of the British Army, even surpassing the brutality exhibited at Hancock's Bridge."[47]

Lacy's troops, which had withdrawn to a deeply wooded area, some miles distant from the encampment, eventually returned to the scene of the first fighting. What they discovered was horrifying. It was a scene more frightful than could be imagined. The bodies of their fellow soldiers littered the field. And they had been terribly mutilated. It was plain that the militiamen had been bayoneted mercilessly and chopped up by cutlasses way beyond any need. Some of the dead had been set on fire, and some of the living also! According to witnesses, "while still alive," soldiers had their bodies covered with straw, which was then ignited. In depositions that were taken it was declared that Redcoats had been observed throwing wounded militiamen into the buckwheat fires; and that British grenadiers had been observed putting the bayonet to men who had already surrendered.

Lacy's report to the Pennsylvania Supreme Executive Council described the atrocities: "Some were Butchard in a manner most Brutal Savages Could not equal, even while Living Some were thrown into Buckwheat Straw and the Straw set on fire, the Close [clothes] were Burnt on others, and scarcely one without a Dozen Wounds with Bayonets or Cutlasses."[48]

John Simcoe

Major John Simcoe (at the time of his writing, a Lieutenant Colonel), who during the Revolution was with his Rangers involved in a number of like episodes, confided an account of the battle to his journal. He fails to mention the brutalities detailed by witnesses: "The excursion [!], though it failed in the greater part, had its full effect of intimidating the militia as they never afterwards appeared but in small numbers, and like robbers."[49]

One British report does acknowledge atrocity, but excuses it: ". . . several grenadiers [light infantry] were so embittered they burned nine rebels." *Embittered* in this account apparently refers to

The Schuylkill

the similar treatment of surrendering British soldiers by Wayne's men at Germantown, which of course was in response to the British savagery at Paoli.[50] Atrocity breeds revenge, and revenge revenge, and revenge revenge, and so on. The time-honored rule of *lex talionis.*

As usual in accounts of any battle, casualty figures vary. Most reports have the American losses at nearly 100 killed and half as many more taken prisoner. One report gives American losses as 26 killed, eight wounded, and 58 missing. *The Royal Pennsylvania Gazette* reports (May 5) that 80-100 Americans were killed, and that "next day" the British received 50-60 prisoners, and 16 wagons loaded with baggage, flour, salt, and whisky."[51] Three other wagons were reportedly burned.

All accounts agree on British losses: not a man killed, six or seven wounded. The Battle of Crooked Billet, for a number of reasons, has never been regarded a glorious moment in the annals of the American Revolution.[52]

Although no real threat from Howe was ever posed for the encampment at Valley Forge, the artillery did have some chances to perform. Upon special occasions the big guns were pressed into service to commemorate the event. The most noteworthy of those that occurred at Valley Forge, indeed surely the most joyous day of the long, hard winter, came when on May 5 there was received the report of the Treaty of Alliance with France. What the army learned was that three months ago, on February 6, the Treaty had been concluded in Paris, with Benjamin Franklin signing for the United States. And just yesterday the Congress had ratified the document. This was most welcome news. The troops were very nearly delirious. Washington ordered a celebration with the regiments at their finest. Lafayette of course became the center of attention. The young officer stood proudly on parade, together with the Continental Army of General George Washington, while, three times, thirteen guns of the Henry Knox Artillery boomed their salute.[53] In the general orders for this day, Tuesday, May 5, in which the alliance was proclaimed, an ecstatic Washington noted the need "to set apart a day for gratefully acknowledging the divine Goodness."

Just how much joy was occasioned in the Commander-in-Chief can be realized from the fact that he promptly pardoned two soldiers who had been condemned to execution, and returned them to their companies. And that night he entertained his officers at the Potts House with the kind of elegant dinner he so much enjoyed.

This news, that France would now be formally and actively supporting the American cause in the war with Great Britain, could not have come at a better time. The prospect of the French naval forces coming into the picture, and perhaps troops as well, heightened considerably the mood of the Valley Forge encampment.

And shortly thereafter, toward the end of the month, the encampment learned that their old nemesis, General William Howe, who had been vigorously criticized by the Crown for "inactivity," had done what Thomas Paine had been urging him to do, that is, to go home. On May 24, Howe said goodbye forever to America. And he made the most of the occasion. His farewell to the city was celebrated in the most extravagant festivity, all orchestrated of course by impresario Major John André.[54] Howe, never on very good terms with his fellow general Henry Clinton, would be succeeded in Philadelphia by the much younger and much more zealous, and perhaps more able British officer.[55] Good news and bad news.

As spring came on more intensely and prospects brightened, young John Harris took stock of his situation. He was now twenty-four years old. He had not been in touch with any member of his family in the year since he left Salem. In fact, he had had no communication from anybody in that time. And he had dispatched none. He did succumb to reverie from time to time, wondering some about "back home." He wondered about Sophie and how she was doing; and he wondered about his brothers, and about his mother. He wondered whether they worried about him. But he could put such musings aside. He rarely permitted himself the luxury of nostalgia.

The common soldier does not always know what is going on, what is being planned for next day or next week. He depends upon scuttlebutt, upon the grapevine. Now, as the time approached for their evacuation of their winter quarters at Valley Forge, Harris heard all kinds of vague and contradictory rumors. It was expected that Clinton would be pulling out of Philadelphia, and it was supposed that whatever his mission or his destination Washington would be forcing an engagement. But what he was hearing over and over was that Proctor's artillery, or at least units of it, would not be marching with Washington.

This, if true, would be bad news for John Harris, and for most of his fellow artillerymen. They had for all the long winter been looking forward to a return to the fighting. Besides, Harris had made a lot of friends during the time at Valley Forge. Of course he was closest to the artillerymen and most especially those eleven of his own hut; but he had come to know a great many others, and he was hoping that they could be kept together.

He thought about the officers too, and he wondered which of those his artillery company would serve. He thought about Lafayette, him whom they all called, without meaning any disrespect at all, "the Frenchman." He liked Lafayette, who was even younger than himself. He liked him for his energy, for the enthusiastic way he went about everything, for his contagious positive attitude. He might have been arrogant and officious, but he wasn't. And it was very plain that General Washington was extremely fond of him, "fatherly,"and inclined to depend upon him. That should be enough for anybody. Certainly he was not short on courage. He must have known that he was always a principal target, and he must have had a thousand bullets whiz by on the fields at Brandywine before one took him down. Harris had heard about Lafayette's clever escape from the trap set for him by Howe two weeks ago. And now, fully recovered from the wound he had suffered in his first battle ever, he would be first in the field again.[56] Harris would like to see that.

And also there was General De Kalb, who, Harris knew, had come to the country with Lafayette, almost like a father to his son, for De Kalb was fifty-six when Lafayette was nineteen. He knew that the older man was driven by the same passion for freedom that impelled the younger, but he could see that he was a very different person. He was inclined to be morose and somewhat sullen. He had been known to express his concern about the site Washington had chosen for the winter quarters. And he had been heard to grumble about the officers, about how many there were. "Everybody here is an officer," he had been heard to mutter.[57] But still he was very pleasant with the ordinary soldier; and he did not order parades for fatigued men. As with Lafayette, it was obvious to everybody that Washington treated him with unqualified respect.

By May, though many of the soldiers remained ill and bed-ridden, conditions had much improved in the Valley Forge encampment. Not only was the health ever so much better, so was the morale, and so was the military stature. By General von Steuben with the infantry and by Henry Knox with the artillery and by the field officers of all divisions the troops had been drilled into a well-oiled machine. The army that marched out of Valley Forge on June 19 was a very different army from that which had taken up residence there in December. If it is too much to say that at Valley Forge during the winter of 1777-78 the United States of America became a legitimate independent nation, let the historians acknowledge at least that from the miseries of that awful winter emerged a new Army, an Army that would shortly win the battle for Independence.

V

THE PASSAIC

> *George Washington, Commander of the American armies, who, like Joshua of old, commanded the sun and the moon to stand still, and they obeyed him.*
>
> — **Benjamin Franklin**

When the Continental Army marched out of Valley Forge on June 19 (the third anniversary of Lexington and Concord), it stepped briskly and purposefully, with confidence and determination. The British force had evacuated Philadelphia (Franklin had been right), and was on its way back to New York City. Washington, feeling very good about his army, and not a little proud, was determined to arrest its march. He was taking the Continental Army back to New Jersey.

But he was not taking the whole of the Continental Artillery. Proctor's 4th Artillery Regiment, although no longer regarded as a strictly Pennsylvania unit, was ordered to take care of Philadelphia.

Together with some small parties of Pennsylvania militia it was to provide the necessary guard and provost duty, and hurry the city back to health, until further notice.[1] It had in its care also a large number of invalids sent from the hospitals at Valley Forge.[2] Perhaps this assignment was ordered because of the size to which the 4th had dwindled. It was way down in June from what it had been in the previous October (and by August 4 it would be even further reduced, to a mere 220 men). But Washington was not merely sloughing off Proctor and his regiment. There was a job to be done in Philadelphia, a very important job.

Whatever the case, the 4th Continental Artillery, except for two or three gun sections, got Philadelphia and not Monmouth.[3]

Clinton had evacuated Philadelphia on June 18. Washington left the winter quarters at Valley Forge the day after. Clinton was headed for New York City, but had not chosen the most expeditious route, and in a week's time had managed hardly more than forty miles. He had 18,000 troops and perhaps as many as 1,000 Loyalists besides. His baggage train, which included an enormous amount of precious personal property stolen from the citizens of the city, was composed of 1500 vehicles and was twelve miles long!

General Knox reported to his brother William on the prospects, should an engagement occur. He noted that Clinton was losing a great many of his fighting force: "Above three hundred German and English have deserted since they left Philadelphia. Had we a sufficiency of numbers, we should be able to force them to a similar treaty with Burgoynes; but, at present, have not quite such sanguine hopes." He went on in his letter to express his characteristic confidence in General Washington: "If general actions had no other

Henry Clinton

consequences than merely the killed and wounded, we should attack them in twenty-four hours. But the fate of posterity, and not the elusive brilliancy of military glory, governs our Fabian commander, the man [to whom], under God, America owes her present prospects of peace and happiness."[4]

Washington, who had been following closely with a force of more than 13,000 officers and men, and harassing the British column by burning bridges and cluttering up the roads, arrived at the John Hunt farm in Hopewell, not far from Englishtown, on the 23rd. While encamped there, Washington called a council of war, as was his wont. Because he felt the British to be extremely vulnerable, the Commander-in-Chief was astonished to find most of his officers voicing opposition to an all-out assault on the Redcoats. But the tactful Washington effected a "compromise," which meant attacking the flanks of Clinton's force, and which of course could turn into the major battle that he wanted and which he felt sure he could win.

By Saturday, June 27, the Continental Army was in Englishtown, not far to the north from Freehold Village (Monmouth Court House), where the British were encamped. Here Washington appreciated his opportunity. But there was no time to be lost. He promptly commissioned General von Steuben to scout the enemy position and to determine what advantages the terrain might afford. The whole day of June 27 the General did just that, reporting to Washington precisely the information that he needed.[5] The strategy having been agreed to, Washington issued the necessary orders.

A portion of the army that was now encamped at Englishtown broke camp at 3:00 in the morning of the 28th, Sunday; and by daybreak had entered the Monmouth Court House region. Other detachments broke camp at 4:30 and at 5:00. The army at this time continued to number some twelve or thirteen thousand.

In faraway Philadelphia a bombardier artilleryman awoke with a start this fateful morning to a strange but vivid vision: Monmouth! Here today, under the scorching sun, pasted in the heavens like the infernal fireball of damnation, boys would become men. Here today the officers whom the young John Harris through the long winter at Valley Forge had studied from a respectful distance would acquit themselves superbly. Perhaps most especially Anthony Wayne, but the Baron von Steuben as well, and Lafayette, and Hamilton and Burr, and the inspiring Generals Lord Stirling and Nathanael Greene. And what a day it would be for his beloved General Washington!

Very early in the morning it was apparent that this Sunday was going to be a very hot day. As it turned out, the battle at Monmouth was played out in a stifling, intolerable heat, that caused almost as many deaths as did the cannon and muskets.

The action, replete with artillery exchanges, commenced at midmorning. As Colonel William Irvine, who had been returned to the army via prisoner exchange in time to participate in the fighting at Monmouth, described it in a June 30 letter to Captain John Davis, who was at the time near Carlisle, Pennsylvania, "The two Armies were formed on two hills about a half mile apart; about Eleven o'clock an exceedingly heavy cannonading commenced on both sides and continued with great vigor till after four in the afternoon."[6]

Knox, in a report on the battle to "My Dearest Love," has the cannonading lasting from "about eleven o'clock until six o'clock, at which time the enemy began to retire on all quarters." Washington, very confident that he could bring up the main body of the army in time to deliver the coup de gras, had commanded General Charles Lee to attack the British forces on the left flank in an all-out effort. And all might have gone well had not General Lee, who had been disagreeing with Washington all along on when and where to assail the Redcoats, settled for a little skirmishing. He even ordered a general retreat. And naturally Clinton promptly ordered a counterattack, which had the American forces in disarray. Doubtless it would have been a complete and catastrophic rout, had not the Commander-in-Chief, with Baron von Steuben, come riding up. A furious Washington was able to restore order, and was able to halt the advance of the British, but the opportunity for a major victory here had been lost. During the night the British recovered their wounded, all except four officers and fifty privates, whose wounds were so serious as to prevent their removal. And then at midnight the Redcoats marched away, as Washington described it "in such silence that tho' General [Enoch] Poor lay extremely near them, they effected their Retreat without his Knowledge."

General Irvine noted that "the enemy drew off about two miles and in the night went off Bag and Baggage." Daybreak the morning of the 29th disclosed no sign of the British forces. Clinton had withdrawn during the night to the heights of Middletown, and, according to Knox and Irvine, was intent on Sandy Hook, "instead of the supposed [route] to South Amboy."[7] Even though Washington was willing, even eager, to continue the fighting, a renewal of the pursuit was apparently not seriously considered. Knox did note in letters to his family that "We have sent out large parties in pursuit, but I believe they will not be able to come up with the main body." And indeed they did not.

Washington's weary army of 12,000 men repaired to the nearby community of Englishtown, and for two days lay quiet in a futile attempt to find refuge from the heat, finally setting out for Spotswood, about seven miles directly north, on July 1 under a continually oppressive sun.

Writing from Englishtown on that same day, July 1, to the President of the Congress, Henry Laurens, the Commander-in Chief provided a full and greatly detailed report of the battle, including an expression of disgust with the conduct of General Lee. He describes his riding up to the scene of the battle: ". . . to my great surprise and mortification I met the whole advanced Corps retreating . . . by General Lee's orders, without having made any opposition . . . ."[8] That Washington was enraged there can be no question. That he vented this rage in an uncharacteristic profusion of profanity there is evidence enough. One witness to the scene was General Charles Scott of Virginia, who commanded a detachment of 1500 men during the fighting, and of whom it was said, there is no man more profane. When, at some time after the war, a friend of his, earnestly bent on reform, raised a question of the General about Washington, the dialogue went something like this: Expecting to embarrass General Scott, his friend asked, "Have you ever known the admired Washington to swear?" General Scott paused briefly to reflect, then exclaimed, "Yes, once; it was at Monmouth, and on a day that would have made any man swear. Yes, sir, he swore on that day till the leaves shook on the trees, charming delightfully. Never have I enjoyed such swearing before or since. Sir, on that ever-memorable day he swore like an angel from Heaven."[9] Needless to report, General Scott's would-be reformer promptly abandoned his enterprise.

Hamilton's unqualified praise of Washington's conduct in this battle was hardly more fervently expressed than was his contempt for Lee. In a letter to Elins Boudinot, written at Brunswick, New Jersey, not long after the battle, on July 5, he described Lee's conduct in command of his corps as "childish," "monstrous," and "unpardonable." He was very sure that the expected Court Martial could not punish him enough.[10]

And after the court martial, when Lee, because of his ugly reflections on Washington, was challenged to a duel by Lt. Colonel John Laurens, son of the President of Congress, Hamilton was quick to offer to serve as Laurens' second. The two met near Philadelphia, in a lightly forested area not far from the four-mile marker on the Point-no-Point Road. And doubtless Hamilton was sorely disappointed when Lee was but slightly wounded.[11]

Colonel William Irvine felt the same disdain and disgust for Lee. After the battle he remembered the difficulty he had experienced in advancing to the position he had been assigned; and he acknowledged that he had, indeed, threatened to charge right through Lee's disordered and retreating soldiers if they did not get out of the way.[12]

At the trial, the guilt of General Lee was declared, and he was relieved of his command for a one-year period. In 1780 he was permanently dismissed. One member of the court martial was in fact the close observer Colonel William Irvine.

But Washington's report was not all about General Lee. Most of what he had to describe of the battle was by way of commendation. He noted for the Congress that the retreating troops were served well by the artillery, "which checked the Enemy's advance and gave time to make a disposition of the left wing and second line of the Army upon an eminence, and in a wood a little in the Rear covered by a morass in front. On this were placed some Batteries of Cannon by Lord Stirling who commanded the left Wing, which played upon the

Enemy with great effect, and seconded by parties of Infantry detached to oppose them, effectually put a stop to their advance."[13]

One British officer, after the close of the action, gave much credit to the Rebel batteries, observing that "No artillery could be better served than the Americans'." And Washington himself had extremely high praise for the conduct of the artillery during the battle of Monmouth. Besides the performance of Lord Stirling's cannon, he singled out the artillery which under General Greene had achieved some high ground from which it produced a withering fire. Also commended in the official reports was Lieutenant Colonel Eleazer Oswald, who had served under Arnold at Ticonderoga and at Quebec. At Monmouth he was acclaimed for his conspicuous gallantry and for his great skills as an artillery strategist. "All the Artillery both Officers and Men that were engaged," Washington reported to the Congress, "distinguished themselves in a remarkable manner."[14]

The man responsible for the artillery, General Henry Knox, was extremely proud of the way in which the guns were maneuvered and fired. He noted that "His Excellency, the General, has done the corps of artillery and me the honor to notice us in general orders in very pointed and flattering terms." While graciously acknowledging the plaudits, Knox declared with not a little pride, "My brave lads behaved with their usual intrepidity, and the army gave the corps of artillery their full proportion of the glory of the day."[15]

In fact, at the Battle of Monmouth, the artillery played a much bigger role than at most other battles of the Revolution, and was more consequential than at any other action, excepting of course Yorktown. The artillery exchanges throughout were heated and most influential in determining the tides of the battle. In particular, it was Colonel John Crane's Third Regiment of the Continental Artillery (800 men) under Captains Thomas Seward, David Cook, and John Compston that performed with such great skill and such extraordinary valor as to make any British gains impossible.

In appraising the battle, in letters home, Henry Knox, continued in his high praise for his artillerymen and recognized the value of the big guns to the fighting. In reports to his brother and to his wife, he declared, "Indeed, I was highly delighted with their coolness, bravery, and good conduct. The effects of the battle of Monmouth will be great and lasting. It will convince the enemy and the world that nothing but a good constitution is wanting to render our army equal to any in the world."[16]

The Battle of Monmouth is particularly memorable also for the participation in it of Pennsylvania's "Mad" Anthony Wayne, who fought a valiant delaying action while Washington reorganized the troops Lee had scattered. Wayne, called "Mad" because he was quarrelsome and hot-headed and impulsive, who rarely looked before he leaped, was, despite Paoli, very rapidly winning the reputation for military skill and daring that by war's end would be second to none. Here at Monmouth, in the late afternoon, he hastily organized three Pennsylvania regiments of infantry to attack the withdrawing Redcoats, and then against a very fierce counter-attack he ably defended the position he had gained along a hedgerow. Washington, while applauding the great courage of his officers and men generally, singled out Wayne for special commendation, noting that he had fought with "good conduct and bravery thro' the whole action."[17] And Hamilton, who himself suffered a hurtful fall when his horse took a musket ball, noted in his letter to Boudinot that General Wayne "was always foremost in danger."

Anthony Wayne

Also impressive in the fighting was Lieutenant Colonel Aaron Burr, who as commander of a provisional brigade composed of the 2nd and 11th Pennsylvania Regiments was able to thwart a major British advance. Burr, though he had served with Arnold and Montgomery in the disastrous Quebec campaign and had participated in the fighting at Long Island and had been at Valley Forge, was still, at twenty-two, a very young man.

The Battle of Monmouth is memorable too because it saw the

return to action of the gallant Lafayette, who had been wounded at Brandywine. And it is memorable, too, because of Molly Pitcher. It was from this battle that Molly Pitcher emerged a heroine. Her name was Mary Ludwig Hays (sometimes wrongly spelled Hayes), but she had always been called "Molly," and here it was Molly Pitcher because it was she who carried pitcher after pitcher of cool spring water to the needy soldiers throughout the intolerably hot day. One soldier or another was always singing out, "Here comes Molly with her pitcher." All through the fierce action she carried water, until the fighting for both armies surrendered to the terrible heat, and the battle mercifully ended.[18]

Aaron Burr

According to legend, and possibly true, the courageous lady was presented to the Commander-in-Chief of the Continental Army after the battle. Washington could only have been deeply moved. And he may indeed have dubbed her "Sergeant Molly," as many people have always believed.

But perhaps most memorable of all that occurred on that unforgettably hot and furious day was the character that emerged in the person of the Commander-in-Chief of the Continental forces. For that, there is the inspired description provided by Washington's aide, Lieutenant-Colonel Alexander Hamilton:

I never saw the General to so much advantage. His coolness and firmness were admirable. He instantly took measures for checking the enemy's advance, and giving time to the army, which was very near, to form and make a proper disposition. He then rode back and had the troops formed on a very advantageous piece of ground. . . . America owes a great deal to General Washington for this day's

Alexander Hamilton

work. A general rout, dismay and disgrace would have attended the whole army in any other hands but his. By his own good sense and fortitude, he turned the fate of the day. Other officers have great merit in performing their parts well; but he directed the whole with the skill of a master workman. He did not hug himself at a distance, and leave an Arnold to win laurels for him; but by his own presence he brought order out of confusion, animated his troops, and led them to success.[19]

Lafayette, who was himself one of the most valiant officers on the field, and who had called for Washington to come to the front at the critical juncture of the battle, also had good things to say of his Commander: "Never was General Washington greater in war than in this action. His presence stopped the retreat; his dispositions fixed the victory; his fine appearance on horseback,[20] his calm courage roused to animation by the vexations of the morning [Lee], gave him the air best calculated to excite enthusiasm."[21]

In recollecting the battle at another time, Lafayette remembered that Washington "rode along the lines, amid the shouts of the soldiers, cheering them by his voice and example and restoring to our standard the fortunes of the fight. I thought then as now that never had I beheld so superb a man."[22]

Time has done nothing to qualify these portraits of Washington. William Scudder Stryker, Adjutant-General of the State of New Jersey, in his definitive account of the action (1927), had this appraisal: "Every act of General Washington in the battle was tactically right. Every move of his, so far as we can now ascertain, was performed in the best possible way. Every disposition of his force after he took immediate control of it has been pronounced correct by skilled military critics who were familiar with the country."[23]

Historians sometimes refer to the Battle of Monmouth as "the longest battle" of the Revolution.[24] What is meant, of course, is "the longest single-day continuous battle" of the Revolution. And that is not only because of the hours involved but because of the intolerable heat, which made every minute seem ten.

Some historians claim the Battle of Monmouth as a victory for American forces, and certainly Hamilton did. And certainly Washington did. And clearly Henry Knox did. But most see it as a draw. The Continental Army suffered casualties totaling 362 killed, wounded, and missing. Among the dead were eight officers, including Lieutenant Colonel Rudolph Bunner of the Third Pennsylvania Regiment and Major Edmund B. Dickinson of the First Virginia Regiment. The British suffered at least 358 battle casualties and perhaps as many as 416, including four officers, one of whom was the Honorable Colonel Robert Monckton, of the Seventeenth Foot, British Army. General Knox, never shy about inflation, had British losses at ten to twelve hundred killed, wounded and taken prisoner.

But the British lost a great many more too, because of desertion. Many of Clinton's troops were Tory colonists, loyal to the King. Some of these were easily discouraged and headed home. Early estimates of the number of deserters had the figure at 600, including 440 Hessians, but some ran as high as 800. All in all, the British may have lost 1200 men on the trip through New Jersey and at the Battle of Monmouth. Washington believed the total to be close to 2000![25]

Of course the heat took its toll as well. It is not known how many of the Redcoats perished because of the incredible heat or because of fatigue; but the Continental Army lost thirty-three privates, two sergeants and two corporals.[26]

By day's end the victor, whoever that was, could look upon the terrain of battle only with great pain. It was a field of carnage and blood. Carcasses of horses were sprawled in all sorts of grotesque positions; and ugly flies were already prowling the lips and eyes of the lifeless. There was scarcely a soldier, redcoat or blue, but had lost a comrade in the battle. Death hung heavy in the acrid air. General Washington of course felt it most. He was responsible, and he was duty-bound to weigh the cost against the gain. Inured as he was to the after-the-battle scene, he felt the great pity of it all.

The Battle of Monmouth was a very critical event of the Revolution. Those who would calculate the effect of it must note that Washington was ready to fight on the morrow, and that there was nobody to fight. The battle of June 28 can be counted a draw if one simply goes by casualties, but the fact is that the British, with far superior numbers, withdrew from the field. The battle ended in the *retreat* of Clinton's army, the British main army of 20,000 men. In fact, the exodus from Philadelphia and the laborious trek across New Jersey to New York City is properly regarded not as a triumphant march but as a flight, and an ignominious one at that, with the long and ponderous baggage train, the constant harassment, and the steady stream of desertions.

What the British (excepting only Henry Clinton) never understood sufficiently through the long years of the war was that the occupation of a principal city in the colonies, like Boston or New York or Baltimore or Philadelphia, counted for very little. And the "capture" of the capital of the United States could never really occur. The capital was simply the meeting place of the Continental Congress. It could be moved easily and speedily and totally, and regularly was. What the British command never realized sufficiently was that the best way to squelch the rebellion, in fact the *only* way, was to destroy the Continental Army under Washington. Their best chance for this occurred early, with the battle of New York City. And another chance occurred at Whitemarsh. But after Monmouth there never did appear another like opportunity.

It was with a kind of arrogant indifference that the British occupied Boston, and then New York City, and then Philadelphia, and then New York City again, almost as if the war could be brought to an end by their mere presence. Howe or Clinton could occupy Philadelphia or New York City until Kingdom Come, but to what avail?

The contempt of King George, and the British generally, for the "insolent rebels," was both ill concealed and clearly genuine. Certainly the military strategy and the military activity of the Redcoats were consistent with the disdain for the Continental Army regularly expressed by General Howe and the British officers. In the end it was this arrogance that blinded them to the policy necessary to win the war.

And it was not because Washington was difficult to locate or to engage that no major destructive effort ever came. After all, it was Washington who pressed the action—at Trenton, at Princeton, at the Brandywine, at Germantown, at Monmouth. History does not provide an account of the all-out British assault on the encampment at Valley Forge. Students of the Revolution and inheritors of American independence and the cherished American freedoms are left to wonder, "What if . . . ?" What if in January of 1778, or in February, or even in the spring, the vastly superior 20,000 regular troops, including the Queen's Rangers of Major John Simcoe, had been launched by General Howe or General Clinton against the inadequately clothed and starving and half-frozen 12,000 colonials struggling to survive the winter? But such speculation is in vain, as nothing like that ever did occur.

The artillery, as Washington was quick to recognize, played a really significant role in the battle of Monmouth, but of course bombardier John Harris missed out on this action. And in fact almost the entire 4th Continental Artillery missed out, for at this time the most of it was occupying Philadelphia, and the rest was much scattered. Captain Isaac Craig, who like Proctor and Duffy, had been born in Ireland (County Antrim), and had enlisted on the same day as Duffy, would soon be in command of the company that included both Samuel Blackwood and John Harris. But he had been sent to Carlisle from Valley Forge, and was in Carlisle from February 1 to August 1 of 1778 as an artillery officer-student of munitions. He did not participate in the action at Monmouth.

Meanwhile the 4th Continental Artillery during the early part of the summer did its job in Philadelphia, the cannon crews grousing a little about the difference between what they had been trained to do and what it was they were doing. They had been warned that the city would doubtless be a mess. And so it turned out to be. And then some!

Of course through the winter, while Washington's soldiers suffered the miseries of Valley Forge, the Redcoats, despite acute shortages of food and fuel, had enjoyed a reckless life of dissipation in the City of Brotherly Love. Philadelphia accommodated at this time a very large Loyalist population, and these welcomed the British to the city, wining and dining the officers. By the Tory ladies the Redcoats were made to feel much at home, and wanton carousing proved the order of the day, and of the night. The dissolute and totally unrestrained behavior of the soldiers, and more particularly the officers, has been charged, properly, to the commanding officer, General William Howe, no wallflower himself.

But the worst of it was the damage done to the city. There are not words, and there never will be, to describe the filth that Benjamin Franklin's city had been reduced to. Perhaps the single word which might convey a proper impression is cesspool. And the word needs to be taken both figuratively *and* literally. The city was hardly more than that. It must be remembered that sanitation systems in those days simply did not exist. An army of 20,000, with almost 2000 prisoners-of-war besides, on top of the normal urban population of 24,000 or a metropolitan population of 38,000–well, that's a lot of pressure on an absent sewage system. Besides, very few houses were left standing in the northern section of the city, and those that could be recognized as houses were in many cases mere shells of their former selves. Throughout the city respectable homes had been gutted, and were missing doors and windows, sometimes even the roof.[25] It was widespread devastation. The first minister dispatched from France to the new United States, Conrad Alexander Gerard, noted that "600 houses" had been destroyed.[28]

Benjamin Rush

All kinds of debris and filth littered the streets. Garbage, even piles of excrement, and the bodies of dead horses were everywhere. The highly esteemed Dr. Benjamin Rush, who had been born in the Byberry section of Philadelphia, and who was an ardent patriot and a signer of the Declaration of Independence[29] did not return to the city until July 21, a month after the disappearance of Clinton's army. But he was appalled by what he witnessed, and of course, as a physician, much distressed by the disease-producing conditions. He woefully remarked, in pained understatement, that "the filth left by the British army in the streets created a good deal of sickness."[30]

Even the air was noxious. The stench, as General Knox immediately discovered, was nauseating, unbearable. In a letter to his brother William, composed at four o'clock in the morning, June 25, just three days before Monmouth, he recalls: "The enemy evacuated Philadelphia on the 19th. Lucy and I went in, but it stunk so abominably that it was impossible to stay there, as was her first design."[31] They vacated posthaste. And John Maxwell Nesbitt, on returning to the city, found Knox's epithet fitting. He perceived "the Town [to be] excessively Dirty and Disagreeable, stinks Intolerably." He declared that Philadelphia was not fit to live in. Another returnee, a man by the name of Richard Peters, promptly complained of illness, and blamed his condition on the "foul and abominable atmosphere of the Place."[32]

Many of those who returned during the first month following the British leaving remarked upon the flies, which were so thick that, as one observed, no matter what you are doing, you do it with one hand, as the other is needed for the constant brushing away of the flies.[33] And naturally rats were abundant, and very active, especially at night.

But the foul air and the littered streets and the ruinous condition of the homes was not all. No, there was plundering as well. It has been recorded that

John André

"virtually every absent American lost some personal articles or pieces of furniture. Benjamin Franklin reported the loss of a painting, books, a printing press, and other items." Franklin's house had been occupied by the charming Major John André, Clinton's Adjutant General.[34] André was actually observed in the stealing of the portrait.[35]

Plundering was standard procedure for those occupying the homes of absent citizens. But in all of this very sordid business one breath of fresh air should be noted. It was produced by General Wilhelm Baron von Knyphausen, John Harris's old artillery "friend" from the Brandywine days. The Hessian, so far as is known, was one of the very few British officers to behave at all honorably during the occupation of Philadelphia. During the winter he occupied the home of Colonel John Cadwalader. At the time he moved in, according to reliable accounts, Knyphausen ordered his steward to compile a complete listing of the owner's property, including even seemingly insignificant items. Then, at the time of his leaving, the General had Cadwalader's agent check the inventory. Not only was everything found to be present, Knyphausen insisted on paying rent for the use of the house![36]

Unfortunately, hardly anybody else among the British army behaved with the respect and good manners of General Knyphausen.

So when the first returning troops entered the city in June, they found themselves overwhelmed by the enormity of the task that confronted them. Not only did they have to restore order, they had to see that the "God-awful mess" got cleaned up. It would be a long time before the city could be made ready for the return of the members of Congress and the patriot citizens.

Many of the Loyalists, fearful of revenge, had boarded the British transports that were headed down river to the Delaware Bay. It has been estimated that as many as 3,000 Tories fled Philadelphia, and it may be that there were as many as 5000. But many citizens remained, Quakers and other neutrals as well as Loyalists, as many as 20,000, and anxiously awaited the return of the patriot citizens. The troops assigned to the restoration of order took a few prisoners, but before embarking on a general plan for the city, they elected to retire to its northern limits, there to await the arrival of General Benedict Arnold, who had just been appointed Military Governor of

Philadelphia.[37]

They did not have long to wait.

General Benedict Arnold at this time was extremely high in Washington's favor. At one of the most important battles of the entire war, the Battle of Bemis Heights, sometimes called the Second Battle of Saratoga, Arnold was something of a hero. It was chiefly because of Arnold that the Americans under General Horatio Gates had been able to repel British General John Burgoyne's attempt to seize the rebels' fortified positions on the heights. Arnold, at the center of the action, had rallied the confused troops of Brigadier General Ebenezer Learned, and with them led a counter-attack. After just about an hour of very sharp fighting, the British fell back. Arnold, not content with simply stopping the British advance, now characteristically led Learned and his men in a charge against the 1st redoubt. Arnold was shot down, wounded in the same leg that had been shattered at Quebec City. But Learned's troops carried the redoubt. And a protesting Arnold was removed from the field by Gates.

On May 21, 1778, General Arnold, still convalescing from the wound suffered in the action at Bemis Heights on October 7 of the past autumn, and dependent upon a cane, reported to Washington at Valley Forge as requested. According to Lieutenant Henry Dearborn,[38] who had served with Arnold in the Quebec campaign and at Saratoga, Arnold arrived "to the great joy of the army." Washington, who had urged him to take his time in coming, not to jeopardize his recovery (signing his letter "affectionately"),[39] was most happy to see him and made him welcome to the encampment, which had emerged from its winter doldrums.

Washington, perhaps with Philadelphia already in mind, had restored Arnold to active service, sending him his commission on January 20 from his Head Quarters at Valley Forge. Arnold was with Major General Benjamin Lincoln at the time, in Albany, New York, very slowly recovering from the wound received at Bemis Heights. That it was taking him so long to get on his feet again may be owing to the fact that this wound was to the same leg that had been damaged at Quebec.

Washington in his letter first inquired into Arnold's condition, expressing the hope that he would soon be up and about again. "I shall expect a favourable account upon the subject," he wrote. "And as soon as your situation will permit, I request that you will repair to this Army, it being my earnest wish to have your Services the ensuing Campaign."

He said that he had nothing of importance in the military line to report, nothing new or interesting. "The Enemy," the letter continues, "still remain in possession of Philadelphia and have secured themselves by a strong chain of Redoubts, with Intrenchments of communication from Schuylkill to Delaware. We on our part have taken post on the West side of the former, about twenty miles from the City, and with much pains and industry have got the Troops tolerably well covered in Huts. We have to regret that we are not in more comfortable quarters, but these could not be found unless we had retired to the Towns in the more interior part of the State; the consequences of which would have been, distress to the virtuous Citizens of Philadelphia, who had fled thither for protection, and the expense of a considerable tract of fertile Country to ravage and ruin."[40]

On May 28, Washington, confident that Clinton would soon be vacating the city, appointed Arnold to the command of Philadelphia. Two days later he was escorted to the area of the Valley Forge camp known as Artillery Park, and there took the famous oath of allegiance that was required of all officers: "I *Benedict Arnold Major General* do acknowledge the UNITED STATES of AMERICA to be Free, Independent and Sovereign States, and declare that the people thereof owe no allegiance or obedience to George the Third, King of Great-Britain; and I renounce, refute and abjure any allegiance or obedience to him; and I do *Swear* that I will, to the utmost of my power, support, maintain and defend the said United States against the said King George the Third, his heirs and successors, and his or their abettors, assistants and adherents, and will serve the said United States

Benedict Arnold

in the office of *Major General* which I now hold, with fidelity, according to the best of my skill and understanding."

Brigadier General Henry Knox administered the oath and signed the affidavit: "Sworn before me 30th May 1778 at the Artillery Park, Valley Forge *Henry Knox B. G. Artillery*."[41]

Historians, with the benefit of hindsight, a luxury not enjoyed by Washington, are of the opinion that Arnold was a terribly bad choice for this post. An officer quite different from Arnold, in temperament and personality, and, yes, in character, was required to mediate the heated contest for authority in Philadelphia which promptly arose between the Continental Congress and the state-conscious Executive Council of Pennsylvania.

Washington certainly knew well enough how impetuous was Arnold, and how vain and arrogant he could be. He may not have known how fond the General was of high living or how greedy he could be. But he was quite well aware, too, of Arnold's bitterness toward the Continental Congress for so long delaying his promotion to Major General. (In February of 1777 Congress had by-passed Arnold to promote five brigadier generals of junior rank to major generalships ahead of him.) Arnold, it would seem then, and it is known now, was an incredibly bad choice for command of the city John Adams was calling a "mass of cowardice and Toryism."[42] The one consideration that must have been front and center in Washington's mind was that Arnold was still unfit for service in the field, could not even ride a horse. And of course Arnold had never fallen out of favor with Washington.

Arnold moved into the home that had been occupied by General William Howe through the winter, the great mansion on Market Street known as the Penn House, and once settled began to live there in a style perhaps even more grand than that enjoyed by Howe. He posted sentries first of all. He brought into his employ a theatrical number of liveried servants. He regularly scheduled formal receptions and dinner parties, and provided lively entertainment. He rode on Sundays, and most other days of the week as well, in a sporty coach-and-four.[43]

Washington had directed Arnold "to take every prudent step to preserve order and to adopt such measures as should appear most effectual and least offensive for compliance with the views of Congress respecting the disposition of property."[44]

But he faced lots of problems. Congress had prohibited the removal of any property. Accordingly, Arnold placed the city under martial law, and attempted to enforce the regulations of Congress by ordering all shops and stores closed. And immediately he was in trouble with the populace. Before long he was in big trouble. He was roundly rebuked for his personal money-making activities, for his favors to the Loyalists, and for his extravagant entertainments, which seemed a distraction from the city's great problems.

Another of these problems was the accommodation of prisoners. What was he to do with the enormous number of prisoners that came his way? As early as June 20 he had 300 Hessian prisoners delivered. Arnold at once tried to exchange these prisoners for Americans who were at that time confined to British vessels. It was known that eighty-one American officers, including General James Irvine of the Pennsylvania militia and Colonel Matthews of the 9th Virginia Continental Regiment, had been conveyed to New York City. He experienced no luck at all in this effort. And then hundreds of additional prisoners arrived in the city for disposition. Happily, a newly constructed prison accommodated some.

Arnold had a great many friends, like John Cadwalader, who appreciated the courage and the patriotic zeal he had seen exhibited at Ticonderoga and at Quebec. But Arnold had his enemies too, and here in his early command of the city of Philadelphia he acquired a great many more.

One of these was the most powerful man in Philadelphia, in fact the most powerful man in all of Pennsylvania, indeed one of the most powerful figures in all the colonies. His name was Joseph Reed. At this time Reed was serving as President of the Executive Council of Pennsylvania, that is, Governor of Pennsylvania.

Reed had served on Washington's staff. And, at the time Washington's army was

Joseph Reed

being forced out of Long Island, he had become the subject of some unsettling rumors. He was still very sensitive to the suspicions that he had conducted treasonous negotiations with the Howe brothers. And certainly from time to time he had been critical of Washington. Now, possibly made ashamed by the heroic patriotism he had been witnessing for two years, he determined to prove himself a passionate supporter of the Cause. He had become a crusader against Tories and all friends of the King.[45] Besides, he was politically ambitious. It was not only that he did not like Arnold nor trust him. He saw in the General a serious threat to his power as President of Pennsylvania.

Eventually the feud, for it had become that, between Arnold and the Executive Council (and particularly Reed) erupted into a trial of the city's commander. On February 3, 1779, after eight months in the city, Major General Benedict Arnold had charges preferred against him by the Commonwealth of Pennsylvania. The complaints were eight in number. The most serious charge was that the General had been issuing authority for government supplies that he clearly intended for his own private purposes. Arnold, of course, was indignant. He declared that Pennsylvania was out to "get " him.

Many thought the charges prejudiced, "unjust," and "unfair." Henry Knox was one of those. Writing on February 13, to his wife Lucy, who had accompanied Arnold to Valley Forge, in the spring of 1778, he advised, "You will see in the papers some highly colored charges against General Arnold, by the State of Pennsylvania. I shall be exceedingly mistaken if one of them can be proven. He has returned to Philadelphia, and will, I hope be able to vindicate himself from the aspersions of his enemies."[46]

But first things first. Back in Philadelphia now, Arnold continued his ardent and energetic courtship of the young Margaret ("Peggy") Shippen, youngest of the three daughters of a zealous and very wealthy, influential Loyalist. Of the girls in Philadelphia, Knox explained to Lucy, "They are the same everywhere,–at least some of them: they love a red coat dearly. Arnold is going to be married to a beautiful and accomplished young lady,–a Miss Shippen, of one of the best families in the place."[47]

One of Peggy Shippen's redcoat friends during the time the British occupied the city was the charming John André, a young man of about her own age. Arnold, a patriot and twice her age, was a very different sort. Arnold was a widower and the father of three sons. His wife (another Margaret), to whom he had been married eight years, had died less than two months after the skirmish at Lexington and Concord. But Knox had been right. On April 8, Major General Benedict Arnold was married to Peggy Shippen of Philadelphia. The ceremony was conducted in the quiet of the home of Peggy's father, Judge Edward Shippen's elegant mansion. Arnold was thirty-eight years old. His bride was not yet nineteen.

Washington, meanwhile, scheduled the court martial of General Arnold for May 1. It was promptly re-scheduled for June 1. It *finally* took place on December 23, in the Norris Tavern at Washington's winter quarters in Morristown. It was a dramatic scene, as can well be imagined. The setting was warm enough – a big stone room with a generous open fireplace, "to which were steadily fed great chunks of oak." Washington was not present. His aide Alexander Hamilton was there, strictly as an observer. The trial ended January 26, 1780.[48]

The court's directed verdict cleared Arnold of all but two of the indictments, one of which, the charge that the wagons requested by the General from Pennsylvania for public service were in fact used for his own personal gain, was quite serious. This is what did him in.

Congress had approved the verdict of the court on February 12, but, remarkably, it was so tardy in notifying Washington of his obligation to carry out the court's instruction (a public reprimand) that not until April 6, one year almost to the day after Arnold's marriage to Peggy Shippen, did the Commander-in-Chief make the announcement.[49]

Arnold had been awaiting the verdict (and the sentence?) impatiently and nervously.

On April 6, Washington read in public the reprimand required by the court.[50] All who knew the circumstances could see that Arnold's Commander-in-Chief was being extremely considerate. He discreetly employed the third person:

The commander in chief would have been much happier on an occasion of bestowing commendation on an officer who has rendered such distinguished service to his country as Major General Arnold. But in the present case a sense of duty and a regard to candor oblige him to declare that he considers his conduct, in the instance of his issuance of the permit, as peculiarly reprehensible, both in a civil and military view, and in the affair of the wagons as imprudent and improper.[51]

Clearly the tone of his words was genuine. Washington really did value Arnold as a field officer. He respected him for his courage and for his military skills, and he was most appreciative of the service he had rendered the rebellion. But the big word here was *But*.

Arnold was stunned. A public reprimand! He had been anxious about the verdict, aware as he was that some wrongdoing could be placed at his door. But he had been confident that his military reputation and his usefulness to Washington would see him completely exonerated. Of course a heavier sentence had been possible. But Arnold did not count himself lucky. A reprimand was a big blow to his pride. And he was not made to feel any happier about his enemies.

On July 20 Arnold said goodbye to Peggy and to his infant son, promising to send for them soon. He said goodbye also to the City of Brotherly Love, a city to which he had given his best service and for which he had been treated rudely and humiliated, a city which he hoped he would never see again.

On the last day of July, 1780, he reported to General Washington at King's Ferry on the west bank of the Hudson, just a few miles down the river from West Point.[52]

Four days later, five years into the Revolution, the General Orders of the Day issued by Washington closed with a postscript: "Major General Arnold will Command at West Point."[53]

Throughout the occupation of the city, desertions and "retirements" continued for Proctor's Artillery. By the 4th of August, the regiment had been reduced to 220 men. By December of that year, the 4th Continental Artillery had lost twelve more men, but that was not the worst of it. Of the 208 men who remained, only 144 (!) could report to muster. Forty-one were ill, sixteen were off on some detached service, and seven were on furlough. And by March 19,

1779, the "present-for-duty" muster would tally only 142.⁵⁴

Still it was a regiment, with guns, and gun crews, and horses, and experience. It was impatient, but it had only to wait its time. A new war was looming for the 4th Continental Artillery.

VI

THE SUSQUEHANNA

On Susquehanna's side, fair Wyoming!
Although the wild-flower on thy ruin'd wall.
And roofless homes, a sad remembrance bring,
Of what thy gentle people did befall;
Yet thou wert once the loveliest land of all
That see the Atlantic wave their morn restore.
Sweet land! may I thy lost delights recall,
And paint thy Gertrude in her bowers of yore,
Whose beauty was the love of Pennsylvania's shore.

—**Thomas Campbell**

In the days preceding the outbreak of hostilities between King George and the colonials, long before the battles at Lexington and Concord, both the British and the rebellious colonists were wooing the Indian tribes of the Iroquois League.

As tensions between the Rebels and the British steadily increased, overtures to the Indians were stepped up. The American colonists seemed not to be interested in the Indians as allies, but they certainly did not want them allied with the British. The American Commissioners urged a neutral course for them. In council after council they hammered home their point: "You Indians are not concerned in it. We desire you to remain at home." They insisted to them that "You have nothing to do with our father-children quarrels." The message to the Iroquois was simple: "Stay out of it."

But the British were determined to have their support, and they most aggressively courted them. They were particularly eager to secure the friendship of the Six Nations of the Iroquois League, and most especially that of the Senecas, who were not only the most populous of the six, but also were known to be the most warlike and fierce. Besides, located as they were at the western end of the "longhouse," as the Federation was called, they exercised an influence over the tribes to the west.

Consequently, during the period 1770-1777 there occurred a steady succession of councils to which the Indians were invited, conducted by both the British and the Americans. The Senecas found themselves scurrying from their homes in the Allegheny region and the Valley of the Genesee in western New York back and forth to Fort Pitt, to Albany, to Oswego, and to German Flats in the Mohawk Valley. In these early councils, and most particularly at German Flats, Cornplanter, war-chief of the Senecas, and his uncle Kyashota regularly pledged to the American Commissioners that the Senecas would remain neutral, and for some time they were able to keep their warriors on the sidelines. But most influential of all in the jousting for Indian favor were the Mohawk Chief Joseph Brant, his brother-in-law (and perhaps father) Sir William Johnson, who for a long time had been serving the Crown as Commissioner of Indian Affairs, and who was to die before the War of the Revolution began, and John Butler.

John Butler had been born in the colonies, in New London, Connecticut, but he had decided when the trouble broke out to cast his lot with the British. He was a Loyalist, a Tory. At the time the courtship began,1770, he was forty-two years old, and already very close to the Indians, particularly to Brant and the easternmost tribes of the Iroquois. As he negotiated with the Indians and sought vigorously to win an alliance with them, he organized the Loyalist troop soon to be called Butler's Rangers.

Butler felt a passionate necessity to win over the Indians, and he would do almost anything to accomplish their allegiance to the British. Certainly he was not above bribery. But where the British were intent upon the favor of the Iroquois, and were constantly urging them to take up the hatchet on the side of King George, the American Commissioners continued content simply to appeal for neutrality.

Butler's chief adversary in all of this was the young war-chief of the Senecas, Cornplanter (Gyantawanka, "By What One Plants"). Cornplanter was a half-breed. He was the son of John Abeel, a Dutch fur trader from Albany, and a Seneca "princess" known as Aliquipiso. He had been born in Canawagus on the Genesee River, nobody knows when, but most probably in the year 1752. During this time, then, he was most likely eighteen to twenty-five years old. He had risen rapidly to prominence among the Senecas and commanded respect from all corners of the Six Nations. He was fond of Washington and always insisted that he was born in the same year as the famous soldier, though in fact he was probably twenty years younger. He was to become the most

Cornplanter

conspicuous figure of all the Indians active during the Revolution, and though born in New York, the best known of all Pennsylvania Indians. He was known to the British as John O'Bail or "Captain" O'Bail, or O'Beel.

Butler's chief support in the contest for the allegiance of the Iroquois was the Mohawk chieftain, Joseph Brant,[1] also *perhaps* a half-breed.[2] The home of Brant's Mohawk parents was at Canajoharie on the Mohawk River, but Joseph had been born on the banks of the Ohio River, not far from present-day Akron. Brant, who was known to the Mohawks and all the Iroquois as Thayendanegea ("He Places Together Two Bets" or "Two Sticks Bound Together in Unified Strength"), had long been close to the British. He had served under Sir William Johnson in the French and Indian War (when he was only twenty years old), and under Johnson again in Pontiac's Rebellion. In fact, he had become something of a protégé to Johnson. Johnson had sent him to the Moor's Charity School for Indians, later to be Dartmouth College, in Lebanon, Connecticut (the only college to remain open during the entire course of the Revolution); and in his British post as General Superintendent for Indian Affairs North of the Ohio, Johnson had enlisted the aid and support of the young Mohawk warrior.

Whereas Cornplanter never learned any English (or perhaps pretended ignorance) and always required an interpreter, Brant had acquired, from his schooling in Connecticut, a rather sophisticated capacity in the language. In fact, he was at the time of all these councils just returned from London, where he had enjoyed an audience with King George himself. He was impressively tall, lithe and strong-limbed. His demeanor compelled respect, and he was at this time the most revered and most influential of all the Iroquois chieftains. He had experienced some difficulty with the Oneidas and the Tuscaroras, but his big trouble was with the Senecas, by far the most savage and warlike of the Six Nations.

The conflict among the Indian factions became steadily more intense, finally reaching the crisis point in mid-summer of 1777, two years into the Revolution, and three years after the death of Johnson. The difference was fully resolved, in July, at the council of Oswego; when the Iroquois commitment to the British, including that of the Senecas, became "official." But the agreement did not come easily, and in fact only after a great deal of drama.

Some 2000 (!) Senecas had made their way to the council site at the fort and trading post on the southeastern

Joseph Brant

shore of Lake Oswego (Ontario to the settlers), there to join representatives of the other tribes of the Six Nations.

Butler, in his ferocious desire to persuade the Indians to his cause, naturally was lavish in the distribution of gifts, most especially rum. It was merrymaking and "getting to know you" that characterized the early going. "After they had been mellowed for two or three days, the Indians . . . were directed to council."[3] Here Butler professed the King's friendship and promised a successful end to the campaign. The Senecas, at first, were not impressed. The old warrior Sayenqueraghta (Old Smoke) and the young warrior known to the British as O'Beal (Cornplanter) were the two chiefs in command of the Seneca warriors. Old Smoke was at this time exactly three times as old as Cornplanter.[4] They made quite a pair. They expressed in energetic language their opposition to the alliance and to the campaign being proposed. Kyashota, Cornplanter's uncle, was also disposed for neutrality. But most of the Indians were inclined favorably toward the British. While they debated among themselves, Butler persisted with his persuasions. Councils continued, and so did the gifting. Now the Indians were presented the most elaborate of gifts: blankets, guns, knives, hatchets, and kettles. Besides, they were promised handsome bounties for every scalp, every prisoner.[5]

Through it all Cornplanter had held his course: "It is none of our business." And the Mohawk leader, Joseph Brant, who was thirty-five years old at this time, was just as adamant for war on the side of the British.[6] The Indians, having repaired to private council of their own, now convened for debate. The exchange which ensued was fierce. Pitted against the powerful Mohawk Joseph Brant were Kyashota, Old Smoke, Cornplanter, and Red Jacket. Cornplanter saw the revolution as a "family quarrel," too complex for the Indians and none of their business. It grew very plain to Brant that the Senecas were strongly united behind their leaders, but he *had* to have the Senecas in camp. Blacksnake, Cornplanter's constant warrior companion, accounting for the affair almost seventy-five years later, remembers the words spoken by the principals, almost as if they had been delivered yesterday. After Brant had spoken hard for war, Cornplanter, subtly making the point that the Americans had not solicited the aid of the Iroquois, addressed the assembly. Here is his speech as Blacksnake remembered it many years later, in the garbled English of

Blacksnake's Indian interpreter, Ben Williams:

> . . . *warriour you must all marked and listen what we have to Say war is war Death is the Death a fight is a hard Business, all I wanted to Say to all of you with others Nations which is combined with one Body–*
>
> *Here is america Says to us, not to lift our hands against to Either Party, because they got in to Difficulty, it is nothing to us, and he also say let him fight it out for his liberty and will Rebel the government of his own Brother in fact we the Indians Nations of Several Differance parts of this continent we Does not Know what is for–and we are a liable to make mistake moved I therefore full Desirous to wait a little while for to heard more the consultation between the two party . . . .*

At this point, Joseph Brant, clearly in great anger, sprang to his feet, and told the young Cornplanter to "shut up." Blacksnake remembers the theatrics:

> . . . *Brant got up on to his feet and Say Nephew, that is called according to his connexionship, to Stop Speaking So planter Did Stop Brant than said to cornplanter you a very coward man it is not hardly worth while to take Notice what you have said to our people you have showed your cowardness &c Cornplanter than Says nothing more till Next Day after . . . .* [7]

Brant had played his trump card. No Seneca, no Iroquois, no Indian (except Red Jacket!) can stomach the term. In the consternation which followed, the Indians met in mini-councils. Neutrality was still popular, but it was not worth the stigma of cowardice. When the vote was taken, a large majority of the warriors, and, more importantly, the women, were for war, for war on the side of the British. It was a dramatic moment in the life of the young Cornplanter, and in the life of the Senecas and for the future of the Six Nations. It was a critical moment, and a very costly decision, for the cause of the American Revolution.

The young warrior Dahgayadoh (who would one day be known as Blacksnake) remembered until his dying day how his "uncle"

Cornplanter rose soberly to his feet to pronounce the verdict for all: "[Let] Every Brave man Show himself Now hereafter for we will find an many Dangerous times During the actions of the war, for we will See a many Brave man amongsth american Soldiers which we Shall meet, with their Sharp adge Stools [swords], ... soon as he fined you out that are against him he than will Show you his wit no mercy on you on us, I therefore Say Stand to your Post where is time come Before you But a gard [agreed] yours be."[8]

The die was cast. Brant next day reported the good news to the British commissioners. And nothing more was done that day. And all retired to dinner, and to "Drink Rum and sugar, and we done so that afternoon our head men was a little too much Rum." And then the Indians, with the Senecas in the van, declared that "We ... shall go to take Wyoming," and America may surrender all at once.

What had begun a week ago in rum now ended in rum, and in a naive and over-confident resolution. But from this time on until the very end of the Revolution and even beyond, the Iroquois, excepting the Tuscaroras and the Oneidas, would stand with the British and the Tories. Old Smoke, though he was now some seventy years along the trail, was remembering well enough his warrior days, the glory and the fame that had been his and that would now continue. Cornplanter, still a young warrior, was destined, as war chief of the Senecas, to play a major role in the American Revolution.

It was not long before it had been made painfully clear to Washington that the Iroquois had come into the war on the side of the British. And the most dramatic announcement of that most unwelcome fact would come in the form of an unspeakable massacre destined to occur in the beautiful river valley known as Wyoming.

The Susquehanna River is one of the principal waterways of the Indian country now known as Pennsylvania. The West Branch of the wandering river flows east from its source at Cherry Tree some 150 miles to Williamsport, then abruptly turns south. The North (or East) Branch flows west a little on its way out of New York State, then south and east to meet its sister at Northumberland before striking out for the Chesapeake. One of the names given by the Indians to the North Branch is M'chewamisipu, "the river on which lie extensive clear flats."

Those broad, clear flats, fertile and lush, are beautiful, spread out as they are on either side of the wide river. Perhaps the most beautiful of all is the valley known as Wyoming. No one has looked upon it but what he or she has sought in vain to account for the rapture of the scene. A noble effort was delivered in 1786 by Colonel Timothy Pickering, who would soon thereafter be named Postmaster General of the United States and after that become Secretary of State in the Cabinet of George Washington. When for the first time he came into a view of the valley he declared it "the most beautiful tract of land my eyes ever beheld!" He insisted that industrious farmers could make the whole a garden.[9] Some years later Reverend Edmund D. Griffin of Columbia University reported: "A scene more lovely than imagination ever painted presented itself to my sight–so beautiful, so exquisitely beautiful . . . ."[10] So it has been for thousands of years, and so it is still.

It is no wonder that those who come to Wyoming long to remain, no wonder that they become so possessive. It should surprise no one to learn that the valley and its embracing forests were for centuries the favored hunting grounds of the first Americans, and were to become the envy of the white settlers.

And perhaps it was inevitable that in this garden spot of the world, one of Nature's choicest bowers, the wrangling that leads to violence and bloodshed should occur. For it is a fatal beauty that is presented by the Valley of Wyoming.

As proof, there are the rival claims of two of the colonies, Connecticut and Pennsylvania, for the land that had always belonged to the Indians. The first recorded Indian massacre for the Valley was a foreshadowing of things to come. In the space of an hour, on the fifteenth of October, 1763, a Connecticut settlement was completely wiped out by a marauding band of Delawares. The discovery that was made by a company of Pennsylvania Rangers has been graphically described. It comes to light as an extract from a letter dated at Paxtamy, Lancaster County, October 23, 1763, and printed in *The Pennsylvania Gazette* for October 27, 1763: "Our party under Captain Clayton is returned from Wyoming, where they met no Indians, but found the New Englanders, who had been killed and scalped a day or two before they got there. They buried the Dead, nine Men and one Woman, who had been most cruelly butchered; the Woman was roasted, and had two hinges in her hands, supposed to have been put in red hot; and several of the Men had Awls thrust into their Eyes, and Spears, Arrows, Pitchforks &c., sticking in their Bodies. They burned what houses the Indians left, and destroyed a Quantity of Indian Corn. The Enemy's tracks were up the River towards Wighalousing."[11]

During the first week of July, 1778, when the 4th Continental Artillery was preserving order in Philadelphia, and Washington was recovering from the fighting at Monmouth, one of the most terrible battles of the Revolutionary War was fought at Wyoming. The battle has fascinated historians for 200 years, and the accounts of what happened there are legion. Not all are accurate; in fact none can be strictly accurate. Some, especially those which appeared early, were composed out of such strong feeling and out of such confusion that they cannot be trusted in their details. Nevertheless, it would be difficult to exaggerate by much the terror of that day and night. The most faithful account, even the most restrained report, would chill the blood. If ever the term *massacre* was apt, it was most fitting for Wyoming on July 3 of 1778.

Butler's Rangers and their Indian allies, who were from the beginning intent on Wyoming, warmed up for their assault with a battle at Oriskany just a month after the council at Oswego, August 6, 1777. In a bloody Indian ambush of American militia, the Iroquois, led by Brant, conducted a devastating raid on a poorly protected white settlement and made plain the kind of warfare in which they would be indulging.

In the succeeding spring, these same Iroquois, led by Brant, in league with Butler and his Rangers, assaulted the helpless village of Cobleskill, and produced a massacre that is now thought of as a practice session for the blood-bath that was to occur at Wyoming. On May 30 the tiny settlement in the Schoharie Valley was approached by a large war party of Senecas and Mohawks. The settlement was defended by patriot forces numbering 30-50 men, under the command of Captains Parker and Christian Brown. The colonials were lured into an ambush prepared by Joseph Brant, who had sent out into the open a handful of his warriors. Under the impression that they were driving off a very small party of Indians, the men under Parker and Brown were led into a trap. It was an old Indian trick.

Twenty-two of the defenders were killed, six were wounded, and two were captured. And the Indians destroyed twenty buildings of the settlement   It was on to Wyoming.

In those days called Westmoreland, Wyoming was a most attractive target for the newly united British and Iroquois. It was quite helplessly exposed, situated as it was some sixty miles from the white settlements east and west.[12]   The British force proceeding to Wyoming was composed of two divisions. One body was made up of 464 warriors. Blacksnake, a half century after the battle recalled the names of the most celebrated: Sagwarithra, a Tuscarora sachem; Gahkoondenoiya of the Onondagas; Fish Carrier, a Cayuga; the Senecas' Little Beard, Hiokatoo, Jeskaka (Little Billy), Honeyeus (Farmer's Brother), Dahgonwasha (Twenty Canoes), Donnegoesha (Jack Berry), Gahgeote (Half-Town), Cornplanter, Ganiodaio (Handsome Lake, Cornplanter's half-brother), and Red Jacket. Cornplanter is at this time not only a celebrated warrior, but a chief, and not only a chief, but one of the two war-chiefs named by the Senecas (their traditional right in the League) to command the Iroquois.[13]   Joseph Brant was not among the Indians in this particular war party.

Butler's party of Rangers had apparently come down river to Bowman's Creek, then, somewhere joined by the Iroquois, across the mountain to Fort Wintermoot, arriving on the last day of June. On the way they came upon the Jenkins, Harding, and Gardner families. What chroniclers now call "the Harding massacre" abruptly occurred. Eight men of these three families, ignorant of any hostile presence, had proceeded out that morning to work the fields. The Indians fell upon them, killing four, and taking three prisoner. John Harding, just a snip of a boy, escaped by secreting himself amid leafy willow boughs which overhung the water.[14] "Remember the Hardings!" was afterwards to become a rallying cry for the defenders of Wyoming.

The war party, and especially the Indians, became somewhat unsettled when upon coming into the valley that was their object they discovered before them a number of forts. These forts, Butler's scouts reported, were manned by some 800 soldiers. While curbing the Indian enthusiasm for plundering, Butler made overtures to the forts and urged their surrender. On July 1, both Wintermoot's Fort, under the command of Lt. Elisha Scovell, and Jenkins' Fort capitulated. Forty Fort, so named for the forty pioneers who had built it, defied the ultimatum.

According to one account of the event, Cornplanter himself led ten warriors into a surveillance position, crawling up a hill overlooking the fort, and "counted the American militiamen within, watching them as they went through their various military exercises."[15]

The defenders, under the command of Colonel Zebulon Butler and Colonel Nathan Denison, fearing a long and perhaps fatal siege, resolved to meet the enemy in the field. When they marched out of the fort, at two o'clock in the afternoon, "they must have presented to the Indians a most gratifying sight." What followed has been vividly described by historian Barbara Graymont:

> Between four and five o'clock, the Rangers and Indians noted that the Americans were within a mile of them. They then resorted to a ruse to throw their enemy off guard. Major John Butler ordered both Wintermoot's and Jenkins' Forts fired to give the impression that he was retreating. They then chose their field of battle, posting themselves in an open wood, with the Rangers on the left and the Indians on the right with their rear edging upon a swamp. Red Jacket [a notorious coward] stationed himself far enough behind the main body of Indians as to afford as little danger to his person as possible. All lay flat upon the ground, quietly awaiting the approach of the Americans.
>
> As they neared the woods, the Americans formed their battle lines. Colonel Zebulon Butler instructed his men: "Stand firm the first shock." They then marched steadily forward, guns at the ready. When two hundred yards off, they gave their first volley. Sayenqueraghta's Indians and Butler's Rangers lay still without returning the fire. The Americans gave three volleys in all, marching forward to within one hundred yards of their silent foes. When they had reached this distance, Sayenqueraghta, from his perch on horseback, gave the signal and the Indians opened fire, followed by the Rangers. The distance was so close and the fire so accurate that the Americans suffered greatly. The Indians closed in around the flanks and the American left wing attempted to fall back to a more advantageous position. The move was mistaken by the rest of the militiamen for a retreat, and the result was a rout. Many threw away their guns in their flight, while the Indians pursued relentlessly, giving no quarter. A few of the militiamen were fortunate enough to reach

Forty Fort. Others were forced into the river where they were tomahawked. A number were able to swim to safety. Others were cut down while they fled from the field of battle. The shooting had lasted only a half hour before the militia fled in all directions. It was a pathetic remnant that made its way back to the fort.[16]

From an earlier historian a similar picture of the frantic flight:

> Men hid under the bushes in the water; some swam down the river with bullets striking around them, others crawled under rocks and in hollow logs, some ran as long as their legs would carry them. They went across the mountains, down the valley, anywhere to escape. They were desperately frightened, as well they might be, for all who did not speedily put themselves out of reach of the Indians' spears, tomahawks, and scalping knives, were murdered without mercy. The individual tragedies on the river and island were as fearful as those on the plain, while those taken prisoner had to face and suffer a fiendish death.[17]

Still the worst was to come. As evening settled over the bloody ground, the Indians, completely out of the control of Butler and his officers, and whether inspired or simply unrestrained by their own chiefs, entered into an orgy of cruelty and torture that violates every sense of the human. Fierce assaults were made upon the individual homes scattered throughout the valley and frightful atrocities perpetrated. And then the savage celebration, about which so much has been written. One historian, while noting the horror, declares he will not turn the picture with its face to the wall. "It is indelibly engraven on the minds of the civilized world and will remain."[18]

Near Tioga Point (present-day Athens), up the river but not far from the battle scene, lay the village of Queen Esther, called Queen Esther's Flats. It was a substantial village of some seventy houses. From her home here came the fiend of the night, to avenge, history infers, the death of her only son, who had been slain just the day before the battle. Queen Esther is the central figure of Wyoming's most awful moment. At the spot where an enormous boulder emerged from the ground she presided, and herself carried out the executions. The scene has been described a thousand times, and doubtless in many

The Susquehanna 151

cases exaggeration occurs, but, as has been wisely noted, no account could ever "convey to our mind an adequate conception of what occurred."[19]

To the rock were brought the prisoners captured from the river and the swamp, some who had given up their persons to the promise that they would not be harmed. There were at least twelve, perhaps as many as sixteen. Reigning over the hideous scene was Queen Esther, inspired by an enraged grief for her only son. Here is one of the many extant descriptions of Queen Esther at the rock:

A fire was built on the level plain. The prisoners brought within the center, where they could witness the delight and feel the hatred of their tormentors. They knew how to get up a dramatic scene of the most fearful and spectacular character. The one at Wyoming was complete in every particular. The Indian was dressed for the occasion. The scalps were gloated over. They struck up their awful music and performed their grotesque dance. They shouted, whooped and grinned, the scene becoming a wild carnival that filled the hearts of the savages with delight. They knew that on the morrow they could turn themselves loose and plunder and burn without restraint. They came to the valley for revenge and plunder, and their day had come. They were wild men and this was their reward. Let us pass over the fate of the victims that suffered and were left mutilated and lifeless when the orgie was over. Queen Esther had presided and the death maul had done its work. The men who escaped at that time give us a good description that leaves little to the imagination.[20]

In another version we have the prisoners placed in a circle with an Indian behind each, and Queen Esther going round the circle and braining each one with a tomahawk, except for one or two who somehow broke away and escaped.[21]

In any version the descriptions of the murders are so blood curdling that some historians are tempted to regard the whole episode as a myth. Too awful to have happened. And Cornplanter's erstwhile comrade Blacksnake absolutely denies Queen Esther's tomahawking.[22] But the Queen Esther episode is perfectly consistent with all that had gone before. Colonel John Franklin, for instance, writing in 1828 for the Towanda *Republican,* declares that a large number of soldiers surrendered on the battlefield and that these were afterwards most inhumanely murdered.[23]

Few survived the massacre, but Colonel Zebulon Butler, who had made his way safely back to the fort from the battlefield, at some time in the night was able with his wife to steal out of the fort and under the blanket of darkness escape from the valley.

For the battle of Wyoming and the cruelties which followed there appears great confusion in the reports, both for the numbers involved, and for the count of casualties. Lossing, in his *Pictorial Field Book of the Revolution*, reports that the red and white men who came down the Susquehanna in canoes under Butler and camped, July 2, upriver from Fort Jenkins, numbered 1100. Richard Cartwright, who was with the expedition, suggests a number half of that. According to his tally, the force was composed of 574, and 110 were Rangers.[24] As late as 1968, one researcher was accepting Lossing's figures, noting that at the time of its assault Colonel John Butler's force numbered "four hundred British and Tories and seven hundred Indians, mostly Senecas."[25] As for casualties, Butler's account does not accord with that of Colonel Denison. It is known definitely that the Indians killed and scalped *at least* 227 persons. This figure cannot be shaken because, as promised by the British, the Indians received ten dollars for each scalp, the records showing the delivery of 227.[26] John Mohawk, a Seneca, in an encyclopedic account prepared in 1996, notes that "more than 300 Americans were killed in this action (and fewer than ten Indians and Rangers!), while eight forts and a thousand dwellings were destroyed."[27]

Some years after the Revolution had come to an end, and the colonists of the young nation had had time to bring some order to their recollections, there began to appear in the newspapers of the Wyoming region a number of letters and editorials urging the fitness of a monument erected to the memory of all who were lost here. In 1843 such a monument was completed. Today a beautiful memorial remembers for the world forever what happened on that day and night. Within the limits of the borough of Wyoming, and between the site of the battlefield and Forty Fort there now stands an impressive monument, sixty-two and one-half feet high and presenting an impressive tablet, on which are recorded the 157 names of the defenders who perished here. Queen Esther's rock remains also, at the southeast of the village. Much of the rock has been carried away by relic hunters, but it is now protected and can be viewed by the curious and the unbelieving.

Like everybody else who heard the horrible news from the Valley of Wyoming, John Harris and his fellow artillerymen, charged with caring for the "City of Brotherly Love," wondered how this could be, and shook their heads in total disbelief. They were not much for philosophizing or intellectual analysis of such events. In vain they tried to assess the carnage that was wrought and tried to explain to themselves how such horrors could be perpetrated by human beings upon each other. John Harris knew nothing about Indians, but by those who did he was informed that the Indian is different. It was explained to Harris and to the others who were new to the Indian country that the Indian is conditioned throughout his life to such cruelty and torture. From the time he is born, he is taught a hardness of heart that renders him inhuman. It is what he expects when he is captured. It is what he practices when the day is his.

Still others noted that the Indian so much reveres courage that he mistakes these hideous acts of cruelty for it, expecting that the more cruelly he treats his victim the more he will be admired. Those who were not persuaded by these explanations just blamed rum for the night of terror. What Harris and his fellows did not know was that very shortly they would walk that bloody ground.

The Battle of Wyoming was not the most crucial battle of the Revolutionary War, but it was definitely one of the most one-sided, and it definitely included, with perhaps one exception, the most cruel and barbarous inhumanity of the entire war. And it was indeed a most significant moment, for now the War of the Revolution was to take a new turn. Because of what happened at Wyoming the Continental Army was forced to acknowledge a new enemy, and the war moved west. A new chapter had begun. John Harris and the 4th Continental Artillery would help to write it.

In the aftermath of the massacre, the Indians, and particularly the Iroquois, remained extremely active all along the Pennsylvania frontier. During the spring and summer leading up to the Wyoming disaster, and during the months immediately succeeding, atrocities occurred in an appallingly regular pattern, that is, with a steadily increasing frequency. In fact, all of the years from this point on to a time long beyond the end of the Revolution would be scarred by the horrors of the Border Wars.

For Northumberland County in Pennsylvania alone there are on record authoritative accounts of eighty Indian depredations for the period 1777-82. Most of the attacks occurred along one or another of the many streams and rivers that flow through the County of Northumberland, an extremely vast territory during the Revolution, when all of Pennsylvania was composed of only eleven counties. The murders and other atrocities were carried out on Pine Creek, Lycoming Creek, both branches of the Susquehanna River, Warrior Run, White Deer Creek, Chillisquaque Creek, Wolf Run, Laurel Run, Middle Creek, Fishing Creek, Buffalo Creek, White Springs, Nescopek Creek, Spruce Run, Muncy Creek, Penn's Creek, Antes Creek, Sugar Creek, Bald Eagle Creek, and the Loyalsock. These were assaults on farmers at work in the fields, hunters in the woods, families assembled in their homes, wagons on the road. No one was safe. John Harris had heard that Indians did not harm women and children. Now he was hearing about women butchered, babes tomahawked while asleep in the cradle, infants torn from their mothers' arms and dashed against the trunks of trees, men and women alike scalped while living and left for dead. For prisoners who were taken only rarely was there ever any report.

The atrocities of course were not altogether the work of the Indians. Whites had their moments too. The account of the infamous Stump the Indian Killer[28] is chilling in its horrors; and the massacre that occurred much later at Standing Stone, where innocent Shawnee women and children were murdered because they were Indians causes the blood to run cold.

Such brutal murders on the part of the whites prompted Old Smoke to declare that the Americans (meaning the rebellious colonists) "gave us great Reason to be revenged on them for their Cruelties to us and our Friends, and if we had the means of publishing to the world the many Acts of Cruelties to us and our Friends, . . . the many Acts of Treachery and Cruelty committed by them on our women and children . . . ."[29]

Unspeakable barbarities were carried out by both Indians and whites. They were avenged by whites and by Indians.

By June of 1778, the atrocities had so much increased in frequency that pioneer families in central Pennsylvania were fleeing in droves to the forts and returning to the east, in what has been called the Great Runaway.[30]

The general anxiety and apprehension that these frequent atrocities caused among the settlers led in the fall of 1778 to organized retribution. Because of a torrent of letters pleading for protection, the Supreme Executive Council of Pennsylvania finally appreciated the necessity of providing a military defense of the frontier. General Washington, who also had heard enough, determined on two expeditions into the Indian country. The locations of the Indian villages, along the Susquehanna and other streams, and across New York State to the Genesee country, were well known. But before Washington's expeditions could be organized, the Eleventh Pennsylvania of Colonel Thomas Hartley, who had been at the Three Rivers fiasco in Quebec, was called into action, together with a number of other troops of militia. One detachment of Hartley's regiment marched from New Jersey to Easton, and united there with Colonel Kowatz. The remainder were ordered to march immediately from Philadelphia to Sunbury in Northumberland County, there to join with two companies lately formed in Wyoming.

Hartley's Expedition, though modest when compared with that of Sullivan later, has to be counted a success. His forces, operating out of Fort Muncy, were able to negotiate the deep gorge of Lycoming Creek and make their way to Tioga. Although he did not catch up with Butler and his Royal Greens, for they had just fled the region, he did set fire to Queen Esther's town and other towns he came upon, including one, unfortunately, which was completely innocent.

After he burned the Indian villages in the region of Tioga, confiscating a great deal of plunder stolen by the savages from Wyoming, he returned toward Sunbury, almost without incident. His forces were assaulted only once, this on September 29, by Indians (possibly including Blacksnake) at Wyalusing (Browntown Mountain). The battle, considered a "sharp skirmish," cost the expedition four soldiers killed and ten wounded.[31]

Hartley's campaign accomplished two things: First of all, it angered the Indians, not surprisingly, inflaming their naturally vengeful disposition, and inspired a fierce attack on the helpless village of Cherry Valley, located some fifty miles northwest of Albany, birthplace of the Dutch father of the Seneca war-chief Cornplanter, and close to the source of the North Branch of the Susquehanna. The settlement was ill-prepared for the savage horde, led by Joseph Brant and Walter Butler, son of John Butler, that attacked on November 11. Some say that the massacre, and it was that, was even more horrible than what had happened at Wyoming. The Indians and Rangers numbered 700. The defenders, under the command of Colonel Ichabod Alden, totaled at best 250, and of these seventy were killed. Certainly it is true that from this time on the names of Joseph Brant and the Butlers were blackened beyond recall, had become anathema to the patriots. But Hartley's campaign also, because of its military tactics and general deportment, and the damage that was done, practically insured the success of the Sullivan Expedition.

All in all, the year 1778 proved to be too much for the American colonials. Pennsylvania had had enough, New York State had had enough, certainly Washington had had enough. It was time to punish the Indians for Wyoming and Cherry Valley and for scores of other atrocities, like the unspeakable murders occurring at Lycoming Creek in June. The Commander-in-Chief was compelled now to avenge these atrocities and to make the settlements along the frontier "safe."

During the late summer and fall of 1778, Proctor's artillery was with Washington's main army. His regiment was at White Plains in September, and marched "with the whole army" at daybreak on September 15 for Morristown. At Morristown, among the assignments given Proctor's regiment was the monitoring of the British movement at Little Egg Harbor and Great Egg Harbor, New Jersey, but the artillery saw little action during these months.[32] Its big assignment would be in answer to the Indian activity.

As spring came on and hostilities intensified, Washington

appreciated the need to address the "Indian problem." He had always felt that for the kind of fighting that characterized the frontier, Indians were needed to fight Indians. But now, even though of course he had no Indians (except for a handful of Delawares, and a few friendlies whom he could use as scouts and guides and runners), he was determined to carry the war to the Indian country. He was beginning to realize how damaging to the cause of the revolution was the alliance between the British and the Iroquois.

In March of 1779, Washington began to search among his generals for the man to handle the Indian problem. After consulting with General Edward Hand (who had been Commandant of the Western Department and headquartered at Fort Pitt), Colonel Zebulon Butler (who had had the command at Wyoming), and the surveyor and one-time captive of the Indians, Lieutenant John Jenkins, he seemed to fix on Horatio Gates. As noted by Washington's biographer John Fitzpatrick, this was a rather remarkable choice, inasmuch as Gates was already known to Washington as vain and ambitious, and the kind of general who directs the battle from his tent. But he must have sensed, or hoped, that Gates would not accept the commission, for he worded his "appointment" letter in such a way as to make plain what would be required and what would be expected; and then he was careful to include in the dispatch to the General another letter addressed to Major General John Sullivan. This letter he directed Gates to forward to Sullivan if he did not himself care for the command.[33] And it worked. The general promptly responded: "Last night I had the honor of your Excellency's letter. The man who undertakes the Indian service should enjoy youth and strength; requisites I do not possess. It therefore grieves me that your Excellency should offer me the only command to which I am entirely unequal. In obedience to your command I have forwarded your letter to General Sullivan."[34]

Sullivan was a good choice. Though he was not in the best of health, he was not yet forty; and he had proved himself most impressively through the first four years of the war. He had served at the patriot siege of Boston, had been captured by the British at Long Island, and had been exchanged in time to fight valiantly at Princeton, at Brandywine, and at Germantown. He had been freed of blame for the failure at Staten Island, and those members of Congress who had urged his removal from the army had been obliged, though it was still felt that he could have done much better at both the Brandywine and Germantown, to revise their estimates of the General. Washington, though not always on the best of terms with him, knew that he could depend upon him, first to accept a big job and, second, to do it.

But even Sullivan had his misgivings. First, he was not all that excited about the prospect of burning Indian villages through the summer; and, second, he was not confident that there was a value to it. But after turning it over in his mind for a week (!) he finally agreed at least to meet with Washington (at Middle Brook) to discuss the enterprise.

As Washington explained it to Sullivan, the campaign was not just for show. It was to be punitive, of course; it was to put the Indians "in their place." But he was hoping that the villages and fields of the Indians could be so completely destroyed as to render their aid to the British negligible. To disable the British war machine, that was the primary mission. The expedition would be two-pronged in its organization, for Brigadier General James Clinton, father of one Colonial governor and brother to another, would lead a force along the Mohawk River west while Sullivan was marching from the south up the Susquehanna. It could even be considered a three-pronged operation, for Colonel Daniel Brodhead would at the same time command a force that would operate in the West, moving up the Allegheny River north from Pittsburgh and into the Seneca country. If all went as planned, these three armies would come together at some convenient point, "advance against the stronghold of the enemy [the villages in the region of the finger lakes] in such force as could not possibly be resisted and then overrun the whole Iroquois country west of the Oneida villages."[35]

The plan called for a junction of Clinton's forces with Sullivan's wherever Sullivan would suggest. Brodhead's campaign for the time would be considered a separate operation.

On May 18, Colonel Proctor at last got some marching orders. Now commissioned by Congress as "Colonel of Artillery in the Army of the U. S," he was promptly pressed into the service he was impatient for. He was ordered by Washington to deliver his regiment to Major General John Sullivan at Easton, Pennsylvania, "for an ambitious expedition against the Indian allies of the British." Proctor had his troops, eager and lusting for some activity, in Easton, within two days. Sullivan promptly advised him that he would be in charge of the flotilla of boats waiting for them at Wyoming, and that he would be expected to transport upriver the stores and provisions of the 3000-man army. It was Colonel Proctor's biggest responsibility yet.[36]

The Sullivan army was proceeding slowly. Since the first of May, its object had been Wyoming, but it did not arrive until the third week of June. Meanwhile the Indians and Tories, having learned of the mission, were fast assembling in the region. They were determined on assaults of their own, hoping to distract the expedition. Before General Sullivan was able to launch his campaign from Wyoming, the tiny fort of Freeland, perched on Warrior's Run on the Susquehanna's west branch, was savagely attacked by Captain John McDonald in command of a force of fifty Rangers and some British Regulars. Leading the major portion of the entire force, at the head of 120 Senecas and Cayugas, was Chief Cornplanter.[37] Besides Cornplanter, among the Seneca participants were such well known names as Handsome Lake, Farmer's Brother, Little Beard, and the ruthless and bloodthirsty Hiokatoo (husband of the famous Mary Jemison, the girl who had been seized at her home in Gettysburg by the Shawnees and had come to live among the Senecas).

Hiokatoo, by this time, had built up quite a reputation. He was well known to the settlements. An impressively large Seneca warrior, Hiokatoo was ferocious and incredibly cruel. At the defeat of General Braddock in 1755 he is supposed to have tortured two white prisoners, "burning them to death in a fire of his own kindling." And he very much enjoyed binding his prisoner to a tree and making him a target for Indian boys just learning to use the bow and arrow.

Warrior's Run enters the West Branch of the Susquehanna four miles upstream from present-day Milton. The stockade was located about two and a half miles still farther up the Susquehanna, but quite close to the smaller stream. The fort, called Freeland, was garrisoned by twenty-one soldiers and was sheltering at this time fifty women and children.

There had been plenty of warning. Ominous neighborhood incidents were being reported with ever increasing frequency, and hostile Indians had been sighted everywhere in the region throughout the spring and early summer. Fort Freeland itself had already experienced trouble. On April 26 it had suffered a fierce assault, called a "massacre" in eye-witness accounts, from unidentified warriors. On the day following, April 27, Colonel Samuel Hunter, writing from his post at nearby Fort Augusta, dispatched a letter to "His Excellency, Joseph Reed, Esqr., President of the Supreme Executive Council," then in session in Philadelphia:

Yesterday, there was another party of Indians, about thirty or forty, kill'd and took seven of our Militia, that was stationed at a little Fort near Muncy Hill, call'd Fort Freeland; there was two or three of the inhabitants taken prisoner; among the latter is James McKnight, Esqr., one of our Assemblymen; the same day a party of thirteen of the inhabitants that went to hunt their Horses, about four or five miles from Fort Muncy was fired upon by a large party of Indians, and all taken or killed Except one man. Captain Walker of the Continental troops, who commands at that post, turned out with thirty-four men to the place he heard the fireing, and found four men kill'd and scalped, and supposes they Captured ye Remainder.[38]

This massacre was on the same day reported to the Council by the surveyor William Maclay: "The whole Force of the six Nations seems to be poured down upon Us. How long we will be able to bear up under such complicated and Severe attacks, God only knows."[39]

Because the Indian activity was actually stepped up through May and June and July, the concurrent removal of supporting troops became a matter of great distress to the settlers. In alarm Colonel Hunter, Commander of the Fort at Augusta, on July 23, directed a dispatch to Colonel Matthew Smith. He recited the calendar of events for the past month:

Dear Sir, we have Really Distressing times at present in this County Occasioned by the late depradations committed by the Savages on our Defenceless Frontiers. Immediately after the Evacuation of Fort Muncy, the Indians began their cruel murders again–the 3rd Inst they killed three men, & took two Prisoners at Lycoming–the eighth Inst., they burned the Widdow Smiths Mills & killed one man, 17th Inst, they killed two men, and took three Prisoners from Fort Brady, the same day they burned Starrets Mills & all the

Princeable Houses in Muncy Township, the 20th Inst, they killed three men at Freelands Fort, and took two Prisoners, them sticking so close to this County after the Continental troops has marched to Wyoming [the Sullivan Expedition] *has intimidated the people so much that they are Really on the Eve of deserting the County intirely as there is no Prospect of any assistance, that the people on the Frontiers Could get their Harvists poot up. I thought the army* [Sullivan] *marching Even to Wyoming would draw the attention of the Savages from us, but I think it never was worse than at present, and without some Reinforcements is sent to this County its not probable the little Forts we have at freelands and Boons can stand long, suppose I never see the people of this County behave more spirited than they do at present, suppose Reduced to a few, I have Just arrived after being on a Scout along Muncy Hill & we make a great Discovery where the Savages had been along the Frontiers & taken off a number of Horses. We are scarce of ammunition Especially Lead there is none.*[40]

Colonel Hunter's letter had not yet been delivered when the trouble came. On July 29, the British Regulars and Rangers under Captain John McDonald, and a horde of Indians under Cornplanter assaulted the tiny fort, garrisoned by twenty-one men. According to one account, the attackers numbered 200 British and 300 Indians; in another the numbers are 100 and 200.[41] Still another provides figures of 100 British Regulars and 300 warriors.[42] In the best case, the battle was an impossible mis-match. The fort was defended by brave men, and they fought stubbornly against the terrible odds, but they were few, and before long their ammunition was expended. In the space of three hours it was all over, "the fort's defenders either victims of the tomahawk or prisoners of war, the women and children objects of charity in the stronger fortification of Fort Augusta."[43]

Once the fort had capitulated, the Indians took possession. Mary Jemison, Hiokatoo's white wife, provided an account: "The women and children were sent under an escort to the next fort below [Boone], and the men and boys were taken off by a party of British to the general Indian encampment. As soon as . . . the firing had ceased, Hiokatoo with the help of a few Indians tomahawked every wounded American while earnestly begging with uplifted hands for quarter."[44]

Scores of eye-witness reports and a great many historical

accounts add their testimony. In one it is noted that the squaws who were with the war party went wild, became "mischievous and destructive." When admitted to the surrendered fort, "they ripped open the feather beds, emptying the contents in a heap and burning them, while they danced about with fiendish glee." Whatever they could not carry away they destroyed. After the fort had been plundered, the squaws rode off on the side saddles they had stolen, "in mockery of the women."[45]

The warriors and Captain McDonald's men meanwhile had assembled on Warrior's Run and were celebrating by feasting. What they did not know is that when the siege was begun the firing could be heard at Fort Boone, which was just four miles to the south. In charge of the garrison there was Captain Hawkins Boone, a cousin of the famous Daniel Boone. At the head of a relief party of thirty-two (some say 70-80) "as brave men as ever fired a gun" he set out for Fort Freeland.[46]

According to one account Boone and his men found the Indians at their feast and carrying on in great glee on the opposite bank of the run and at once fired a volley into them, killing about thirty. The forces of McDonald and Cornplanter, however, surrounded the small party, and dispatched almost half, including Boone himself.[47]

Mary Jemison's version of this part of the battle is very different and gives more prominence to her husband, Hiokatoo: "The massacre had just finished when Capts. Dougherty and Boon[e] arrived with a reinforcement to assist the garrison. On their arriving in sight of the fort they saw that it had surrendered, and that an Indian was holding the flag. This so much inflamed Capt. Dougherty that he left his command, stepped forward and shot the Indian at the first fire. Another took the flag, and had no sooner got it erected than Dougherty dropt him as he had the first. A third presumed to hold it, who was also shot down by Dougherty. Hiokatoo, exasperated at the sight of such bravery, sallied out with a party of Indians, and killed Capts. Dougherty, Boon[e], and fourteen men, at the first fire. The remainder of the two companies escaped by taking to flight, and soon arrived at the fort which they had left but a few hours before."[48]

But in every version of the battle, the fall of Fort Freeland is complete, and the tragedy was extended far and wide. Cornplanter and McDonald had marched from the vicinity of Wyalusing, in

Bradford County. After the surrender of the fort, the war party plundered freely, and burned much of the country between Muncy Hill, north of Freeland, and Northumberland, down river from the fort. According to one report, the expedition, following the taking of the fort, "burnt thirty miles of a close-settled country, which inhabitants had abandoned."[49] The ravaging included the killing of sixteen additional men and the capture of thirty, who were carried back to Niagara as prisoners. Records contained in the *Pennsylvania Archives* append this note: "As usual [!], women and children were left unharmed."[50]

The fall of Fort Freeland excited consternation in central Pennsylvania, and settlers as far away as Williamsport and Lock Haven and the Great Island in the Susquehanna began to evacuate their homes and join the mass exodus that has been called the Great Runaway. Dispatches describing the destruction of the fort went out in a steady stream to General Sullivan and to the President of Pennsylvania's Executive Council.

With Wyoming and Cherry Valley fresh in his mind, the surveyor William Maclay was inspired by what had happened at Freeland to revitalize the suggestion made twenty-four years earlier by Benjamin Franklin that these Indians should be hunted down by dogs.[51]

Certainly it would be difficult to exaggerate when attempting to assess the significance of the collapse of this frontier fort. There is first of all the terrible toll that was taken in human lives. One tally shows 108 settlers killed or led away as prisoners, "not alone by the Indians in their savage and cruel treachery, but as well by the organized militia of Great Britain." Besides, there is the toll taken of the attackers, numbering perhaps as many more. Then, too, the collapse of the fort had the effect of cutting off support for the rear of Sullivan's army; it also increased the pressure on magazines and stores in the neighboring forts. For these reasons the assault on Fort Freeland, on July 29, 1779, must be regarded an important battle of the Revolution.[52]

History bristles with "what ifs." What happened so tragically at Freeland inspires a big "What if . . . ?" Supposing that General Sullivan had been able to reach Wyoming just a week or two earlier, and had been able to set out for the Indian towns closer to the schedule he had hoped to be on. Perhaps then there would have been no assault upon the Fort at Freeland; for the Indians would be compelled to get between Sullivan's army and their villages.

In the real case, Fort Freeland goes down as the first battle of the Sullivan Campaign – even though it was to the rear of Sullivan and did not directly involve his forces. For Butler and Old Smoke and Joseph Brant and Little Beard, and Cornplanter, who would head up the resistance throughout, it was to be the only engagement of the campaign that they could possibly feel good about.

Finally the Expedition of Major General Sullivan, including the 4th Continental Artillery under Colonel Proctor, lumbered into motion. Sullivan had arrived at Easton on May 7 and there had very soon assembled some 3500 men in three brigades under Generals Maxwell, Hand and Poor. Proctor's artillery had arrived on May 20. But not for almost a month was Sullivan provisioned and ready to go. At last, at 5:00 in the morning of June 18, the General broke camp at Easton and began the trek to Wyoming.

With all the pack horses and some of the necessary stores (more to be picked up along the way), the army made twelve miles on this first day, encamping at the foot of the Blue Mountains. According to the Reverend William Rogers,[53] who, though still not twenty-six years old (only a little older than John Harris), was to serve as Chaplain for the whole of the mission, "On the road from Easton . . . nothing is to be seen [for the first twenty miles] but hills, stones, trees and brush, except here and there a scattered house and a lake near the mountain." And the remainder on the way to Wyoming he found almost completely uninhabited, "except by wild beasts and roving animals." But from a mountaintop in the Poconos "we had a fine prospect of nature's works. We discovered the water gap of the Blue Mountains, and hill upon hill surrounding us."[54]

The army on its march from Easton to Wyoming proceeded in an order which had General William Maxwell's brigade in the van, followed by Proctor's regiment of artillery, then Poor's brigade, and last the baggage train, General Hand having been dispatched to round up provisions. On the third day out, Harris and his fellow artillerymen killed some rattlesnakes, and according to one report "made a good meal of them." But this day's march was extremely difficult, the soldiers passing through thick stands of pine, poplar, oak, and chestnut, as well as some very dense mountain laurel. The artillery horses suffered most, and by early afternoon had gone as far as they could. The Reverend Rogers noted in his journal that he had done "no preaching to-day on account of the fatigue of the troops."[55]

The next day, if anything, was worse. The road which they followed was a recent but hardly adequate enlargement of the very narrow path that led though the Great Swamp and a different kind of timber—ash, locust, maple and hemlock. Because the trees reached so high, no sunlight penetrated the forest, and the constant gloom had inspired for their maps the name "Shades of Death." The troops somehow made twenty miles on this day, but by the time they were setting up tents they were so exhausted that Sullivan named the place Camp Fatigue. And because they had marched so far, and because some of the supply wagons did not reach the encampment until midnight, Sullivan declared a day of rest. One of the sentinels who were posted at the camp reported the sighting of a bear and a wolf, but no Indians. This day was Tuesday, June 22.[56]

Only a few miles remained to Wyoming, and the soldiers marched briskly through the early morning Wednesday. Three miles along the road, however, they had a bad moment. They had come to the place "where Captain Davis and Lieutenant Jones, with a corporal and four privates were scalped, tomahawked and speared by the savages, fifteen or twenty in number." The site had been marked by two boards fixed in the ground where Davis and Jones had fallen, with their names upon them, and that of Jones besmeared with his own blood. Reverend Rogers later confided to his journal his recollection of the scene: "In passing this melancholy vale, an universal gloom appeared on the countenances of both officers and men without distinction, and from the eyes of many, as by a sudden impulse, dropt the sympathizing tear. Colonel Proctor, out of respect to the deceased, ordered the music to play the tune of Roslin Castle, the soft and moving notes of which, together with what so forcibly struck the eye, tended greatly to fill our breasts with pity, and to renew our grief for our worthy departed friends and brethern."[57]

When, after five days, at last the army reached Wyoming, on Wednesday, June 23, all were afforded from "a fine eminence" a most thrilling view of the settlement on the river. "There it is," exclaimed an officer. "That is Wyoming." And young John Harris murmured to himself, "So this is where it happened." Most of the soldiers by the scene which lay before them, which included the remnants of log houses, were reminded of the massacre which had occurred here just a year ago. What they all were remembering the Reverend Rogers turned over slowly in his own mind: "At the battle . . . about two hundred and twenty were massacred within the space of an hour and a half, more than one hundred of whom were married men; their widows afterwards had all their property taken from them and several of them with their children were made prisoners. It is said that Queen Esther, of the Six Nations, who was with the enemy, scalped and tomahawked with her own hands in cool blood eight or ten persons. The Indian women in general were guilty of the greatest barbarities. Since this dreadful stroke they have visited the settlement several times, each time killing, or rather torturing to death, more or less. Many of their bones continue yet unburied where the main action happened."[58]

Sullivan was disappointed to discover that the stores and provisions he required were *still* not here in Wyoming. He was impatient to get the mission underway, but he would have to wait. He would have to wait perhaps a long time.

After the troops were settled in the community and had feasted on great quantities of freshly baked bread, produced by a bake-house, which had been specially constructed, the soldiers got acquainted with the settlers. One of these presented to Dr. Rogers one of the most fearsome of the Indian weapons, what he called a "death maul." At the end of a crooked and limber handle appeared a solid ball, "about the bigness of a three pounder," which had once been a maple tree knot. This instrument, he explained, "is used to knock people on the skull with, when overtaken in a chase."[59]

As it happened, this day, their first in Wyoming, was St. John's Day, and a number of Freemasons had been called to a meeting at Proctor's quarters. Although Reverend Rogers was not a mason himself, he read for those present, at Proctor's request, the "excellent sermon" on Masonry composed by the Reverend Dr. Smith. And he was rewarded next day by an invitation to dine with the officers of the artillery.

During this last week of June, Sullivan continued to stock provisions and to ready the army for the expedition up the

Susquehanna. On the 29th some of the supplies that he had been awaiting, upwards of thirty fully loaded boats, arrived from Sunbury down river. Meanwhile Colonel Proctor was readying his artillery and studying the possibilities of river warfare. With Sullivan's permission he endeavored an experiment. He wanted to find out just what his capacities were when firing from boats on the water. Having discharged four rounds of canister and eight of ball from a grasshopper on one of the flat-bottomed boats, he found himself much pleased. Even though the axletree of the cannon was every bit as wide as the boat itself, no damage to either gun or boat had occurred.[60]

Sunday, July 4, the Reverend William Rogers preached a vigorous Independence Day Baptist sermon to his brigade and to the regiment of Artillery. Bombardier John Harris loved a good Baptist sermon, and by this, which had as its text Psalm 32:10 ("But he that trusteth in the Lord, mercy shall encompass him about."), and which included an exaltation of General Washington, he was thrilled.[61]

While provisions continued to arrive, some of the officers (General Maxwell, Colonels Proctor, Butler, and Israel Shreve), with a number of other gentlemen, were given a tour of the region, visiting the remains of Forty Fort and discovering skulls and bones on the field of battle, now twelve months old. Particularly gruesome was the "place of skulls" near Wintermoote's Fort (up the river four miles from Forty Fort), where Colonel Zebulon Butler's routed soldiers were horribly butchered. They came to a grave where seventy-five skeletons were buried; and farther on they discovered a plot where the grass was distinctly different from the grass everywhere else. Here, it was explained to them, "Fourteen wretched creatures, who having surrendered upon being promised mercy, were nevertheless made to sit down in a ring, and after the savages had worked themselves up to the extreme of fury in their usual manner, by dancing singing, halloaing, etc., they proceeded deliberately to tomahawk the poor fellows one after another."[62]

For these barbarities which they were hearing about, and for which there was ample evidence, Reverend Rogers blamed King George. "Good God!" said he, "Who, after such repeated instances of cruelty, can ever be totally reconciled to that government which divesting itself of the feelings of humanity, has influenced the savage tribes to kill and wretchedly to torture to death, persons of each sex and of every age–the prattling infant, the blooming maid and persons of venerable years, have alike fallen victims to its vindictive rage."[63]

But one of the most chilling stories to come out of the entire American Revolution does not involve Indians. It involves only two people and it also belongs to the Wyoming experience. Still living in the Wyoming settlement at the time the forces of Sullivan arrived from Easton were the widow of Henry Pensell and his seven children. The Pensells had come to Wyoming from lower Smithfield on the Delaware, some twenty miles from Easton. The story is of Henry and his brother John. John was a Tory and Henry was a Whig. Incredibly, they came together after the battle at Wintermoote's Fort, on a small island in the Susquehanna down river a little from the field of action. A witness to this meeting was the young man Giles Slocum, who had miraculously escaped from the Indians and here on this island had secreted himself in the marsh grasses. Colonel Zebulon Butler, who had the story from Slocum, related it to the officers whom he was escorting about the battle sites:

> Henry, having lost his gun, upon seeing his brother John, fell upon his knees and begged him to spare his life; upon which John called him a damned rebel. John then went deliberately to a log, got on the same and began to load his piece, while Henry was upon his knees imploring him as a brother not to kill him. "I will," said he, "go with you and serve you as long as I live, if you will spare my life." John loaded his gun. Henry continued, "You won't kill your brother, will you?" "Yes," replied the monster, "I will as soon as look at you, you are a damned rebel." He then shot him and afterwards went up and struck him four or five times with a tomahawk and scalped him. Immediately after, one of the enemy coming to him said, "What have you been doing, have you killed your brother?" "Yes," said he, "for he was a damned rebel." The other replied, "I have a great mind to serve you in the same manner." They went off together.[64]

After waiting for darkness, Slocum withdrew from the horrors of the island and made good his escape.

On the 9th of July, more boats, fifty of them, loaded with supplies, arrived from Sunbury. These boats were guarded by the Eleventh Pennsylvania Regiment, under the command of Colonel Adam Hubley. Once the boats were unloaded they whipped back out into the river and headed downstream to secure more provisions.

Toward evening of the next day Colonel Proctor was at it again. From one of his flatboats he launched several shells from a five and one-half inch howitzer. Happily, again there was no damage to the boat, and, remarkably, one of the shells traveled 900 yards. The spectators who had assembled for the fireworks were treated to a most spectacular sight when it burst so far away.

On Wednesday the 14th of July thirty-three soldiers of the German regiment abandoned the expedition, declaring that their time was up. On Monday next, a great many horses arrived for the army; and twenty-nine of the German deserters, who had been captured, were returned as prisoners.[65] On the next Wednesday some really good news came to the encampment. It was reported, to the great joy of Sullivan's idle soldiers, that General Wayne had in a surprise attack with light infantry, captured the British garrison at Stony Point. According to the report, this meant 600 men captured, with all their stores, guns, tents, and baggage. And still more good fortune arrived the same day, as in the evening a number of wagons fully loaded with supplies for Sullivan, arrived from Easton.

And when on that Saturday, the 24th, General Hand showed up with 112 loaded boats, General Sullivan sent word throughout the army, "Get ready to march!"

It had required more than a month for Sullivan to acquire all that he needed, including 1200 pack horses and more than 700 cattle. It was not until the last day of July that the Sullivan Expedition was completely assembled and equipped and pronounced ready.

As the Expedition moved out from Wyoming, it moved in two parts, one on the river, and one on the shores. The artillery, together with "the ammunition, the salted provisions, flour, liquors, and heavy baggage," was consigned to a flotilla of boats. These boats, of all shapes and sizes, some of them newly built, numbered 214.[66] They were manned by 450 enlisted boatmen, together with 250 soldiers and Proctor's artillery. Those of Proctor's artillery who were not required in the boats were ordered to march in the rear of Maxwell's brigade.

The artillery was modest. It consisted of eight brass field pieces only: two six-pounders and four three-pounders, two howitzers, and a cohorn (a portable, light piece for firing either grapeshot or shell).[67] The firing piece called a cohorn is quite small, generally made of brass, and mounted on a wooden block provided with handles, "so that it could be carried a short distance by hand." It had been the idea of Colonel Proctor to equip it with legs. Borrowing the term from the British, he called it the "Grasshopper," because of its habit of leaping backwards from the discharge. It was carried to one of the lighter vessels which were to run at the head of the fleet.[68]

Sullivan's instructions were conveyed to all officers on the 25th: "The main army will keep as nearly abreast of the boats as possible; the horns in the boats must be frequently sounded to give notice of their situation. A captain and sixty men will advance a mile in front of the boats on the west side of the river to scour the country and give notice of ambuscades. In case of their being attacked by a superior force they are to retreat across the river, for which purpose four light boats will keep ahead of the fleet, nearly abreast of the party to transport them across the river in case of necessity; in these boats there will be a trusty officer and twelve armed soldiers, who are to be answerable for their conduct."

For the artillery: "Colonel Proctor will take part with his pieces of artillery, which will be fixed in the boats and have the direction of the whole fleet, he will take such officers and men with him as he shall find necessary. When a warm firing commences against the light party on the west side of the river the armed boats will immediately proceed to the place to cover the party by their fire." And further, "Should a firing begin with the main army, Colonel Proctor will wait for orders; he is also directed to establish signals to notify the fleet how to conduct in case of attack or other emergencies. The brigadiers must see that a covered wagon be filled with ammunition and put into proper boats for their respective brigades."[69]

This fleet of vessels and all that they carried were under the command of Colonel Thomas Proctor.

At precisely 1:00 in the afternoon, on this last day of July, the expedition got underway. The signal for the boats to weigh anchor was sounded from one of the guns aboard the *Adventure*, which was Proctor's "flagboat." As the flotilla passed the fort at Wyoming, it was saluted by the firing of thirteen cannon; and Proctor ordered a proper response. By the time the army on shore had all moved forward, it occupied a distance of some two miles. The parade of vessels on the waters of the Susquehanna was probably also two miles long.[70] The pack horses, about 2000 in number, it has been estimated, extended the column another six miles![71]

All in all, it made quite a show, with drums and fife, and flags aloft, "and Colonel Proctor's regimental band playing a lively air."[72] It doubtless dazzled whatever Indians were able to view it, or to hear it.

Unfortunately, before long, two of the boats, one heavily laden with ammunition, the other with provisions, went to the bottom. Happily, most of both the ammunition and the provisions was saved. And while the boatmen found rowing against the very strong current more than a little difficult, spirits continued high. After nearly three months of preparing and waiting, the expedition was on its way. Most of the soldiers were enjoying their first-ever view of the beautiful Susquehanna Valley.

Most of the boatmen were, like Harris, relishing a totally new experience. Few had ever been on the Susquehanna, and of course none ever before as a member of such an awesome army.

This was as far west as John Harris had ever been, and it was his first venture into "Indian country." He was happy to be riding the boats, so happy in fact, that from time to time he would spell one or another of the soldier-boatmen in the poling or the rowing, the civilian boatmen having been left behind. And he was constantly reminded by the Susquehanna of his own river, the Delaware, which had been growing a little foggy in his memory. The country through which they were passing, with the deep forests on either side, and the lush riverbanks, seemed beautiful to him. But he was not a poet. For a really memorable impression of the army on the march the historian Joel Tyler Headley provides the poetry:

So imposing a spectacle those solitudes never before witnessed. An army of three thousand men slowly wound along the picturesque banks of the Susquehannah–now their variegated uniforms sprinkling the open fields with gay colors, and anon their glittering bayonets fringing the dark forest with light; while by their side floated a hundred and fifty boats, laden with cannon and stores–slowly stemming the sluggish stream. Officers dashing along in their uniforms, and small bodies of horse between the columns, completed the scene–while exciting strains of martial music rose and fell in prolonged cadences on the summer air, and swept, dying away, into the deep solitudes. The gay song of the oarsmen, as he bent to his toil, mingled in with the hoarse words of command; and like some wizard creation of the American wilderness, the mighty pageant passed slowly along. The hawk flew screaming from his eyrie at the sight; and the Indian gazed with wonder and affright, as he watched it from the mountain-top, winding miles and miles through the sweet valley, or caught from afar the deafening roll of the drums, and shrill blast of the bugle. At night the boats were moored to the shore, and the army encamped beside them–the innumerable watch-fires stretching for miles along the river. As the morning sun rose over the green forest, the drums beat the reveille throughout the camp, and again the pageant of the day before commenced. Everything was in the freshness of summer vegetation, and the green forest rolled its sea of foliage over their heads, affording a welcome shelter from the heat of an August sun. Thus, day after day, this host toiled forward, and on the twelfth from the date of their march, reached Tioga.[73]

The best way to appreciate just exactly what happened during the months of the Sullivan Campaign, from July 31, 1779, through October, is to march with John Harris and Samuel Blackwood[74] and the soldiers who formed the various companies. One can experience the campaign almost as if he were participating. Happily, anyone who wants to can do exactly that, for the journal accounts of twenty-seven officers who served with Sullivan and Clinton are available. And, besides, there are the recollections of some of the common soldiers, like those of John Harris, made later on. Taken together, these provide *vivid* day-by-day (almost hour-by-hour) impressions of the marches and the battles, of the burning of the Indian villages, the destruction of the fields of corn and squash and cucumbers, of peach trees and other fruits. Of course there will occur for the reader a great deal of repetition, for the writers are observing the same thing. And perhaps the descriptions will not seem quite so rhapsodic as that with which the march was begun. But in these diaries the campaign comes alive.

What strikes one as he or she pores over these pages is the awe by which the officers are overcome. They revel in the beauty of the forests, the white pine and the spruce, and in the sparkle of the mountain streams. They are impressed by the size of the Indian buildings, and even more so by the vast fields of corn (some extending to 200 acres), with the stalks reaching to seventeen feet (!). Lieutenant William Barton declares early in the march that this "is the best part of the country I have seen since I left Wyoming." He speaks of the rich and fertile flats, of the lush mountains which embrace them. And Lt. Colonel Adam Hubley sets down a striking impression of the valley of the Chemung. He has his view from a mountain height: "The summit was gained with the greatest difficulty; on the top of the mountain the lands, which are level and extensive, are exceedingly rich with large timber, chiefly oak, interspersed with underwood and excellent grass. The prospect from this mountain is most beautiful; we had a view of the country, of at least twenty miles round; the fine, extensive plains, interspersed with streams of water, made the prospect pleasing and elegant from this mountain."[75]

It rains every day, or it seems to. Sometimes the rains are heavy; sometimes the days are simply dismally damp, shrouded in fog. The officers describe in their diaries the picking of huckleberries, the sighting of rattlesnakes and blacksnakes, fishing parties, corn roasts, the execution of deserters and traitors, the monotonous hours of sentinel duty. They have news that Spain has declared war against Great Britain.

But they never lose sight of their mission. Even the common soldier knows exactly what he is there to do. Years after the end of the war Bombardier John Harris reported in his recollections: "In the fall of 1779 I was with General Sullivan up the Susquehanna to destroy the Indians' corn. As they were partly civilized and farmed a good bit, it was thought that they had an extra amount planted to feed Burgoyne's army, that was expected to come from Canada down that way; and also [we were] to retaliate for the massacre of Wyoming. But General Gates defeated Burgoyne at Saratoga, New York. It was splendid corn, about forward enough for roasting or boiling, when we [ripped] it up and set fire to their wigwams."

Proctor's artillery, including John Harris's company under Lt.

Colonel Forrest, had plenty to do. Besides the normal work of the artillery in "softening up" the hostile forces who may be making a stand, or lurking in ambush, the cannon crews had General Sullivan's program to follow. This program called for announcing to the Indians and to Butler's Rangers just exactly where the Army was–morning and evening. Through the booming of the cannon, the location of the army was precisely established for all who were interested. Apparently it was Sullivan's intent, first, to let the Indians know that this army was on the march, that it was moving so many miles a day, and that its march was unrelenting. This army is coming on! Second, it seemed to suit General Sullivan to avoid actual battles. His mission was to destroy the corn and to destroy the habitation, livestock and fruit trees; to do all he could to make life for the Indian difficult if not impossible. If the warriors chose to make a stand, so be it. If they preferred simply to withdraw and leave the army to its work, well, maybe all the better. He would make it easy for them. Besides that, Sullivan seemed to understand that the sound of cannon, which the Indians called "thunder trees," was an unsettling disturbance to them. Anyway, John Harris and his fellow artillerymen were sounding the cannon morning and evening.

  The order of march was precisely defined. It was in that formation known as the hollow square. Sullivan's arrangement called for this marching organization: At the head of the army, generally one mile out front, marched a strong advance guard of light troops commanded by the Irish-born Brigadier General Edward Hand, who though the youngest of the generals, at thirty-five, served as second in command to Sullivan throughout the campaign. Hand was a good man to have out front. He enjoyed fighting Indian style, and it was he who had in that manner bought precious time for Washington at Assunpink with his Pennsylvania riflemen. Following these troops was, after it came ashore from the river, the artillery, commanded by Colonel Thomas Proctor, and eight lines of led pack horses, and the beef cattle. On the left flank marched the New Jersey brigade of Brigadier General William Maxwell; on the right flank marched the brigade of General Enoch Poor. General James Clinton's brigade, once it joined the army, marched at the rear.[76] The rate at which the army moved was determined by the flotilla of boats at first, and then by the artillery, which necessarily trudged at the proverbial snail's pace.

As Lt. William Barton recorded in his journal for a typical day, "At half past 12 p.m. began our march with several pieces of cannon, which caused us to move slowly, as we had formed a hollow square, in which the pack horses and cattle were all driven, together with the cannon."[77]

The army moves four to sixteen miles a day. There are occasional glimpses of Indians and sometimes actual skirmishes, but the enemy stays about two days ahead of Sullivan.

By August 6 the army had reached Wyalusing, which the soldiers found to consist "of about one thousand acres of clear land amazingly fertile and containing beds of extraordinarily fine English grass . . . . On this fine open plain, like a bed of down, the main army encamped." On this day Reverend Rogers visited Colonel Proctor on board the *Adventure*, and was very glad to find all the fleet safely arrived and tied up along the shore of the Wyalusing plains.[78]

After some time at Wyalusing, because of the incessant rain, the army moves on some ten miles upriver to Standing Stone Flats and on to Rush Meadow Creek. Through this region the soldiers enjoyed wild gooseberries, crab apples, may apples, flocks of mergansers, an occasional osprey, and wild turkeys.

Bombardier John Harris was not all that big on the creatures of the forest. As a boy growing up in Salem, New Jersey, he had never seen a wolf, nor an elk, nor even a black bear; and his first timber rattlesnake had made its appearance on this expedition. But, thanks to the interest his mother had awakened in him, he knew a little about birds, a great deal more than did most of his fellow artillerymen. He was very much enjoying the bird life along the river. And he was quite happy to discover the soldiers depending upon him for identification. He delighted in pointing out to members of the gun crews the various swallows and waxwings which dipped and dived and darted, in pursuit of flies, above the water. He knew birds by their call too, and the high-pitched, drawn out whistle that they were hearing all the time he declared was that of a little brown sparrow known "back home" as the "whitethroat." Once when one of his buddies, noting some large, ominous black shapes lazy in the sky above the river, asked, "Harris, whaddya call them things up there?" he explained: "Them? Them's vultures, so they are. Buzzards, folks call 'em. Only bird that can smell, so they say. Smell you-uns—if you was dead—from five miles away, or more, so they would." When he was stumped by a call, or by a silhouette, Harris was quick to invent a name, and in doing so would thus inflate his reputation. In this way he was particularly resourceful on the wild ducks which from time to time suddenly exploded from the river sallows, and on the herons which stalked the river shores. He had names for them all.

Such was the soldiers' excitement during the first days of the expedition. And so the army inched its way up river, the soldiers poling the boats through the shallows, and trudging the Indian trails. And so the long days dragged their weary lengths along.

On the ninth day out, General Sullivan was taken so ill that he could not proceed any farther on his own. When the fleet of boats caught up to the main army at Standing Stone, he was taken aboard, and for the time of his illness (which fortunately turned out to be less than two days) was transported upriver, a royal member of the fleet.[79]

The army did not always have the boats in sight. It was sometimes marching by the river, but much of the time it found itself a considerable distance from it, and of course well ahead of the boats. But sometimes the soldiers were actually in the water. From time to time the men had to ford the river. This required them to take off their overalls, secure them around their neck, and, while clasping the hand of a comrade, grope for a footing the necessary distance. It was a dispiriting experience for most, and General Hand, for morale, got in the habit of dismounting and wading with the men.

On August 10th a flour boat was lost, but all barrels except two were salvaged.

On August 11th, Sullivan has a fort constructed at Tioga. Called Fort Sullivan naturally, it was built at "the carrying place," a shallow water canoe portage linking the Susquehanna and Chemung Rivers. To strengthen the position further, Sullivan installed in the stockade some of the cannon from Proctor's artillery. Command of the fort was given to Colonel Israel Shreve.[80]

On the thirteenth day out, in the region of Tioga (present-day Athens, Pa.), the forces come upon the first of the Indian settlements, and the work of devastation commences. The army has reached the Chemung River, but Sullivan judging that it would not be safe for the infantry to attempt a crossing, even though here was a shallow ford, ordered a bombardment of the far shore. Accordingly, the company of artillery under Lieutenant Colonel Forrest (including bombardier John Harris) was pressed into action. The cannon, including the six-pounders, were wheeled into position for firing into the banks on the far side of the Chemung, and not until a substantial barrage had been fired were the infantry given the green light to move forward.[81]

About a week later Sullivan's main force is joined by the troops of General James Clinton, and his huge flotilla of boats.[82] Clinton's arrival, on Sunday, August 22, at 10 a. m., is noted in almost every journal account of the expedition. He had brought his five regiments (1800-

James Clinton

2000 men) down the Susquehanna from Lake Otsego, which he had left on August 9. That Clinton's force had made the appointment this close to the proper time was due in large measure to one of Proctor's artillery officers, the same Captain Andrew Porter who had been commended by Washington at Trenton and who had lost his company at Germantown.[83] Porter, who was very talented in mathematics and engineering, had suggested to General Clinton that he construct a dam at the outlet of Otsego Lake, which is at the headwaters of the Susquehanna near present-day Cooperstown, New York. Porter's idea was that after the dam had been constructed and the water level raised, the breaking of the dam would supply a rush of water which Clinton's fleet could ride down the river. The plan was ingenious. And it worked. The lake water was raised a whole foot, and then released. The boats were hurried to Tioga Point. And "when the head of his column came in sight of the main army, and the boats [208-248 of them] floated into view, there went up such a shout as never before shook the wilderness."[84]

Clinton's boats had arrived at the head of Sullivan's column, which was composed of General Hand's detachment of light troops. When the boats were perceived by Proctor, who was following Hand, he ordered an artillery salute of thirteen rounds from the six-pounders. And on top of that he had his drummers and fifers produce a celebratory music that made it all a grand occasion.

The union took place within a mile of Tioga,[85] that narrow wedge of land that lies between the Chemung River and the North Branch of the Susquehanna.

Now the army, with Clinton's regiments, boasts probably 5,000 men.[86] Sullivan has laid waste the village of Chemung; which had been abandoned by the Indians; Clinton has destroyed a settlement of the Onondagas. Butler and the Indians under Cornplanter, Old Smoke, and Brant, have yet to make a stand. On August 26, the expedition moves up the river toward the Indian village of Newtown. The campaign is about to heat up.

For at Newtown (present-day Elmira) Butler and the Indians have resolved to make a fight. Their force, it was discovered from captured men, was now 700 strong ("500 savages and 200 Tories, with about 20 British troops, commanded by a Seneca chief [Old Smoke, presumably, or possibly Cornplanter], the 2 Butlers, Brandt, & McDonald."[87] The battle, joined on Sunday, August 29, was to be the closest thing to a real engagement during the whole expedition. It was also to be one of the most important battles of the war for Cornplanter and the Seneca Indians. For young John Harris it was to be a battle that would provide him a great deal of meaningful action, as Proctor's artillery here would fire the first salvo, and would play a very strategic role, actually making the difference in the battle.

With the strong impression that a stand was going to be made by the Indians on the next day, the Sullivan army made camp near the ruins of Chemung. The customary patrols were not long in reporting evidence to confirm the feeling. Major Jeremiah Fogg recalled for his journal that the patrol led by Captain Jason Wait perceived smoke from a number of fires that evening; and that six miles up the trail (north) fortifications were recognizable.[88]

As one historian put it, "As morning dawned on 29 August, every soldier in Sullivan's army expected he would find himself in a fight before the end of the day."[89] Certainly young John Harris was counting on it. The artillery had been alerted to the role they would be expected to play.

After some two hours of sporadic musketry exchange, General Edward Hand ordered Proctor to bring his field pieces forward to some high ground just about 400 yards from the ambuscade the Indians had thrown up. That turned out to be much easier ordered than accomplished. The extreme difficulties were later recalled by Samuel McNeill, who was twelve days older than John Harris[90] and had been serving as Quartermaster in Hand's Brigade: "General Hand would, after Putting himself in a proper Position, have attacked their works, sword in hand, had not General Sullivan Sent orders to the Contrary. General Hand Continued Transmitting his Discoveries to General Sullivan from time to time, while the Artillery was Crossing an Exceeding bad Defile, and the men had to hitch wagons, and with the help of Horses, it took one hundred and Twenty men to each waggon to draw it up the Hill. At 12 o'clock the artillery was brought before the enemy's works. The Riflemen kept up a slow fire, amusing the Enemy, and in order to keep them from Turning out of their works to make Discoveries, the artillery was planted in the most advantageous Place at about 400 yards Distant. The artillery Consisted of Pieces as follows, viz: Two Howitz's and Four Threes."[91]

It was Sullivan's hope that the artillery could produce enough of a barrage to keep the Indians pinned down and buy enough time for Poor to outflank them. So he had Proctor's artillery deployed about 300 yards away and "directly in front of a long breastwork," which was manned by Indians; and then he dispatched the flanking force of infantry to the left of the ambuscade, to cut off retreat. At just about three o'clock in the afternoon, he ordered the cannon to fire. It is thought that Captain Craig, who, after Lt. Colonel Thomas Forrest, was second in command of the field artillery, was the officer to give the actual signal to fire the cannon.[92] Captain Isaac Craig had been observed studying his watch by William Earl of Pittsburgh, who was passing by on his way to deliver a message to General Hand.

McNeill stated that "once the gun crews found their mark, they proceeded to pour a combination of solid shot, iron spikes, grape, and exploding shells into the ambuscade which proved so intense that the Indians chose to abandon their positions long before Gen. Enoch Poor could reasonably be expected to be in position."[93]

In the notes of General John S. Clark, who carefully studied the whole of Sullivan's campaign, conducting meticulous inspections of the entire line of march, can be found a full and fine account of the battle staged on the left bank of the Chemung River, some six miles southeast of Elmira, New York:

> The enemy's force of British regulars, two battalions of Royal Greens, and Tories, were left by Colonel John Butler with Captain Walter N. Butler and Macdonald as subordinates; the Indians by the great Mohawk Captain Thayendanegea, alias Joseph Brant, Butler being chief in command. The design of the enemy appears to have been, primarily, an ambuscade. They had artfully concealed their works, and posted their forces in positions to attack simultaneously, both flanks. Front and rear; the position naturally strong was admirably adapted to their purposes. From Elmira, extending southeasterly for several miles is a mountainous ridge running parallel with the river, something over six hundred feet in height near the Indian village, but gradually melting away to the level of the plain where it terminates about a mile below; on this southeastern slope was the village of Newtown. To the north and east of this ridge is a similar one, which also terminates near the battlefield, and between them is a considerable stream, which, running parallel with the river in its general course enters the Chemung a mile and a quarter below. The river here sweeps around in a graceful curve, making a full semi-circle, enclosing several hundred acres of rich bottom lands on which were the Indian cornfields; the Wellsberg north and south road dividing it into two nearly equal parts. Rising abruptly from this plain is a sharp, narrow ridge, known locally as the Hog Back. This extends from the river across the plain nearly to the creek, a distance of about a third of a mile. The crest of this ridge was occupied by the enemy in force, protected by rude, log breast works and rifle pits, which extended to the eastern extremity, and from thence turning north, connected with the steep banks of the creek above. The lines to be defended were those two sides of a triangle, their right resting on the river, their left on the mountain, the path of the army passing between the two lines, along which was also the enemy's line of retreat. From the angle in the works a thin line extended to the mountain, on which was a body of the enemy and also another small body on the mountain to the east. The results at Chemung a few days previous led the enemy

to hope that a like blunder might be repeated, and that Wyoming and Minnisinks were to be re-enacted. Presuming that the army, after crossing the creek, would follow the Indian trail without discovering their works, they flattered themselves that an unexpected fire on the exposed flanks would create great confusion, which if augmented by simultaneous attacks in front and rear by the forces in that quarter, might result in a panic, and a possible stampede of the pack horses and cattle, which would be quite as disastrous as the defeat of the army. But three companies of Morgan's riflemen, the pride of Washington, were in the advance; these veterans of a hundred battles were in no way inferior to the enemy in Indian craft; the works and position of the enemy were discovered when afar off, and this ingenious device of drawing our forces into an ambuscade was frustrated. The ambuscade failing, the alternative was presented of forcing a direct attack in front, under great disadvantage, or of a flanking movement, over very difficult ground, where nearly the entire force of the enemy could be brought to bear on the attacking force at any point on interior lines possibly in time to repulse one division of the army before the other could come to its relief. The attack in front was invited by repeated sorties of a body of about four hundred of the enemy, who would deliver their fire, and immediately retreat to their works. After three hours of skirmishing, deliberation and reconnoitering, General Sullivan determined to divide his force, turn the enemy's left, and attack simultaneously in front and flank.

The artillery was posted on a rising ground, three hundred yards from the enemy, in order to enfilade their works, and sweep the ground in the rear. Gen. Hand was to support the artillery, the left flanking division to threaten the enemy's right, and Gen. Maxwell's brigade to be held in reserve. Gen. Poor's brigade of four regiments, the right flanking division, and the three companies of riflemen, were to make a circuit of about two miles and turn the enemy's left and attack in flank and rear, to be supported by General Clinton's brigade of four regiments following as a second line. One hour was allowed for this movement, at the expiration of which, the artillery was to open, to be followed by a general assault of the two divisions. Poor almost immediately after commencing his march, found himself involved in a thicket of underbrush, almost impenetrable, but after great difficulty reached the foot of the hill on which the enemy was *posted, just at the moment the artillery fire commenced. Forming the line of battle with Lieut. Col. Reid's 2d N. H. on the extreme left, next to him Lieut. Col. Dearborn's 2d N. H.,[94] then Alden's 6th Mass., and Col. Cilley's 1st N. H. on the extreme right. To the right of the brigade was the right flanking division of two hundred and fifty men under Col. Dubois, the whole preceded by three companies of riflemen under Maj. Parr. General Clinton's brigade formed line of battle with Col. Gansevoort's 3d N. Y., on the left, next Dubois 5th N. Y., then Livingston's 4th N. Y., with Van Courtland's 2d N. Y. on the extreme right, following in the rear of the first line. Poor when about halfway up the hill encountered the enemy, but not in sufficient force to materially check the advance of the flanking division, or the regiments on his right; on reaching the summit of the hill, these rapidly pushed forward to seize the defile near the river, a short distance above Newtown, which was the only avenue of escape for the enemy. Almost at the commencement of the cannonade, the main force of the enemy adroitly abandoned their works with out being discovered, and precipitated themselves on Col. Reid's regiment in greatly superior numbers. They swarmed about him in a semi-circle, and for a few moments made the forest ring with their exultant shouts, but for a few minutes only; for Col. Dearborn having reached the summit of the hill, and missing Col. Reid on his left, on his own responsibility, faced his regiment to the rear and moved to his assistance. At the same moment the two regiments on the left of Clinton's brigade by a left oblique movement, came up from the rear to Reid's support, and the enemy soon found themselves dangerously threatened. The conflict was short, sharp, and decisive, and the war whoop soon gave place to the retreat halloo. Poor with the remainder of his brigade, followed by the two regiments on the right of Clinton, had pushed rapidly for the defile. In the meantime Hand had advanced in front, and the left flanking division under Col. Ogden had worked its way along the river on the enemy's flank, when, the enemy, admirably commanded, and wisely discreet, sounded the signal for retreat just in time to escape.[95]*

    Actually, the Indians and Tories were able to withdraw before Sullivan's flanking force could get around them to cut them off. One account notes that they "retreated from their works with the greatest precipitation."[96] And a British report on the situation makes very plain how close the Indian-Butler forces were to great catastrophe, to a total wipe-out: "In this action Col. Butler and all his people was surrounded, and very near being taken prisoners. On the same day a few miles from this he attempted again to stop them, but in vain. The Colonel lost four rangers killed, two taken prisoners and seven wounded."[97]

General Clark's description of the battle continues:

Twelve Indians were found dead on the field, the number of wounded unknown. The enemy were pursued for two or three miles above Newtown by the light troops, where . . . they made another stand, which appears to be confirmed by the report [of the British], but no details are given, and the matter is not alluded to in Gen. Sullivan's official report. The loss in killed according to the Indian official account, found four days after, near Catherine's town is as follows: "Sept. 3d–This day found a tree marked 1779, Thandagana, the English of which is Brant, 12 men marked on it with arrows pierced through them, signifying the number they had lost in the action of the 29th ultimo. A small tree was twisted round like a rope and bent down which signified that if we drove and distressed them, yet we would not conquer them."[98]

Noting that the casualty figures for the action vary some in the many reports of the battle, General Clark cites Major Livermore, who is his journal for Aug. 29 reported that "but four or five" were killed, and perhaps as many as thirty additional were wounded. The impression recorded by Lieutenant Barton in his personal journal is similar, for he noted that "but four or five" [of ours] were killed, and that three officers and thirty-four or five wounded. Lt. Robert Parker reported: "Our loss was three killed and thirty-six wounded–Sixteen of the enemy were found dead and a great number must be wounded."[99] Lt. Obadiah Gore had the army losses at five killed and twenty-three wounded.[100] On the day following the battle, General Sullivan, in his report produced the official figures. For his troops he had the total loss at three killed and thirty-nine wounded.[101]

The artillery did not lose a man in this engagement, but they did have one wounded. A cannoneer named Thomas Tweedy was shot through the right leg. This same Thomas Tweedy, almost a year later, on July 1, 1780, in the action at Bergen Heights, N. J., at the Block House, was shot through the *left* leg.[102]

Colonel John Butler, who had been in charge of the Indian defense at Newtown, had afterwards great praise for Sullivan's artillery. He attributed the general consternation of the Indians to the effect of Proctor's six-pounders. He noted that the Americans had "six pieces of Cannon & Cohorns," which began "discharging shells, round & grape shot, Iron Spikes &c. Incessantly which soon obliged us to leave . . . ." He describes the flight: "The shells bursting beyond us, made the Indians imagine the Enemy had got their Artillery all round us, & so startled & confounded them that [a] great part of them run off." In fact, Butler notes, they panicked and were pell-mell in their flight: "Many of the Indians made no halt, but proceeded immediately to their respective Villages . . . ."[103] No wonder General Sullivan had the cannon fired morning and night, all through the expedition.

But the great irony here is that Sullivan did not want the Indians to flee. In a way, the artillery was too effective, perhaps too zealous. While it was actually the element that won the battle, Proctor's artillery could be blamed for the failure of the army to achieve the kind of victory that was desired.

Lt. Obadiah Gore, in his account, written the day of the battle, confirms Butler's impression of the disarray attending the Indians' departure. His version of the battle's beginning differs only slightly from that of General Clark: "Marched at 8 A. M. and our advanced parties frequently discovered Indians in front, and at the distance of about 4 miles, they had a breast-work situated on a very advantageous height. The rifle corps crept up, and amused them with a scattering of fire for 2 or 3 hours, attended with some execution, while our artillery could be brought up to play upon them." And on the critical timing of the operation he noted: "Meantime Genls. Poor and Clinton's brigades advanced to gain the enemy's rear. At 3 P. M. we began a cannonade upon the breast-work, and in about 6 minutes [!] they began to run and quit their works, which our advance party took possession of immediately." That it was a panicky exit which ensued, just as Butler had described, Gore's description confirms: "The right flank of the enemy, in their flight, fell in with General Poor's brigade, who gave them a warm reception, which put them in such precipitation, as to leave packs, blankets, guns, powder and even an officer's commission etc. We found 9 dead and took 2 prisoners, and have reason to think that considerable other execution was done, as there was great quantities of blood found in their paths."[104]

It has been suggested that General Sullivan at Newtown ordered the artillery fire a little too early, for General Enoch Poor had not yet out-flanked the Indians, and they were able to retire, albeit in confusion. But Sullivan had given Poor, he thought, plenty of time; and of course, besides that, he could hardly have expected the Indians to flee so early in the cannonading. Explained the General: "Fear had given them too great speed to be overtaken."

And the Aug. 29 journal entry made by Lieutenant Robert Parker, far from finding fault with Sullivan, blamed bad roads for Poor's delay and the unfortunate timing: "It must be allowed that our plan of attack was judiciously laid, well executed and must reflect great Honor on those that conducted it–but the badness of the road with some other circumstances, prevented the right wing [Poor] from gaining their post as soon as could be wished for & thereby part of the plan proved unsuccessful."[105]

At another place, Lt. Parker, in describing the beginning of the battle, shows that he at least felt that Poor had been given plenty of time to complete his flanking movement. He writes: "In this situation we remained near an hour keeping up a small fire of musquetry on the enemies front until the time allowed the right wing [Poor], to gain the post they intended, was expired–our Artillery was then ordered to advance upon the eminence, about two hundred yards in front of the enemies' works, where we began the attack by opening upon them two 5 and one-half Irish Howitzers & 6 three pounders, when a pleasing piece of Music ensued." Most amusing is his version of the effect: "But the Indians I believe did not admire the sound so much, nor could they be prevailed upon to listen to its music, although we made use of all the eloquence we were masters of for that purpose, but they were deaf to our entreaties and turned their backs upon us in token of their detestation for us."[106]

Of the Battle of Newtown, Blacksnake, Cornplanter's companion here as ever, and a participant in the action, many years later reported that "the Indians did not manage well." In fact, he seemed in his recollections to be most impressed by a shameful collateral episode, for it was during the Battle of Newtown, Blacksnake discloses, that Red Jacket suffered one more costly blow to his already much sullied reputation as a warrior. As the story goes, Red Jacket, having slaughtered a cow in the field, showed up among his fellow Senecas with the bloody tomahawk conspicuous. He was suggesting that he had slain an enemy soldier. According to Blacksnake, he was promptly exposed for a coward and had to suffer the shame, being known as "the cow killer" for the rest of his life.[107]

Almost twelve years later, while he was on a mission into the Indian country for Washington, March 27, 1791, Colonel Proctor recalled the battle of Newtown: "Dined at Mr. Isaac Baldwin's [near Tioga Point], and halted for the night and reviewed the ground on which the British and Indians were intrenched for better than a mile, against the forces under the command of Major General Sullivan. I also saw many traces made by our round and grape shot against them, and a large collection of pieces of five and one-half inch shells, which I had the pleasure of formerly causing to be exploded, amongst them."[108]

On the next day after Newtown there were no Indians to be seen anywhere. So almost the entire army was employed in cutting down the corn of the neighborhood, several hundred acres. And General Sullivan commended the army for its performance in yesterday's action, and thanked the soldiers for their fine execution of the battle plan. "In the afternoon," Lt. Parker confided to his diary, "it was proposed to the troops whether they would consent to live on half allowance of provisions, which was unanimously agreed to–the smallness of our Magazines & the impossibility of procuring another supply in season rendered this measure absolutely necessary–The troops in testimony of their approbation gave three huzzas which re-echoed from Regiment to Regiment."[109]

As darkness began to fall that day, Sullivan determined on a shipment down the river. And by eleven o'clock the soldiers, a little weary from the razing of the cornfields, had dismantled the wagons and carts and loaded them into the boats, together with two howitzers and two of the three-pounders. Then the wounded as well, and everything superfluous, were placed in the care of Captain McClure, whose job was to get the flotilla down river to the garrison at Tioga.

Newtown dealt a devastating blow to the Butlers and to their

Indian allies. The battle pretty much marked an end to any organized resistance to Sullivan. Certainly it contributed to the feeling of resignation and sense of futility which was steadily coming over Cornplanter, the most influential of the savage Senecas, and which would one day totally consume him.

The Expedition now moved forward with great confidence and high morale, "much animated with this day's success." Intent now on the villages located on both sides of the finger lake called Seneca, the army arrived at Catherine's Town on the first day of September. The town had taken its name from Catherine Montour, the wife of a noted Seneca chief, Telenemut (Thomas Hudson), and sister of the "fiend of Wyoming," Queen Esther. Like that at Chemung, this village had earlier (in the autumn of 1778) been wiped out by Colonel Thomas Hartley. It was promptly destroyed again.

As the army moved up the eastern shore of the beautiful lake, it came to Kendaia (Appletown), Blacksnake's birthplace, a small village about a half mile from the lake itself and on both banks of a small stream. After erasing this community the army moved on along the shores of Seneca Lake, coming on September 7 to the capital of the Seneca nation, the home of the chief sachem. It was composed of nearly sixty solidly built houses and stood on both sides of Kanadaseaga Creek. Called Kanadaseaga (the *grand village)* it reposed about a mile and a half to the east of present-day Geneva.[110]

Cornplanter had persuaded the Indians to make a stand on the beaches of the lake at this castle, but as a detachment of Sullivan's forces approached, the warriors grew skittish. Cornplanter tried to rally them. Leaping in front of the infamous Red Jacket, he insisted that the warrior stand and fight. When Red Jacket indicated that he certainly did not mean to do so, the enraged chief "turned to the young wife of the recreant warrior" and exclaimed in great heat, "Leave that man–he is a coward!"[111]

No battle occurred here. It required Sullivan only two days to put an end to the chief city of the Senecas.

Next to be destroyed were the villages of Kanandaigua, Hanneyaye, Kanaghsaws (Great Tree's town), and Gathtsegwarohare.[112] But while the army was still in the region of Kanaghsaws, delayed because of the necessity to build a bridge over a large sunken place, so that the troops might cross the swamp, the

Indians, under the leadership of Old Smoke, Cornplanter, Brant, Sagwarithra, Little Beard, Fish Carrier, and Blacksnake, prepared an ambush.[113] Only because Lieutenant Thomas Boyd and Michael Parker, who had been sent out on a scout with twenty-six men, stumbled into this ambush, was the plan of the Indians frustrated. Nine soldiers of Boyd's party escaped, but others, including Lieutenant Thaosagwat, whose brother was fighting on the side of the British, were killed, scalped, and mutilated. Boyd and Parker, having been questioned by Butler, were dispatched under the guard of Butler's Rangers to Genesee Castle, the village of Little Beard.[114]

On the next day, Tuesday, September 14, bombardier John Harris and the rest of the men of Sullivan's army came upon the most grisly sight of the entire expedition. How it all happened is a gripping, chilling story. John Salmon, who was from Pennsylvania's Northumberland County, and had heard of and seen his share of Indian barbarities, was serving as a First Sergeant in the company commanded by Captain Michael Simpson and Lieutenant Boyd. He was with the company as the army, after the battle of Newtown, moved to the head of Seneca Lake, down the lake to its mouth, and from thence past the outlets of Canandaigua, Honeoye, and Hemlock Lakes, to the head of Connisius Lake. Here the army had set up camp on some ground that is now called Henderson's Flats.

Salmon, regarded by James Seaver, to whom his account is addressed, as "a hero in the American war for Independence," was at the time of this writing living in Groveland, New York, which is in Livingston County, the scene of the drama he is recalling. Salmon's home is but a stone's throw from the grave of his fellow soldiers. He is writing on January 24, 1824, almost a half-century after the event. Here is his story:

Soon after the army had encamped, at the dusk of the evening, a party of twenty-one men, under the command of Lieut. Boyd, was detached from the rifle corps, and sent out for the purpose of reconnoitering the ground near the Genesee River, at a place now called Williamsburg, at a distance from the camp of about seven miles, under the guidance of a faithful Indian pilot. That place was then the site of an Indian village, and it was apprehended that the Indians and the Rangers might be there or in that vicinity in considerable force.

On the arrival of the party at Williamsburg, they found that the Indian village had been recently deserted, as the fires in the huts were still burning. The night was so far spent when they got to their place of destination, that lieutenant Boyd, considering the fatigue of his men, concluded to remain during the night near the village, and to send two men as messengers with a report to the camp in the morning. Accordingly, a little before daybreak, he despatched two men to the main body of the army, with information that the enemy had not been discovered.

After day-light, Lieut. Boyd cautiously crept from the place of his concealment, and upon getting a view of the village, discovered two Indians hovering about the settlement, one of whom was immediately shot and scalped by one of the riflemen, whose name was Murphy. Supposing that if there were Indians in that vicinity, or near the village, they would be instantly alarmed by this occurrence, Lieut. Boyd thought it most prudent to retire, and make the best of his way to the general encampment of our army. They accordingly set out and retraced the steps which they had taken the day before, till they were intercepted by the enemy.

On their arriving within about one mile and a half of the main army, they were surprized by the sudden appearance of a body of Indians, to the amount of five hundred. [!][115]

Upon discovering the enemy, and knowing that the only chance for escape was by breaking through their line (one of the most desperate enterprises ever undertaken), Lieut. Boyd, after a few words of encouragement, led his men to the attempt. As extraordinary as it may seem, the first onset, though unsuccessful, was made without the loss of a man on the part of the heroic band, though several of the enemy were killed. Two attempts more were made, which were equally unsuccessful, and in which the whole party fell, except Lieut. Boyd and eight others. Lieut. Boyd and a soldier by the name of [Michael] Parker were taken prisoners on the spot, a part of the remainder fled, and a part fell on the ground, apparently dead, and were overlooked by the Indians, who were too much engaged in pursuing the fugitives to notice those who fell.

When Lieut. Boyd found himself a prisoner, he solicited an interview with Brandt, who he well knew commanded the Indians.

This Chief, who was at the moment near, immediately presented himself, when Lieut. Boyd by one of those appeals which are known only by those who have been initiated and instructed in certain mysteries, and which never fail to bring succor to a "distressed brother," addressed him as the only source from which he could expect respite from cruel punishment or death. The appeal was recognized, and Brandt immediately, and in the strongest language, assured him that his life should be spared.

Lieut. Boyd, and his fellow-prisoner, Parker, were immediately conducted by a party of the Indians to the Indian village called [Little] *Beard's Town, on the west side of the Genesee River, in what is now called Leicester. After their arrival at Beard's Town, Brandt, their generous preserver, being called on service which required a few hours absence, left them in the care of the British Col. Butler, of the Rangers; who, as soon as Brandt had left them, commenced an interrogation to obtain from the prisoners a statement of the number, situation and intentions of the army under Gen. Sullivan; and threatened them, in case they hesitated or prevaricated in their answers, to deliver them up immediately to be massacred by the Indians, who, in Brandt's absence, and with the encouragement of their more savage commander, Butler, were ready to commit the greatest cruelties. Relying, probably, on the promises which Brandt had made them, and which he undoubtedly meant to fulfill, they refused to give Butler the desired information. Butler, upon this, hastened to put his threat into execution. They were delivered to some of their most ferocious enemies, who, after having them put to very severe torture, killed them by severing their heads from their bodies.*

The main body [of Sullivan's army], *immediately after hearing of the situation of Lieut. Boyd's detachment, moved on towards the Genesee River, and finding the bodies of those who were slain in Boyd's heroic attempt to penetrate through the enemy's lines, buried them in what is now the town of Groveland, where the grave is to be seen at this day.*

Upon their arrival at the Genesee River, they crossed over, secured the country for some distance on the river, burnt the Indian villages on the Genesee flats, and destroyed all their corn and other means of subsistence.

The bodies of Lieut. Boyd and Parker were found and buried near the bank of Beard's creek, under a bunch of wild plum-trees, on the road, as it now runs, from Moscow to Geneseo. I was one of those who committed to the earth the remains of my friend and companion in arms, the gallant Boyd.

Immediately after these events the army commenced its march back, by the same route that it came, to Tioga Point; thence down the Susquehanna to Wyoming, and thence across the country to Morristown, New-Jersey, where we went into winter quarters.

Gen. Sullivan's bravery is unimpeachable. He was unacquainted, however, with fighting the Indians, and made use of the best means to keep them at such a distance that they could not be brought into an engagement. It was his practice, morning and evening, to have cannon fired in or near the camp, by which the Indians were notified of their speed in marching, and of his situation, and were able to make a reasonable retreat.

The foregoing account, according to the best of my recollection is entirely correct.

John Salmon[116]

Almost every journal that was kept by the soldiers on this expedition includes an image of this scene, or at least some reference to it, and while there may be some inconsistency in details, it is a gruesome picture in every account. It may be presumed that John Harris and his companion Samuel Blackwood knew all about it and were horrified.

John Salmon's account of the torture and murder of Boyd and Parker is awful in its description, but Salmon has discreetly omitted the most blood-curdling details. From the journal of Lt. Erkuries Beatty, who one day would be present at the surrender of Lord Cornwallis, emerges a much fuller, eye-witness account of the terrifying scene, as the soldiers discovered it. Sullivan's forces are arriving at Genesee Castle, Little Beard's town:

The whole Army was under arms this morning an hour before Day & remained so till sunrise; about 7 oClock fatigue parties was sent out to Destroy Corn which was there in great Abundance and beans. about 12 oClock we marched crossed over the branch of the

Jinasee River and came upon a very beautiful flat of great extent growing up with wild Grass higher in some places than our heads. we marched on this flat 2 Mile and Crossed the Jinesee River which is about as big as the Tyago but very Crooked. left the flats and march'd thro the woods 3 Mile and arrived at Chenesee Town which is the largest we have yet seen; it lies in a Crook of the River on extraordinary good land about 70 houses very compact and very well built and about the same number of out houses in Cornfields &c: on entering the town we found the body of Lt. Boyd and another Rifle Man [Parker] in a most terrible mangled condition they was both stripped naked and their heads Cut off and the flesh of Lt. Boyds head was entirely taken of and his eyes punched out. the other mans hed was not there. they was stabed I supose in 40 Different places in the Body with a spear and great gashes cut in their flesh with knifes, and Lt. Boyds Privates was nearly cut of & hanging down, his finger and Toe nails was bruised of and the Dogs had eat part of their Shoulders away likewise a knife was sticking in Lt. Boyds body. They was immediately buried with the honour of war.[117]

Mary Jemison, who had been living among the Senecas for almost twenty years, most of the time in Little Beard's Town, and was at the time of the Sullivan Expedition thirty-five years old,[118] provides an even more horrifying account. She tells how Boyd and Parker were brought to Little Beard's Town, "where they were soon after put to death in the most shocking and cruel manner." Jemison in describing such scenes, particularly when her ruthless husband Hiokatoo is

Mary Jemison

the agent of the cruelty, rarely registers much feeling. Here she seems to be moved to pity:

> *Little Beard, in this, as in all other scenes of cruelty that happened at his town, was master of ceremonies, and principal actor. Poor Boyd was stripped of his clothing, and then tied to a sapling, where the Indians menaced his life by throwing their tomahawks at the tree, directly over his head, brandishing their scalping knives around him in the most frightful manner, and accompanying their ceremonies with terrific shouts of joy. Having punished him sufficiently in this way, they made a small opening in his abdomen, took out an intestine, which they tied to the sapling, and then unbound him from the tree, and drove him round it till he had drawn out the whole of his intestines. He was then beheaded, his head was stuck upon a pole, and his body left on the ground unburied. Thus ended the life of poor William [Thomas] Boyd, who, it was said, had every appearance of being an active and enterprizing officer, of the first talents. The other prisoner was (if I remember distinctly) only beheaded and left near Boyd.*[119]

Boyd, who was born in Washingtonville, in Pennsylvania's Northumberland County, had first marched into the wilderness in the failed invasion of Quebec. A sergeant then, he served under Benedict Arnold, in Captain Matthew Smith's Pennsylvania Company of Riflers, and survived the torturous march through Maine to Quebec. He was still only twenty-two years old when he was murdered at Genesee Castle. He has been described: "Of fine physique, engaging manners, brave almost to recklessness, he was endowed with the qualities which would command attention, without the cool judgment of firmness which would fit him for a leader."[120]

Michael Parker had been a corporal in the First Pennsylvania Regiment, from which he was promoted to sergeant in Captain Michael Simpson's company.[121]

Skeptics are many ("too horrible to be true"), but the story is preserved by the locals, and to this day one may stand next to the tree ("the sapling") to which Boyd was bound. It is a huge tree now, a white oak, said to be 240 years old, and called "the torture tree." It is designated by an historical marker at the old site of Little Beard's

Town. Doubtless the sight of this scene of torture and mutilation and murder impelled the soldiers of General Sullivan to a greater zeal as they went about their business. It required the army only until the middle of the afternoon of the next day to destroy the enormous town of Little Beard, called Genishau (Genesee Castle). There were many sturdy houses (Lt. Beatty had counted seventy, and Lt. Thomas Blake counted 180 !), and a very, very expansive field of corn. At the close of the day, satisfied that they had reached the end of the trail of villages, the army of General Sullivan marched only about four miles farther. It never did reach the village of Cornplanter's birth, which lay just a few miles beyond the town of Little Beard, and a number of other villages had escaped their attention altogether, but it seemed enough. They had been burning cornfields and firing villages for six long weeks, all of August and well into September. Next day, September 16, they set out on the return trip.

The expedition traveled, by water and along the river shores, by the same route it had followed into the Indian country. It reached

Historical Marker

Catherine's Town in one week, and arrived back at Wyoming just two weeks after that, on Thursday, October 7, to a big celebration, which included the firing of cannon for every toast. On Saturday, the 9th, at 6:00 a.m. it began the march to Easton.

Lt. Robert Parker's journal entry for the date of September 16 provides a short summary of the expedition and a vision for the future of the beautiful Susquehanna River Valley:

Thus had we advanced 140 miles in the Enemy's country from Tioga and carried fire, sword and destruction in every part, that we could possibly find out or approach, in the prosecution of which, we had to encounter many and almost insurmountable difficulties, such as forcing a march all the way, cutting a Road for the Artillery, in many places a continued swamp for several miles, want of provisions, hard marches, and fatigue.

But here let us leave the busy army for a moment and suffer our imaginations to Run at large through these delightful wilds, & figure to ourselves the opening prospects of future greatness which we may reasonably suppose is not far distant, & that we may yet behold with a pleasing admiration those deserts that have so long been the habitation of beasts of prey & a safe asylum for our savage enemies, converted into fruitful fields, covered with all the richest productions of agriculture, amply rewarding the industrious husbandman by a golden harvest; the spacious plains abounding with flocks & herds to supply his necessary wants. These Lakes & Rivers that have for ages past rolled in sacred silence along their wonted course, unknown to Christian nations, produce spacious cities & guilded spires, rising on their banks, affording a safe retreat for the virtuous few that disdains to live in affluence at the expense of their liberties.[122]

Meanwhile Colonel Daniel Brodhead had not been idle. His assignment had been to drive a stake into the heart of the Seneca country, which lay up the Allegheny River to the north of Pittsburgh. Brodhead was a Pennsylvanian. Though he had been born in Albany, his father had emigrated to Danbury (now East Stroudsburg, Pa.). He

Daniel Brodhead

had commanded a detachment of militia in the Battle of Long Island, and he had endured the winter at Valley Forge. An older man than Sullivan, by fifteen years, he would after the war serve the Commonwealth for eleven years as Surveyor General. In the Surveyor General's office at Harrisburg, a half century after his death, were discovered the letters he wrote during the time of the Sullivan Campaign. They date from early in 1779 to the end of 1780 and provide important details not only of the conduct of the war but also the relationships among the Indians, in particular those of the Six Nations with the Delawares and the "western tribes."

The letters are addressed in the main to his superiors, to John Jay, to Thomas Jefferson, and to General George Rogers Clark, as well as a number to his Commander-in-Chief, General Washington. He is writing from his headquarters at Fort Pitt.

In the time some months before Sullivan set out from Wyoming, Brodhead complains about the hostility and the depredations of the Indians in the region around Fort Pitt: " . . . the Indians at present are daily Committing Murders in Westmoreland to such a degree that I have ordered ranging parties to cover them [the inhabitants] and drive out the Indians." He suggests that the Delawares, though not so numerous, may be persuaded to fight against the Six Nations, but appreciates the need to pay them in goods and trinkets.[123]

He notes in July that he is sending out runners regularly to keep track of Butler and his Rangers. He urges at the time the building of a fort at the Delaware town of Kittanning on the Allegheny, and recommends that it be named for Colonel Jack Armstrong. And he must have been pleased to see the completion of the fort before the month was out.

In a letter to Thomas Jefferson, then Governor of Virginia, he expresses his need for troops from Virginia and reports: "About the fifth of next month [August] I intend to make an excursion against some of the Seneca settlements, they being the most hostile and warlike nation, and if I am successful it may establish the Tranquility of our frontiers for years to come." To Governor Joseph Reed of Pennsylvania on August 3 he affirmed this plan. "As I have leave from his Excellency [Washington] I shall set out on an expedition against the Seneca towns, up the Allegheny River, within a few days. I expect to have a number of Delaware Warriors to join me, but have nothing to reward them with, and therefore cannot expect their future service." Three days later he informed General Sullivan of this plan and indicated that Washington was urging a coordinated effort between the two armies.

On August 11, at just the time Sullivan was reaching Tioga-Chemung, Brodhead, with 605 Rank and File left Pittsburgh for Mahoning, fifteen miles upriver from Kittanning (Fort Armstrong). Small garrisons of regular troops were left at Forts McIntosh, Crawford and Armstrong, as well as at Fort Pitt. To Washington he reports from Pittsburgh five weeks later, in a greatly detailed, long letter, dated September 16, at just the time Sullivan is arriving at Little Beard's Town, the results of the mission. He explains that one engagement with a party of canoes on the Allegheny came to nothing, and that very little resistance did he encounter on the whole course of the expedition. Actually, there were few Seneca warriors at home to oppose the Brodhead expedition, for almost all, including Cornplanter, had gone east and north to join those Indians of the Six Nations who were offering resistance to the Sullivan forces. Colonel Brodhead found that towns had been deserted long ago, or were abandoned upon the approach of his troops. The upper-river Seneca villages, numbering eight, he destroyed, together with the fields of corn, totaling at least 500 acres. Brodhead declares to Washington that "I never saw finer Corn, altho' it was planted much thicker than is common with our Farmers."[124]

The one engagement that "came to nothing" occurred just after he had returned to the Allegheny River, having struck out overland for a little distance, seven days into the mission. On the river, not far from where it receives Brokenstraw Creek, they found a party of warriors numbering at least forty and perhaps fifty, headed down river in canoes, apparently to assault settlements in Westmoreland County. The Indians made for shore to attack the Brodhead forces, but were met rudely. Before they could abandon the field they lost five warriors. It is thought that the notorious Dehguswaygahent was the leader of this war party. It could not have been Cornplanter, of course, as he was on this day in the Genesee River valley contending with Sullivan.

Allegheny River, at Red Bank Creek

Brodhead got as far north as Yahrungwago, some forty miles short of the Genesee, and thus very close to the expedition of Sullivan. He would have continued on to "Jenesseo" but for want of shoes for his men. On his return he followed the old Venango Road and laid waste to Indian villages at Conawango (present-day Warren), Buchloons (Buckaloons, near present-day Youngsville), and Mahusquechikoken, upriver from the entry into the Allegheny of French Creek. Brodhead judged from the houses, which he found "much larger than common, and built of square & round logs & frame work," and from the quantity of corn and a number of very new buildings, that the Seneca and Muncy nations were intending to assemble at this spot to establish a permanent settlement, which might extend some eight miles along the river. He concludes his long letter by expressing his eagerness for an undertaking against Detroit (a request he is constantly repeating) and his willingness to make additional excursions against "any of the Indian nations." He wants to know, too, how he should react should the Seneca and Muncy sue for peace.[125] The Brodhead expedition began on August 11, almost two weeks after Sullivan set out from Wyoming, and ended on September 14.

In October, Brodhead responds to a letter he has had from Sullivan, who in the last week of September had been at Catherine's Town on his way home. In reply to Sullivan's curiosity, he repeats the report he has made to Washington, which adds up to great success; and he is very quick to congratulate Sullivan for what he takes to be a big step toward "lasting tranquility on the frontier."

On the 18th of October, Colonel Brodhead himself received congratulations. Writing to express the gratitude of the nation, Washington extended his compliments: "The activity, perseverance and firmness which marked the conduct of Colonel Brodhead, and that of all the officers and men of every description in this expedition, do them great honor, and their services entitle them to the thanks and to this testimonial of the General's acknowledgment."[126]

It is difficult to assess the effect of the Sullivan-Clinton-Brodhead campaign. Some historians insist that the campaign did little more than to exacerbate the Indians, that it was in fact a failure. More than a decade later, it has been noted, " . . .the Seneca chief Cornplanter reminded Washington of the legacy of the general's decision [to invade the Indian country on the Susquehanna]." In 1790 Cornplanter declared to the President in Philadephia: "When your army entered the country of the Six Nations, we called you Town Destroyer and to this day when that name [Sullivan] is heard our women look behind them and turn pale, and our children cling close to the necks of their mothers. Our counsellors and warriors are men, and cannot be afraid, but their hearts are grieved with the fears of our women and children, and desire that it [the pain inflicted by the campaign] may be buried so deep as to be heard no more."[127] To the very end of his long life, which was closed out in extreme bitterness, the venerable Iroquois chieftain inveighed against the inhumanities of the Sullivan expedition.

But the campaign did more than simply anger the Indians. They clearly suffered an almost total devastation of villages and grain fields and vegetable plots and fruit trees. Before the Battle of Lexington/Concord, the Indians of the Six Nations lived in thirty-some widely scattered villages. By the spring of 1780, most of them had been reduced to ashes, had simply disappeared. Sullivan alone claimed to have destroyed forty (!) villages; and thirty is the total, with villages named, in another report.[128] Only two of all the Indian villages known to the settlers survived undamaged.[129]

And when it is considered what the casualty figures might have been, the official tally of forty soldiers lost is most remarkable.[130]

Noteworthy, too, is the prominence that was given to the artillery during the campaign. One historian, in assessing its role, declares that from the Sullivan campaign it was learned how vital to success is artillery in such operations:

> *Artillery proved important to the army's military tactics, and Sullivan went to considerable trouble to ensure its presence. The effort Proctor expended on mounting a howitzer as well as some small grasshoppers on his bateaux provided the first indication of high priority. With its ability to fire all the standard ordnance of the day, Proctor's river fleet could provide covering fire to the infantry company clearing the river's opposite shore. Though the artillery left Wyoming by boat, only muscle and sweat could move the pieces beyond Tioga. Sullivan ordered one coehorn hand carried along on the raid on Chemung. At Newtown the artillery played a key role in driving the enemy from its positions. Sullivan had most of his heavy artillery taken back to Tioga after Newtown but proceeded to carry several small cannons all the way to the Genesee River. A reliance on overwhelming fire support has characterized the U. S. Army during the wars of the twentieth century. Sullivan's fixation on keeping artillery with him even at the expense of speed indicates a similar attribute in the eighteenth century.*[131]

When the object of the campaign is brought to mind, "to put the Indians in their place," and to render the Indian aid to the British negligible, and to disable the British war machine, it would seem that the Expedition was a success. Certainly the common soldier who served throughout the campaign, if John Harris can be thought typical, thought that the army had done its job. Harris declared that these six weeks had "ruined them [the Indians], and they never recovered from the blow."

It had been expected by many, in high places and low (but not by those who knew Sullivan), that, because the whole campaign was in essence in retribution for the Wyoming massacre and other atrocities suffered by the settlers on the frontier, horrible acts of cruelty would occur. In fact, what is remarkable is that almost nothing of that kind was carried out by Sullivan's soldiers. Just the contrary.

Owing probably to the insistence of General Sullivan, who had himself been a prisoner of war, captured women and children were treated most kindly. For one aged squaw, whom the Indians had left behind, and who expected to be murdered, the soldiers built a house and equipped it with a healthy store of food and blankets. Samuel McNeill reported that "We found some Cattle, such as Horses, Cows and Hogs, also found in one of the houses an old Squaw Scarce able to walk, Supposed to be about 100 years of age. Our Indians took great care of her During our Stay at that place, and by General Sullivan's order built a Bark Cabin near the waterside and gave her Bread, meat and Indian Corn sufficient to last her six weeks. I confess I think she was the greatest object of Pitty I ever Saw."[132]

This occurred at Catherine's Town, during the forward march upriver. On the return march, this same squaw "greeted the soldiers with a smile of gratitude." And General Sullivan ordered that from the troops' meager supplies there be left "a keg of pork and some biscuit &c for the old creature to subsist on."[133] Besides the skinning of two dead Indians to make boots, only two instances of barbarity occurred for the whole campaign, and one of these, the murder of a squaw found on the army's return to Catherine's Town, is "generally believed" to have been the work of express riders from Tioga.[134] The other is definitely a bad mark for the campaign.

For the most part, villages that the Army came upon were totally abandoned, but occasionally women or children would be left behind. According to a well documented account, at Cayuga Lake, on the forward march, Colonel Dearborn discovered three Indian women and a badly crippled Indian lad. He ordered that one house in the village be allowed to stand to accommodate them. But, somehow, his orders were not followed. Two of the squaws were taken along as prisoners; and the remaining squaw, apparently the oldest, together with the crippled boy, was locked in the house, which was then burned down.[135] While that inhumanity is a blemish for the campaign, it clearly was an aberration, and should not be taken as a reflection generally upon the behavior of Sullivan's soldiers.

Unfortunately, it was rumored among the Senecas that many atrocities had occurred, and such beliefs assuredly did little to improve relations between Indians and whites.

But the campaign can be judged a success, too, for what it did not do. It did not do what it might have done, that is to unite the Indians generally, and to bring closer together the fragments of the Six Nations. Besides, it had the beneficial effect (from the Americans' point of view) of making the Iroquois tribes increasingly dependent upon the British. And the blow to morale must have been heavy. Certainly the feeble, token resistance put up by the British under the Butlers and by the Indians under their war chiefs must have sounded to them all a note of futility.

Yet neither Brodhead nor Sullivan reached Canawagus, the home village of Cornplanter and Blacksnake.[136] Brodhead never did become a real part of the Sullivan-Clinton Expedition. He had left Fort Pitt on August 11, about the time Sullivan's army was coming to the Chemung, with 605 "rank and file" to invade the Seneca country and to form a junction with Generals Sullivan and Clinton somewhere in the Genesee region. And despite the fact that Brodhead destroyed a number of the Seneca villages and met with no resistance, and had a generally easy time of it on the Allegheny, the Indians had not submitted, nor had they ceased their hostile activity in the Fort Pitt region.

The border wars did not end with the campaigns of Sullivan and Clinton and Brodhead on the rivers of the west. Hostilities all along the frontier continued, and in many areas, like especially Northumberland County in central Pennsylvania, actually seemed to increase in frequency. Hostile Indian activity in the neighborhood of Fort Pitt kept Brodhead constantly edgy, so uneasy that he feared an all-out Indian assault from Detroit. It is putting it all too simply, but it might be remarked, with respect to the Six Nations, that their back was broken, but not their spirit. Or to put it another way, the road to despair was merely paved, not traveled. For the chiefs, like Cornplanter and Brant, it might one day be time to cast off the attitude of force and to adjust to all that the inevitable loss of their lands would mean. But not yet.

The Susquehanna

The war was not over, not by a long shot. There were critical battles yet to be fought. Harrowing raids on the settlements continued. Bombardier John Harris and his fellow artillerymen were not going home. Not yet.

One of the most dramatic moments in the aftermath of the Sullivan Expedition occurred in August of 1780. Some 400 Indians and Tories under Old Smoke, Cornplanter, and Brant burned the Canajoharie District of the Mohawk Valley, the region of Brant's own home. Sagwarithra of the Tuscaroras and Fish Carrier of the Cayugas were also participating, at the heads of small parties. The Senecas, however, made up the largest percentage of the warriors, and among them were the familiar names: Handsome Lake, Red Jacket, Farmer's Brother, Little Beard, Jack Berry, and Blacksnake.

Canajoharie is on the Mohawk River, sixty miles northwest of Albany and twenty miles northeast of Cherry Valley. The region had been settled primarily by Dutch and German immigrants in the early days of the eighteenth century. The area gets its name (an Indian expression meaning "washed pot") from a large pothole conspicuous in the nearby Canajoharie Creek Gorge. A 45-foot waterfall is a feature of the gorge and can be viewed from Wintergreen Park. As with the beauties of the Wyoming Valley, these scenic delights in no way accord with the events of August 2, 1780.

Among the homes razed by fire was one in which was residing the father of Cornplanter, the Dutch trader John Abeel, now almost sixty years old. In one account of what happened here, the old man was simply taken captive by the Indians, along with everybody else, and only later was by the Senecas recognized among the prisoners.[137] According to another, earlier, version, Cornplanter knew in advance that the elder Abeel resided here, and "repairing with a detachment of his warriors to his father's house, he made the old man a prisoner, and marched him off."[138] In the first version, after the warriors explained to Cornplanter that one of the prisoners was his father, the chief "apologized profusely" for burning his house. In the second, Cornplanter said nothing to him until the march of the captives had proceeded ten or twelve miles. In both versions he presented his father the choice between returning home with him to his Indian village or going back to his white family. The oft-quoted speech by Cornplanter, by which he identified himself and expressed the hope that his father would come to live with him, was included in her narrative by Mary Jemison, who had herself chosen to live among the Senecas:

> *My name is John O'Bail, commonly called Cornplanter. I am your son! You are my father! You are now my prisoner, and subject to the customs of Indian warfare. But you shall not be harmed: you need not fear. I am a warrior! Many are the scalps which I have taken! Many prisoners I have tortured to death! I am your son! I was anxious to see you, and greet you in friendship. I went to your cabin and took you by force. But your life shall be spared. Indians love their friends and their kindred, and treat them with kindness. If now you choose to follow the fortune of your yellow son, and to live with our people, I will cherish your old age with plenty of venison, and you shall live easy. But if it is your choice to return to your fields and live with your white children, I will send a party of my trusty young men to conduct you back to safety. I respect you, my father: you have been friendly to Indians, and they are your friends.*[139]

John Abeel elected to return to his home among the whites, and, as promised, was provided an escort, which took him safely out of harm's way. Cornplanter never again saw his father. It was a touching moment in an otherwise time of terror.

But that fierce assault on the region was only a small part of the Schoharie Expedition, the major British campaign of the year 1780. This campaign was led by Sir John Johnson himself. Historians regard it as "comparable in size and destructiveness" to the Sullivan Expedition of the year before. And clearly it was by way of answer to the Sullivan campaign. "Tory Rangers and Indians, converging from north, west, and south, met to make up an army of 1500 men, well armed and even carrying mortars."[140] One historian describes how this "formidable force" moved first, almost entirely unopposed, down the Schoharie to where it merged with the Mohawk River, and then proceeded up the Mohawk in a wave of destruction. The Indians burned everything that they found along their route, including forts and barns, churches and gristmills, not to mention scores of houses. This raid has been regarded as the culmination of three years of "incendiary incursions." It had an effect comparable to that of the Sullivan Campaign in that it "virtually wiped out all white settlements in the Mohawk Valley west of the environs of Schenectady."[141]

As the end of the war approached, raids upon the frontier settlements did not cease. As late as 1781, historians report, there were sixty-four war parties (almost 3000 warriors) active on the frontiers of Pennsylvania, New York, and what would be Ohio. Most of the war parties were small. One, which was headed up by the powerful Sayenqueraghta (Old Smoke, of Wyoming and Oriskany fame), numbered generally only about thirty-six warriors; but that war party operated in the region of Fort Pitt, and it was able at one time to attract to its force so many additional warriors that it actually posed a real threat to Fort Henry at Wheeling, Virginia.

These raids upon the settlements all along the New York and Pennsylvania frontiers in the wake of the Sullivan Expedition, devastating as they were, may be viewed as the last gasp of the Senecas. Roving bands of warriors continued depredations and were involved in some skirmish action through 1782. But Cornplanter and Blacksnake did never again participate in any formal military action.

VII

THE OHIO

We finally arrived at Pittsburg, a poor place then,–not even a frame house in it. There was a line of soldiers' barracks, frame-work. There were several log houses, with a quarter of an acre of ground attached, which formed the city at that time. . . . Not much there but whisky, and it would take a month's wages to buy a gill with the money we were paid with! About eighty dollars good money would buy a quarter of an acre of ground with a log house on it then, but I would not have had one even for a gift if I had to stay there; it was such a poor place and I thought always would be.

— John Harris

At the close of the Sullivan Campaign, the 4th Continental Artillery was dispersed in all directions. A great many members at this time retired from the Army for good, and for the remainder of the war the regiment would operate in four different sections of the country. One element of the Artillery was stationed in Carlisle, Pa., at the ordnance depot; some companies were dispatched to nearby Lancaster; one was ordered from Carlisle to Fort Pitt; and the remainder continued with the main body of Washington's army, under Generals Horatio Gates and Nathanael Greene, operating in the South.[1]

But before they got so much scattered, Proctor's 4th Continental Artillery spent the winter with Washington's main army at Washington's favorite wintertime encampment, Morristown. Some soldiers had been referring to the January-April months of 1777 as the "coldest winter ever," and some would always remember Valley Forge, "the coldest winter of the war." But the winter of 1779-80 came as if it were the end of everything. This, declared old-timers, was the "worst winter in 100 years." When General De Kalb marched into the Morristown encampment on November 26 of 1779 with his division, he began the experience of the "harshest winter" he had ever known. The bitter cold, without let-up, dictated privations for the soldiers equal to or greater than those suffered at Valley Forge. The mutiny that Washington had feared and had expected at Valley Forge, was, here at Morristown, because of the impossible conditions, even more likely to occur.

It was a familiar countryside for most of the soldiers. Some were returning to their huts in the popular Jockey Hollow, and some were locating again at Fort Nonsense. But most of the necessary huts had to be rebuilt or built from scratch. For a time the soldiers slept out in the open, in the snow. Only some days after the arrival of troops did the wagons appear with the tents. They had to make do with the tents until the huts were completed. Most men moved into their huts around Christmas time.

It was the second winter that Washington had elected to make his headquarters here at Morristown, and the region around Morristown was beginning to be known as The Revolution's Military Capital.[2] The advantages remained the same as on the first occasion, but the encampment this time was more vast. The principal elements of the Continental Army were here, 13,000 men. And they had to be provided for. Fortunately, Quartermaster General Nathanael Greene was a good provider. He was able to acquire, besides the essential military supplies, food and clothing sufficient to see them through. And he was able to ensure that provisions were fairly distributed. Greene was their salvation.

Here in the encampment also was General Arthur St. Clair. He made his headquarters the big farmhouse on the Wick Farm, which that summer had produced, together with adjacent farms, great quantities of grain (buckwheat, oats, rye, wheat, and corn), and lots of apples. Major General Knox was in camp, and so was Colonel Proctor with his 4th Regiment of Artillery, and Lord Stirling. Serving still in Proctor's Regiment as one of the company commanders was Captain Isaac Craig, and members of his company were Sergeant Samuel Blackwood and Bombardier John Harris. All in all, General Knox had in his Artillery Park a corps of forty-nine companies (1607 men and sixty cannon).

Washington, paying a generous rent, had made his headquarters the Jacob Ford mansion. Jacob Ford had died on January 11, 1777, but his wife and their four children continued to reside in the house. Washington would be headquartered here from December 1, 1779, until June 10, 1780.

It was a tough winter, because of the extreme cold, and because there was very little activity for the enlisted men. But the British were still in New York City, and their patrols were out, and foraging for provisions produced the familiar run-ins and skirmishing. One incident of the war that is not well known occurred in January of this winter.

Washington had the impression that the British troops quartered on Staten Island, some 1200 strong, were not in good communication with the British forces in the other areas of greater New York. Perhaps remembering the success at Trenton, he resolved to make a surprise wintertime assault on these forces. Placing Lord Stirling in command of 2500 men, he scheduled the attack for the night of January 14-15. He ordered Brigadier General Henry Knox to provide the artillery support.

Knox promptly detailed Captain Isaac Craig, in whose company bombardier John Harris was presently serving, to command the artillery unit, which was to include four six-pounders and two five and one-half howitzers. Craig was ordered to leave Morristown not later than one o'clock p.m. on January 14, and was advised that "Your order must be so regulated as to reach Elizabethtown by ten or eleven o'clock that night."[3]

Captain Craig with his men did arrive on schedule, joining there the infantry forces, whereupon the whole detachment crossed the ice to Staten Island. But "the best laid plans . . . ." The operation was promptly aborted when it was discovered (1) that the British troops were impregnably fortified, and (2) that communications with British forces elsewhere in New York were in fact open, so that reinforcements could be easily brought up.[4]

In the retreat that followed, the patriots suffered some losses to the pursuing British cavalry, but no major battle ever did occur, and Craig's company of artillery was able to salvage all of its field guns.

Both Bombardier John Harris and Sergeant Samuel Blackwood must certainly have participated in this mission, and it can be thought likely that they were members of the gun crew manning one of Craig's six-pounders.

Four weeks later, in the same week as Washington's birthday, there occurred at the encampment a big celebration. Organized by John and Eleanor Hodge Boylan, the affair was to celebrate, on its first anniversary, the Alliance between France and the United States, which had been consummated on February 6 a year ago; but because Washington, who was to be the honored guest, was unable to be in camp at that time, the festive event was postponed to the 18th.

General Knox, whose headquarters were not far from the Boylan home, had pledged the participation of the artillery. The Artillery Park was handy, and Knox had earlier ordered the clearing of some avenues at the rear of the Boylan house, for easier access to the Park, which occupied the vast fields beyond. These avenues were known as General Knox's Lanes.

The Boylans were calling their entertainment the Grand Alliance Ball. Four hundred people had been invited, seventy ladies and three hundred and some gentlemen.

The affair was held on the grounds of the Boylan estate, on the northwest side of the Cornelius Eoff Farm. The letters of General Knox provide a very full description of the occasion. The "genteel entertainment" was provided by his artillery, with their fifes and drums. It all began at four o'clock in the afternoon with the discharge, by Knox's artillery (including bombardier John Harris), of thirteen cannon. After dinner, which was opened with some polite toasting and many expressions of patriotic sentiment, the artillery supplied some extravagant "illuminating" fireworks, which "were more than pretty." Then the dancing was begun, with Washington (who loved to dance) and Lucy Knox the first couple, in an elegant room of the

Academy Building of the village of Pluckemin.[5] "We danced all night," remembered Henry Knox.

No such festivity was being enjoyed by Colonel Daniel Brodhead, Commander of the Western Department, who had long been appealing to Washington for more men and supplies for the garrison at Fort Pitt. Washington, of course, had nothing in the way of artillery to send him. In fact, as before noted, on December 21, 1778, before the Sullivan Expedition was formed, the Pennsylvania State regiment of artillery showed a complement of only 208 men, and of these, seven were absent sick, and seven were on furlough. By March 19 of 1779, the total offensive force, officers and men, had dwindled to 142.[6]

But by March 29 of 1780, five months after the close of the Sullivan Campaign, numbers had improved a little. A general return of the Pennsylvania regiments of artillery, signed by adjutant Samuel Storey, showed 188 names under that of the commanding officer, Colonel Thomas Proctor. One of the seven company captains listed is Captain Craig; one of the nine bombardiers is John Harris. And demands had so much diminished that the War Office began to make arrangements for a detachment of Proctor's artillery to remove to Fort Pitt. From the War Office, at some time early in the spring, Captain Isaac Craig, then at Morristown, received relayed orders from Washington to take command of a detachment of artillery and to proceed from Carlisle to the support of the Fort Pitt garrison.

Craig, who, like Proctor, had been born in Ireland, and who, again like Proctor, had become a Philadelphia carpenter, was at this time thirty-eight years old. He had served as a company captain in Colonel Thomas Proctor's regiment since March 3 of 1777, and had crossed the Delaware with Washington and had fought at Trenton and at Princeton, as well as in the battle of the Brandywine, where his company suffered severely, and in the battle of Germantown. He had been in Carlisle, as a student of munitions, learning the art of the military laboratory, from February 1 through August 1 of 1778. After a month-long stint as commander of the Billingsport Fort on the

Delaware, he served under Proctor on the Sullivan Expedition, and had been at Morristown for the past six months.[7]

In response to the appeal made by Craig on April 20 for specific instructions, Colonel Timothy Pickering,[8] at the time a member of the Board of War, promptly replied:

Sir, in answer to your request of this day for sundry matters relative to your march to Fort Pitt, we have to inform you–

Forage is to be obtained in the usual way at the several posts by application to the quarter and forage-masters.

You have herewith an order on the several quarter-masters to supply you with the necessary teams and carriages for conveying to Fort Pitt the artillery and stores under your care and a particular order on Col. Davis, at Carlisle, for that purpose, and the supply of horse shoes and any other articles necessary for repairing the carriages on the way.

The eight men of Capt. Coren's company at Carlisle and Fort Pitt or other place westward of Philadelphia, you will take with you, and cause them to do duty in your company, subject, however, to the future orders of the Board or of the Commander-in-Chief.

We have no money, nor can we get any to defray the expenses of your march. If Col. Flower. C. G. of U. S., thinks it reasonable to make you an allowance for conducting the artillery and stores to Fort Pitt, we shall not object to it; the money so allowed you to be applied in the same manner as if given to a conductor of military stores.[9]

And in a second communication, dispatched on the very same day, Secretary Pickering, for the Board of War, provided Craig with the necessary authority: "Sir; You, having under your charge a quantity of artillery & artillery stores destined for Fort Pitt, all quarter-masters and forage-masters on the route are hereby directed to furnish you with the necessary forage for your horses, and also with horses to replace any that may fall on the march. We expect you will use this order with great prudence & economy, that the distresses of the public may not be increased, but in case of absolute necessity."[10]

And four days later authority went out from the Supreme Executive Council, in session in Philadelphia, ordering aid to Captain Craig all along the way:

To all concerned:

Capt. Craig, ordered by his Excellency Gen'l Washington, to Pittsburgh, with artillery and stores, applied to the Council for aid and assistance therein; on consideration,

Ordered, That the Lieutenants, Sub-Lieutenants, Justices of the Peace, and others of the respective counties thro' which Capt. Craig shall pass, do give him such aid & assistance in transporting the said stores & artillery as the occasion may require.[11]

On that same date, April 24, Colonel Brodhead from Fort Pitt expressed to Washington his gratification: "I am honored with a line from the Honorable Board of War, informing me that an officer of Procter's regiment with some stores and cannon were in readiness to be sent down as soon as the roads would permit and the means of transportation can be procured."[12]

When all seemed finally arranged, on May 13, the impatient Brodhead wrote directly to Captain Craig from his headquarters at Fort Pitt to acknowledge the ardors of the expedition, to urge him to come with all possible speed, and to advise him on the best route:

Sir: It is some weeks since his Excellency, the Commander-in-Chief, and the Honorable Board of War wrote me that you were ordered to this department with a number of cannon and military stores. I am aware of the difficulties you must meet with in obtaining carriage, &c., to enable you to proceed expeditiously, yet as the enemy are very troublesome to the settlement and it is becoming highly expedient for me to counteract their designs by some effective operation, I must request you to exert yourself as much as possible to reach this point before the first of June. It will be very hazardous to come up the Pennsylvania road, wherefore you are to come up the Virginia road, and if you find that the artillery and stores will be too much exposed upon any part of that road, you will halt and give me notice, so that a sufficient convoy may be sent you. I wish you to send me by the first conveyance a return of your strength and of the number and calibres of your ordnance, and the quantity of stores you have with you, or expect to be forwarded, that in case of deficiency I may make further applications.[13]

On the same day Brodhead, obviously in a big hurry for Craig's artillery, dispatched a memo to Washington: "I have wrote to the artillery officer [Captain Craig] to hurry up the artillery and stores, but I hear he is badly furnished with carriages and forage, which must prevent his marching with the expedition."[14]

But Captain Craig was shortly ready to go, and he was fully determined to follow a southern route. He understood that if he were to set out from Carlisle to pick up the regular road across Pennsylvania (the Great Road, known also as the Forbes Road),[15] he would have the shortest distance (160 miles) to negotiate; but he knew that Brodhead was right to caution him, that the hazards were real, that the Indian activity in central and western Pennsylvania was at this time intense. Besides, there was the terrain. The Forbes Road, though it had been traveled for nearly twenty years, was still only a woodland trail really, widened where necessary to permit the passage of wagons, and bristling with treacherous defiles, and formidable mountains, like Laurel Hill and Chestnut Ridge. But whatever route was followed, Craig knew, and so did his men, that it would be a rough trip, a test for the most hardy.

Years afterward Harris remembered that "A part of the army, I among them, was sent across the mountains to Fort Pitt, now Pittsburg. What route we went I cannot tell. There was not even a wagon road farther than Gettysburg."

In the end, Craig elected to proceed south and then west and then north to Fort Pitt, following a course that would take him chiefly through Maryland and only barely into Virginia.

On May 23, from the way station known as McAllister's,[16] just south of Carlisle, Captain Craig, at the head of a modest company of some fifty soldiers (many fewer than the standard complement) of Proctor's 4th Continental Artillery, which included Sergeant Samuel Blackwood and Bombardier John Harris and which was equipped with the guns and supplies it had been provided, and furnished with pack horses and cannon carriages, and ammunition wagons, set out for Fort Pitt, 230 miles away.

Harris had got close to home, but not home; and he still had had no communication with any member of his family. He was not aware that his mother had died, and he did not know anything about the British occupation of Salem or the Battle of Quinton's Bridge, in which three of his brothers had participated. He was now on his way to Fort Pitt. He understood that he was being returned to the Indian country, and he did not particularly relish the prospect.

The first day of the long march, because the men and the horses were fresh and more than eager to be moving, would turn out to be its best. The detachment, moving southwest, marched a remarkable fourteen miles, almost reaching Shippensburg. On the next day, at Shippensburg, they lingered some, to rest the horses and to work out improvements to their methods of transport.

By the 26th the expedition had reached the Little Conococheague Creek in the oak and hickory hardwoods regions of present-day Washington County, Maryland, on what is today the Ashton Road.

On the 27th the company encamped at the Pauling's settlement, a little west and north of the confluence of the Conococheague Creek and the Potomac River, the site of Williamsport, which village had been founded by General Otho Holland Williams, a close friend of Washington.

They had reached the Indian country, and now the prospect of hostile savages became an everyday concern. As they were following the trail the Indians regularly used, the possibility of ambushing warriors was ever in their minds; but Captain Craig, unlike General Sullivan, did not sound the cannon each morning to announce the progress of the expedition. He much preferred to move through the wilderness quite undetected. And so he urged extreme caution, "as little disturbance as possible." He regularly dispatched scouts forward, and not until he had the "all clear" would he order the company to proceed.

Fresh venison would have been a welcome treat for the soldiers, but Craig preferred not to alarm whatever Indians might be in the vicinity, and, besides, he felt amply provisioned.

Remembering that the supplies were carried by pack mules, Harris recalled that "We would start a train when the path was reported clear of Indians. They could run almost equal to a deer or lie flat as a rabbit and hide where there was almost nothin'. I did not admire the Indians' character. They would lie and steal anything they could lay their hands on. We had a great many skirmishes with them, but not much we could call a battle. Their warfare was to get behind trees and shoot from cover. In one of our skirmishes I was not feeling very good and an Irishman said to me, 'Braize up, Harris: This day a golden chain or a wooden leg.' I told him I thought the prospect for a golden chain was not very bright, fighting Indians, when they could carry all they had on their backs and run with it."

Fortunately, Harris and Blackwood and Captain Craig, and those who had been with them on the Sullivan Expedition, as well as a few who were veterans of Hartley's campaign, knew something of the Indian methods, and were able to size up situations promptly. And fortunately, the Indians never seemed to appear in great numbers.

As they left the flat country of Carlisle, and eastern Pennsylvania, and proceeded through Maryland west up the Potomac River, the soldiers found the terrain increasingly difficult. Even though they favored the river valleys, they had somehow to traverse the Shenandoah Mountain range, and that would only bring them deeper into the endless Alleghanies. The road, or more properly the trail, was rough beyond description, here and there swampy, and much of the time rocky and mountainous. The artillery, pulled by horses, slowed the train considerably, and fatigue, in the horses, in the pack mules, and in the men themselves, regularly showed up early in the afternoon.

Because they followed the Potomac and the lesser streams, they had lots of mosquitoes to contend with, and great clouds of gnats, and deer flies and greenheads. These did little to lessen their woes; and the swampy places could be depended upon to intensify even more their insect agonies. From time to time, one soldier or another would exclaim, the irritation resounding to both ends of the column, "These *dang* flies. I'd rather see a mess o' Indians come charging out of them woods there yonder, than have to fight these *dang* flies. *Damn* them. *Damn* them all to hottest hell."

Somebody wanted to know how the Indians managed with all of these flies and mosquitoes. "Hell if I know," said one soldier. "Eat 'em probably."

"Bear fat," explained another.

"Ugh," grunted his neighbor.

Sergeant Blackwood, who had assumed responsibility for the pack mules and the horses, felt for the animals. He knew that they had thick hides, but endless waves of flies and mosquitoes were everywhere about them all the time, and that constant thrashing of the tails could only mean that the animals were not indifferent to the bites. Besides, in the ever growing heat the horses wanted water. Blackwood never missed an opportunity to get the horses and mules to whatever stream they came to, and fortunately the company was never very far from the Potomac, or from some tributary.

But the springs! What a joy it was for the company to come upon a mountain spring, a tiny pool of clear, cold water, with clean sand at its bottom, and sometimes embraced by a structure of stones fashioned by some wayfarer, with a large flat one provided for kneeling. More precious than his musket, or his tent, or even his boots, was the soldier's leather or wooden canteen; and at such a spring he would fill it gratefully.

Happily, the ever cautious Captain Craig did permit swimming. And whenever the company elected to camp near the Potomac, most of the soldiers, Harris and Blackwood among them, were quick to gambol in the refreshing water, a refuge from the heat and from the relentless flies.

From time to time they sensed the presence of Indians, and from time to time they had their suspicions confirmed. Wraith-like, the savages would float among the shadows, vanishing so abruptly and completely as to make their appearance seem unreal. But what Harris would later recall as "skirmishing" was hardly ever that, and though some run-ins did occur, no real assault was ever made upon the caravan. The Indians seemed more curious than hostile. "Uneventful" was the tag that Craig would finally place upon the trip.

But the night sounds. Although wearied as they always were at the end of the day's march, and though they knew sentries were posted, sleep did not come easily. From the forest darkness emerged an unsettling symphony of sound: the *hoohoohoo hoohoo hoo* of the great horned owl, the mournful howling of the wolves, and the haunting call of the spectral whippoorwill. Sometimes so close would sound the *whip-poor-willll* that the soldiers could make out the little cluck at the end of the call. And often this call, as well as the hooting of the owl, would produce in them the chilling wonder whether it might not be a signal sounded by some cunning savage. John Harris had been told that the Indians never attack at night, and his experience on the Sullivan Expedition had tended to confirm that. Nevertheless, on the nights when they were "camping out," the soldiers fell into their fitful sleep "with finger on the trigger."

From Pauling's three more days were required to pass beyond Jacquese's Furnace and to reach Licking Creek, still in Washington County in the north-central section of the state. On the last day of May the detachment found itself at Old Flint's, not far from Sideling Hill Creek in Allegany County.

Now as they proceeded up the Potomac, they found the roads hilly but in general clear of stone and passable. The flats along the river they found indifferent but at times very narrow.

By June 3, almost two weeks into the march, the artillerymen had reached Old Town (present-day Oldtown), a settlement situated on the banks of the Potomac, some 160 miles upriver from present-day Washington, D.C., and near the point, just west of the junction of the North and South branches of the Potomac, where the Warriors' Trail crossed the river. It was the Warriors' Trail which accommodated the Iroquois on their expeditions south. Here at Old Town, Colonel Thomas Cresap, an agent for the Ohio Company, had established a trading house almost forty years before. Craig's company discovered the place to consist of only about a dozen houses, set back about one-

The Potomac River, at Oldtown

quarter of a mile to the north of the river.[17]

Because of the nasty weather and the need for rest, Captain Craig's company spent three days and part of a fourth at Old Town. Then, much refreshed, the detachment set out, still upstream on the north branch of the Potomac. They experienced a great deal of difficulty in crossing at a narrows, a place where the mountain reaches down so close to the river as to provide only a very thin strip of land for the road . Here it could be seen that only the slightest rain would result in washouts and extreme difficulty for travelers. Fortunately the gorge through which they were forced to pass at this point was not so very long.

Wills Creek presented another problem, for it was surprisingly deep and swift. Still the column made remarkably good time upstream along the river, accomplishing fifteen miles fast enough to reach Fort Cumberland on the 8th of June.

As they came into view of the historic fort, a giant redtail, as if to put a period to this first portion of their long journey, made great lazy circles high in the air above them. And the clamorous honking of a gaggle of geese lifting off from the river, seemed, to soldiers made vain by achievement, a generous welcome.

The settlement at Cumberland had grown up on the site of the trading post which had been established here, at the junction of Wills Creek and the north branch of the Potomac, in 1750 by the Ohio Company. The village was considered the gateway to the west. Roads ran out from the cluster of houses in all directions, south into Virginia, north into Pennsylvania, east through Maryland, and west through the Appalachians toward the Ohio Valley. Trails used by the Indians ran close along the streams. It was a busy place.

John Harris and his fellow artillerymen could not have known, but they were now assembled at the very spot from which their General George Washington twenty-seven years ago, when he was but twenty-one years old, had set out on his historic mission in the service of the Honorable Robert Dinwiddie, the colonial governor of Virginia. With the famous frontiersman Christopher Gist as his guide, Washington was headed for Fort Le Boeuf, about twelve miles south of present-day Erie, Pa., to advise the French to withdraw from the territory, as it belonged to the British. And Captain Craig's artillerymen could not have known that on this expedition the wily and resourceful Gist twice saved the life of the young Washington.[18]

It was Washington who later proposed the site for a British fort, and in 1754 a kind of rude stockade was built and called Mount Pleasant In the very next year, when General Edward Braddock had the fort enlarged, he also had it renamed after his close friend the Duke of Cumberland. It was Fort Cumberland that provided the starting point that year (1755) for Braddock's ill-starred campaign against Fort Duquesne. This British army post at Cumberland was in its early years garrisoned by Colonel George Washington's Virginia Regiment and by the soldiers of Braddock's successor, the colonial governor William Shirley. In fact, it was from Fort Cumberland that the twenty-three-year-old soldier George Washington returned from the dead. By a hair's breadth he had escaped from the ambush of Braddock on the banks of the Monongahela in July. He had had two horses shot from under him, and four bullets had pierced his coat. To the colony of Virginia he had been reported lost. Now from the fort in Cumberland, in a letter to his brother, he rather whimsically observed: "As I have had since my arrival in this place, a circumstantial account of my death and dying, I take this early opportunity of contradicting both . . . ."[19]

Cumberland, because of its strategic location, was a very important frontier fort. It was an essential stockade to the settlers for protection and refuge; and, naturally, it was constantly being harassed by Indians.[20]

Craig's company had marched by this time about 125 miles in seventeen days, but still had almost that much farther to go to reach Fort Pitt.

At Cumberland, the soldiers said goodbye to the Potomac and continued their westward trek. Happily, they now had a "pretty good" road to follow. This was the wagon road that had first been opened in 1752, running from Cumberland to the Youghiogheny River in southwestern Pennsylvania. In 1755 it had been improved and extended. By the time of Craig's expedition it could be considered a "well traveled highway." The pack horses were glad to see it.

During the next two weeks the artillery train passed through settlements or farms in western Maryland known as Hall's, Tittle's, and Tomlinson's. Everywhere the men were received warmly, and the horses were provided for and replaced by fresh ones. Captain Craig very rarely had to present the authority provided him by the Board of War.

Eventually Craig turned north into Pennsylvania in what is today Fayette County, reaching on June 16 the site of the settlement established by Washington's guide the pioneer Christopher Gist, with eleven other families, in 1753. This settlement was close to the communities that are today known as Connellsville and Uniontown. It had been destroyed by the French at the outbreak of the French and Indian Wars.

On June 22, the company finally reached the Forbes Road, which it had abandoned at Carlisle. It had arrived at the fort known as Walthour's. This stockade, which included an array of buildings, one of which was a blockhouse, had been built by Christopher Walthour in 1774 in what is now Penn Township in Westmoreland County to provide protection to the mostly German settlers from Indian attacks. It was located about equidistant (one and one-half miles) from Adamsburg to the west and Harrison City to the south.[21]

Captain Craig was not going to have his artillery at Fort Pitt by June 1, as Colonel Brodhead had hoped, but the troop was getting very close.

The next place of rest, a little north and west, was the stagecoach stop known as Widow Meyers'. Sometimes called Widow Meyers' Wayside Inn, or Tavern, it was located at what is today the corner of Sycamore and Sixth Streets in Turtle Creek.

As the artillery train got ever closer to Fort Pitt, it slowed down dramatically, presumably because of fatigue. On the next day it managed only five miles, coming to rest at Bullock Pens, just ten miles east of Fort Pitt. At that time Bullock Pens was a small settlement in what is now greater Pittsburgh in Allegheny County. It had acquired some little fame because of the vibrant preaching of the pioneer Presbyterian minister the Reverend Charles Clinton Beatty, who had been with General John Forbes' army after the fall of Fort Duquesne. The church here and the settlement were called Bullock Pens because the community had developed in the area where General Forbes penned his beef cattle during the French and Indian Wars. Bullock Pens is today known as Churchill.

The expedition had but ten miles of its 230-mile journey yet to traverse. It had not reached Fort Pitt at the hoped for time, but it had made the trip in just a little over a month, averaging over seven miles a day. Dragging cannons and toting supplies and ammunition, with the need to care for the horses and the pack animals, and the concern for Indians, and rugged terrain, the soldiers had acquitted themselves well. The company had not lost a man, nor a piece of artillery. The mission, though tardy, had to be considered a success.

But by the end of this laborious and nervous trek across western Maryland and a portion of what was then Virginia and a chunk of western Pennsylvania it certainly would have taken a spectacle more ravishing than what finally appeared before the weary soldiers to lift their spirits. As they neared their destination, Bombardier John Harris was not impressed: "We finally arrived at Pittsburg, a poor place then,–not even a frame house in it. There was a line of soldiers' barracks, frame-work. There were several log houses, with a quarter of an acre of ground attached, which formed the city at that time. There was no road across the mountain, and from Gettysburg everything was carried by pack-mules. Not much there [in Pittsburg] but whisky, and it would take a month's wages to buy a gill with the money we were paid with! About eighty dollars good money would buy a quarter of an acre of ground with a log house on it then, but I would not have had one even for a gift if I had to stay there; it was such a poor place and I thought always would be."

Nevertheless, Captain Craig had the company pause at the first view of the fort, which had for so long been their object. Craig was not much for pretty speeches. He never adorned his instructions with any kind of inspiriting phrase or commendation. Here he said only, "Boys, there she is. We've made it." Then after a moment, he issued the troop's last directive: "We're not going to march in at quick-step, but we are going to march in smartly. Everybody straighten up. We're here."

So, on the 25th day of June the little company, footsore and fatigued, heavily bearded and weathered in the face, marched smartly into Fort Pitt. The enthusiastic welcome which they received from Colonel Brodhead and the Fort Pitt garrison made them all feel pretty good about what they had accomplished, despite their heavy weariness. A happy Brodhead promptly advised Washington of the successful appearance of Captain Craig's detachment: "The artillery has arrived and the military stores are safely lodged."[22]

And it was not long before the soldiers realized just how much their presence was needed. They were quickly made to know that they were expected to make a difference.

Actually, Harris could not know just how very bad conditions were in the region protected by Fort Pitt. To make themselves more secure from the Indians, families were bunching up, two or three to one log house or cabin. Because men were afraid to work the fields, or to go into the forest to hunt, food was always in short supply. Those fathers and sons who did venture into the fields often never returned; and sometimes when they did come back to the house it was to find the family disappeared or murdered. Westmoreland County historians report that "from 1778 to 1782 there was scarcely a family within the limits of our present county that had bread sufficient to subsist on from fall to spring."[23]

The Indian threat had been for many years so serious that bounties were being paid for scalps. The bounty hunters were most active in the years 1781 and 1782, when the going rate was $100 for a dead Indian's scalp, and $150 for an Indian brought into the garrison alive. Even the scalps of women and children appeared![24]

Desperately endeavoring to protect the families settled in western Pennsylvania was Daniel Brodhead, of the Sullivan-Clinton-Brodhead Expedition fame, who was at this time in command of the Western Department, with headquarters at Fort Pitt. Brodhead had succeeded Brigadier General Lachlan McIntosh, who had on August 8, 1778, succeeded Brigadier General Edward Hand. He was responsible for Fort Pitt of course, and for the many other forts and stockades in the Western Department. Besides Pitt, the two most important forts were Fort Laurens (named after Henry Laurens, President of Congress), which had been built late in November 1778 on the banks of the Tuscarawas River, in the heart of the Indian country, near present-day Bolivar, Ohio;[25] and Fort McIntosh (named for General Lachlan McIntosh) twenty miles down the Ohio from Fort Pitt, at present-day Beaver, Pa. Lesser forts were Crawford, Shippen, Allen, Wallace, Armstrong, and Lochry's Blockhouse. These garrisoned forts of course were to provide protection for the settlers, and refuge. Brodhead felt that the building of both Laurens and McIntosh was a mistake, as they were so difficult to maintain.

Captain Craig and his artillery company found him a nervous

and anxious man. Certainly he had his hands full with the hostiles and with the ever more unhappy "friendly" Delawares. In February of 1780, more than four months beyond the close of the Sullivan-Clinton Campaign, he had been still sounding the alarm from Fort Pitt. He had for a long time been expecting an expedition of hostile Indians to emerge from the fort at Niagara to come down the Allegheny "to pay me a visit early in the Spring."

While that assault did never occur, Brodhead had *many* depredations in Westmoreland County to report. So numerous were these incursions, together with the familiar atrocities, that the Colonel had very seriously considered mounting an expedition against the Shawnee and the Wyandot.

He also had continued in his designs on Detroit. He remained hopeful that he could launch a successful expedition against the British stronghold, and thus put an end to the Indian hostilities. On February 11, he expressed his concern in a letter to Pennsylvania's President Joseph Reed: "I sincerely wish to see a reinforcement from the main Army, for I am really apprehensive of a visit from Niagara."[26] But in the middle of March, Washington, advising that no support would be forthcoming from the East, had insisted that Brodhead give up his plans to proceed against Detroit. The Commander-in-Chief urged him to meet the Indian threat through "short excursions against hostile tribes."[27]

Brodhead was not discouraged. Two weeks later he penned to George Rogers Clark a letter in which he expressed his great confidence that before the year was out he would possess Detroit: "I think it is probable that before next Winter I shall have the pleasure of taking you by the hand somewhere upon the waters of lake Erie."[28] But the dream was dashed by an April 29 letter from President Reed. He explained to Brodhead that while the Pennsylvania legislature had voted four companies for the defense of the western frontiers they would not be coming, because there were simply no supplies.[29]

Less than a week after Brodhead had received the letter from Reed, the expected trouble arrived. It came in the form of a wanton destruction leveled by the Iroquois at the settlements along Brush Creek, a small stream that enters the Monongahela east of Pittsburgh.[30]

Captain Craig with his artillery unit, arriving at Fort Pitt on June 25 of 1780 plunged right into the middle of the Indian depredations which had been continuing since the Brush Creek affair and well into the summer. While John Harris and the 50-man detachment from Proctor's artillery had been trudging to Fort Pitt to carry on the war against the British and their Indian allies in the Western Theater, the principal action had moved steadily south from the New England colonies and New York and New Jersey into the Southern Campaign. But Harris and his fellows had heard nothing of Charleston and Savannah, and of that elusive patriot general called the Swamp Fox. Since setting out for Pittsburgh they had in fact had almost no news at all from the East; but in August there came to Fort Pitt the report of the disaster suffered by the Continental forces at Camden, South Carolina.

Harris was much saddened by the news that General De Kalb had been mortally wounded. He had not ever had to answer directly to De Kalb, and actually had not had any close association with the General during the winter at Valley Forge, but he had known him well enough, and had known enough about him, to know that he genuinely liked the bluff German-Frenchman. And when you go through something like Valley Forge, and survive, you naturally become very close to those who suffered with you, regardless of any difference in rank.

De Kalb battlefield monument

Few details of the battle at Camden were available from the account that came to Fort Pitt, and only a very sketchy impression of the disastrous defeat suffered by the Continental Army was possible. Later the garrison would learn that the battle was fought in the wooded swamps of South Carolina, in the Gum Swamp and at Sanders Creek, a few miles to the north of Camden, and that it was General Gates[31] against Lord Cornwallis, who had marched from Charleston. They learned that it was indeed a catastrophe for the Continentals, that the battle, owing chiefly to mismanagement on the part of Gates, was turned into an utter rout. Though of course he was grieved over the death of De Kalb, Harris was, when he got the story much later, gratified, though not surprised, to hear of the gallantry of the General. De Kalb, who was second in command to Gates, had been placed in charge of the right wing, at the head of one regiment of Delaware troops and two brigades of the Maryland Division. Even though, unbeknownst to them, the other divisions of Gates's army had fled the field in panic, De Kalb's soldiers offered a fierce and very stubborn resistance to the advancing Redcoats, fighting on, even while totally surrounded and enveloped by fire. The heroic death of General De Kalb, for his friend Lafayette, and for Bombardier John Harris, and for anybody who knew the courageous officer, would always be one of the most memorable and saddest moments of the entire Revolution. De Kalb, after his horse had been shot from under him, continued to fight on foot, shoulder to shoulder with his loyal troops of the

General De Kalb monument in Camden, South Carolina

Maryland Second Brigade. Finally he fell, mortally wounded, stricken with three musket balls, and pierced eight times by British bayonets. The General was saved from instant death by his lieutenant Charles Dubuysson.[32] As he was being carried away, he could not believe what he was being told, that for the Americans all was lost.

This news did little to lift the spirits of the Fort Pitt garrison. For some it seemed, indeed, that the War of the Revolution had been lost, and easily it could have been that. The Battle of Camden, fought on August 16, 1780, was possibly the most disastrous defeat suffered by the Colonials in the six years of fighting.

And one thing it meant for certain sure, there would be no more relief coming from the East to Fort Pitt.

Depredations continued throughout the summer, and in September Brodhead repeats from Fort Pitt to Washington his growing anxiety: "I have this moment rec'd intelligence that the Enemy from Detroit is paying a visit to this frontier . . . . The Delaware Runners add that a party of twenty Indian warriors have been discovered about six days ago marching toward these settlements & that a large party of Senecas may soon be expected down the Allegheny River. Last week seven persons were killed & taken by the Savages in an interior settlement on Ten mile creek." He expresses again the hope that Washington may be able to send reinforcements to Pittsburgh.

At about the same time, in another communication to Washington, Brodhead disclosed just how desperate the situation had become: "The whole Garrison, with Serjeants to lead them, came to my quarters a few days ago to represent that they had not rec'd any bread for five days together."[33] For those who remembered the winter of 1778 it was Valley Forge all over again.

Later that month, on the 23rd, he repeats his chronic worry to Jefferson, at that time Governor of Virginia: "I have received intelligence that a Thousand British Regulars and a great number of Indians are on their March towards this Frontier." Fortunately for Fort Pitt, which could not have been defended against such a force, this report was apparently the product of somebody's lively imagination. No such army ever appeared.

As the year 1780 wound down, conditions at Fort Pitt worsened dramatically. Looked for reinforcements had not arrived, provisions, including food and clothing, were in desperately short supply.

Hunting parties that were dispatched up the Allegheny and down the Ohio produced woefully inadequate amounts of game. Desertions were occurring at an ever-increasing rate, and replacements for the garrison were almost impossible to secure. The Delawares, the Indians most friendly yet to the Americans, were becoming increasingly uneasy and less eager to supply runners and information. Fort Pitt, by December of 1780, would have been easy pickings for any well organized force of Butler's Rangers and the Iroquois. It was most surprising that British victories in the eastern theater had not yet inspired such an expedition in the west against Fort Pitt.[34] This was the situation into which Captain Isaac Craig had brought his artillery company. And prospects for improvement were difficult to perceive.

It was not the war that was being fought in the East. It was war against the Indians. Fortunately for John Harris and his fellow soldiers, it was a familiar war. They had had some experience with Indians, and were accustomed to their duplicities and tricks. This experience would stand them in good stead.

As Brodhead had been expecting, negotiations with the ever more hungry and ever more impatient Delawares finally that winter collapsed altogether. Aware that the Delawares were planning to assault settlements in his territory of the western frontier, and perhaps even Fort Pitt itself, Brodhead got up one of those striking forces that Washington had recommended. With 150 regular troops of the Continental Army and that many more (some say three times that many more!) from local militia units, and sharp-shooting Indian fighters from the Fort Henry area of Virginia (now West Virginia), he marched from Pittsburgh on April 7, bound for the largest community of Delawares in the region. This was the town of Coshocton, which had been built at the junction of the Muskingum and Tuscarawas Rivers, more than 100 miles west of Pittsburgh, in what is now Ohio.[35]

It is not known whether John Harris was a member of this expedition. He makes no mention of it. If indeed he was, it is to be hoped that he was not a party to the cruelties which were practiced on the Indians by Brodhead's soldiers. Not only was the village of Coshocton wiped out, but the nearby town of Lichtenau was destroyed as well. And, besides the rampant pillaging which characterized the behavior of the troops, there occurred the cold-blooded murder of many, perhaps all, of the captive Delaware warriors.[36] And even all of that was not, apparently, enough for Brodhead. According to one account he was eager to lay waste some additional Delaware towns, "but his troops, feeling that they had accomplished enough, were unwilling to accompany him,"and thus all returned to Pittsburgh.[37] The campaign was not one of the war's most glorious events. It was not Colonel Brodhead's finest hour.

The Coshocton affair took place in April. From a time long before, as early as February, George Rogers Clark, who in March had established headquarters in the home of Washington's friend William Crawford on the Youghiogheny near Connellsville, and also with Dorsey Pentecost on Chartiers Creek, had been trying to assemble sufficient men and supplies to outfit an expedition down the Ohio. He had drawn up a plan to put an end to the Indian threat. What he hoped to do was to invade the Indian country, there to burn their houses, destroy their crops, and do whatsoever damage could be effected. It sounded to Brodhead and to Archibald Lochry, who was the county lieutenant, very like the expedition Brodhead had himself conducted up the Allegheny, and very like the Sullivan campaign up the Susquehanna.

Washington's reaction to the proposal gave the project some expectation of success. Writing to Jefferson, who was also being counted on for help, the Commander-in-Chief indicated that he was ready to give the plan his blessing. "I have ever been of the opinion," he wrote, "that the reduction of the post of Detroit would be the only certain means of giving peace and security to the whole western frontier, and I have constantly kept my eye upon that object . . . . I shall think it a most happy circumstance, should your State, with the aid of Continental stores which you require, be able to accomplish it."[38]

Brodhead, who was lukewarm on the enterprise, having himself such an expedition in mind, also had a communication from Washington on the matter. Washington made it plain that he expected Brodhead to lend every possible assistance, declaring that he expected Clark's requests for whatever supplies or troops he may need to be fulfilled, including a company of artillery, just as large as could be spared. Washington's orders to Brodhead on the question of artillery were unequivocal: "You will likewise direct the officers with the company of artillery to be ready to move, when Colonel Clark shall call for them."[39] And then he added a line which, because Brodhead seemed always a little embarrassed by Clark, or envious of him, might have annoyed the Commander of the Western Department some. "I do not think," wrote the Commander-in-Chief, "the charge of the enterprise could have been committed to a better hand than Colonel Clark's. I have not the pleasure of knowing the gentleman; but, independently of the proofs he has given of his activity and address, the unbounded confidence, which I am told the western people repose in him, is a matter of most importance."[40]

But Washington, noting that most of the men who might be available to Clark from the Continental Army were already in great need by General Nathanael Greene, made it clear that he could not promise much beyond the troops that could be supplied by Fort Pitt.

Still the plan was approved by those who mattered, and Clark continued with his arrangements. Originally, it was expected that a sufficient force would be assembled at Fort Pitt by March 1, and that by March 15 the expedition would rendezvous at the Great Falls on the Ohio with the 500 militia men promised by the Kentucky regions known as Fayette, Lincoln, and Jefferson.

Now, obviously, it was not going to operate on that schedule. All kinds of delays occurred, in the securing not only of troops, but of supplies. There was a long wait for powder being shipped from Philadelphia and other provisions were not showing up in the hoped for time. Appalled by the condition of Craig's artillery company, Clark, on April 2, from Crawford's home on the Youghiogheny, penned a letter to the "Gentlemen of the Congress," in which he expressed his dismay. Besides, as spring came on, Brodhead, fearing both an attack from Detroit and a revolt of the Delawares, withdrew the promised regiment of Colonel John Gibson. And, worse, the pledge of Jefferson to contribute 2000 men to the expedition was squelched by no other than Patrick Henry. To the Virginia Assembly, Henry presented a resolution "to put a stop of the Expedition lately organized against Detroit, and to take all necessary steps for disposing of, or applying to other uses, the stores and provisions laid in for that purpose."[41]

And on top of all that, Clark was having absolutely no luck at all in trying to collect fighting men from Westmoreland County. He was impatient to get going and a little discouraged by the response to his recruiting efforts. He was accustomed to cooperation and the kind of enthusiastic support for his cause that characterized the small band of daring Virginians which under his command had taken the British-held installations of Kaskaskia, Cahokia, and Vincennes.[42] He was made most unhappy by the unwillingness of Brodhead and the militia units in the neighborhood of Pittsburgh to provide him the troops that he needed.

But Clark was a difficult man to discourage when he got hold of something. And he did have the support of Colonel Archibald Lochry, who commanded the militia in Westmoreland County, and, though Lochry could raise only one hundred men, and Clark had managed only four hundred, they decided to launch the expedition. Before setting out, Clark expressed his disappointment with the people of western Pennsylvania. To the governor of his native state, Thomas Jefferson, he described his feelings: "The anxiety I have, and the probability of loosing [sic] the fair prospect I had of putting an End to the Indian war Occasion me to View such Charracters in a most Dispickable light and to make this Representation. I do not suppose I shall have anything more to do with them, but should it be the case and had [I] the power [I] should take the necessary steps to teach them their duties before I went any farther."[43]

"Clark's Plan," as it was known, called first for an assault on the Shawnee and Delaware Indians settled to the west of the Scioto River, in what is now Ohio, and, second, the destruction of the Sandusky tribes. It was his idea that with his soldiers he would hit the Shawnees, with Lochry attacking the Sanduskies. At the close of these two campaigns the forces were to unite and consider further invasions of the Indian villages in the Ohio River valley.

The Colonials were forever launching expeditions against the Indians on the rivers, on the Susquehanna, on the Allegheny, on the Ohio. With the original plan suspended because of the unfortunate mis-timing, this expedition by Clark was now intended to go down the Ohio River to the Great Falls (Louisville),[44] where his force could be enriched by troops from Kentucky. His army at this time numbered four hundred, including the artillery company under Captain Isaac Craig, which had been delivered to Clark by Fort Pitt at the command of Washington. But Craig's company, though he had been appealing to Washington for more men, was horribly under quota, both in officers and enlisted men.

George Rogers Clark

On April 15, Craig had dispatched to Washington a request for more men. Washington ten days later advised Major General Arthur St. Clair that "Capt. Craig of Colo. Procters Regt. Of Artillery, who is stationed at Fort Pitt has applied to me to have his Company compleated; that cannot be done in the present state of the Regt. but you will be pleased to consult the Commanding Officer of it, and let Capt. Craig have as many men as will put his Company on a level with others."[45] At the same time Washington wrote directly to Craig on this matter (Washington was compelled, of course, to write hundreds of letters of this kind.), and enclosed letters for Craig to relay to General George Rogers Clark and Colonel Brodhead. The letter reads: "Sir, I have recd. your favr. of the 15th. The present State of Colo. Procter's Regt. does not admit of your Company's being made up to its full complement, but I have, by this conveyance desired Genl. St. Clair to let you have as many Men as will put you on a level with the others. This is all that can now be done. I have already desired the Board of War to send six Artificers to Fort Pitt, you may wait upon them with this letter and ask three or four more, if they can be spared."[46]

So the artillery company made available to Clark was not only short of men, it was painfully lacking in equipment (cannon, shells, and shot). In fact, in the way of cannon Clark would have only the three pieces supplied by Craig.

On June 8, Washington, troubled by what Clark's recent requests seemed to indicate about the state of the campaign, wrote directly to General Clark: "Sir: I this day received your favors of the 20th. and 21st. of May by Capt. Randolph and am sorry to find that your intended expedition against Detroit stands upon so precarious a footing. When Govr. Jefferson first proposed the plan to me he only asked for the Artillery and Stores and an Artillery Officer, but as I wished to give every support in my power to the undertaking which I deemed of great public import, I ordered Colo. Brodhead to detach Captain Craig with his whole company of Artillery and as many Men from the 8th. Penna. and 9th. Virginia Regts. as he could safely spare. That command I did not imagine could amount to more than a Captain's or Major's at most. Your present request of augmenting the number of Continental Troops to the whole of the 9th. Regiment and Heath's [Captain Henry Heth's] independent Company is what I cannot think myself at liberty to comply with, as it would be leaving the post of Pittsburgh in too defenceless a state to resist any attempt of an open enemy, to say nothing of the disaffected in the Vicinity, who from intelligence which comes from the same Quarter as that which I communicated to you, are numerous and ready to join the enemy whenever an opportunity offers."[47]

Washington, apparently under the impression that Clark, so much in need of additional men and supplies, is throwing in the bag, then closes out the letter expressing his regret that the expedition cannot go forward.

But it was going to go forward. Only some little change in plans. Because of all the delays in getting started the fleet was now composed of two separate forces, Clark's and Lochry's, which, however, were supposed to come together on the river. At the end of July, Clark, impatient to get going, pushed off, with his modest army, into the sweeping currents of the Ohio, "the beautiful river," which is formed at Fort Pitt by the junction of the Allegheny ("stream of the Alligewi") coming from the north, and the Monongahela ("high banks, breaking off and falling down at places"), coming from the south.

In all, his force consisted of about three hundred men, volunteers and militia rounded up from Westmoreland County and a regiment of Virginia state troops, together with the detachment of artillery from Fort Pitt commanded by Captain Craig. The artillery company, which included John Harris, carried three field pieces, a most inadequate ordnance, and the necessary horses and supplies.

By Ephraim Douglass of Pittsburgh, in a letter written to Brigadier General James Irvine of Philadelphia (who after four years a prisoner of war, had just returned home), Clark's setting out upon the river was vividly described about a month after the embarkation: "He left this place a month ago with a great many boats, large and small," remembered Douglass, "a very large quantity of flour, some salt, a good deal of Whisky and very little beef, and that little he chiefly lost before he got to Wheeling where he continued some days. When he left this place his force amounted to something more than three hundred–comprised of draughts from the militia, from Volunteer infantry and a small troop of Volunteer Horse,–Captain Craig's company of Cont. Artillery [from which one officer, one sergeant, and six matrosses had been withdrawn!], and colonel Crocket's regiment of Virginia State troops, with three pieces of field ordnance, including one Howitz, ordnance and other stores etc. etc. At and about Wheeling, he was joined by numbers from that country, to what amount I cannot tell, and deserted by near an hundred of the militia who left this [place] with him."[48]

Lochry had assembled his men, 106 experienced Indian fighters, at Carnahan's blockhouse, some ten or eleven miles northwest of Hannastown, on July 24. The next day he set out by way of Pittsburgh for Fort Henry (Wheeling, Virginia), where he was supposed to join Clark. He reached Fort Henry on August 4, only to discover that Clark had already moved on, leaving instructions for Lochry to meet him twelve miles down river. But Lochry was further delayed at Fort Henry, as he needed to outfit some additional boats. When he did finally get to the appointed meeting place, Lochry found only another note. This time he was urged to join Clark farther down the Ohio, at the point where the Kanawha enters the larger stream. Tenaciously Lochry set out again in pursuit of the phantom Clark. Too late again. This time he found that Clark had erected a conspicuous pole in the riverbank, and to it had pinned a letter which directed Lochry to proceed now all the way down river to the Great Falls (Louisville). Through all of this what neither was sufficiently aware of was that bands of Indians were from both banks of the river constantly observing the boats, watchful for any opportunity for ambush. As it turned out, these war parties, composed of savages from a number of different tribes, were "watching and waiting,"hopeful as they were of additional warriors. One party, numbering perhaps thirty, was, unbeknownst to either Clark or to Lochry, lying in wait for the expedition at that point on the river where the Great Miami enters the Ohio from the north.[49]

Just how sensitive Clark and Lochry were to the Indian presence is not clear. Certainly they had had premonitions. Reports of Indian sightings on the river had been coming into the settlements. Shortly after Clark had left Pittsburgh, William Croghan noted that "From Every Account we have the Indians Are preparing to receive him [Clark] And if they should attack him in his present Situation, either by land or Water, I dread the Consequences."[50] Unfortunately, whatever Clark and Lochry had been advised was not sufficient to inspire in them the requisite caution.

What they did not know is that the British had been well informed, over five months, on the expedition, its route and its purposes. Accordingly, they had provisioned a force of 100 Rangers under Captain Andrew Thompson and 300 Indians with orders to intercept Clark somewhere on the river. At the same time the ubiquitous Mohawk war-chief Joseph Brant was rounding up warriors with the same in mind.

Bombardier John Harris was in the first force, Clark's, under Major Isaac Craig, whose Fort Pitt troops had been delivered to Clark. Although he had fought at Long Island, and at the Brandywine, and at Germantown, and had suffered Valley Forge, and had experienced the summer's campaign up the Susquehanna and back with Sullivan, and had marched over the mountains from Philadelphia to Pittsburgh, John Harris felt that the Ohio River Expedition of George Rogers Clark was the most arduous of all his Revolutionary War experiences. Recollecting his time spent in the neighborhood of Pittsburgh, for the last three years of the war, he remembers, "We made an expedition down the Ohio river. That was the hardest campaign of all. It was not very much work to go down with the current, as we were in a flat-boat of some kind, with oars to row it. It was reported that a settlement of white people was along the river on the Ohio side at one place, perhaps Marietta; but we did not know certainly. We were in two divisions and I was in the first; and our officers ordered every one to be ready with his finger on the trigger, and so we drifted by, never seeing any one. The other party, carelessly thinking the advance had stopped, rowed up to the shore and the Indians sprang out and killed and took every man! We heard the reason the Indians did not attack us; they thought we were only a small advance party and they felt able for the main body and expected our general was in the rear; and as he had a red head they wanted his scalp particularly; but they were deceived in that; and if they had attacked us they would have met with a warm reception."

What Harris is reporting here is the ambush of Lochry by the Indian war party, largely Shawnees under the Mohawk Brant, and including James Girty, which occurred on August 25, three weeks into the expedition. Clark had been experiencing a number of desertions (which explains his desire to keep moving), and one group of nineteen was actually apprehended by Lochry as they made their way back up the river. Lochry could do little but release them, as they were most unwilling fighters, and so he did. Unfortunately, these deserters somehow got next to the ambushing Indians and apparently gave up valuable information in exchange for their "permission" to go home.[51] What happened after that has been described by the Westmoreland County historians:

Nothing was left for Lochry to do [after getting Clark's message at the mouth of the Kanawha] *but to go down the river. Yet, without provisions and with but little ammunition and nothing in the country to draw from, his advance must indeed have looked very gloomy. Nor could he now hope to overtake Clark, for his boats were clumsy and poorly manned by pilots who knew nothing of the channel or the surrounding country. The best he could do was to dispatch Captain Shannon in a boat with three or four men hoping that a lighter craft might overtake Clark's army and secure supplies, etc. Shannon and his party were captured by the Indians, and with them a letter from Lochry to Clark, which gave them some idea of the weak condition of Lochry's forces. The Indians, as was afterwards learned, were only prevented from attacking Lochry's army by a fear that Clark might have forces near enough to assist him. Moreover, while Lochry was in the middle of the river, an attack would have been very serious on the part of the Indians. But from deserters from Clark's army whom they captured, they learned pretty nearly the true situation, and rapidly collected large forces of Indians near the mouth of the Miami River. They then stationed their prisoners on a small island on the Ohio side of the river, where they could see any craft which might pass down the Ohio. They* [the prisoners] *were to hail the expedition as it came down the stream and induce them to land on the island. Should they succeed in this treachery, they were to be set free, and if they failed to perform their part they were to be put to death.* But Lochry's men landed on the Ohio side, about three miles above the island, about nine miles downriver from the mouth of the Miami, near the mouth of a small creek which yet bears his name, being known as Lochry's creek. He has been criticized for landing at all, and thus making his capture possible. [But] *he knew more about Indian warfare than any of his modern critics do, and his landing was probably a matter of necessity. He landed at a place of peculiar beauty even to this day* [1882], *and his starving horses were turned out to graze, for the bank was rich in herbage. One of his men killed a* [woods] *buffalo, and there was plenty to eat for all his forces. This was about 10 o'clock a.m., August 24, 1781. Clark, if at the falls* [present-day Louisville] *was yet one hundred and twenty miles down the river, but with refreshed troops and horses this distance might easily be covered in three or four days and the hopes of the soldiers ran high. But the Indians had their scouts out along both banks, and the news of the landing was then made known to their main forces. Without the slightest warning, as was the Indian custom, came the leaden hail and the well known Indian yell from a bluff nearby. This bluff was covered with large trees, and from behind these and among their branches the six hundred and forty-eight assailants fought at a great advantage. Lochry's men sprang to their guns, and while their ammunition lasted defended themselves as well as they could. When it was exhausted they made for their boats, but by this time the Indians had closed in on them, and at once took them prisoners. Not one of them escaped capture. Lochry was killed soon after being taken. He had with him one hundred and six men when he landed, of whom forty-two were killed and sixty-four were captured. The prisoners, their arms, etc., were divided among all the tribes represented in the attack, in proportion to the number of each tribe. They were thus separated, but nearly all were held captive until the fall of 1782, when they were collected by the British officers and exchanged for prisoners whom the American army had captured. All whom the English ransomed were taken to Montreal, but in the meantime a few had escaped. In the spring of 1783 most of them sailed for New York, and thus returned to Westmoreland county, after an absence of twenty-two months.*[52]

The Indians, feeling either that they did not have warriors enough to stage a successful attack, or feeling that this was not the main body, which they preferred to assault, had permitted the first fleet of flat-boats and canoes to go by. And Clark's party drifted all the way to the Great Falls without incident. Here, however, Major Isaac Craig[53] found that for his troops the mission was over. After coming all the way down the Ohio River, from Fort Pitt to the Great Falls, in order to mount a campaign against the Indians in the west, under the leadership of the renowned George Rogers Clark, they found all was for naught. The Kentucky troops which were supposed to be here, to augment Clark's force substantially, had failed to show up.

Clark, naturally, was very much disappointed. He found that the conditions among the settlers here in Kentucky were just as troubled and confused as they were in Pennsylvania. Disheartened, he gave up completely his plans to capture Detroit; but he would not give up on the enterprise altogether. Now he began to consider an expedition up the Wabash. But that would have to wait. While he was still at the fort (which he had built and named Fort Nelson), in October of 1781, he penned a message to the new Governor of Virginia, his close friend Thomas Nelson. How close he has come to despair is evident: "But I would not wish to trouble your Excellency with my remarks. I have lost the object that was one of my principal inducements to my fatigues and transactions for several years past–my chain appears to have run out. I find myself enclosed with few troops, in a trifling fort, and shortly expect to bear the insults of those who have for several years been in continued dread of me."[54]

Clark had released the company of Major Craig and the soldiers from Fort Pitt. Weary, and disappointed too, the now very modest force, lingered at the Falls for about two weeks. When by October 17 they had at last summoned up sufficient strength and resolve, they returned to the river. This time it would be upstream. There would be a lot of poling and rowing before they would see Fort Henry or Fort Pitt.

In fact, because the river was so low now in the fall of the year, the boats were able to make way up the river only with great difficulty; and Craig, though he was able to save the cannon and most of the stores, was obliged to discard the gun carriages. The trip upriver required forty days. It was fatiguing and dispiriting. Happily, the men had no way of knowing that George Rogers Clark had reported to the governor of his native Virginia that "Captain [Isaac] Craig and company of artillery return to Pittsburgh, anxious for a second attempt in the Indian country."[55]

Harris recollects how difficult and frustrating was this return trip, upriver against the current and in the unrelenting consciousness of Indians on either bank, though the artillerymen as yet knew nothing of the Lochry mishap: "We went as far as Louisville, then called the Great Falls, but were not there but a short time before we were ordered back to Pittsburg, just as the setting in of winter and the river low and full of ripples. We would have to jump out and push our boats over and then get in and row, sitting with wet clothing on and almost freezing. As we went down [river] one of our number died, and we had no shovels to bury him. We placed him in a hollow in the ground made by the blowing down of a tree, and put what dirt we could on him; but as we came back [upriver] we saw that the wolves had dug him out and picked his bones!"

Now a little more anxious about Indians than they had been in coming down river, Craig's party is more than a little careful. Harris remembers that they would "stay out in the middle of the river all day pulling up till, toward night, we [would] work in[to] shore and land a party to scour the woods for Indians and post our sentinels around, and camp for the night. The wolves would come up around the sentinels and howl and appear as if not farther off than the length of our guns; but we dared not shoot them; it would be giving a false alarm."

It is apparent from Craig's reports later that he was very sure that all the way up the river his party was being closely watched by the Indians. He believed that the savages would have seized any opportunity to assault the flotilla, and that only a constant vigilance on the part of his men saved the party from attack.[56]

Harris remembers too that "We also had another thing to contend with, worse than any I have mentioned, hunger; we came very near starving. There was a settlement at Wheeling . . . , and a temporary mill that would grind corn, which was run by man power. So we made great calculations when we reached there; but pretty soon after we got to work the soldiers got hold of some whisky and got so drunk that they could not work, got nothing done, and we came nearer starving than before!"

Winter could be read in the winds coming from the west, but the remnants of Clark's failed expedition were still a long way from home and struggling with the current. Fortunately for the boatmen, some relief was provided from time to time by some amusing incident. Harris remembered one: "Pittsburg was a hundred miles yet before us. We were working up the Ohio. In one canoe was a sick Irishman and the current catched and upset it. We lamented his fate, supposing he was drowned, of course: but when we came to turn up the canoe there he was under it, not any the worse,–only wet! Some one asked him if he could take a little whisky. He said, 'By the Lord! Try me.'"

Without further incident the company finally, on November 26, reached Fort Pitt. They discovered that there was in place a new Commander of the Western Department. Brigadier General William Irvine, who had been promoted from Colonel on May 12, 1779, had replaced Colonel Brodhead. Major Craig and his men somehow still had not learned anything about Lochry and his troops, and, not seeing their boats on the return trip upriver, had always naturally supposed they had turned back long ago. They were astonished to learn from Irvine of the tragedy, and simply could not believe it.

What Irvine informed them he reported to Pennsylvania President William Moore a week later, on December 3: "I am sorry to inform your Excellency that the country has got a severe stroke by the death of Colonel Lochry, and about one hundred–it is said–of the best men of Westmoreland, including Captain Stokely and his Rangers. Many accounts agree that they were all killed or taken at the mouth of the Miami River,–I believe chiefly killed. This misfortune, added to the failure of General Clark's expedition, has filled the people with great dismay. Many talk of returning to the east side of the mountain in the spring. Indeed there is great reason to apprehend that the savages, and perhaps the British from Detroit, will push us hard in the spring, and I believe there never were parts of a country in a worse state of defence."[57]

And indeed the failure of the George Rogers Clark anti-Indian mission, so awkward in its beginning, and suffering the tragic loss of Lochry and his one hundred and six men, meant disappointment and a continuing sense of despair to the settlers in the region near Fort Pitt.

Major Isaac Craig and his artillery company certainly returned disheartened..

But there was big news waiting for them. For quite a long time they had been conducting their own little war on the Ohio River, and had been out of touch with the "real"war against the British. Now, back in Fort Pitt at last, they learned that the war of the Revolution was "over." They had arrived too late for the Commander's announcement to the garrison at Fort Pitt and to the people of Pittsburgh, for it was on November 6, while they were still down river from Fort Henry, when he reported: "General Irvine has the pleasure of congratulating your troops upon the great and glorious news–Lord Cornwallis, with the troops under his command, surrendered as prisoners of war upon the 19 of October last to the allied armies of America and France, under the immediate command of his excellency, Washington. The prisoners amount to upward of five thousand regular troops, nearly two thousand Tories and as many negroes, besides a number of merchants and other followers. Thirteen pieces of artillery will be fired on this day at ten o'clock in the fort, at which time the troops will be under arms with their colors displayed. The commissaries will issue a gill of whiskey extraordinary to the non-commissioned officers and privates upon this joyful occasion."[58]

John Harris and Samuel Blackwood and Major Craig and the artillery company that had made the trip down and up the Ohio had missed out on the "extraordinary whiskey," but they were made ecstatic by the news from Yorktown, Virginia.. Eagerly they sought out the details. And what Harris learned was that those generals with whom he had endured the winter at Valley Forge, the Frenchman Lafayette and the German von Steuben, and Chester County's Anthony Wayne, had driven the British forces down the Virginia peninsula to a place called Yorktown, and had thereafter distinguished themselves in bottling up the Redcoats right there.

And he learned that the French had made the difference. Two French officers whom he had never heard of were apparently in large measure responsible for the surrender of the British army. One was an admiral, whose long name ended in de Grasse.[59] Fresh from his defeat of the British at Tobago, Admiral de Grasse had brought his fleet from the West Indies to the colony of Virginia, there to blockade the York and James Rivers, which form the York Peninsula, and bottle up Cornwallis. The other French officer had an even longer name, and Harris made himself content to remember just Rochambeau.[60] He had been dispatched to the colonies by King Louis XVI, with 6000 regular French army troops to aid Washington. He reached Newport, Rhode Island in July of 1780 with his thirty-six troop transport ships, in the convoy of seven capital ships and three frigates, under the command of the Chevalier de Ternay. But he was not able to achieve a meaningful meeting with Washington until September 21. On that day Rochambeau met with the American Commander-in-Chief at Hartford, Connecticut, in order "to concert the details of a plan of operations."

Washington at Yorktown

Washington of course had been concentrating on Clinton in New York City, and in fact through the fall and winter continued to make New York his top priority. But Rochambeau had apparently laid out before Washington and his officers a strategy very different from what was presently being employed. It was Rochambeau's idea to forget Clinton, and instead head south to join the Southern Army and attack Cornwallis, who having failed in the Carolinas, had come north to join the other British forces at Yorktown. When Washington was finally persuaded, a massive army of French and Americans hastened south.

Early in September, Admiral de Grasse reached the Chesapeake Cape. Within a week he had landed three thousand troops upon the York Peninsula. By late September, Washington found himself in command of a truly colossal force, composed of three times as many

Frenchmen (perhaps 29,000 soldiers and sailors) as Americans. This huge military power, with Washington's regular troops and Virginia militia at its core, now laid siege to the British army of seven thousand in Yorktown. With this massive force enveloping the garrison, and the French fleet blockading the rivers and presiding over the sea, and the failure of a number of British efforts to break through, and the defeat by the French navy of the British squadron that had been bringing reinforcements from General Clinton, and supplies running low, and weariness from the incessant and merciless fire of the French artillery and that of Henry Knox, whose heavy cannon were described as "extraordinary," Lord Cornwallis finally requested surrender terms. The date was October 17, 1781. Finding the conditions for surrender "acceptable," he agreed to deliver his forces to Washington. The date was October 19, 1781.

The British had been winning the war. In December of 1778, they had taken Savannah, Georgia; in the following December some 7,000 British soldiers, dispatched by sea by General Clinton from New York City, laid siege to Charleston, South Carolina, and took the city in May of 1780. By the spring of 1781, despite defeats at Kings Mountain and Guilford Courthouse, the British felt good enough about the Carolinas to move on Virginia. Cornwallis soon had established a base and strongly fortified Yorktown and had designs on Richmond. But trouble appeared in the person of Lafayette. General Lafayette had been holding Virginia, with a very small force of the Continental Army. He was able to contain Cornwallis until late in September, when Washington and Rochambeau arrived with their awesome force.

Charles Cornwallis

With the surrender of Cornwallis at Yorktown a number of ironies promptly appeared. One was that New York City, which had always seemed so critical and which had been fought for so hard, and which Washington had hovered over for five years, and which Clinton continued to occupy, was now totally irrelevant.

But the biggest irony, and the most grim, would be recognized later, in the fact that the weary war, which had dragged itself along through six long winters and seven long summers, and which had *seemed* to end with Yorktown, was not over. Because no large-scale fighting occurred after October 19, 1781, it might be argued that the capitulation of the British forces in Virginia meant the end of the long war. And most certainly it did. It *meant* the end; but it was not the end. The defeat of the British at Yorktown only implied the end; it defined the ultimate victory and defeat. General Lafayette, after the Cornwallis surrender, observed to his Commander-in-Chief that "The play, sir, is over." But the war was not over, not by a long shot. Soldiers who had committed "for the duration" were not going home. Bombardier John Harris was not going home. Sergeant Samuel Blackwood was not going home. Not for a long, long time yet.

The War of the Revolution was not over for the frontier settlements. No one had suggested to the Indian allies of the British that they lay down their tomahawks and give up their lands to the westward-moving settlers. Formal hostilities, with rival forces arrayed against each other, would continue for almost two more years! As it turned out, the war had run three-quarters of its course only. Hundreds of lives would be lost, and the horrible pains that attach to every war would be suffered – by the British serving the King, by the rebellious colonists, by the native American Indians. For the garrison at Fort Pitt, and its fellow frontier forts, and for settlements like Hannastown, and for the Tuscarawas Indian villages the war was not over.

William Irvine

Of course the news from Yorktown was great news for the soldiers of Craig's company, who had returned from the Great Falls.

But for them there was still a job to be done, here at Fort Pitt and for the frontier settlements. And they would now be answering to a new Commandant of the Western Department. William Irvine was a good choice for the position. Like Colonel Proctor, and Daniel Brodhead, he had been born in Ireland, and, like General Sullivan and Lord Stirling, he had been a prisoner of war. At the time of his appointment (September 24, 1781), which was made upon the recommendation of Washington, he was not yet forty years old, but he was rich in beneficial experience. He had attended Trinity College in Dublin, and afterwards studied medicine. As a Royal Navy surgeon he served at sea for a time during the Seven Years' War. He came to America at the age of twenty-three determined to practice medicine.

Settling in the eastern Pennsylvania frontier town of Carlisle, he promptly established a medical practice, and for a time was one of only two physicians practicing in the entire Carlisle region. With Lexington and Concord and the outbreak of the war, he organized the 7th Pennsylvania Regiment and participated, as above described, in the early invasion of Canada and the disastrous Quebec campaign. He had fought well at Monmouth. On May 12, 1779, he was commissioned Brigadier General and given the command of the Second Pennsylvania Brigade.

Although his appointment to the command of the Western Department had been made in September of 1781, he did not actually assume the post until early in November. Irvine, of course, stepped into the same situation Brodhead had left. Accordingly, he would have to deal with the Indian threat, with the condition of Fort Pitt, and with the maintenance of Fort McIntosh, which was a new fort, it having been built in 1778 by General Lachlan McIntosh, then Commander of the Western Department. Fort McIntosh, he learned, was thirty-five miles northwest of Fort Pitt, at present-day Beaver, Pennsylvania, north side of the Ohio River.

There was also Fort Laurens, as well as a number of other smaller forts, all with the problem of provisions. But for Irvine, the first order of business was the repair of Fort Pitt. This he got accomplished so well that on at least two occasions expeditions by hostile Indians were discouraged simply by the formidable appearance of the fort.[61]

He had not been long in his new office when there was written in his territory perhaps the bloodiest chapter in the whole of American history. Certainly it is the bloodiest chapter ever produced by citizens of Pennsylvania.

It concerns the Indians who had been converted to Christianity by the Reverend John Heckewelder and ministers of the Moravian Church. These Indians lived in three villages on the Tuscarawas River in what is today Tuscarawas County, Ohio. They were peace-loving and were gracious hosts to all passers-by. Generally their right to live on their river in their passive way of life was respected. Colonel Brodhead, for example, when passing by the three villages in 1780, had directed his soldiers not to disturb them in any way.

Abruptly all was changed for the Moravian Indians. Apparently in retaliation for Indian raids on the settlements, a militia force in what is now Washington County, south of Pittsburgh, determined to destroy these settlements. Organized and led by Colonel David Williamson, a party of ninety men early in March of 1782 set out from Mingo Bottom,[62] down river from Fort Henry (Wheeling), for the three villages known as Gnadenhuetten, Salem, and Schoenbrun.

On March 6 the company neared the village of Gnadenhuetten ("huts of mercy"). That night the men secreted themselves in the forest about one mile away. Next morning, pretending to themselves that they were attacking a fierce war-party led by Cornplanter or Old Smoke, instead of innocent and harmless women and children at work in the fields, Williamson's "soldiers" stole cautiously closer to the village. From time to time they would come upon an Indian in the forest. These, six in all, including one squaw, were killed.[63]

Having effectively surrounded the village, Williamson ordered his men to move in as if they intended no harm. The Indians, given the impression that they were to be removed to Pittsburgh, somewhat indifferently submitted. Meanwhile, by an Indian who had discovered the body of one of the six slain by Williamson's men in the woods an alarm had been sounded at the village of Schoenbrun. These Indians, possibly fifty in number, promptly fled into the forest and escaped. Those at Salem were not so lucky. Like those at Gnadenhuetten, they were won over by the seeming sincerity and friendliness of the white men, and were persuaded to join the others at Gnadenhuetten.[64]

Here all were confined to the chapel in which they had regularly attended the ministry of the Moravians Heckewelder and Zeisberger.

In all, ninety Moravian Indians had been rounded up, men, women, and children. Still supposing that the white men were friendly (even though they knew some of them as Indian haters), and that they were being taken to Pittsburgh, they waited. Meanwhile, outside the chapel, Williamson and his men deliberated over what to do with them. After some discussion, which grew steadily more heated, Williamson put it to a vote. The question was simple. Should these prisoners, these ninety men, women, and children, be put to death, or should they be transported, by us ninety, to Pittsburgh, as we have been promising? To hear of what thereafter transpired requires a very strong stomach:

So they lined up the militia and allowed them to vote as to whether the prisoners should be put to death or taken in captivity to Pittsburgh. Only eighteen voted in favor of taking them, the others, about seventy, voting that they should be put to death The cringing Indians were then told to prepare for death. On hearing this they began to sing and pray as they had been taught by the pious minister. To make a show of reason for this outrage, they were charged with many things they had not done, such as harboring hostile Indians and stealing property. To this they answered that they had not refused shelter to either the white or the Indian race, and had never knowingly aided any one who was intent on committing depredations. To all charges they answered equally well, offering, by the way, to show all the property they had to prove that none of it was stolen. But they were told to prepare for death. They then asked for more time to sing and pray and this was granted. They asked forgiveness as they had been taught to do, and bade each other good-bye, but in the hope of a speedy reunion after death. Some of the murderers outside were impatient for the slaughter, and they moreover could not agree as to the manner in which they should be put to death. Many wanted to burn the houses in which they were imprisoned, and shoot all who would attempt to escape the flames. This was objectionable because it would destroy the scalps, from which they hoped to realize a handsome revenue. The eighteen members of the militia [who had voted against death] *washed their hands of all complicity in the affair* [and withdrew to a distance], *and there is no evidence that any of them took any part in it.*

After the night that was granted the Indians for their prayers, Williamson's men reassembled. That morning they herded the Indians into two of the mission buildings (the slaughter houses) and began their deadly work.

One of the murderers [a gross and repulsively ugly man, "Captain" Charles Bilderback by name] *took a cooper's mallet and* [starting with Abraham, the very elderly leader of the village] *began killing them by breaking their skulls. He kept this up until he had killed fourteen, and then complained that his arm was tired and handed his mallet, wreaking with blood, to another. In this way all were put to death save two boys, one of whom had hidden in a cellar* [and who saw blood flowing down the walls in streams]; *the other, surviving the stroke of the mallet and the removal of his scalp* [and left for dead in the piles of bodies], *escaped that night. Thus quotes one writer on the subject: "By the mouth of two witnesses shall these things be established." When all had been murdered the dead bodies were put in one house, which was fired. They then started home, and on their way met a body of friendly Delawares, all but a few of whom were killed.*[65]

In all, ninety innocent Christian Indians (not counting the six slain on the way to the village or those killed on the way home) were here murdered. Twenty-seven of these were women, and thirty-four were boys and girls. All were scalped.[66] Only two boys escaped.

The Commandant of the Western Department, Brigadier General William Irvine, was at home in Carlisle when the sordid affair occurred. When he had news of "the mallet murders," as they were being called, he was thunderstruck. He knew the Moravian Indians and understood them. He knew them to be a peaceful, innocent people. Indeed he had himself, not all that long ago, released from captivity a company of Moravians who had been brought to Fort Pitt as prisoners. He was on horseback at once, and in a remarkably short time was back at the Fort. There he promptly launched an investigation, determined as he was to identify and bring to justice those responsible for the incredible barbarity. Shocked and horrified by what was being described to him, he felt, as he declared in a letter to his wife, that those responsible for the murders should be "hanged."

He conducted interviews with some he had reason to believe "knew something," among them "the best citizens," like County Lieutenant John Canon (the founder of Canonsburg), who, it is now known, was a central figure. But at length a very discouraged and much disheartened Irvine wrote to William Moore, Chief Magistrate of the State, declaring that it was impossible to identify any of the men responsible, "as they would neither confess nor tell on each other."[67] That may very well have been the reason that General Irvine did not press the investigation any further. But it is also true that while he was searching out the truth and trying to identify those responsible, he was getting the very strong impression that the people of Westmoreland County were sustaining what Williamson's party had done, and that they would resist any public condemnation of it. His investigation was aborted. He was giving up on it because he had been made to realize that not only were the frontier families passively accepting what had happened, a great many of the settlers were actually applauding the murders. Not everybody felt this way, he knew of course, but he had the impression that if a vote were taken it would accord very closely with that taken by Williamson's men.

Actually, the whole business does not look all that good for General Irvine. During the years after the war, when Irvine was engaged in surveying lands northwest of the Allegheny, he got to know the Seneca war-chief Cornplanter quite well. A high regard, each for the other, developed, Cornplanter declaring that General Irvine was one of the few white men of his acquaintance who spoke the truth.[68] But here, in his correspondence with the authorities, Irvine does not appear to be perfectly candid. He must have known who was responsible for the massacre. *Everybody* knew. Indeed, almost immediately after, Irvine informed Washington that he was campaigning covertly against the election of Williamson as head of the militia mission now being planned against the Ohio Indians. The General was clearly in a most awkward position, but he settled for a cop-out. It was shameful that those responsible were never brought to justice, and, it would seem, the blame must be laid at the door of the Commander of the Western Department.

No officer, no soldier, of the Continental Army was involved in this sordid affair. Indeed, Isaac Craig and John Harris and Samuel Blackwood, and all other members of the Fort Pitt garrison must have been horrified, like their commander, when they heard about the massacre. One would have to search long and hard, very long and very hard, the annals of American history before he or she would ever come upon an episode reflecting such cowardice and such cruelty. The Wyoming massacre, awful as it was, can hardly be said to match the Williamson atrocity. One writer, declaring it the blackest deed in the history of Pennsylvania, noted a terrible irony: "How the patriotic and justice-loving Washington must have blushed with shame when he learned that these murderers had sought to perpetuate his name by giving it to their newly formed county!"[69]

In the end, nobody was punished for the murders, not by the authorities. But in time all of the settlers living in the Western Department, the innocent as well as the guilty, were punished. By this terrible slaughter the Indians throughout the region, the warriors of all tribes, were whipped into a frenzy, and hostilities more fierce than ever before occurred in the settlements. As one historian observed, "The crimes which followed were too many to enumerate."[70] And they proved that cruelty is not the special province of any one race. And they proved that "blood will beget blood," that one atrocity is answered by another.

One of the most blood-curdling scenes from the long War of the Revolution occurred not long after the Williamson massacre, and *definitely* in revenge. Its central figure is Colonel William Crawford, who had been a good friend and partner of the young George Washington, serving as his land agent in the surveying activities. Crawford, who had fought at Trenton, at the Brandywine, and at Germantown, and who had been with the forces of Colonel Brodhead when they attacked Coshocton in 1781, was a well known and popular figure in the region protected by Fort Pitt. He had held the seat of presiding judge in the Westmoreland County Courts.[71]

An expedition against the Delawares, the Shawanese, and the Wyandots in the Sandusky region had been in the works for a long time. Washington had hoped to launch a regular army, Sullivan-type, punitive mission against the villages of the Indians known to be conducting raids. Such an expedition doubtless would have included soldiers from the Fort Pitt garrison, and some of Craig's artillerymen, surely John Harris. It would have been commanded by General Irvine. But Washington, recognizing that he could not provide the necessary regular army personnel or the necessary supplies to support such an undertaking, had discarded the plan.

Both Washington, however, and Irvine knew that *something* had to be done. Both therefore gave their approval to a militia mission, to be composed strictly of volunteers, Washington insisting that he could not provide any men or supplies, and Irvine, who at first was thought of as a commander, declining that post. In a letter to Washington, dated May 21, 1782, Irvine laid down a number of conditions under which he would approve the mission, even as the militia men were assembling at Mingo Bottom, on the Ohio River: (1) They were not to extend their settlements; nor (2) to do anything more than to harass the enemy sufficiently to protect the frontier; and (3) that any conquests that they might make should be "in behalf and for the United States"; and (4) that (remembering Gnadenhuetten) they would be governed by military laws as militia; and (5) that they must go in such numbers as promise success; and (6) that they equip themselves at their own expense.

Irvine notes that Crawford "has pressed me for some officers. I have sent with him Lieutenant Rose,[72] my aid-de-camp, a very vigilant, active, brave young gentleman, well acquainted with service; and a surgeon."[73] And "These two," writes Irvine, "are all I could spare."

He let Washington know that "Several were solicitous for my going." But, as he explains, "I did not think myself at liberty, consistent with the spirit of your excellency's instructions,"and of course the General well knew how difficult was the command of a company of militia. "Nor are we," he laments, "in such a situation that I could take a single continental soldier, particularly as the volunteers are all mounted."[74]

While organization for the expedition was getting underway, "in secret," Irvine met with many of the men who would likely be officers. Though, ostensibly, these meetings were of the briefing kind, it is very clear that the Commander of the Western Department was doing some hard politicking. To Washington, in that same letter of May 21, he had written: "As they will elect their own officers I have taken some pains to get Col. Crawford appointed to command, and hope he will be."[75] It was apparent that Irvine, with Gnadenhuetten up front in his mind, was much determined that Williamson would not be elected to the command of these militia forces. The Sandusky campaign was not to be another Gnadenhuetten. The speculation is that had Williamson been placed in command, General Irvine would have nixed the operation altogether.

Late in May, the force was finally composed, 480 men, all volunteers (many, like Crawford himself, veterans of the battles fought in the early years of the Revolution), each supplying his own rifle or musket, his horse, thirty days' worth of provisions, and the necessary equipment. Almost all were from Westmoreland County and what is today Washington County, some few from the Virginia panhandle. Only three were from the Fort Pitt garrison. These were the two mentioned in Irvine's letter to Washington, Dr. John Knight and Lieutenant John Rose, and Irvine's gardener-servant, a Negro named Henry, who was assigned to Rose. By order of General Irvine, who painfully repeated his insistence that he really did not have any regulars to provide, Knight was detached from the Seventh Virginia, which was then stationed at Fort Pitt, and made available to the party being assembled. Crawford, to whom Knight was a good friend, had requested that he be made surgeon for the expedition.

In the balloting for the command of the force, Williamson received 230 votes, and Crawford 235 (!). Williamson was appointed one of the four majors of the militia.

The force had agreed to assemble at Mingo Bottom, a kind of plateau on the banks of the Ohio River, some two and one-half miles below present-day Steubenville. It was precisely the spot from which Williamson's men had launched their assault on the Moravian villages less than three months ago. On the 25th of May the militia war party, 480 strong, set out for Sandusky. Colonel William Crawford, before leaving Mingo Bottom, composed his will.

On June 6 the militia force led by Crawford came to the Moravian towns on the upper Sandusky. At Olentangy they were able to fight off the Indians and their British allies. But next day on the Sandusky plains Crawford's force was attacked again by Indians. The fighting continued throughout the night.[76] When it appeared next morning that the numbers of warriors had increased dramatically, Crawford ordered a retreat. After some discussion it was agreed to withdraw in broken up small parties, rather than as a single force. The party under Colonel Williamson made good its exit from the territory; and Crawford's command was in orderly and safe retreat as well. But, after going some distance, Colonel Crawford became aware that he had not seen his son John, or his nephew William Crawford, or his son-in-law William Harrison.[77] Concerned for them, he stopped, permitting the horsemen to pass by; then, still not perceiving any of them, he endeavored to catch up. But he was unable to do so, and, on falling in with his friend the surgeon Dr. John Knight, and two others, and later with two officers, he proceeded.

But by a small band of Delaware warriors, seventeen, they were surprised and captured. Crawford and Knight, together with nine others, were then walked thirty-three miles to the old Indian town at Sandusky and the camp of their chief, Wigenund, who had once been an overnight guest in Crawford's home! Before setting out on the trek, the warriors blackened the faces of most of the prisoners, to indicate the fate intended for them. This was June 7. Here they remained three days. On the 11th they began a forced march through the Delaware country. Along the way, they came upon the corpses of four of the prisoners, who had been murdered by the tomahawk and scalped. By and by they caught up with the remaining five of the original nine, all with blackened faces. In the region of Little Tymochtee Creek all seven were ordered to sit on the ground. Crawford and Knight were compelled to watch in horror the butchery of their remaining five companions, who had been turned over to the savagery of the squaws and to the boys of the village.[78]

Colonel Crawford's fate was pending. "Perhaps of all outrages committed by the Indians," declares one historian, "his cruel death is the one which will dwell longest in the memory of civilized people."[79]

For savage cruelty and inhumanity it will remind one of the pitiful death of Lieutenant Thomas Boyd of the Sullivan Expedition and the torture tree.

Presiding over the scene was the Delaware Chief Pipe (Pimoacan), who, not all that long ago, had been encouraging his people toward friendship with the whites. Thirty to forty warriors were present, and sixty to seventy squaws and boys. Colonel Crawford was stripped naked, and bound to a post some sixteen feet high, and fires were built to encircle him. The squaws, who took an insane delight in the sport, knifed off his ears and his nose. The warriors then, as Dr. Knight remembered it, "took up their guns and shot powder into the Colonel's body, from his feet as far up as his neck. I think that not less than seventy loads were discharged upon his naked body."[80]

Simon Girty

Then from the fires the squaws secured red-hot burning embers, with which they showered him. From time to time he was obliged to walk in his bare feet upon the coals. This torture continued for the space of three hours, from four o'clock in the afternoon until the setting of the sun, Crawford enduring excruciating pain with great courage.[81] The infamous Simon Girty,[82] who had been observed among the Delawares during the fighting, astride a white horse and in his characteristic ruthless glee, was present throughout the torture. He might have interfered, but he did not. He did not even oblige Crawford, who had pleaded, "Please shoot me."

As Dr. Knight recalled the scene, the Colonel, "being almost exhausted . . . lay down on his belly; they then scalped him and repeatedly threw the scalp in my face, telling me 'that was my great captain.' An old squaw (whose appearance every way answered the ideas people entertain of the Devil) got a board, took a parcel of coals and ashes and laid them on his back and head, after he had been scalped, he then raised himself upon his feet and began to walk around the post; they next put a burning stick to him as usual, but he seemed more insensible of pain than before."[83]

At this point Dr. Knight was led away and did not witness the last, when Crawford, now only semi-conscious, his last energy spent, "commended his soul to God, and lay down on his face . . . and . . . sank into the welcome arms of death."[84]

All of this awful torture of course Knight knew would be his to suffer also, and within two days. But . . . . he had been consigned to a single man, a strong-limbed, lithe Shawnee warrior named Tutelu, whose villainous countenance, made more hideous by garish daubs of war paint, belied his stupidity. As Knight remembers,

> . . . the Indian fellow who had me in charge now took me away to Capt. Pipe's house, about three-quarters of a mile from the place of the Colonel's execution. I was bound all night, and thus prevented from seeing the last of the horrid spectacle. Next morning, being June 12th, the Indian untied me, painted me black, and we set off for the Shawanese town, which he told me was somewhat less than forty miles from that place. We soon came to the spot where the Colonel had been burnt, as it was partly in our way; I saw his bones lying amongst the remains of the fire, almost burnt to ashes; I suppose after he was dead they laid his body on the fire.
> The Indian told me that was my Big Captain, and gave the scalp halloo. He was on horseback and drove me before him.
> I pretended to this Indian I was ignorant of the death I was to die at the Shawanese towns, assumed as cheerful a countenance as possible, and asked him if we were not to live together as brothers in one house when we should get to the town? He seemed well pleased, and said yes. He then asked me if I could make a wigwam? I told him I could, he then seemed more friendly. We went that day as near as I can judge about 25 miles, the course partly Southwest. The Indian told me we should next day come to the town, the sun being in such a direction, pointing nearly South. At night, when we went to rest, I attempted very often to untie myself, but the Indian was extremely vigilant and scarcely ever shut his eyes that night. About daybreak he got up and untied me; he next began to mend up the fire, and as the gnats were troublesome I asked him if I should make a smoke behind him, he said yes. I then took the end of a dogwood fork which had been burnt down to about 18 inches long; it was the longest stick I could find, yet too small for the purpose I had in view; then I picked up another smaller stick and taking a coal of fire between them went behind him; then turning suddenly about, I struck him on the head with all the force I was master of; which so stunned him that he fell forward with both his hands into the fire, but seeing him recover and get up, I seized the gun while he ran off howling in a most fearful manner. I followed him with a determination to shoot him down, but pulling back the cock of the gun with too great violence, I believe I

broke the main spring. I pursued him, however, about thirty yards, still endeavoring to fire the gun, but could not . . . .[85]

Tutelu, as is known from another survivor, arrived at his village in disgrace, and having concocted a story that no one would believe, was made to suffer the ridicule of his fellow warriors.

Almost delirious in his great relief, the surgeon promptly set out for Fort Pitt. When coming upon the trail taken by the retreating militia, he declined to follow it for fear of Indians. For twenty days he traveled through the wilderness, guided only by the sun and by his sense of the "beautiful river." As Tutelu's gun, which he carried throughout, could not be made to work, for food he had to depend upon what he could catch with his hands, small birds and turtles, which he consumed raw. Though his wanderings required three weeks, he finally came to the big timber for which he was searching, and on the evening of July 3 struck the Ohio River "about five miles below the mouth of Beaver," and the site of Fort McIntosh, twenty to thirty miles down river from Pittsburgh . On the 5th of July he arrived safely at Fort Pitt. Here he was quick to report the details of Crawford's horrible death, and of his own miraculous escape.[86]

Another account of the murders of the captives taken by the warriors was dictated to Hugh Henry Brackenridge, a prominent Pittsburgh attorney. This is the story of John Slover, who served as a guide for the expedition. Also captured and scheduled for torture and execution, like Dr. Knight, he made, like Dr. Knight, an incredible escape.

During the retreat of the militia forces Slover's horse got mired down in a swamp, and Slover had to abandon it. He fell in with six others who had suffered the same predicament, and together they made their way through the wilderness. They escaped capture very narrowly on one occasion, but were caught up to about twelve miles from the Tuscarawas, still 135 miles from Fort Pitt. Slover was one of the three men taken by the Indians in a brief scuffle. They were taken in a march of three days to Wachatomakak, a town of the Mingoes and Shawanese. As Slover recalled, "The inhabitants from this town came out with clubs and tomahawks, struck, beat, and abused us greatly. One of my two companions they seized, and having stripped him naked, blacked him with coal and water. This was the sign of being burnt; the man seemed to surmise it, and shed tears. He asked me the meaning of his being blacked; but I was forbid by the enemy in their own language [which Slover understood], to tell him what was intended."

After running the gauntlet, this man was murdered. That same evening Slover saw three other bodies brought in, "black, bloody, burnt with powder." Two of these he knew to be the bodies of Crawford's son-in-law and his nephew. Next morning "the bodies of these men were dragged to the outside of the town and their carcasses being given to the dogs, their limbs and heads were stuck upon poles."

Slover's remaining companion was taken off to another town, and as Slover presumed probably tortured and burnt. Slover himself was obliged to sit through fifteen days of councils, fifty to one hundred warriors normally present. As Slover was conversant in the various Indian dialects, he understood that the Indians were agreeing to take no more captives. They were to show no mercy to any white, not even a child.

In the succeeding days he saw twelve Kentuckians brought in, three of whom were burnt at this village, and the rest dispatched for the same at other villages. One day he saw a warrior coming into the town to report that the prisoner (a doctor) whom he was bringing in to be burnt had escaped. This Indian, Slover perceived, was suffering from a wound in his head some four inches long. Of course it was Tutelu, and Slover, who could know nothing of Crawford's ordeal or of Knight's escape, could tell that the story he was offering by way of explanation was far from the truth.

On the day following the final council, some forty warriors, with George Girty, Simon's younger brother,[87] in their company, showed up. "The squaws gave me up, I was sitting before the door of the house; they put a rope around my neck, tied my arms behind my back, stripped me naked, and blacked me in the usual. George Girty, as soon as I was tied, damned me, and said that I now should get what I had deserved many years. I was led away to a town distant about five miles, to which a messenger had been dispatched to desire them to prepare to receive me."

At the roofless council house in the town to which he was taken, he was bound to the familiar post, always about sixteen feet high. And the fires were lit. Something very strange occurred at this point. It was late in the afternoon on a perfectly clear, cloudless day, and Slover heard no thunder nor perceived any sign of approaching rain. Yet, just as the fire began to blaze, the wind blew a "hurricane," and a violent rain fell, and the fire was extinguished. The Indians stood amazed. They might have taken it all for a sign that they were making a mistake. But they didn't. They simply rescheduled the burning for the next morning, when they "would take a whole day's frolic" in it.

So Slover was delivered to three warriors for safekeeping. In the block house, he was securely bound, with a rope around his neck and secured to a beam above him. While the warriors prepared themselves for sleep Slover worked away at his bonds, but they were of buffalo hide and gave little. When at last he sensed from their snoring they were asleep, he worked more earnestly. Just as he had despaired of any chance, and just as he heard the cock crow, he made one more effort. And, lo, he was free. In a moment he slipped by the guards and by a squaw asleep outside with many children, seized a horse and was away.

After fifty miles the horse gave out, and Slover was forced to run now, to run for his life. Somehow he managed to elude pursuit, and eventually, in the same manner as Dr. Knight, was able to make his way to the Ohio. Never had the river looked so beautiful. He was at Fort Henry, and hailing a man whom he perceived on an island, he was rescued by canoe.

Slover, having dictated this story to Brackenridge in Pittsburgh, felt obliged to add a thought about it all. He knew that what happened to the officers and men captured by the Indians was in consequence of the merciless murders of the Moravians. And he knew that the Crawford Expedition, which he had served as guide, included the commander of the forces responsible for Gnadenhuetten. This is how he concluded his account of his terrifying experience: "At the same time, though I would strike away this excuse which is urged for the savages, I am far from approving the Moravian slaughter. . . . the putting to death the women and children, who sang hymns at their execution, must be considered as unjustifiable, inexcusable homicide; and the Colonel who commanded the party, and who is said perseveringly, contrary to the remonstrances of officers present, to have enjoined the perpetration of the act, has not yet been called to an account, is a disgrace to the State of Pennsylvania."[88]

Both Slover's and Knight's narratives were published in the year succeeding their incredible escapes. They were printed in a pamphlet entitled *Narrative of a late Expedition against the Indians; with an Account of the Barbarous Execution of Col. Crawford; and the Wonderful Escape of Dr. Knight and John Slover, from Captivity, in 1782.* The pamphlet was printed by the Market Street shop of Francis Bailey, who was the printer of Philadelphia's *Freeman's Journal.*[89]

The defeat of the Crawford expedition, together with the torture of Colonel Crawford, is sometimes regarded the "worst blow of the Revolutionary War in the Northwest."[90] It was terrible news for Washington, who had approved the mission, and it must have pained him deeply to hear of the horrible death of his close friend and associate, Colonel Crawford. From General Irvine, writing on June 16, three weeks before the return of Dr. Knight, Washington had the news of the failure of the campaign, and the report of Crawford's death; but of course Irvine did not yet know himself the gruesome details. He did note in the letter that he had been informed by "a number of people" that the tortures were in retaliation for the Moravian murders.[91]

In his letter to Washington, July 11, the day after Slover's return to Fort Pitt and six days after the arrival of Dr. Knight, General Irvine, still sparing Washington the graphics of Crawford's torture, informs his Commander-in-Chief that both Knight and Slover report that they were assured by sundry Indians "that not a single soul should in future escape torture; and gave, as a reason for this conduct, the Moravian affair."[92]

In a letter from President William Moore of Pennsylvania, July 27, Washington receives a note on Crawford's death. Perhaps aware of how close Washington was to Crawford, President Moore writes in a consolatory way: "It is with the greatest sorrow and concern that I have learned the melancholy tidings of Col. Crawford's death. He was known to me as an officer of much care and prudence, brave, experienced and active. The manner of his death as given in letters of Gen. Irvine, Col. Gibson, and others was shocking to me; and I have this day communicated to the honorable, the congress, copies of such papers as I have regarding it."[93]

Both Irvine and Washington had been horrified by the massacre of the Moravian Indians, and while not excusing the Indians for their cruel treatment of their prisoners because of that barbarity, there is a pained understanding running through their communications. On August 6, from his headquarters at Newburgh, New York, Washington expresses himself to Irvine: "I lament the failure of the . . . expedition, and am particularly affected with the disastrous fate of Colonel Crawford. No other than the extremest torture that could be inflicted by savages, I think, could have been expected by those who were unhappy enough to fall into their hands; especially under the present exasperation of their minds, for the treatment given their Moravian friends. For this reason, no persons, I think, should at this time, submit themselves to fall alive into the hands of the Indians."[94]

The Crawford Expedition against Sandusky was eventually described in great detail for Washington in a series of preliminary letters and reports.[95] One can only imagine the reaction by Washington to the horrible death of his close friend, Colonel William Crawford. It could not have made him any warmer toward the Indians and their rights to the land.

The darkest and most horrible period in the history of Westmoreland County and western Pennsylvania generally was that time from the spring of 1781 to the spring of 1783. Called the "night of darkness," these twenty-four months for the settlers were never free from fear, nor from widespread suffering. This is the period which included the massacre of the Moravian Indians, the torture of Colonel Crawford, the tragic end of the Lochry expedition, and countless additional frontier atrocities including the murder of farm families, and the equally cruel acts of vengeance in the murder of Indians, both hostile and friendly. This is the period which saw an alarming number of desertions from the garrison at Fort Pitt and other lesser forts, and even from the forces of George Rogers Clark. This is the period during which the settlers were constantly threatening to return to the east.

And into this doom and gloom had marched the company of Captain Isaac Craig, of Colonel Thomas Proctor's Artillery. Over the mountains they had come, from Carlisle to Pittsburgh, to serve in the garrison of Fort Pitt, and to provide support to those efforts meant to reduce, and, hopefully, end the depredations occurring on the western frontier. Unable to do all that much, still their presence was a real boon to the Pittsburgh settlement and to the farms and villages of the

Western Department; and these fifty men,[96] with their cannon, indeed may have supplied support sufficient to discourage Indian assaults on Fort Pitt itself.

But, in general, conditions in the region of Fort Pitt had been deteriorating steadily since Captain Craig's arrival. By the spring of 1782 they had gone from bad to very bad, both in the number and in the severity of the Indian depredations. Morale along the frontier was at its lowest. General Irvine had been at home in Carlisle during the late winter of 1782. On March 8 he was ordered posthaste back to Pittsburgh. Washington's orders were "to proceed with all convenient dispatch to Fort Pitt." And Irvine knew how to interpret the "convenient."

He had also received a communication from Captain John Finley of the Fort Pitt garrison. Dated Saturday Evening, Feb. 2, 1782, the letter read: "Dear General: This evening we are informed that the troops which compose this garrison, intend to mutiny, and have appointed Monday next to put it into execution. It appears to be general throughout all the corps."[97] The disorder was inspired chiefly by the failure of long overdue pay to come through.

By March 25 Irvine was back at the Fort, where, as he reported, he found "people in a frenzy of excitement because of Indian raids."

Worse, he discovered that the soldiers at both Fort Pitt and Fort McIntosh had indeed become unruly and even mutinous. The General was quick to restore order. He did it the way he knew how. He scheduled a number of courts-martial. And whenever the sentence dictated, he was ready with the lash. One soldier was sentenced to 100 lashes on his bare back for abandoning his guard post. And the order was carried out.

Two of the most rebellious soldiers were sentenced to death. Irvine's order to the Fort Pitt Guard House, dated April 30, 1782, read: "John Philips and Thomas Steed, soldiers in the seventh Virginia regiment under sentence of death, are to be executed to-morrow forenoon between the hours of eleven and twelve o'clock."[98] Before the sentence could be carried out, Irvine, moved by the extreme youth of Philips, pardoned him. Steed was executed.

In a very short time Irvine, with his no-nonsense rule and his characteristic firmness, and his insistence on stern discipline, had the garrisons at both Fort Pitt and Fort McIntosh shaping up in military style. Now he returned to the necessary repairs.

Since coming back to Fort Pitt from the Great Falls in November, Isaac Craig (now Major) had been given a number of important assignments. On May 15, 1782, Major General Benjamin Lincoln of the War Office, out of concern for the unnatural ratio of officers to men at Fort Pitt, addressed a letter to Irvine: "You will please to divert the commanding officer of your artillery [Craig] to take charge of all the military stores, which is certainly a part of his duty. Such assistance as he may want must be afforded by some of the other officers, of whom, I observe there is a great proportion to the number of men at the post."[99]

At about the same time Washington relayed to General Irvine reports that he had had suggesting that a huge British-Indian expedition, probably under the command of the notorious Colonel Connolly, was being aimed for Fort Pitt. It was enough to urge Irvine to the immediate repair of the buildings within the stockade and the fortifications themselves. Of particular concern to Irvine was the old magazine, constructed of logs, now much decayed and insecure. He determined to replace it altogether with a very substantial stonework,[100] and to make certain that the work was done as it should be he placed Major Craig in charge.

On July 16, Irvine addressed to Benjamin Lincoln (with a copy to Pennsylvania's President William Moore a report on the improvements that had been made to the Fort. The letter included this passage: "This fort has been much repaired in the course of the summer. A new row of picketing is planted on every part of the parapet where the brick revetment did not extend, and a row of palisading nearly finished in the ditch; so far, also, with sundry other small improvements; but, above all, a complete magazine, the whole arched with stone. I think I may venture to assert, it is a very elegant piece of workmanship as well as [a] most useful one. It has been executed under the direction of Major Craig."

John Harris and Samuel Blackwood and the other members of Craig's artillery company who had been doing the work under carpenter Craig's supervision had good reason to be proud.

But Irvine was not done. The letter continues: "I have used the most rigid economy in every instance. The whole expense is but a trifle. Though the troops labored hard, yet, from the smallness of their number[101] and unavoidable interruptions, some necessary repairs remain yet unfinished. Some parts of the ramparts and parapets are much broken down. A new main gate and drawbridge are wanted and some small outworks are necessary to be erected, which cannot be effected this winter, as it is now time to lay in fuel and make some small repairs on the soldiers' barracks to make them habitable."

He also in this same letter appealed to the Secretary of War for a leave of absence: "If I am to be continued in service and command here, I shall be much obliged to your excellency for leave to visit my family in Carlisle at the dead of winter when I suppose there can be no risk in my being absent from the post. Besides, I shall then be directly on the line of communication to this place, and will not stay longer than you may judge proper."[102]

But while Irvine was completing his repairs to Fort Pitt, which was the chief refuge and protection from the hostile Indians of the Western Department, and while he was considering a leave for the winter months, one of the settlements in his charge was completely wiped out.

This was Hannastown.

The account of the burning of Hannastown, a small, largely Scotch-Irish settlement snuggled in the hilly farmlands midway between present-day Greensburg and Crabtree, and the county seat of Westmoreland County, is the extraordinary story of miraculous escapes and sacrifice, of remarkable courage and horrible cruelty.[103]

At two o'clock in the afternoon of Saturday, the 13th day of July, 1782, there appeared at the little cluster of houses called Hannastown a war party of some 100 Muncy warriors and renegade Tories. Their appearance was so sudden that settlers later described it as "like a clap of thunder."

Many of the settlers on this afternoon were in the fields helping with the harvest on the Michael Huffnagle farm. Fortunately, Captain Matthew Jack had had a report of Indians, and on horseback in a circling scouting mission had discovered the approach of the war party. He was able to spread the alarm, and, though great confusion erupted among the residents of the village, all were ushered safely into the stockade.

The war party was composed of approximately 100 Indians and white renegade Tories. By the time they had emerged from the surrounding forests and come up to the town the people of Hannastown were all secure in the small stockade. Done out of their hoped-for barbarities, the Indians, disappointed and enraged, settled for grotesque mockeries of the settlers. One warrior by his wild gesticulations was carried a little too close to the stockade and was promptly dispatched by a single rifle shot. No other member of the war party showed any inclination to encourage fire from the barricaded settlers.

After some excited consultations, the warriors promptly put torches to the whole town, composed of some thirty cabins and houses.

Stockade at Hannastown

They set their fires in a number of different places, and, because of very strong winds, in no time at all the settlement had been reduced to ashes. Only the stockade itself and the two small houses closest to it, one of which was Hanna's, were untouched.

Within the stockade now were forty to fifty men, women, and children. No more than twenty of these could be considered fighting men, and these were equipped with only nine guns. Fortunately, the Indians seemed not to know how weakly defended was the refuge, for they made no assault on the stockade itself. Instead, some members of the war party, forty to fifty, made their way to another stockade, called Miller's Fort or Miller's Station, where that afternoon some festivities, possibly those of a wedding, were in progress. Here a number of settlers were captured. Among them were the famous Indian fighter John ("Jack") Brownlee, who was a lieutenant in Captain Joseph Erwin's company of the Eighth Pennsylvania Rifle Regiment, and his wife and infant child. Brownlee was well known to the Indians who were active in the area of Fort Pitt, and he was among the most hated of all white men. He had a reputation for ruthless ferocity, and had been known to declare that he felt obliged to shoot any Indian that he saw. At the same time, among his own kind he was a very patient, kind and gentle man, and something of a hero-protector to the settlers.

Here Brownlee, who might have saved himself, instead surrendered meekly, in order to protect his wife and family, and continued to behave quite passively. Consequently, he was not at first recognized. Like the other men who had been captured he had his hands tied behind his back, but he carried his three-year-old son John upon his shoulders. It was only when one of the women captives used his name that he became known to the warriors. She had said, "I am glad, Captain Brownlee, that we have got you along with us." The Indians stared at each other, and some were observed grumbling to each other. What followed has been graphically described: "At a descending ground he [Brownlee] stooped to adjust his child upon his shoulders, drawing his tiny arms up more closely around his neck. As he was so doing, one of the Indians that had eyed him so closely sneaked up behind him and dashed the hatchet into his head. Brownlee fell headlong, and the child rolled over him. The next instant the child was killed by the same savage with the same hatchet which had laid open the skull of the gentle and tender-hearted father. The wife of Brownlee, full of horror, witnessed the death of her husband and child. Another woman shrieked out as she fell swooning to the ground. And she met the same fate, the Indians, as was supposed, taking her to be the real wife of the dead man."[104]

The only casualty at the Hannastown Fort was the heroic Margaret (Peggy) Shaw, whose father and brother were renowned Indian fighters. Peggy, who was only twelve or thirteen years old, was shot by the Indians while she was trying to save an infant which had crept too close to the picketing of the stockade.

By nightfall the whole countryside had been roused, and a relief party of some thirty men, all armed, had been formed. This party was able to reach an unwatched side of the fort and make itself known to those inside. Once they had been safely admitted, they gave through the night the impression that the garrison was now a formidable one.

The Indians that night entered into their characteristic torture rituals and carried on a good bit, but as the gray dawn was breaking, now under the impression that reinforcements had arrived at the fort, they slipped away with the prisoners they had taken at Miller's. The pursuit party that was promptly organized was able to follow the trail between Congruity Church and Harvey's Five Points, all the way to where the warriors with their captives crossed the Kiskiminetas River, not far from present-day Apollo.

For a long time it was not known who was responsible for the destruction of Hannastown. By some it was supposed that the leaders were renegade Tories, for it had been perceived that among the party were a number of whites dressed in Indian garb. Many felt that the principal figure in it all was the infamous Simon Girty. Then it was believed that the command of the warrior force was that of Cornplanter's uncle, Guyasuta,[105] the aging war-chief of the Senecas and long active in the west. Now it is thought that the raid was led by the Seneca warrior known as Farmer's Brother.

Because of what had happened at Hannastown and a subsequent, less successful, assault upon the settlement at Fort Henry, and a terrific build-up of the British-Indian army, there occurred during the remainder of the year a lot of talk about an expedition against the Indians, not unlike what George Rogers Clark had proposed. But that was all that it was, just talk. As Irvine complained in letters to his wife, nothing will come of this. "The militia will not go without regular troops, and there are no troops. It is only talk."

Irvine himself had intended an expedition, and apparently had laid plans for it He reported to Washington on October 29 of that year (1782): "Sir: I would have marched the 20th of Sept. into the Indian country with about eight hundred militia and a small detachment from the post, had I not received letters on the eighteenth from the secretary at war [Benjamin Lincoln, letter of September 7, 1782] and council of

Pennsylvania . . . ."[106]

Irvine in later years recollected in a letter to Washington that his expedition planned for September might have been pre-empted anyway. According to information that had come to him both from a Seneca chief and from "a white man named Matthews,"a detachment of 300 British and 500 Indians sometime in that summer of 1782 had been assembled in Canada and had come south in canoes to Lake Jadaque (Chautauqua) in southern New York State. What Irvine was given to understand is that this army had actually left Chautauqua with twelve pieces of artillery in a determination to attack Fort Pitt.[107]

As confirmation, General Irvine reports in the same letter, "I remember very well, that in August, 1782, we picked up, at Fort Pitt, a number of canoes which had drifted down the river [the Allegheny]; and I received repeated accounts, in June and July, from a Canadian, who deserted to me, as well as from friendly Indians, of this armament; but I never knew before then where they had assembled."[108]

To some it will always seem a mystery that Fort Pitt was never through these violent years, 1777-1783, ever seriously assaulted. But the Seneca chief who reported all of this to General Irvine was of the opinion that this particular campaign was abandoned because of reports the British had received about the increased strength of the garrison and the repairs that had been made to the fort. In any case, the attack did not come, the Indians contenting themselves with small war-party raids on the settlements, like that carried out against Hannastown.[109]

And so it was. No large-scale expedition was launched that summer from Fort Pitt; no assault was suffered that summer by the garrison at Fort Pitt. But the War of the Revolution continued fiercely in the Western Theater.

The last major battle of the Revolutionary War did not involve the Continental Army. It was not fought on the York Peninsula in the Southern Theater; it was not fought near New York City, nor at Boston; it was not fought at Fort Pitt. It was fought in the wilderness, on the "dark and bloody ground"of Indian warfare, in a region called Kentucky, at that time a county in the State of Virginia.

The date was Monday, August 19, 1782.

The battle was fought between two forces very different in their make-up. Pitted against a company of 182 Kentucky militia was the largest army of Indians and British Regulars and Queen's Rangers ever assembled, numbering almost 1000 strong, the very force that *might* have made an assault on Fort Pitt.

Simon Girty had organized the British-Indian force, rounding up the warriors of the Ohio Nations and the Iroquois, and bringing them together with the Redcoats to follow the battle plan he had himself drawn up. At the head of the army was the Tory officer Alexander McKee. The chief figure among the Indians was the ubiquitous Mohawk war-chief Joseph Brant.

Daniel Boone

At the head of one company of the Kentucky militia, along with John Todd, was Daniel Boone, at this time not yet forty-eight years old. Only a few years ago he had been captured by Shawnee Indians at the Blue Licks saltworks and held prisoner in Detroit until he was able to accomplish his escape. At the head of other units were Hugh McGary, who had lost his family to the Indians, and Stephen Trigg.

The battle site, as determined by the Indians, was the area of some salt springs in a bend of the Licking River known as the Blue Licks,[110] not far north of Boonesborough, the settlement which Boone with a company of thirty men had founded in 1775.

The Indians employed their favorite trick, inviting the Kentuckians to follow what was meant to seem a small party of warriors into the ambush prepared by the main force. In spite of cautions expressed along the way by Boone, who could read in the "too obvious" trail signs that the Indians wanted to be followed, that is, wanted an engagement, the militia fell into the trap. What followed was an incredibly costly battle for the Americans. The Kentucky militia lost seventy of their riflemen killed or captured, including eighteen officers, more than one-third of their whole force. Colonel John Todd and Colonel Stephen Trigg were both casualties; and

The Ohio

Boone's son Israel was mortally wounded. As the militia retreated, Israel, mounted upon a horse his father had found for him, paused for one last shot at the pursuing Indians. It cost him his life, as he was fatally wounded. Daniel carried his dying son to a cave, and, seizing a riderless horse, led the remnants of the militia force to safety on the far side of the Licking River.

The battle had lasted only a few minutes; it ended in a total rout of the Kentucky militia. The British-Indian army lost only three men killed, some few wounded.

So the British won the last battle of the rebellion, as indeed they had won most of the military engagements throughout the long eight years. But the victory at Blue Licks did nothing toward the King's advantage. Actually it inspired a revenge mission, led by George Rogers Clark at the head of more than one thousand (!) experienced riflemen. This force was able to drive the Shawnee from their villages on the Ohio River north of the Blue Licks battle site. With this huge army Rogers was able to destroy the Indian village of Chillicothe, as well as a number of lesser towns.

The Battle of Blue Licks, though horribly tragic for the colonials, was not a crucial battle of the War. In a way, the battle did not even belong to the war, for the Revolution had "ended" with the defeat of Cornwallis at Yorktown, ten months earlier. The war in the west was the war in overtime, and way past the time for King George III to remove the British presence from the colonies and to acknowledge the truth of the new and independent United States of America.

By October news of a preliminary peace treaty had reached America, and in fact the preliminary articles of peace were signed in Paris on November 30. So the British interest in continuing the fighting subsided to nothing. And of course the Indians were not prepared to do anything full-scale without the British support. The peace was not fixed and final yet, but the end was in sight.

Still, it was business as usual at Fort Pitt. Craig was asked during these months to serve on the judgment boards of a number of courts-martial, and even to preside. Irvine, who obviously had great confidence in Craig's executive abilities, in September of 1782 appointed the major to the full command of the Fort, for the time of his upcoming absence, to the chagrin of Craig's superiors. When he finally took leave of the Fort, in late November, to return for the winter months to Carlisle, General Irvine supplied Craig with fully detailed instructions for the defense and the maintenance of the Fort, and expressed to Washington his great confidence in him.

Major Craig felt himself ready for the responsibility. Although he was an artillery officer, he had been handed all kinds of assignments during the time he had been at the Fort, and he felt he was sufficiently familiar with the routine. But of course it was never routine at Fort Pitt. Just as he was ready to leave for Carlisle, General Irvine was advised that the British had established a military post at Sandusky, and it was suggested to him that the enemy was planning to put into place another such fort at Cuyahoga or at the mouth of the Grand River. Accordingly, determined to discover the truth of this report, he turned to Craig.

On November 11 he ordered Craig to enlist seven men, including Irvine's aide, Lieutenant John Rose, who had survived the Crawford Expedition, and proceed to the hostile Indian country of Cuyahoga (the "crooked river") "to ascertain whether any such attempts were being made by the British," at the mouth of the Cuyahoga, or at the mouth of the Grand River, which empties into Lake Erie at present-day Fairport Harbor, northeast of Cleveland. On the 13th the party set out, with one horse and the necessary provisions. Crossing the Big Beaver and the Little Beaver, they proceeded, without incident, toward Muskingum (to deceive the Indians) and then north through the country that is now northeastern Ohio, reaching finally a point just a day's journey from the mouth of the Cuyahoga, which is at present-day Cleveland, on Lake Erie. Incredibly bad weather, however, compelled Craig at this point to abort the mission. When the party returned to Fort Pitt, in the evening of December 2, Craig, having journeyed 240 miles in three weeks, reported that there was as yet no sign of any British presence at the mouth of the Cuyahoga.[111]

It is extremely doubtful that bombardier John Harris was one of the six men enlisted by Craig for this expedition. Harris was not a skilled musketeer, nor a particularly able woodsman, and in his recollections which survive there appears no mention of this scouting expedition.

Two months after the return of Major Craig's party to the Fort, there arrived the most welcome news that King George III had issued a Proclamation of Cessation of Hostilities. The formal negotiations which had begun on September 27 in Paris had produced preliminary articles of peace, and the document had been signed by Britain and by the American Peace Commissioners, John Jay, John Adams, and Benjamin Franklin, on November 30. The excitement generated by this news was muted some by the realization that until a *final* agreement was reached, and ratified by Congress, and that could be a while, the war was not altogether over.

But a permanent peace seemed assured. Throughout the late fall the prospects for an actual peace between the rebellious colonies and the mother country had steadily increased. The peace negotiations which had for long, long months been carried on in Paris seemed at last to be bearing fruit. And now at least a temporary treaty of peace had been agreed to. Writing from Carlisle on April 1, 1783, General Irvine expressed himself buoyantly to his stand-in, Major Craig, at Fort Pitt: "*Dear Major*:–As Mr. Rose[112] will carry you all the particulars of peace, etc., the present is only to congratulate you on the glorious end to the war. It has been with hard work and much assiduity, in Mr. Rose, that subsistence and pay have been obtained for the post. But after all, you will find the post has been, on the whole, better supplied than any other part of the army. Not a rag has the main army got this winter. A late commotion of the officers at headquarters has occasioned some attention from congress."

He concluded with the confidence (hope?) that the soldiers would have their long overdue back pay upon discharge from the Continental Army: "It is said the army will be settled with before they are disbanded. I will wait here [in Carlisle] some time and watch every motion. Everybody must remain in *statu quo* for some time. A peace establishment is talked of. What do you think of that? Do let me know your intention soon."[113]

Craig let Irvine know immediately what his thinking was. He made it abundantly clear that as far as he and the Western Department were concerned, the prospect of peace was just that, a prospect. There is still lots of trouble out here. On April 5, immediately upon receiving the General's letter, he responded: "*Dear General*:—Notwithstanding General [Guy] Carleton's assurance of the savages being restrained and the Indian partisans being called in, we have almost every day accounts of families being murdered or carried off. The frontier inhabitants of Washington and Ohio counties are moving into the interior settlements. The inhabitants of Westmoreland, it is said, will follow their example, and we have reason to believe that the post of Wheeling is or will shortly be evacuated."

The hostilities appeared to Craig to be widespread and serious: "It appears there are several parties of the enemy, or detachments of some large party, as they are ranging the country in several places at the same time. . . . Applications and petitions for ammunition and assistance have come in from all quarters."

And he closes out his letter, not in the happy anticipation of peace, but in the gloomy expectation of continuing engagements throughout the summer at least. And, though inadequately equipped, he pronounces his artillery company ready to proceed against the hostiles. There is *still* talk of an expedition against Detroit: "Prospects of peace on this side the mountains seem to vanish. The British either have very little influence over their savage allies or they are acting a most deceitful part. I hope, however, that the assurances we have of a pacific disposition of England will give congress an opportunity of sending a sufficient force to extirpate or at least properly chastise these marauding rascals. Should an expedition be determined on in which artillery is to be employed, I hope it will be remembered that there is not a three-pounder fit to be carried into the field at this place, and that at least two of that calibre will be wanted, according to my opinion. I hope I shall have the pleasure of battering the Wyandot blockhouses in the course of the ensuing summer and perhaps of taking possession of Detroit."[114]

But on April 19, exactly eight years from the war's beginning at Lexington and Concord, the Commander-in-Chief of the Continental Army, General George Washington, from his headquarters at Newburgh, New York, proclaimed the end of the war.[115] It was peace at last. The Proclamation announced to the weary soldiers and to all the world the birth of a new nation.

A jubilant General Irvine returned to Fort Pitt from Carlisle in May, confident that his responsibilities to the Western Department would soon be ended.

And the War came to an end. It had ended finally, formally and absolutely. It ended on September 3, 1783, with the signing by the adversaries, Great Britain and the newly organized United States, of the agreement made in the "Treaty City," Paris, France.[116] It had been two years since the American victory at Yorktown, and in that time many lives had been lost and a great deal of suffering experienced. But it was here at last. Peace. Independence.

The final document was composed of nine articles, and in its language was the same as that of the preliminary document negotiated and signed by John Jay, John Adams, and the principal architect Benjamin Franklin on November 30 the year before. It was a signal moment in the history of civilization.

The treaty first, of course, recognized the independence and the sovereignty of the world's newest nation, the United States of America. Article I read as follows:

His Brittanic Majesty acknowledges the said United States, viz. New Hampshire, Massachusetts Bay, Rhode Island, and Providence Plantations, Connecticut, New York, New Jersey, Pennsylvania, Delaware, Maryland, Virginia, North Carolina, South Carolina, and Georgia, to be free, sovereign and independent States; that he treats with them as such, and for himself, his heirs and successors, relinquishes all claims to the Government, proprietary and territorial rights of the same, and every part thereof.

Most important in the agreement was this portion which recognized the sovereignty of the United States and which established boundaries for the new nation. Benjamin Franklin had pressed for the inclusion of Canada, but he had not really expected it, and he didn't get it. In addition, fishing rights were defined; creditors of each of the two nations, Britain and the United States, were permitted payment by citizens of the other; those colonials who had remained loyal to the King (Tories) were guaranteed the restoration of their rights and property; and the Mississippi River was opened up to citizens of both parties. Finally, the articles provided for the evacuation of all British forces (New York City was still occupied by the British army, and would be well into the next year.).

But consider what the Treaty did not do. Conspicuously absent was any acknowledgment of Indian interests. When it ceded the Crown's claim to the land south of the Great Lakes and accepted terms of peace that included no reference whatsoever to Indian rights, Great

Britain totally forsook its Indian allies (its only allies in the war). And because the Treaty of Paris did not respect the boundary line fixed along the Ohio River by the Treaty of Fort Stanwix, signed by the Indians and Americans in 1768, big trouble was unavoidable Not for many years after the war would the new nation mature sufficiently to appreciate that if it were to acquire the lands to the west, lands that the Indians had lived on for thousands of years, it would most properly and honestly be done by amiable and responsible purchase rather than by force and military conquest.

All in all, a most momentous date in the history of nations, September 3, 1783.

And all of this was glorious news for the garrison at Fort Pitt. But good news in those days traveled no faster than bad news. It was at some considerable time after Bombardier John Harris's birthday (September 10) that the glad tidings finally made their way to the extreme west of the young country. And it was not until the end of the month that the Continental Army relieved the garrison at Fort Pitt of its duties, and turned the brave old fort over to the people of Pittsburgh.

Bombardier John Harris was but dimly aware of how long he had been serving the Cause. He was but dimly aware of this birthday, his thirtieth, which put an end to his youth, his "best years." He was not counting birthdays. If he had been, he would have discovered that this was the eighth on which he could be found tending his cannon. Only Washington himself, and perhaps a very few of his officers, and perhaps a very, very few of the "ordinary" soldiers had served longer. And, unlike the officers, Harris had never been granted a furlough or been relieved of duty. Except for the short period of illness between his days with the Flying Camp and his tour with Proctor's artillery, his service was continuous. The time between battles he simply spent awaiting the next engagement. He slept in a tent, or in a hut, or in a fort, or in the open air. But he was not a professional soldier. He was a farmer, a new world, New Jersey farmer. And now . . . now he was going home. Home at last.

It was time for General William Irvine to go home to Carlisle. It was time for Bombardier John Harris and Sergeant Samuel Blackwood to go home to Salem, New Jersey. It was time.

VIII

THE DELAWARE

*Peace and rest at length have come
All the day's long toil is past
And each heart is whispering, "Home,
Home at last."*

— **Thomas Hood**

With his health much impaired by anxieties and the burden of his command, General Irvine left Pittsburgh on October 1, 1783. He carried with him a letter which had been hand delivered to him on the eve of his departure. It was from the people of Pittsburgh, who had been surprised by notice of the General's leaving and were thus unprepared to give him the send-off they felt he so richly deserved.

Addressed to "Brigadier General Irvine, Commanding at Fort Pitt and its Dependencies," the letter, couched in warm notes of affection, read:

Sir:–The inhabitants of Pittsburgh having just learned that you intend to retire from this command to-morrow, would do injustice to their own feelings if they did not express their thanks to you, and their sense of your merit as an officer. During your command in this department, you have demonstrated that amidst the tumults of war, the laws may be enforced and civil liberty and society protected. Your attention to the order and discipline of the regular troops under your command, as well as to the militia, your regard to the civil rights of the inhabitants, the care you have taken of the public property, and your economy in the expenditure of the public money, we have all witnessed. This conduct, we assure you, has given general satisfaction to a people who, before your time, were, unfortunately for them, much divided, but now united.

As you are now about to quit the military life (in which your ability and integrity have been so conspicuous), we wish you all possible happiness, and that your fellow citizens may long enjoy your usefulness in civil life, in which we doubt not you will deserve their utmost confidence.[1]

We regret that we were not sooner informed of the time you intended to set out, as we are confident the whole country would have, with pride, joined us in this or a more animated and better drawn-up address.

We sincerely wish you health and a happy meeting with your family and friends at Carlisle;—and are, with great esteem and respect, sir, your obedient and very humble servants."

The letter is then signed by twelve of Pittsburgh's most distinguished citizens.

Upon receipt of the letter, General Irvine, much touched, promptly replied in kind, expressing appreciation for the writers' generous expression, and declaring his determination constantly to "facilitate the public service."[2]

Pennsylvania was soon to acknowledge formally her gratitude for his labors by the donation of a very rich expanse of land on the shores of Lake Erie, south of present-day Erie. It has long been known as "Irvine's Reserve."

At Fort Pitt, on September 30, 1783, with his signature, Brigadier General William Irvine, Commander of the Western Department, honorably discharged Bombardier John Harris, of Salem, New Jersey, from the service of the Continental Army. This was among General Irvine's last official acts as Commander of the Western Department. Indeed, it may well have been the very last of his official duties.³

The certificate of discharge reads:

*These are to certify that the bearer hereof
John Harris Bombadier* [sic]
*in the Penna. Artillery regiment, having faithfully
served the United States Six years five months
and thirteen Days and being inlisted for the war, is
hereby discharged from the American army.*

*Given at Fort Pitt Sept. 30. 1783
Wm Irvine B. Genl
Registered in the books of the* regiment, *Detachment.
Izac Howell L¹ and adjutant.*

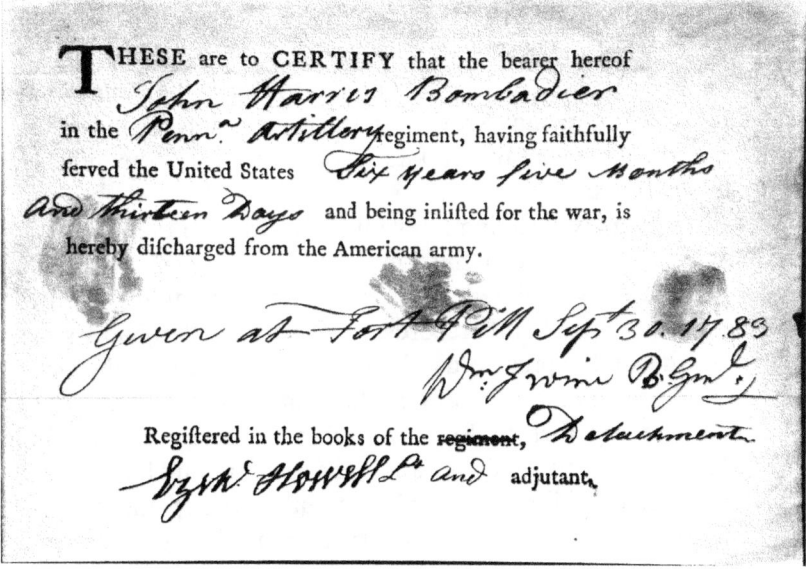

Harris had served in the militia for six months at the beginning of the war, and he had served in the Continental Army of George Washington for six years, five months, and thirteen days. He had fought in six, perhaps seven, major battles – at Long Island, at White Plains, on the Brandywine, at Germantown, at Whitemarsh, in the Sullivan Campaign (including Newtown)—as well as in countless skirmishes. He had endured the winter at Valley Forge and the march across Maryland and Pennsylvania from Carlisle to Fort Pitt and the trip down the Ohio with General George Rogers Clark. He manned the boats on two major river expeditions; he did the work of the Valley Forge encampment; he participated in the recovery of Philadelphia; and he contributed his willing service to the repairs of Fort Pitt.

Bombardier John Harris was witness to desertions and mutinous behavior and insubordination and indolence and meanness, but was never a party to any of that. He was witness to incredible acts of courage and generous sacrifice and fierce determination, and he marveled at all of that.

He saw a lot of violent action, and lost many members of his various gun crews, but he was never even wounded himself (only knocked down once by a "very tired old cannon ball that had nothin' better to do").

In all of the time he served in the artillery of the Pennsylvania Line and the Continental Army (almost seven years), he never heard from a single member of his family or from any acquaintance in Salem, New Jersey.

Now as he was saying farewell to the army of the Revolution, he had from General Irvine the army's regrets that the back pay long promised the active soldiers would not be forthcoming right away. Instead, according to family records, he was offered "probably several acres" of the land in present-day Pittsburgh which is now the Golden Triangle, at the Point, where the Allegheny and the Monongahela Rivers come together to form the Ohio. There are no official documents to present the facts of the matter, but family letters and the John Harris family bible, and word-of-mouth have kept the story alive for more than 200 years. Says Harris's great-great granddaughter, "We don't have all the details, but there is one letter in which he was offered a considerable portion of the Point, apparently in payment from the Government as back pay and a bonus."[4]

These "several acres" were presumably just east of the location of Fort Pitt, and must have included the Duquesne heights along the

The Delaware

Monongahela, for Harris insisted that "the bluffs . . . were too steep," and that "it would be too hard to get the cows down to water." Besides, he declared that "Pittsburg would never amount to anything anyway." So he turned down this remarkable offer! And as his great-great-great granddaughter has ruefully observed, "He just missed the Point."[5]

Instead Bombardier John Harris accepted 200 acres in what is today Mercer County, north of Pittsburgh. In this way the soldiers were being compensated for payment owed to them for service in the army. The problem was that these lands which were being parceled out did not belong to the United States or to Pennsylvania. They belonged to the Indians, or at least the Indians thought so.[6]

Here is what happened in the months just before Harris's discharge: "By act of the Legislature in 1783, even before the Indian title to the lands in this section of the State was claimed to have been either negotiated for or extinguished, a strip of land along the north and west side of the Ohio and Allegheny Rivers, commencing at the place where the western boundary of the State crossed the Ohio River, and thence up said rivers to the mouth of Mogulbughtiton Creek, thence by a west line to the western boundary of the State, and thence south to the place of beginning, was set apart for the purpose of being surveyed into numbered lots, each containing from 200 to 350 acres, to be sold for 'certificates of depreciation,'[7] given in settlement to the soldiers of the Pennsylvania Line in the Revolutionary Army. These certificates were assumed to be the special value of all claims against the State for military service, and for those lands thus set apart were to be received in specie." These bounty lands which were defined in this fashion, when surveyed, were discovered to be located in what is today Mercer County.[8]

In October of 1784 Fort Stanwix, in New York State, played host a second time to a treaty session. On this occasion, Congress-appointed commissioners met with the principal chiefs of the Six Nations, to negotiate a peace, and to define boundaries. At this time the commissioners of Pennsylvania were able to purchase the right and title of the Six Nations to all their lands within the Commonwealth of Pennsylvania. However, the Delawares and Wyandots, who had been thus disenfranchised, continued to profess ownership of lands within the State. It was not until January of 1785 that all Indian rights to lands within Pennsylvania as it was then defined were extinguished. And this was done by purchase. This occurred at the treaty session held at Fort McIntosh (present-day Beaver).

Still the rights were contested. When in the spring and summer of 1785, not long after the Indians' title had been extinguished by the Treaties of Fort Stanwix and Fort McIntosh, surveyors began to define and to number the plots that were to be turned over to the Revolutionary War soldiers, the Indians expressed their dissatisfaction in no uncertain terms. And by the time Washington was elected President they had worked themselves up to an acute sense of injustice. The Seneca chiefs Cornplanter, Half-Town, and Great Tree sought and won an audience with Washington. In Philadelphia, the new nation's capital, they registered their dissatisfaction and put forth their claims. With Cornplanter as chief spokesman, they made quite a speech.

Washington replied with great tact. The Indians replied to him without tact but with a good bit of logic. Washington now made reference to Fort Stanwix and to the agreements that had been reached in the treating. In the end, Washington did not restore to them the lands ("this little piece") they were requesting.

In all of this there were a number of ironies. One was that these "Bounty Lands," which were to go to "officers, surgeons, chaplains, musicians, and privates," were actually settled by only a very few of the soldiers to whom they had been donated. They were sold to others.[9]

What John Harris did with his 200 acres is not clear. Apparently he never did take the trouble even to see the land, and he may not have paid taxes,[10] but he did always assume his ownership, for at the time of his death he willed the acres to his son Peter.

Bombardier John Harris was in extremely poor health as he left Fort Pitt, suffering as he was from exposure and experiencing the familiar and ever recurring bouts of the chills and fever. Besides, he was penniless, as the Continental money with which he had been paid over the last many months had depreciated so much as to be next to worthless. Nevertheless, clutching his discharge securely, and conscious of his 200 "Indian" acres, he set out on foot for Salem, New Jersey, 300 miles away. With him was Sergeant Samuel Blackwood, with whom he had served throughout the long war. Whether the two managed to hitch rides on farm wagons, or were able to secure horses, is not known. Nor is it known just exactly when it was they finally showed up in Salem. Presumably it was near the middle of November in the first days of winter. In the very best case it was unquestionably a most arduous trip for them.

John Harris returned to an excitedly warm welcome. His family had long presumed him dead. And of course he knew not what or whom he would be finding. He did not find his mother, who had died before the war's end, just a few years after the death of his father. But here, all living in the Salem area, were his five brothers, Abraham, Isaac, Jacob, Parmenas, and Nicholas. And here was sister Sophia, just married.

All, of course, were eager to hear about his experiences in the war, and he very early got into the habit of narrating his adventures. He was not shy about his service, and in fact felt rather proud to have been a part of the effort that had produced a new nation. But he was startled to hear how the war had come to Salem.

The first thing he learned, from his brothers and from Sophia, was that during the time he was at Valley Forge he was eating food that had been produced from his own land, and from the lands of his family and their neighbors right here in Salem. What he had not known then was that the foraging expeditions carried on by his own General Mad Anthony Wayne out of Valley Forge had regularly brought Wayne to Salem, New Jersey. And what he was very happy to hear was that the people of Salem had generously provided whatever they could in foodstuffs and supplies.

What made him unhappy was the report of the British invasion of Salem County and of British offenses. His brothers told him all about the fighting at Quinton's Bridge, and the massacre at the Hancock House, and the burning of Colonel Benjamin Holme's home. He learned that three of his brothers had actually fought at Quinton's Bridge. And he learned about the exploits of Captain William Smith, whom he had known before he set out for the war.

He learned, much to his surprise, that Captain Smith had participated in the Battle of Long Island, and that he had been at White Plains, and that he had had all kinds of militia experience both before and after the battles for New York.

His brothers referred to the bridges. Of course John Harris was well acquainted with Alloway's Creek, and with the three bridges that spanned it: Quinton's Bridge, three miles below Salem; and the old bridge a little farther south that had been built in 1709 and was known as Hancock's Bridge; and the one at Alloway's called Thompson's Bridge.

It was the Battle of Quinton's Bridge that Isaac and Jacob wanted to tell him about. And it is the defense of Quinton's Bridge that Captain Smith was most famous for.

With the engagement at Quinton's Bridge at the center, the battle for the Salem, New Jersey, farm produce has been called "the most decisive battle of the American Revolution."[11] The point is that without the food that General Wayne was able to carry back to Valley Forge from the Salem County farmlands, "there would have been no Yorktown." And "had it not been for the sacrifice which the massacre at Old Hancock House typifies, the Revolution would have been a failure."[12] George Washington himself publicly acknowledged the critical worth of Salem and South Jersey to the war effort, insisting that if it had not been for the generosity of these people the troops at Valley Forge would have starved to death.[13]

General Wayne, though regarded by most historians as a skillful, while impetuous, field general and strategist, was known to the people of Salem as "Drover" Wayne, for his great ability to secure beef and other food for the troops; and it may very well be that in his foraging expeditions into New Jersey, as well as through Pennsylvania and Delaware, he rendered his greatest service.[14]

General Wayne's excursions for food and supplies were begun from Valley Forge on February 16, 1778. On this day, Washington, who would be in constant communication with Wayne, wherever the General found himself, dispatched a letter to Governor George Clinton of New York:

> *It is with great reluctance I trouble you on a subject, which does not properly fall within your province but it is a subject that occasions me more distress than I have felt since the commencement of the war; and which loudly demands the most zealous exertions of every person of weight and authority who is interested in the success of our affairs. I mean the present dreadful situation of the army for want of provisions and the miserable prospects before us with respect to*

futurity.

It is more alarming than you will probably conceive for to form a just idea of it, it were necessary to be on the spot. For some days past there has been little less than a famine in camp. A part of the army has been a week without any kind of flesh and the rest three or four days. Naked and starving as they are, we cannot enough admire the incomparable patience and fidelity of the soldiery that they have not been ere this excited by their suffering to general mutiny and desperation.[15]

Two days later Washington appealed in highly emotional language to the people of New Jersey, Delaware, Pennsylvania, Maryland, and Virginia. He urged farmers everywhere to do all they could to preserve cattle for the immediate and future needs of the Continental Army.[16]

But the British, too, had learned about the bounty that might be acquired from the farmlands of South Jersey. In fact, an invasion had been planned for a long time, and had only been put off because of extremely inhospitable weather. Finally the time seemed right. In March of 1778, while John Harris was fighting cold and hunger at Valley Forge, carefully selected regiments from the British army occupying Philadelphia boarded the ships of an armada preparing a foraging invasion of Salem and Cumberland Counties. It was a most ambitious operation. The fleet included sixty-three transport vessels of all sizes and was headed up by the frigates *Camilla* and *Pearl* and the flagship *Roebuck*.

It required two days for the somewhat ponderous flotilla to reach Mud Island and three more days to proceed past Billingsport and Marcus Hook and to reach Reedy Island, which stood out from the mouth of Salem Creek. Here, at the shoulder of the shore known as Finn's Point, the British forces under Colonel Charles Mawhood, who had performed so ably in the defense of Princeton, and including a company of the Queen's Rangers, under the command of Major John Graves Simcoe,[17] disembarked. The total number of troops was close to 1300, and the Queen's Rangers were particularly to be feared. As one historian's description accounts for them, "They were trained as guerila fighters, they wore green [were often called the "Greens"] for camouflage and were adept at living off the land, surprise attacks by night and stealth, cunning use of terrain, and swift, deadly, bayonet raids, all of which tactics made them exceptionally dangerous against militia in the marsh and woodland of South Jersey."[18] The Queen's Rangers was a corps composed chiefly of Loyalist colonists from Connecticut, New York, and Pennsylvania. These men were mostly foot soldiers, but the corps included also some thirty light horsemen, known as Huzzars, who served as scouts and as advance guards.[19]

The British proceeded promptly, without any real resistance, to occupy Salem, and thereby double the size of the community. Colonel Elijah Hand, in command of the militia forces of Cumberland and Salem Counties had been expecting the British assault at Cohansey, but on the morning of March the 18th the first engagement actually occurred in Quinton. It was the battle fought at Quinton's Bridge.

Fortunately, Colonel Benjamin Holme, understanding that the British in order to reach the rich farmlands they had designs on, would have to cross Alloway's Creek, had persuaded Hand the night before to prepare for attacks at all of the bridges on Alloway's Creek. At Quinton's Bridge the defense was commanded by thirty-six-year old Captain William Smith.

When the British became aware that these rude farmers were actually planning to resist the invasion, they could not conceal their contempt. The British commander, Colonel Charles Mawhood, hearing of this "insolence," promptly sent out 50-man companies to challenge the defenses at each bridge, and to "chastise" the ridiculous militia. To Quinton's Bridge was dispatched one battalion of regular troops.

At Quinton's, as at the other two bridges, the British were met by a hail of gunfire from the well-entrenched militia on the far side of the creek. Though no damage was done by either side, there was no crossing of the bridge. Hearing the shots, Andrew Bacon, who had been plowing in his fields, came running to the bridge, and, sensing the situation, seized an axe, and promptly began to sever the draw which supported the bridge. He continued to work while the British sniped away at him, and even though wounded was able to complete the job and collapse the bridge, all before he was finally captured.

One account comes from the 1903 files of the *Salem Sunbeam*: "Andrew Bacon was captured in the hollow of the present road, just below the road which intersects the one going to Hancock's Bridge.

He, being a large powerful man, resisted the order to surrender, and shot one English soldier and knocking another from his horse with the breach of this gun, but being bayoneted in the back, he was disabled, captured and sent to Philadelphia as a prisoner of war."[20]

Although there occurs a great deal of confusion in the accounts of Bacon's heroism, in all versions he resisted his capture savagely before becoming the first casualty of the battle of Quinton's Bridge. But conflicting impressions of Bacon's activity at the bridge have been published. It is not clear, for example, whether he disabled the bridge and then went home unscathed, to return to the bridge at sounds of battle, or whether he was wounded at the time of the cutting of the draw and captured then. Moreover, in one account he is imprisoned on the *Jersey*; in another he is confined in Philadelphia prisons. Likely he went from Philadelphia to the *Jersey*.[21] In any case, it is known that he survived the war and lived to a very ripe old age.

What followed was disastrous for the patriots. Colonel Mawhood, having heard of the trouble at Quinton had rushed a large force of his regular troops and some 200 of the Queen's Rangers as well to the forested region of Quinton known as Mill Hollow. Here he had the Rangers take over the home of Benjamin Weatherby. Herding the family into the cellar, the Rangers prepared an ambush.

Meanwhile the British at the bridge, having shown so far only a modest force, now, under orders apparently from Mawhood, feigned a retreat from the bridge in the direction of the Weatherby house. It was an old Indian trick.

Captain William Smith was the senior officer at Quinton's Bridge. He well deserved the command. Smith had been very active already in the cause of the Revolution. After serving as Lieutenant in the Second Battalion of the Salem County Militia, he was commissioned, May 24, 1776, by the Provincial Congress of New Jersey, as Captain of the Lower Company of Foot Militia in Upper Alloway's Creek Township (Colonel John Holme commanding). Later that year he served as Second Lieutenant in Brigadier General Nathaniel Heard's Brigade, New Jersey State Troops, in the division of the Continental Army headed up by Major General Nathanael Greene. He had taken part in the Battle of Long Island and in the Battle of White Plains. He had served a tour of duty from February 4, 1777, to April 20, 1777. On July 1, 1777, he was commissioned

Captain of a company of militia in Lower Alloways Creek Township, Second Battalion of the Salem County, New Jersey, Militia (Colonel Benjamin Holme commanding).

Perceiving the withdrawal of the assaulting force, and noting how few they were in number, Captain Smith, despite orders to the contrary, called for an advance. The militia laid down planks to span the bridge and, crossing the stream, pursued the "retreating" British troops. As Smith's militiamen passed the Weatherby house, one of the ambushing Rangers could not stifle a mocking laugh. Smith, in this way made aware of the deception, now tried to rally his men, but the Rangers opened fire, instantly killing several members of the militia.

Smith, having too late recognized the ploy, now ordered his men to fall back to the bridge. The British of course followed at white heat. But just as they were about to charge the bridge, Colonel Elijah Hand with a very strong force of his Cumberland Militia arrived, and delivered such a lethal musket fire that the Rangers were thrown into confusion. In the disorder which followed most of Smith's militiamen were able to cross the bridge. But Captain Smith himself, who had stood courageously at the bridge to muster his men across, had a lock of hair shot from the back of his head, and another bullet creased his loins. His horse was struck with two bullets, but, incredibly, was able to carry the captain over the bridge before collapsing and falling dead under a tree.

The patriot casualties tallied seven dead, nineteen wounded, and seventeen captured. The wounded Andrew Bacon was marked by the British "not available to prisoner exchange," and, as noted, was eventually placed aboard the notorious British prison ship *Jersey*, which was anchored in New York Harbor, and was probably the vessel to which Colonel Robert Magaw had been consigned since November.[22]

Among the patriot participants in the action at Quinton's Bridge were three of John Harris's brothers, Corporal Jacob Harris, and Privates Abraham and Isaac. From Abraham, his oldest and most articulate brother, John heard about Jacob, how he had lost his gun, and how he had been very severely wounded by saber cuts and actually left behind for dead.[23]

From Isaac, who was John's senior by five years, John heard about Abraham, about how he had been stationed with Captain

Smith's militia at Elsinboro with Jacob in January, when John was at Valley Forge, and about how valiantly he had conducted himself during the rout at the bridge.

From Jacob, who was now obviously fully recovered from his wounds, and happily married, John heard about Isaac, whose experience at the bridge was perhaps the most dramatic. In the return flight to the bridge from the Weatherby house, Isaac not only lost his gun but was so nearly overtaken that he was compelled, amid a hail of bullets, to launch himself into the creek and swim to the other bank to escape. Just before brother John's return to Salem from Fort Pitt, Isaac was reimbursed by the Assembly of New Jersey for his lost gun.[24]

"Brother Nicholas was there too," reminded Abraham. And so he had been. Nicholas was only eighteen years old at the time of the action at Quinton's Bridge, but he was there. He was there with a gun on his shoulder.

Of course the episode of Quinton's Bridge was not all that Isaac and Jacob and Abraham had to report to their long lost brother John. Not by a long shot. Salem County had been a hotbed during the time Washington was encamped at Valley Forge.

Colonel Mawhood, made insanely angry by news of the British failure to take the bridge and by reports of heavy losses (though in fact the British had lost only one man killed at Quinton's Bridge), resolved on revenge and promptly embarked on a campaign of terror. Seizing upon the information delivered to him by a Tory, that rebels were hidden in the old Hancock House, he dispatched a company of soldiers under Queen's Ranger Commander John Graves Simcoe, the "hero" of Crooked Billet, with orders to kill every man.

Simcoe had done a preliminary surveillance, and he had drawn up a plan perfect for the talents of the Rangers. His idea was to proceed in boats on Salem Creek downstream to the Delaware River. Once in the river, he expected they could drift downstream until they reached that point at which Alloway's Creek enters the river. Then, if they could muffle their oars they could move without detection upstream to the region of Hancock's Bridge. But, as it happened, when they came to the mouth of Alloway's Creek they found the tide strong against them. Simcoe might have given up at this point, but instead he here abandoned the boats and with Tory guides led his

Rangers sloshing through the marshes the remaining two miles to Hancock's Village. Here, at about five o'clock in the morning, they reassembled. They took the single sentry by surprise, killed him,[25] and entered the house, by both the rear door and the front, to fall upon the sleeping men. Apparently the men, thirty in number, were herded into the attic, and were there mercilessly bayoneted to death. No quarter was given. No one was spared. Even unarmed noncombatants, including three Quakers, and Quaker Judge William Hancock himself, were slain, all by bayonets. The only shot fired was discharged at a man trying to escape.[26] Visible to this day is the grim evidence of the massacre, black bloodstains everywhere in the attic.

Hancock House

It is very difficult to justify what happened at the Hancock House. Nobody has done it yet. Some try to excuse the officer in command, Major John Simcoe, noting that "he had no more control over his partisan troops than any officer who commanded irregular troops." But Simcoe did not try to absolve himself, admitting only that "Some very unfortunate circumstances happened here," and lamenting that "Events like these are the real miseries of war."[27]

John Harris was used to horrible stories. He had heard about those that involved savages, like Wyoming and Cherry Valley, and because of Gnadenhuetten he knew how merciless and inhumane his fellow whites could be. But this news chilled him to the bone. Some of those men whose names he was now hearing had been acquaintances of his.

The heroism exhibited at Quinton's Bridge by Captain Smith and Colonel Benjamin Holme and the militiamen, together with the report of the massacre at the Hancock House, so strengthened the spirit of the farmers that they vowed to die rather than to permit the British a particle of their goods, though even gold was offered.

So the enraged Colonel Mawhood had to be content with random depredations, like driving the wife and family of Colonel Holme out of doors, absconding with the family clock and burning down the farmhouse.

Shortly following the massacre, March 21, Colonel Charles Mawhood sent a dispatch to Colonel Elijah Hand, Commander of the Cumberland County and the Salem County Militia. In this letter he urged the militia, as well as private men, to lay down their arms and depart to their homes. Failure to do so he declared would result in extreme punishment. He would, he insisted, arm the Tories, and attack all of the militia who persisted in arms, burn their homes and destroy their property. And then he even appended a list of the names of the seventeen men who would be the first objects of his vengeance.

In the reply that Colonel Hand returned to Mawhood is expressed the spirit with which the people of Salem and indeed all of South Jersey had been resisting the British invasion of their farmlands. Actually the spirit of this letter is the spirit which characterized the patriots throughout the entire Revolution. Here are scorn and defiance, stout courage, fierce devotion to the cause, with an unshaken confidence that the cause is right, and a stubborn refusal to acknowledge the odds against patriot success. The tone of the reply is that with which Colonel Robert Magaw promptly rejected the first British order to surrender Fort Washington.

The letter was composed with Quinton's Bridge and the Hancock House murders very vivid in the writer's eye:

Sir–I have been favored with what you say humanity has

induced you to propose. It would have given me much pleasure to have found that humanity has been the line of conduct to your troops since you came to Salem. Not denying quarters, but butchering our men who surrendered themselves prisoners in the skirmish last Thursday, and bayoneting, yesterday morning, at Hancock's Bridge, in the most cruel manner, in cold blood, men who were taken by surprise, in a situation in which they neither could nor did attempt to make any resistance, and some of whom were not fighting men, are instances too shocking for me to relate, and, I hope, for you to hear. The brave are ever generous and humane. After expressing your sentiments of humanity, you proceed to make a request, which I think you would despise us if complied with. Your proposal that we should lay down our arms we absolutely reject. We have taken them up to maintain rights which are dearer to us than our lives, and will not lay them down till either success has crowned our arms with victory, or, like many ancient worthies contending for liberty, we meet with an honorable death. You mention that if we reject your proposal you will put arms in the hands of Tories against us. We have no objections to the measure, for it would be a very good one to fill our arsenals with arms. Your threats to wantonly burn and destroy our houses and other property, and reduce our wives and children to beggary and distress is a sentiment which my humanity almost forbids me to recite, and induces me to imagine that I am reading the cruel order of a barbarous Attila, and not of a gentleman, brave, generous, and polished, with a genteel European education. To wantonly destroy will injure your cause more than ours; it will increase your enemies and our army. To destine to destruction the property of our most distinguished men, as you have done in your proposals, is, in my opinion, unworthy a generous foe, and more like a rancorous feud between two contending barons than a war carried on by one of the greatest powers on earth against a people nobly struggling for liberty. A line of honor would mark out that these men should share the fate of their country. If your arms should be crowned with victory (which God forbid!) they and their property will be entirely at the disposal of your sovereign. The loss of their property, while their persons are out of your power, will only render them desperate, and, as I said before, increase your foes and our army, and retaliation upon Tories and their property is not entirely out of our power. Be assured that

The Delaware

these are the sentiments and determined resolution, not of myself only, but of all the officers and privates under me.

My prayer is, sir, that this may reach you in health and great happiness.

Given at headquarters at Quinton's Bridge, the 22d day of March, 1778.

And the letter is signed *Elijah Hand, Colonel.* [28]

Some consider this reply one of the most memorable letters of the entire Revolution. And historian Frank Stewart feels that "a memorial of some character should be erected at Roadstown and the famous reply of Col. Hand to Col. Mawhood emblazed on it."

In what temper Colonel Mawhood read this letter is not recorded. And though for a little while yet he sent out raiding parties and continued to occupy Salem, his high hopes for a bountiful harvest here in South Jersey were terribly disappointed. And he did not hunger so much for another engagement with Colonel Hand's militia as to force one. In all of this action during the invasion of South Jersey, the British lost only thirty-one men. But it can be noted for history that the Battle of South Jersey, or the Battle of Salem, or the Battle of the Three Bridges, or whatever it may one day be called, was not a victory for the King's Men.

John Harris, hearing all of this, felt a strange sensation. He couldn't but think that he might have done a great deal in the cause of the Revolution simply by staying home. What his brothers had told him made him very proud of the people of Salem.

A fine monument now stands on the main street of Quinton, only a short distance from the bridge across Alloway's Creek. The inscription reads: "In memory of Col, Benjamin

Quinton Monument

Holme, Col. Elijah Hand, Capt. William Smith, Andrew Bacon and those other patriots who defended the bridge at Quinton, March 17, 1778." The Hancock House, still standing, was turned into a shrine by the State of New Jersey in 1932 as a memorial to the men who gave their lives there.[29] Its idyllic charm is in great contrast to the horrors of that night.

Captain Smith served continuously throughout the Revolution, but he survived it and was able to enjoy the later years of his life at his homestead on the Quinton-Jericho Road some two miles from Quinton. He was wedded twice (marrying sisters), and had nine children. The eighth-born (1780) he named Washington, who became thus possibly one of the earliest of the children born in the United States to be named for the central figure of the Revolution. And this Washington Smith, who himself was father to eleven children, named one of his seven sons Washington.

On September 28, 1784, to the "consternation" of his large family, Captain William Smith, at age forty-two, obtained a tavern license, in Upper Alloways Creek, although there were already twenty-six licensed taverns in Salem County, whose population was a mere 8172.[30]

In his very last days Captain Smith moved from the plantation to a home in the village of Quinton, now supposed to have been located just east of the bridge and near the spot of the DAR monument which commemorates the battle. His will was composed, witnessed and registered in Salem County on May 1, 1815. He died in 1820 and was buried on the Old Hill Farm, that his father, Peter Smith, had left him, among many members of the family,

Hancock House historic marker

in a little family graveyard. The old farmhouse is still standing, but gone is the familiar buttonwood tree which for so many years presided over it.

Captain William Smith home

John Harris, returning at the age of thirty to his native Salem from Fort Pitt and the War of the Revolution, had good reason to be interested in anything having to do with Captain William Smith.

When John returned to his New Jersey home, he had of course that portion of his father's farm which had been left to him, but as his health had been so much impaired, and as he was penniless, he simply stayed off and on with his brothers, all five of whom were living close by. He was particularly well cared for by Nicholas' wife Sarah, who was a most energetic and able woman of the house. But he was welcome at every one of the family homes, and he delighted in his many nephews and nieces. One caution he did not need to be advised of: He had to conduct himself as a Baptist. Everybody in the large Harris family was a Baptist.

For a little more than a year, as his health steadily improved, he managed in this way. As he had a most capacious and retentive mind, he was constantly sought out, by family and friends, for stories of the

Revolution. He was only too happy to oblige. He delighted in recalling episodes of the war, and he saw no need ever to embellish his account. He would invite an audience by curling up in a rocker, and lapsing into a kind of trance. "I was with Washington at Valley Forge, you know," he would begin.

Before long, he fixed on a very special audience. He began to squire around the first-born of Captain William Smith, the hero of Quinton's Bridge. Lydia, always a tiny woman, was very lucky to be living, for when she was born she was given no chance. Amos Harris, Lydia's grandson, writing in 1907, recalls the family story that Lydia was "so small when she was born that they put her in a quart pitcher and put the cover on it . . . and she lived to have eleven children afterwards." Lydia had been only thirteen when, standing with her younger sister Hannah under the enormous buttonwood (sycamore) tree which presided over her father's farmhouse, she heard the booming of the guns fired at Brandywine. At the time John Harris returned to Salem she was nineteen.

Lydia Smith Harris

It was not long before the two were married. The ceremony was conducted by the Reverend Peter Peterson, Pastor Van Horn of the First Baptist Church of Salem. The date was January 12, 1785. The bride was some ten years younger than her husband.

For a little more than ten years John and Lydia eked out a living on the farm. In this time Lydia gave birth to four children, only two of whom, Stretch and Benjamin, survived infancy. In 1795 they scraped together enough money to purchase Round Island from Joshua Eaton, who had owned it for three years. Not so much an island really as an extension of marsh land, Round Island stood a little offshore in the Delaware River two miles south of Alloways Creek Neck.

Although in size it measured some 1000 acres, there were only about thirty acres so far up out of the marsh as to permit farming. The island was bounded by Hope Creek on one side, a passage called Cat Gut on another, Fishing Creek on a third, and by the Delaware River to the west.

The island was called "round," not so much for its own shape, as indeed it is not round, but for the circle effect produced by the island's dense thicket of trees at the center.

When John and Lydia came to their new home with their little ones, Stretch, who was then seven and one-half years old, and Benjamin, who was barely two, they found only a very small two-story frame house and the necessary out-buildings.

But the sight was most pleasing to John. He had always loved the water, and his wartime experiences on the Susquehanna and on the Ohio, had done nothing to dampen his enthusiasm for rivers and lakes. And he had always preferred trapping and fishing to straight-out farming. He was confident that his family would fare well out here.

The island, as he had known it would, turned out to be alive with waterfowl. Here were the great blue heron and the bittern, all kinds of ducks, blackbirds, gulls and terns. As the land was almost entirely marsh, adorned with cat-o'-nine tail and swamp grass, it abounded with muskrats. Their tunnels were everywhere. And as he surveyed the marsh, John supposed that his trapping might even occasionally produce a mink.

There was the river too. In a few steps one could be swimming in the Delaware, or boating, or fishing. John meant to fish. He figured to fish plenty, and he'd make the boys fishermen too.

He did not mean to neglect farming altogether. In fact, he made a farm of the island in a hurry. He assembled the standard chickens and pigs, and even a few geese, a team of oxen, four cows, and a few sheep. There was good soil enough, he surmised. Maybe a little corn, and timothy for the stock. An orchard, or at least a few fruit trees, to keep Lydia busy, and a vegetable garden, to keep her really busy.

He looked forward eagerly to winter. That would be muskrat trapping season, and visions of beautiful glossy pelts flitted through his imagination. And so the little family began a new life. And as it turned out it was a good life. Turned out there were indeed plenty of muskrats, and each year brought a better price; and the fishing was productive too. The biggest problem for the Harris family came in the form of mosquitoes, which were a whole lot more numerous in the marshes even than muskrats, and in a number of other biting flies. These took some getting used to.

They had been on the island only three years when there came the sad news of the death of John's younger brother Parmenas. Although they had not seen much of his brothers since they moved to Round Island, they had known that Parmenas had not been in very good health for some time, and they were not surprised to learn that the dreaded yellow fever had taken him.

During the nine years that John and Lydia lived on Round Island, four more children were born to them, all robustly healthy. And while the family did not really prosper, in the fine sense of that term, it was a close-knit, happy, outdoors life that they lived.

Unlike his older brother Abraham, who was passionate about reading, John kept no books in his home. Lydia, who apparently had never learned to read or to write very well, had little chance to improve in these abilities, and the children had no chance at all for education. Except for the Bible. The family bible, the 1768 edition of John Wesley's 1755 version of the King James Bible, which was published in Dublin, is well worn and doubtless was much read by all members of the family. The birth dates of the children of John and Lydia are all recorded at the beginning of the New Testament.[31]

By 1804 John and Lydia had laid aside enough money (much of it from furs) to make the move they had been longing for. To Elijah Fogg, John paid $1400 for a nearby island called Ragged Island. Like Round Island, this island was named for its trees. It was not called Ragged Island because of a serrated shoreline, as one might suppose, but rather because of the manner in which the few trees had appeared, scattered and willy-nilly.[33]

John did not have any desire to join the westward movement that so many of his fellow Salem Countians found compelling. His brother Jacob, a very small and wiry man who had taken up the weaver's trade, was constantly talking of it. And John heard regularly about "the new life out west" from Jacob's eldest daughter, Sarah, who while a little girl lived with John and Lydia. Jacob, however, was not just talking about it. In 1807 he packed up the family, his second wife and seven children (including Sarah), and headed for Ohio.[33]

So the John Harris family, excepting the eldest son, Stretch, moved just a short way across the water and into some fresh muskrat country. Stretch, who was left to fend for himself, was married eight years later, to Rebecca Padgett, and with their four children lived on Round Island for a good many more years.[34]

John was fifty-two when he took his family to Ragged Island. He was at this time in fairly good health, except that he had become somewhat hard of hearing. He could hear well enough the hoarse croak of the blue heron as it left one stalking station for another, and he could hear well enough the rattling call of the kingfisher, and he could hear the booming of the bull frogs through the nighttime, but he could not hear the call of the white-throated sparrow, even when Lydia called his attention to it. And it bothered him a lot that he could not always hear Lydia's voice distinctly. Her voice had ever been one of her many charms.

To Lydia and John on Ragged Island there were born two more children, Clarissa, who would live two days beyond her 81st birthday, and Beulah, who lived only four years. Lydia was forty-five years old, when the last of her eleven children was born. Clarissa, with her husband, David Ellett, in 1834 (twenty years after the death of her father and ten years beyond the death of her mother) joined the westward movement that had taken her Uncle Jacob and her seven cousins out of Salem. They settled at Bunker Hill in Goshen Township (now in Mahoning County), Ohio.

John saw little of his brothers and his sister Sophia during his last years. Sophia, who was a good bit younger than John, had married a man by the name of William Paulin (sometimes rendered Pacelin), and had borne five children. John's oldest brother, Abraham, continued for his whole life to live on the land given him by his father. He was "a remarkable sober temperate man," an extremely devout Christian, and a deacon in Salem's Baptist Church for many years. Even at ninety years of age he could be seen trudging to the Sunday church service from his farm, a distance of seven miles!

After Abraham's Scotch wife, Herenhappuch Blackwood, died, the elder of his two daughters, Margaret, who never married, stayed on in the home to care for him, but her father outlived her too.

Isaac, too, was happily married (and a Baptist) and extremely hard-working. He and his wife, Mary Young, were busy rearing nine sons, the eldest of whom, when only five years old, had watched his father swim for his life amid a stream of bullets fired from the other side of Quinton's Bridge.

John knew that Nicholas, seven years his junior, longed to get to the city, that is, Philadelphia, and open up a feed store or a livery stable. But as yet he was still living on the farm with his good wife, Sarah Sheppard, by whom he had had eight sons and one daughter.

Although John Harris, on Round Island or on Ragged Island, or even in Salem, was not in close touch with the outside world, from time to time this veteran of the Revolutionary War heard of officers and men with whom he had served, and had reports too on a number of people whom he had fought against. He was of course extremely happy with the young country's insistence that it be governed through its infant years by its champion, George Washington. And it pleased him, too, to learn that serving in the Cabinet of the nation's first president were two of his old "friends" from Valley Forge, Alexander Hamilton and Henry Knox.

Somehow he got news from the west of the dreaded Cornplanter. He learned, much to his surprise, that Pennsylvania had actually made a friend of the Seneca war-chief. The Commonwealth of Pennsylvania, noting that Cornplanter had after the war worked most zealously for peace along the frontier, participating in all of the important treaties since 1784, provided a sanctuary for the great Cyantwahia. In 1795, a grateful Commonwealth extended to Cornplanter the right to select 1500 acres "in this tract [the upper Allegheny River] or country on Lake Erie." As he and his people had already been happy on the Allegheny for the thirteen years they had been settled there, naturally the chief chose this ground, and it continued to be known as Cornplanter Town.

On February 18, 1836, the long and vigorous life of the great Seneca Indian chief, who had allied his people with the British in their effort to squelch the rebellion in the colonies, and who had worked after that for peace with the white settlers, was laid to rest, amid much ceremony near the great river he had always loved. Embittered in his late years, he had requested an unmarked grave, but that could hardly be. In fact, only thirty years after his interment, the Commonwealth of Pennsylvania elected to establish a monument to his memory, and in 1866, there was erected at this grave site a beautiful stone. It has been regarded as the first monument ever erected to an American Indian. This monument was moved in 1960, together with the remains of Cornplanter, to higher ground, in order that it might be spared the inundation that would come with the closing of the newly built Kinzua Dam. It is the same monument that stands now, still overlooking the Allegheny River. Its inscription, now, after forty-six years, is much weathered. But on the stone, on one side, can still be made out the words:

Cyantwahia, The Cornplanter,
John O'Bail, Alias Cornplanter,
DIED
At Cornplanter Town, Feb. 18, A.D. 1836
Aged about 100 years.

Cornplanter Monument

Upon another side a capsule account of his life and character is engraved: "Chief of the Senaca [sic] tribe, and a principal chief of the Six Nations from the period of the Revolutionary War to the time of his death. Distinguished for talent, courage, eloquence, sobriety, and love for tribe and race, to whose welfare he devoted his time, his energy, and his means during a long and eventful life."[35]

And what of that other notorious Indian chief, equally prominent in the War of the Revolution, the most able Mohawk leader of the Iroquois, Joseph Brant? Well, just before Christmas in the year 1807, John Harris heard that Brant, after adopting Christianity and preaching it forcefully, had passed away in Ontario.[36] His post-war story was much the same as what Harris had heard for Cornplanter. Like Cornplanter, Brant had finally come to see the need for his people to adopt the ways of the whites. Having failed to do much for the Mohawks in the new United States, he turned to Great Britain, whose cause he had supported most energetically and ably throughout the Revolution. The British responded. By Canada's Governor Sir Frederick Haldimand, Brant was in 1784 awarded a 675,000-acre grant of land on the Grand River, in that region now including the city of Brantford.

Brant promptly brought his people, as many of the Iroquois tribes as cared to come, to the Grand River Basin. As they had to cross the river to reach the land that had been set apart for them, the crossing became known as "Brant's ford," and the village which appeared there by and by naturally was called Brantford. In all there were 1843 Indians, most of them Mohawks from the Mohawk River region of New York State, who composed the original settlement. It was called the Grand River Reservation for the Mohawk. Today there stands on the original grant site the Joseph Brant Memorial Hospital. In the lobby hangs a portrait of the great Mohawk chieftain.

Brant, while very active in the community, like Cornplanter in Cornplanter Town, especially in the interest of religion and education,[37] lived somewhat apart, near present-day Burlington, at Burlington Bay. In fact, he lived royally, in the style that he had observed of King George. His home was conspicuously elegant, very spacious, and replete with ornate furnishings. It was said that his servants were everywhere in his attendance, and that they dressed him in the finest clothes and served his dinners with linen towels on their arms. It was rather unlike the life lived by John Harris in the muskrat marshes. Happily, Harris had no notion of all of this. All that he knew was that the dreaded warrior chief who had so savagely assaulted the frontier settlements, ruthlessly laying waste to Cherry Valley, and who had so stubbornly resisted the Sullivan expedition, and who had wiped out the militia force which had been trying to catch up with the boats following George Rogers Clark down the Ohio, had gone to the Happy Hunting Ground.

But the most exciting news, the news that interested John Harris most, came from the Ohio Valley, at the end of August, 1794. And its central figure was the much revered General Anthony Wayne, he who had done so much to bring the rebellion to a triumphant close. Harris never learned the details. All he knew was that General Wayne had won a big victory over the Indians at some place called Fallen Timbers, which he learned eventually was somewhere close to the Maumee River.[38] What he had not been able to follow since his discharge from the army was the intense activity in the region west of Fort Pitt. The Indians had been resisting with force the westward movement of the settlers, and in the Maumee River region of Ohio had dealt devastating defeats to the American forces. A powerful federation of tribes, including the Chippewa, some Delawares, the Shawnee, the Mingo, the Wyandots, the Ottawa, and the Potawatomi, had been assembled and placed under the leadership of Michikinkna (Little Turtle).

From the moment of his inauguration Washington naturally had a great many most difficult problems to address, including slavery. The national census that was conducted in 1790, during his first term as President, revealed that of all the states only Massachusetts was free of slaves. And the administration of every one of his next fifteen successors would have this problem to address, under a steadily increasing pressure. Washington had been troubled by the matter of slavery for a long time, all through the Revolution, when blacks were set free in return for service, and because of his own situation at Mount Vernon. Both the morality of slavery and the economics of slavery were constantly on his mind. By the time of the Revolution, he was certainly principled toward emancipation, and, as he himself declared; certainly he favored an end to slavery. Even without the arguments of Lafayette and of John Laurens, and the anti-slavery example of Benjamin Franklin, he could appreciate that the institution of slavery was flagrantly inconsistent with the goals of the Revolution and the endorsement of freedom set down so beautifully in the 1776 Declaration. In the writing of his will he set free all of the slaves that remained to him.

Still, for Washington and the infant nation there was a matter even more urgent. Certainly the most unpleasant and the most perplexing and most immediate of all the problems posed for the new nation was the Indian question. It had been plain ever since the Treaty of Paris that the Indians west of the Ohio River were bitterly opposed to any further United States expansion westward. The domain of those tribes known as the Shawnee, the Wyandot and the Miami would have as its eastern limits "the beautiful river," the Ohio.

These natives presented a big problem for Washington, who found his young nation already at a crisis crossroads. Although the new president earnestly desired a peaceful solution to the problem, and had always (at least for the short term) genuinely hoped for a fair and honorable accommodation, there can be no question that he never did regard its resolution as anything like what the Indians had in mind. Washington was operating out of a visionary view which had the Indians ultimately displaced by the European white settlers.

Long ago, during the French and Indian Wars, Washington's attitude toward the Indian lands had taken shape. The young Washington's epithet for the Indians was "wolves." He was pretty much of the same mind as Franklin and Jefferson. As they were not a civilized people, these savages were entitled to the same respect as animals, little more. Certainly they should not be thought of as proprietors of the land.[39]

All his life he had been driven by a great passion for land, and he was constantly alert to any opportunity to acquire it. He was never respectful of the Proclamation issued October 7, 1763, by King George, who was attempting to ease tensions between white settlers and the native Indians. The edict, which was binding on the settlers of all thirteen colonies, was unequivocal in its language. Although it did allow 5000 acres apiece to those British officers who had served the King during the French and Indian Wars,[40] it plain and simply forbade any other settlement of the region west of the crest of the Appalachian range of mountains. Moreover, the Proclamation required those already settled in these regions to return east. But in its pronouncement it had little effect, and during the years leading up to the Revolution it continued to have little effect.

And, in fact the Treaty negotiated in 1768 at Fort Stanwix (now a national monument in Rome, New York) made the Proclamation null and void. The Council was presided over by Sir William Johnson, the General Superintendent for Indian Affairs North of the Ohio, and the agreement signed by British officials and various chiefs of the Six Nations was nothing short of astounding. The Indians here made incredible land cessions. In return for guaranteed rights to the lands in western new York State which they had long occupied, the Iroquois surrendered to the British all of their "claims" south of the Ohio and Susquehanna Rivers, regions in what is now western Pennsylvania, West Virginia (then Virginia), and Kentucky (at that time not a colony). The amazing thing is this: the Iroquois had absolutely no authority to cede these lands, as they had no claim to them whatsoever. These lands that were being ceded to the British belonged to the Shawnee, the Miami, and Delaware tribes, who were not represented at the negotiations. The Iroquois at Fort Stanwix simply sold out the Indians of the west.

The Iroquois through this agreement felt that they were solidifying their right to the lands they had long occupied in western New York State. The treaty opened up the lands west to the Ohio; opportunities were boundless. But, needless to remark, the Ohio Indians were embittered and resentful, and naturally, as settlers moved into these lands (1770-1795), organized resistance appeared and frequent Indian attacks occurred. As noted above, in a second Treaty of Fort Stanwix (1784), negotiated after the end of the war, and this time with the Americans, the Indians, made additional cessions, now agreeing to give up lands in western Pennsylvania and Ohio to the new American government. The Seneca war-chief Cornplanter was among the Indians signing this document. Naturally relations between the Six Nations and the Ohio tribes were never again cordial.

Washington did a lot of speculation in lands during the decade

1765-1775, a habit that was resumed during the years following the Revolution. He had employed his good friend and land agent William Crawford, to whom he had taught the art of surveying[41] "to investigate and survey for me various new locations." When he learned that Crawford himself had gone through with his determination to buy himself a farm along Braddock's Road, Washington wrote him to "look me out" a good piece of the same. This Crawford did, securing some 300 acres for him for thirty pistoles, roughly a dollar per acre, at the very spot on which he had suffered, by the French and Indians, his first military setback.[42]

Washington at one time, shortly after the King George Proclamation, had confided to Crawford: "I can never look on that proclamation in any other light (but I say this between ourselves) than as a temporary expedient to quiet the minds of the Indians. It must fall, of course, in a few years, especially when those Indians consent to our occupying the lands."[43] Washington felt that nobody who desired land should neglect this opportunity.

Historical Marker

With total disdain for the Proclamation, Crawford, at Washington's bidding, had as early as 1767 begun to survey some of the most desirable lands in the region near the Monongahela and Youghiogheny Rivers, at Great Meadows, and on Washington's Run and Chartiers Creek.[44] Eventually the two entered into a partnership, the arrangement requiring Washington "to supply the necessary funds and give Crawford a share of the land for his efforts."[45]

And after Crawford was well settled on his farm on the Youghiogheny River, in the region of present-day Connellsville, Washington expressed to him the hope that he might one day have some 2000 acres in Pennsylvania. He even suggested in this letter that Colonel John Armstrong[46] ("an acquaintance of mine"), who was

The Delaware

serving in the Surveyor's Office at Carlisle, might be of some help. And, "leaving the whole to your discretion and good management," he added "Keep the whole matter a profound secret . . . . I might be censured for the opinion [of the King's Proclamation]. It might give the alarm to others . . . before we could lay a proper foundation in for success ourselves . . . . All of which may be avoided by a Silent Management and [operation] carried on by you under the pretence of hunting other Game . . . ."[47]

During these years, because lands were being sold in Pennsylvania on a first come first served basis,[48] naturally, great confusion occurred, and claim jumping was rampant. Washington, because he was so active, was much involved in disputes and rival claims.

William Crawford cabin

Hopeful of viewing the acreage that Crawford had purchased for him in western Pennsylvania, Washington arranged to visit his friend at his home in Connellsville on the Youghiogheny. For four days in October of 1770, the 13th through the 17th, Washington, with a great sense of proprietorship, was conducted through southwestern Pennsylvania by his land agent-partner-friend, who provided very pleasing impressions of the lands he had acquired for him and his younger brothers, Samuel and John.[49]

In 1771, Crawford notified Washington that he had selected for him a tract of 2800 acres on Miller's Run, which is a branch of Chartiers Creek, near present-day Canonsburg in Washington County. The typical problem appeared, however, when a buyer by the name of George Croghan also laid claim to the land, and "proceeded to sell portions of it to settlers." When Washington learned of this, he promptly filed a suit against Croghan. During the court proceedings Croghan and the settlers to whom he had sold chunks of the tract were represented by the most able attorney in Pittsburgh, Hugh Brackenridge, the same Brackenridge to whom John Slover would later dictate the account of his escape from the Indians. Washington, however, with the documentary evidence to prove his claim, won the case and recovered his lands.[50]

An additional sense of the ardor with which Washington searched out land, and how jealously he guarded his holdings, may be gained from a letter he wrote, in 1772, to Dr. John Briscoe, concerning property on the Ohio which Washington had "claimed." To the founder of the village on the banks of the Ohio known as Briscoe's Settlement he vented his indignation:

> *Sir, I have been informed that a Survey which Captain Crawford made for me on the Ohio (being the first bottom on the Sou. East Side of the river) above Capteening and nearly opposite Pipe Creek, at my particular request, you have either gone or intended to go and take possession of. Such a step as this, I cou'd hardly have expected from you. However as it is a piece of land I viewed in Nov 1770 before you had ever explored that Country, have had it surveyed by an officer legally appointed by the Surveyor General of the Colony and am resolved to take out a patent for it (notwithstanding any improvement you either have or may make upon it) as soon as Rights are to be had, I have judged it expedient to serve you with this notice thereof (which I am told is not the first you have had) and to assure you at the same time that I am determined not to relinquish my right to this tract, which contains 587 acres, and which I am ready to pay for at any time till I have at least spent the full value of the Land in support of my claim.[51]*

The land in question here is Washington's Round Bottom tract down river from present-day Parkersburg, West Virginia, an expanse of some 20,000 acres. When learning in this way of Washington's claim, Briscoe bowed out, and simply moved to the tract adjacent.

During these years in which the colonists were steadily moving west, claims continued to be filed willy nilly, and of course if the "owner" was not settled on the land, challenges and disputes occurred. Washington, who was so active in all of this, was naturally regularly involved. He was even accused of cheating. George Muse, who had actually served as one of Washington's early military instructors, apparently confused by one of their dealings, charged him with stealing from him his share of the bounty lands. Washington, his character impugned, exploded. He slept on the letter one night, and then, his temper having failed to cool, replied in extreme heat:

Sir: Your impertinent letter was delivered to me yesterday. As I am not accustomed to receive such from any man, nor would have taken the same language from you personally without letting you feel some marks of my resentment, I advise you to be cautious of writing me a second of the same tenor; for though I understand you were drunk when you did it, yet give me leave to tell you that drunkenness is no excuse for rudeness. But for your stupidity and sottishness you might have known, by attending to the public gazette, that you had your full quantity of ten thousand acres of land allowed you; that is, nine thousand and seventy three acres in the great tract, and the remainder in the small tract.

But suppose you had really fallen short, do you think your superlative merit entitles you to a greater indulgence than others? Or if it did, that I was to make it good to you, when it was at the option of the governor and council to allow but five hundred acres in the whole, if they had been so inclined? If either of these should happen to be your opinion, I am very well convinced that you will be singular in it; and all my concern is that I ever engaged myself in behalf of so ungrateful and dirty a fellow as you are.[52]

When it came to the acquisition of property, Salem County's Bombardier John Harris was clearly a piker next to his beloved George Washington. Two little islands in the Delaware River he was able to buy. At the time of his death in 1799, Washington held in his estate the following: 9200 acres in Mount Vernon; 1,000 in Maryland; 4000 in the Dismal Swamp; 10,000 on the Ohio River between Fort Henry (Wheeling) and Point Pleasant; 23,000 on the Great Kanawha–river bottoms for forty-eight miles on either side; 1000 in New York's Mohawk Valley; 3000 near Cincinnati; 5000 in Kentucky, and 234 in Pennsylvania; and 7500 in tidewater Virginia and the Shenandoah.[53]

Washington through these years of course could have no idea that down the road a little way he would be compelled to respond to the Indians' claims to the lands west and north of the Ohio, and that, one way or another, he would have to establish the government position on settlement. He would have to make his own proclamation on this subject at the highest level.

Even though most of the American Indians had been his fierce adversary during the French and Indian Wars, and through the last six years of the Revolution, and even though as a young man he had accorded them little respect, now seven years after "the end of the war," as President of the United States, he was obliged to take a different view.

Washington now assumed a moral responsibility for the Indians. His earlier vision of colonial settlement ever westward was now enlarged to provide for the land's first inhabitants. As one historian has put it, the President "envisioned multiple sanctuaries under tribal control that would be by-passed by the surging wave of white settlers and whose occupants would gradually, over the course of the next century, become assimilated as full fledged American citizens."[54]

To testify to his sincerity and good faith, as well as to clarify what he intended for the Indians, Washington in 1790 issued a Proclamation (remarkably similar to that of King George twenty-seven years earlier) in the form of an executive order which forbade "private or state encroachments on all Indian lands guaranteed by treaty with the United States."[55] And, like the Proclamation of King George, there was never any good chance that it would prove the least bit effective.

At the same time, the continuing belligerence of the Indians in the Ohio Valley region offended him. And though the use of force was distasteful to him, Washington made it clear to the Indians that he would resort to whatever means necessary to put an end to hostile activity.

The Delaware

The Indians were unmoved. They made it equally clear to the young government that force would indeed be necessary.

The President of the United States responded to the incessant hostility as promised, and promptly suffered two most embarrassing defeats. The two expeditions dispatched by the War Department of Henry Knox against the Indians of the Ohio Valley were virtually annihilated. The first, a somewhat modest and largely untrained military force, composed of some Federal troops and militia and backwoodsmen, under the command of General Josiah Harmar[56] on October 20-22, 1790, was ambushed and wiped out by the Miami war-chief Little Turtle[57] at the head of a confederation of tribes in the Maumee Valley, north of the Ohio River.

Josiah Harmar

In the succeeding year, on November 4, the second expedition, led by General Arthur St. Clair,[58] was likewise overwhelmingly defeated, again by Little Turtle, this time on the Wabash River, near present-day Fort Recovery. Washington had warned St. Clair to "beware of surprise," and to "be sure to build fortifications" at every encampment. But the General did not require fortifications of the weary soldiers, and he went to sleep feeling secure. The attack came at daybreak, St. Clair's troops awakening in the bitter cold to find

Little Turtle

the encampment almost completely surrounded by a sea of savages, one thousand warriors made hideous by the garish war-paint, and fired to a battle frenzy by the cunning Miami war-chief Little Turtle and the Shawnee Blue Jacket. What happened during the next three hours has been many times called "the bloodiest battle ever fought against the Indians." In the melee, St. Clair lost 900 soldiers (including almost all of the eighty-six officers), seventy-five per cent of his fighting force, killed or wounded. Besides, there were slaughtered a great many of the soldiers' wives, who had accompanied the expedition; and many children were carried off. The General himself only barely escaped, finding refuge in Fort Jefferson, which lay to the south. The Indians lost 66 (!) warriors.

One does not have to imagine Washington's reaction to the terrible news when it arrived in Philadelphia. His early biographer, Washington Irving, has recorded it. The President had had the news earlier in the day and had sat on it through a dinner party, but after Mrs. Washington had retired and the guests had all left, about ten o'clock, Washington, left alone with his private secretary, Tobias Lear, erupted. Here is Irving's account:

Arthur St. Clair

The general walked slowly backward and forward for some moments in silence. As yet there had been no change in his manner. Taking a seat on the sofa by the fire he told Mr. Lear to sit down; the latter had scarce time to notice that he was extremely agitated, when he broke out suddenly: "It's all over! — St. Clair's defeated! –routed! The officers nearly all killed, the men by wholesale; the rout complete; too shocking to think of, and a surprise into the bargain!" All this was uttered with great vehemence. Then pausing and rising from the sofa, he walked up and down the room in silence, violently agitated, but saying nothing. When near the door he stopped short; stood still for a few moments, when there was another terrible explosion of wrath.

*"Yes," exclaimed he, "**HERE**, on this very spot, I took leave of him; I wished him success and honor. 'You have your instructions from the Secretary of War,' said I. 'I had a strict eye to them, and will add but one word, **BEWARE OF SURPRISE!** You know how the Indians fight us. I repeat it, **BEWARE OF A SURPRISE.**' He went off with that, my last warning, thrown into his ears. And yet!! To suffer that army to be cut to pieces, hacked, butchered, tomahawked, by a surprise–the very thing I guarded him against–O God! O God!" exclaimed he, throwing up his hands, and while his very frame shook with emotion, "He's worse than a murderer! How can he answer it to his country! The blood of the slain is upon him–the curse of widows and orphans–the curse of heaven!"*[59]

Certainly this unthinkable, crushing defeat was a terrible blow to the young government. Disappointment and discouragement settled over Washington and General Knox and the Cabinet and the Congress. And, in fact, the army of the United States, by this single battle had been almost totally destroyed, reduced as it was to hardly more than 300.

But now Washington, as he had done so many times during the war with Britain, reached for a trump card. The President and Commander-in-Chief of the United States forces, looking still for a clear and decisive victory and an end to the intolerable hostilities, finally fixed on an officer who (except for Paoli) had never disappointed him. That was General Anthony Wayne, whom Washington regarded as still a young man.

On the 25th day of May, 1792, Wayne, equipped with his instructions from President Washington, which included the admonition that "another defeat would be inexpressibly ruinous to the reputation of the government," set out for Pittsburgh.[60] By late fall he had organized his army (in spite of a steady stream of desertions), and had closely studied the Indian situation. From Pittsburgh he marched his forces to the Miami territory down river on the Ohio, establishing headquarters at Legion Ville and at Hobson's Choice, and intending first to open negotiations with the war-chiefs of the hostile tribes.

Expecting negotiations to fail, Wayne was left with one big problem to resolve before he could even think about an engagement. That problem was the Six Nations, and particularly the Senecas. The Six Nations had to be persuaded to "stay out of it." Both Washington and Wayne clearly understood that a victory over the western Indians would be most difficult to achieve if the Iroquois tribes, who so far had remained on the sidelines, were to come in on the side of the Ohio Indians. Consequently Washington and Wayne and Secretary of War Henry Knox engaged the influential Cornplanter in a number of tete-a-tete conferences, as well as a constant interchange of letters, many of which included invitations to the chief to come to Philadelphia. Just how important Chief Cornplanter was to the hostilities in the Ohio River region is readily apparent from the letters which passed between General Wayne and the Secretary of War, Henry Knox. For the period July 27, 1792–August 8, 1793, in no fewer than thirty-four of these communications is Cornplanter a serious subject. In many he is *the* subject.

Knox is of course writing from Philadelphia, which had succeeded New York City as the capital of the infant nation. Wayne is communicating first from Pittsburgh and after that from Legion Ville and Hobson's Choice, as he worked his way ever closer to the Indian villages at Cincinnati. The letters were requiring, generally, about one week to make the trip.

President Washington is a party to the correspondence, as he is kept well informed by Knox, who in many cases simply relays the letters which have arrived from Wayne.

But Washington decides that it will not be necessary for Cornplanter to come to Philadelphia (Colonel Thomas Proctor, who has been mediating with the Indians, was to have been his escort.). He is content with the dispatches from Wayne, who has met with the Seneca chieftain. Anyway it is quite clear to him by this time that the Ohio Indians are unshakably at odds to any expansion of the United States westward from their present position. The Indians continued to draw the line at the river, the "beautiful river," the Ohio. And, though it may have been wishful thinking, the President had the tenuous impression that the Senecas were going to remain neutral.

The Delaware 315

It is not easy to define exactly the feelings of Washington for the Indians. His observations are not all that consistent. Are they cruel and ruthless savages who should be annihilated? Are they a nuisance merely, to be tolerated? Are they fellow human beings with very legitimate claims to the land which they occupy, and have occupied for a long, long time?

But at this time, in this moment of extreme crisis, with the immigrant nation on a collision course with the first Americans, history sees the President working genuinely and industriously for a peaceful settlement. On February 25, after he had determined that it was too late to make any more use of Cornplanter, he assembled the Cabinet to ask of them two questions pertaining to the trouble on the frontier. He wanted to know, in the first place, whether the Executive had the power to relinquish to the Indians any lands beyond the Ohio acquired by previous treaty. He wanted to know, in the second place, whether the commissioners should be instructed to effect such recessions if necessary to the achievement of peace. On both questions Alexander Hamilton, Henry Knox, and Edmund Randolph responded in the affirmative. Jefferson dissented on both.[61]

But by the middle of March, Washington and Knox were made uneasy again by communications from Wayne. Typical was the letter in which the General informed them that the Iroquois *still* remained a big question mark. He reported that the representatives of the Six Nations "generate a nervousness when they appear." Wayne did acknowledge one condition that favored his army. That was that the Ohio Indians intensely hated the Iroquois, and most especially the Senecas, by whom they felt betrayed. For the western Indians (the Miami, the Shawnee, the Chippewa, the Ottawa, the Sac, the Wyandot the Fox, and the Potawatami), Wayne wrote, there is no question. They have long ago written off the Iroquois, whom they regard as cowards. Their disgust is undisguised. They are not likely to welcome the Iroquois.

And so matters stood. The armies were now assembled. Councils had met. Negotiations had been carried on. Intermediaries had functioned. The warriors of the Six Nations were not committed. Some skirmishes through June and July had taken many lives and had provided intimations of the cost to come. But it was plain to all that a battle would be fought. Wayne made one more effort. "I have thought proper," he said, "to offer the enemy a last overture of peace; and as they have every thing that is dear and interesting at stake, I have reason to expect they will listen to the proposition mentioned in the enclosed copy of an address, despatched yesterday by a special flag, under circumstances that will insure his safe return, and which may eventually spare the effusion of much human blood. But should war be their choice, that blood upon their own heads. America shall no longer be insulted with impunity. To an all-powerful and just God, I therefore commit myself and gallant army."[62]

But not only did the Ohio Indians spurn the overture, the confederation replaced the Miami Little Turtle, a most skillful and resourceful chief, with the Shawnee Blue Jacket. Actually, Little Turtle pretty much replaced himself, because he had been trying to persuade the western Indians to bury the hatchet. The popular warrior-leader, who had described Wayne as "the chief who never sleeps," had been urging his people, the Miamis, as well as members of the other Ohio tribes, to sue for peace. In the battle that was to follow, though he provided his presence, he was not in command, and his heart was not in it.

In the Battle of Fallen Timbers, fought on August 20, 1794, Wayne won a decisive victory, and promptly filed with the Secretary of War a highly detailed report of the action. What the General did not remark on was the well founded rumor that a large body of Senecas had been hovering on his flank, studying the tide of battle apparently. And Seneca runners were ever at the ready to return to the villages for warriors if indeed it seemed an Indian victory was possible. Historians are agreed that, Cornplanter notwithstanding, had the western Indians begun to carry the field as they had under Little Turtle against Harmar and against St. Clair, the Senecas would have joined with the Miamis and the rest.

By the first day of the new year negotiations had come forward so far that preliminary articles of peace could be agreed to. But it was not until the 7th of August, almost one year to the day from the time of the battle, that the historic Treaty of Greenville was signed. Signing for the Indians were the chiefs of the Ottawa, the Chippewa, the Wyandot, the Sac, the Fox, the Delaware, the Shawnee, the Miami (including Little Turtle) and the Potawatami. Of course General Wayne represented the United States.

The treaty meant chiefly the ceding of a large part of the Old Northwest to the United States. The terms included the immediate surrender to the United States of the British posts at Detroit, Michilimackinack, Oswego, and Niagara. Most significant was the provision by which all previous treaties ceding land to the United States were recognized, for here for the first time was signed a treaty which acknowledged the Indian claim to lands within the boundaries of the United States. The Indian threat to the white settlers of the west was not ended (two more decades would be required), but the Battle of Fallen Timbers and the Treaty of Greenville made very plain what the end would be. And Cornplanter, who had fought so fiercely against the patriot forces during the years of the Revolution, had played a major role in the Battle of Fallen Timbers – by staying out of it.

After the battle, Wayne had made a triumphant trip to Philadelphia, but later returned to the West in order to effect the terms of the treaty. He was sailing from Detroit for Presque Isle in Lake Erie, the very last post which it was his duty to visit, when he was cut down by illness. Just the day before he came ashore, on November 17, he suffered a violent attack of the gout. He died one month later, on December 15, 1796. This war-scarred veteran of the Revolution and the attendant Indian wars, a friend to Washington and to Cornplanter, the patriot hero of a new country, was only fifty-one.

The War of the Revolution was inspired by a concern for rights and freedoms. It was fought between the British King and his rebellious colonists. The war ended in a concern for land. It was fought at the last between the Old World immigrant citizens of the new United States and the native peoples who had lived on the land for thousands of years.

These reports of the people he had known throughout the eight years of the Revolution, now thirty-five years distant, helped to refresh in Harris's mind his many memorable experiences, and inspired in him also a reflection on the meaning of it all. While lamenting the terrible cost of the war, he felt good about the revolution. He had been thrilled to learn that his General Washington had agreed to serve as the infant nation's first President. He would be disappointed by the President's decision to forego a third term, but he was satisfied that the struggling young country was in good hands, and he knew that the future was bright.

But he knew, too, that he had been as much a part of his country's future as he would ever be. He was feeling "poorly."

Harris had suffered bouts of fever, "the chills and fever" people called it, off and on through his lifetime, and twice particularly, once just after the Battle of White Plains, and again at the time of his discharge from the army. But now, in the early spring of 1814, when he was in his 61st year, a new kind of fever assaulted his system, and this time it came with a vengeance. It was the dreaded typhus.[63]

Son Benjamin and the family, fearing the worst, urged him to prepare a will. This he hastened to do. The will was written by Joseph Holliday. Dated March 28, 1814, the will of John Harris of Lower Alloways Creek Township, Salem County, N.J., ". . . devises to sons Stretch and Benjamin Harris land, woodland and marsh where I live, equally divided; to wife Lydia her thirds during lifetime; to son Peter Harris 200 acres in Penna.;[64] to son Stretch Harris a plantation wagon, pair of 3-year-old steers, 2 young and 2 old cows, and all female sheep of his earmark; to wife Lydia and daughters Lydia, Elizabeth, Margaret, and Clarissa Harris the rest of moveable estate; and appoints wife Lydia and son Stretch the executors." His personal estate had been appraised at upwards of $1900.[65]

The next day Bombardier John Harris delivered his soul to his Maker. He was interred, without ceremony, in the Canton Baptist Churchyard.

Because he served for so long a time, and served willingly, even eagerly, without complaint, Salem's John Harris might be thought an exceptional patriot soldier. But it is better to see him as typical of those young men of immigrant families who won for the colonies their independence. One of his descendants, writing of him fondly for *Pittsburgh* magazine in 1990, one hundred and seventy-six years after his death, provides a fitting epitaph. In reflecting on the life that John Harris led and on his service to his country, she put it this way: "My great-great-great grandfather was not what you would call famous. He was not a national hero. But he has always represented for me, in his devotion to the Continental Army and the diligence with which he served the Revolution, the qualities the Colonials stood for then and the freedoms we cherish now."

APPENDIX A

The Truth about Molly Pitcher

Confusion in the literature on Molly Pitcher is boundless. So many contradictions and errors have been perpetuated that it is almost impossible to put together a factual account of her life, or even of her role at Monmouth. For example, "In a series of ten papers on her life, it is stated in five that her husband was 'wounded at Monmouth,' in one that he was 'mortally wounded,'[!] in three that he was 'killed,' [!] and in one that he 'died from the heat.'" [!][1]

The problem is that Molly Pitcher did not begin to achieve her lofty place in American history until nearly six decades beyond the Battle of Monmouth. By the time the story was first emerging there were few veterans of the action to consult, and very few even who remembered Molly in her later life in Carlisle. Consequently, for this most fascinating figure of the American Revolution, the romantic imagination ran rampant; and it has become extremely difficult to distinguish between fact and myth.

To begin the labor, it is very obvious that she has often been confused with Margaret (Molly) Corbin, who in the Battle of New York City, at Fort Washington, did indeed replace her fallen husband (whose name was John, same as Molly Pitcher's husband) and served the cannon as gunner. Margaret Corbin did survive the assault on Fort Washington, and, though among the surrendered, was released by the British to her home in her native Pennsylvania. She later was granted a pension by the Commonwealth.

The truth about the other Molly *seems* to be the following: Mary (Molly) Ludwig Hays was born to German immigrant parents October 13, 1744, in what is today Mercer County, New Jersey, very near Trenton. (Some accounts have her born in 1754, which would make her fifteen years old at the time of her first marriage.) Her father, John George Ludwig, was a dairy farmer. (But even this ancestry is disputed; and some have made her Irish–Molly Corbin again–rather than German). At some time, but probably when she was quite young (biographers have her at age 15, 16, 20, and 25), she became a domestic in the home of Dr. William Irvine (later Colonel and Brigadier General Irvine) in Carlisle, Pa. Irvine had, apparently, been much taken with Molly on a visit to his wife's cousin, schoolmaster Ralph Remy, in Trenton.

On July 24 or 25 of 1769, Mary married John (often called William) Casper Hays, a Carlisle barber, whose shop was very near the Irvine home. On December 1, 1775, Hays enlisted for one year in Thomas Proctor's First Pennsylvania Artillery, and served for that year as a gunner, reaching the rank of sergeant. Shortly after his term expired, in January (some biographers say June) of 1777, he re-enlisted, but this time as an infantryman (a private) in Captain John Alexander's company of the Seventh Pennsylvania Regiment, Continental Line, which by the time of Monmouth was commanded by Colonel William Irvine, in whose home Molly had served as a domestic.[2] His wife Mary (Molly) toward the end of that year, when she was thirty-three years old, may have accompanied John to Valley Forge, and from nearby the encampment with a number of other women helped with the washing of uniforms, the preparation of food and the care of the sick.

At some time she caught up with the forces of Washington (a great many women marched with the army from Valley Forge), which included her husband, as they pursued the British from Philadelphia to Freehold. For the fighting at Monmouth, because of his artillery experience, John Hays was temporarily detached from the Pennsylvania 7th and assigned to the cannon. He was not "mortally wounded" at Monmouth. He appears not to have been wounded at all. He may have been felled by the terrible heat, as were so many. Whether Mary's husband was among those to whom she delivered water is not certified. Presumably he was. That she took her husband's place at the cannon and used the rammer has not been certified. She *may* have served the cannon, and, if so-called eye witness accounts which have been preserved can be trusted, she did. But the later historians (see the 1956 edition of *The Columbia Encyclopedia)* feel that the report that Molly took over her husband's role on the gun is "apocryphal." Cokie Roberts, in her recent *Founding Mothers*, goes a great deal farther. Even while noting that Molly was granted a pension, she, amazingly, allows the possibility that Molly Pitcher "may not have ever existed."[3]

After the war's end Mary Hays lived with her husband in Carlisle, bearing him a son in 1783, when she would have been nearly forty. When her husband died, in 1787, she remarried. But her second husband, Sergeant George (most often rendered "John") McCauley (McAuley, McKolly, McCauly), also a veteran of the war and sometimes a comrade of her first husband, proved, if Carlisle community reports are right, to be "cruel and heartless," treating her as a servant.

Her son, John Ludwig Hays, participated in the War of 1812. He had two sons, John and Frederick, both of whom lived in Carlisle, and one daughter, Polly. John, Sr., died in Carlisle in 1853.

On February 21, 1822, when Mary was in her 77th year, the Pennsylvania Legislature awarded her a pension: "That the State Treasurer be, and he is hereby directed to pay to Molly M'Kolly, of Cumberland County, or her order, forty dollars immediately, and an annuity of forty dollars to commence on the first of January, one thousand eight hundred and twenty two, payable half yearly during life for her service during the revolutionary war." The act was signed by Governor Joseph Hiester.

The heroine of Monmouth died on a Sunday, January 22, 1832, aged eighty-seven. She had lived her last years in her son's old stone house near the southeast corner of Bedford and North Streets, at the location popularly known as Lougheridge's Corner. Her ten-year-old grandson, John A. Hays, who had been born in that house, was living with her at the time.

She was interred, with military honors, in the Old Graveyard, or, as it was then known, the English Graveyard of Carlisle, at the present-day streets of Bedford and South. Her grave marker, installed long after, is now much weathered. There is good reason for preserving it of course; and there is good reason, too, for placing a new one. Upon the centennial of the War's beginning, on July 4, 1876, a long overdue monument to Molly was placed at her grave site. It is inscribed "MOLLY McCAULY. Renowned in history as MOLLY PITCHER, the Heroine of Monmouth, died Jan 1833, aged 79 years. Erected by the Citizens of Cumberland County, July 4,

1876." The stonecutter, a local named Peter Spahr provided the monument at a cost to the community of $100.00. Inexplicable are the clearly erroneous age at her death and her death date. And during World War I, on June 28 (the anniversary date of the Battle of Monmouth), 1916, a most beautiful statue, designed by J. Otto Schweitzer, of Philadelphia, and representing Molly with a rammer was placed atop the granite marker at her grave site in the Old Graveyard in Carlisle. It was unveiled by Molly's granddaughter, Polly McCleester, of Mount Holly Springs, near Carlisle, who apparently remembered her grandmother well. It is supposed that the face of the statue is inspired by a composite picture of five of Molly's great grandchildren. The Patriotic Order of the Sons of America have added drama to the scene with a cannon, a flagstaff, and bronze relief

Molly Pitcher Monument

to feature the deeds of Molly Pitcher.

The battlefield monument in Freeport, New Jersey (formerly Monmouth Court House), which memorializes the battle, is a very tall, granite shaft with the figure of "Liberty Triumphant" at the very top. Along the base of the monument there have been included five commemorative bronze tablets. One of these, in a compelling bronze bas-relief, portrays Molly Pitcher at her husband's cannon. It is a beautiful memorial.

The historic spring from which she carried water is today marked as Molly Pitcher's Well. However, Samuel C. Cowart, on August 12, 1926, in conversation with William Starr Myers, the editor of William Stryker's definitive book on the Battle of Monmouth, said this: "I am satisfied that this spring was in the edge of Gordon's woods near what is known as Gordon's Bridge on the Pennsylvania Railroad, and not where 'Mollie Pitcher's Well' is today pointed out, for the reason that Ramsey's guns were near these woods and the well was not dug until fifty years after the battle, by Dr. J. C. Thompson, who himself years later told me he dug it."[4]

A china pitcher, which was in Molly's possession at the time of her death, is now a treasured exhibit at the Hamilton Library of the Cumberland Historical Society in Carlisle. But it is not thought to be the pitcher which she carried on the battlefield at Monmouth, which supposedly was pewter.

Surely the whole truth about Molly Pitcher will never be known. But enough is known to place her among the immortals of the American Revolution, an enduring symbol of the passion which inspired the rebellion and of the incredible courage which gave birth to the nation.

APPENDIX B

Lafayette Returns

When the Marquis de Lafayette, at the formal but very warm and friendly invitation of Congress and President James Monroe, returned to the United States in 1824, he discovered a country very different from the one whose independence he had fought for. The thirteen stars in the flag had become twenty-four as the nation now known as the United States expanded westward. His own country had sold to the United States a vast tract of land along the Mississippi River in the south, and north to the Rocky Mountains, 800,000 square miles, and thus had exactly doubled the size of the country at the time. The purchase (from the Emperor Napoleon) made possible the creation of a number of new states, including Louisiana, Mississippi, and Missouri. Missouri, the most recent of the new states, had applied for statehood in 1821, and had been admitted to the Union on August 10 of that year. The General had not only the old colonies to re-visit, but a lot of new country with which to become acquainted as well.

He had been back to the country for five months in 1784, at that time visiting with Washington at Mount Vernon, and saying good-bye to him for the last time when they parted at Annapolis; and even then he found the nation much changed. But now it was ever so much larger and ever so much more vigorous and forward looking.

But, besides that, he now had nobody from his Revolutionary War experience with whom to visit. His mentor and always close friend Major General (Baron) Johann De Kalb had been a casualty of the war, mortally wounded at the Battle of Camden, August 16, 1780, in South Carolina. The Quartermaster General of the Continental Army, whom he had gotten to know so well at Valley Forge, Major General Nathanael Greene, had lived only three years beyond the close of the war. And Benjamin Franklin, who had helped to win France to the Cause, and who had been serving as the Governor of his beloved Pennsylvania, had died at his Philadelphia home in April of 1790.[1]

The Prussian Baron von Steuben, who had delivered his fortune to the cause of the colonies, had become an American citizen in time to live his last years under the Constitution. But he was dead at sixty-four. Major General John Sullivan, after a distinguished post-war career, died in 1795 at age fifty-five. The energetic and tempestuous life of the General known as "Mad" Anthony Wayne was even shorter, for the victor at Fallen Timbers lived not long after he had settled affairs with the Ohio Indians at Greenville, dying at age fifty-one.

Patrick Henry, whose rhetoric was inspiring to the young Lafayette, had died in June of 1799. His life ended at his plantation home, known as Red Hill, before he could assume in the Virginia Legislature the Federalist seat that he had just won.

Dearest to the Frenchman of course was Washington. But his Commander-in-Chief had died just a few months after Patrick Henry, only two years beyond the end of his second term as the first President of the new nation. Lafayette was remembering that Washington had died calmly, just before midnight, speaking of his passing as "the debt we all must pay."

General Benedict Arnold he did not expect to find in the United States, and indeed Arnold had died in London long ago, in June of 1801. Thomas Paine, whom he had met at Valley Forge, and whom he knew well because of Paine's later activity in the French Revolution, had died, unpopular and virtually friendless, in New York City and had been buried on his farm in New Rochelle. Alexander Hamilton, whom Lafayette knew extremely well and very much admired, and whose political fortunes he had followed closely, was long lost, too, tragically killed as he was by Aaron Burr in a duel in Weehawken, New Jersey, July 11, 1804.

Both General Henry Knox, who had built up the artillery, and who had served for ten years in the young government as Secretary of War, and General Horatio Gates, who had defeated Burgoyne and who had commanded the Southern Army in the time before Yorktown, had died two decades ago, in 1806, Gates expiring on a farm in what is now New York City.

Dr. Benjamin Rush, for a time the Army's Surgeon, and during his last years regarded by many as the most considerable person (after Washington and Franklin) for the Revolution, had died at age sixty-eight, in 1813. The hero of Vincennes and of the war's activity in the "Old Northwest," the Virginia militia's Brigadier General George

Rogers Clark, after completing his memoirs, departed from this life at age sixty-six, in 1818.

Bombardier John Harris, of course, had been dead for a decade. And most of the youngest of the common soldiers who had endured Valley Forge were gone; those yet living were well into their sixties.

And what of the British whom General Lafayette had fought against?

General Sir Henry Clinton, who had been born in the same year as Washington, had died at his post as Governor of Gibralter on December 23, 1795. General Charles Cornwallis, after a *most* distinguished post-war career, had died in India, where he had been reappointed Governor-General, on October 5, 1805. William Howe, who after his recall never returned to America, had died in 1814. The Tory leader John Butler had died in 1796. The Mohawk leader, Joseph Brant, the most prominent of the Indian allies of the British, died in his home at Burlington, Ontario, in 1807. King George III had died just a few years before Lafayette set sail for the United States, on January 29,1820, at Windsor Palace. He was blind when he died, and for many years had been suffering from dementia, and perhaps porphyria. Because he was unable to reign in the last nine years of his life, his son had governed in his stead.

Among the very few principal figures of the Revolution still living when Lafayette set foot on shore in New York were John Adams and Thomas Jefferson, Cornplanter and Aaron Burr. And of course President James Monroe, with whom Lafayette had served at Valley Forge and at Monmouth. Adams and Jefferson, who had had their disagreements but who had been happily reconciled, would die on the same day, the 50th anniversary of the Declaration of Independence, July 4, 1826. Adams, the second President of the United States, still supposing that "Jefferson lives,"died just a few hours later than did the third President of the United States.

Of all the figures prominent in the War of the Revolution, only two, Cornplanter and Aaron Burr, would outlive Lafayette. Lafayette died in Paris, May 20, 1834, nine years after his return from the United States. Aaron Burr, just one and one-half years older than Lafayette, died on September 14, 1836. Cornplanter, though his monument proclaims that he lived "about"100 years, in fact lived only eighty-four, maybe eighty-five. He died on February 18, 1836.

Lafayette made port in New York City on August 15 of 1824, arriving aboard the merchant ship *Cadmus*, and commenced his "triumphant tour" with visits to New Haven, Providence, Boston, Concord, Hartford, New York City (again), Albany, Philadelphia, and Washington. Then he proceeded to the southern states. In one of these states, South Carolina, he enjoyed one of his most tender moments. In Camden, the site of the calamitous battle that took the life of his dear friend and mentor General Johann De Kalb, he was asked to lay the cornerstone for the monument that had been erected to his memory. He must have been deeply moved by the inscription, which he could appreciate applied to himself as well: "His love of liberty induced him to leave the old world to aid the citizens of the new in their struggle for independence."

In all, he would travel more than 5000 miles in 400 days.[2] Everywhere he was welcomed with unbridled enthusiasm, every community turning out en masse and entering wildly into celebration, ten million citizens of the new nation paying homage to the "savior of the country," the "champion of liberty." The Marquis de Lafayette, at age sixty-seven, was the last surviving general of the War for Independence, and as such he became for all the citizens of the young country a symbol of the freedom that had been so dearly won by the colonials.

Meadville, Pennsylvania, just north of Pittsburgh, was typical. The community, which was the county seat of Crawford County (which had been named for Washington's friend Colonel William Crawford), was on the General's schedule, and the people waited patiently. Huge crowds lined the streets, men, women and children waving their strips of bunting, and shuffling for improved positions. The news that raced through the small town was that General Lafayette had been in Pittsburgh, and had gone on north to Butler, and that he had stayed the night (June 1) in Mercer. His carriage, replete with military escort, but without his little dog, which had been lost in a riverboat accident on the Mississippi, could appear at any minute. But the folk of the community knew that they would have to make the most of the moment, as the General, after visiting Allegheny College, would be on his way promptly to Erie and then to Buffalo. He was due in Boston June 17, the 50th anniversary of the Battle of Breed's Hill. It turned out to be a day that the townspeople would never forget.

Historical Marker

On June 26, 1825, General Lafayette visited Brandywine Battlefield in Chester County, the site of his first battle and of his first battle scar. He had revisited the battle scene twice before, and the house that had served as his headquarters, in 1780 and 1785. Now vivid recollections of that September 11, forty-eight long years ago, came rushing over him. From the battlefield near the Brandywine Lafayette visited the community of West Chester, and there reviewed troops assembled and parading in his honor.

Although the General, because of his Brandywine wound, had missed out on the battle of Germantown and the siege of the Chew Mansion, he was now entertained at a lavish reception held for him at that very Chew house.

And so it was, in community after community, the famous Lafayette, wounded in his first battle, narrowly escaping abduction by the Philadelphia British, a force for morale at Valley Forge, heroic at Monmouth, magnificent in the campaign to Yorktown, influential in bringing his native France to the Cause, the "savior of the country," was lionized and celebrated as he should be.

Just before he was to leave the country for his native France, his birthday, September 6, was celebrated in Washington, now the capital of the United States. And on the next day he departed forever from the country he had come to love as his own. For the voyage home he was, most appropriately, placed aboard the sparkling new frigate the *Brandywine*.

Image Credits

George Washington in 1795. Frontispiece. Portrait by the Swedish artist Adolf Ulric Wertmüller. Oil on canvas, 1795. Courtesy of Philadelphia Museum of Art. Bequest by Allen Munn, 1924.

Israel Putnam, courtesy of Stephen Shaw and the Connecticut Sons of the Revolution.

Thomas Gage, portrait by an unknown artist, 19th century, after original by John Singleton Copley. In the State House, Boston. The Massachusetts Art Collection. Courtesy Commonwealth of Massachusetts Art Commission.

Benedict Arnold in Maine, Sydney Adamson artist ("Working against the Flood on Dead River"). Engraving by Harry Davidson, *The Century Illustrated Monthly Magazine*, January, 1903. Prints and Photographs Division, Library of Congress.

Richard Montgomery, portrait by Charles Willson Peale, possibly after an engraving, 1784-86. Independence National Historical Park.

William Howe, courtesy of Clements Library, University of Michigan.

Richard Howe, courtesy of Clements Library, University of Michigan.

"Forcing the Hudson River Passage–1776," painting by Dominique Serres the Elder (1779). Serres, of French origins, was in 1780 appointed the marine painter to King George III. Pictured in the painting are Fort Lee and three British vessels: the HMS *Roebuck* (which would become in March of 1778 the flagship of the armada which under Colonel Charles Mawhood transported the British foraging expeditions into Salem and Cumberland Counties, New Jersey); the HMS *Phoenix*; and the HMS *Tartar*. To the captains of these three ships the painting was presented. One of these three is on exhibit at the U. S. Naval Academy Museum on the Academy grounds in Annapolis, Md. A reproduction hangs in the main chamber of the Edgewater (N.J.) Borough Hall. Image is by courtesy of the U. S. Naval Academy Museum.

The *Jersey*, British prison ship. Sketch. Courtesy of Clements Library, University of Michigan.

Hugh Mercer, portrait by W. A. Greaves (ca. 1900), from a sketch by John Trumbull. Courtesy of The Mercersburg Academy, Mercersburg, Pa. Photo by Robert M. Kurtz, Jr.

Thomas Clarke House. Photo by Lincoln Bittner.

George Washington at Princeton, the 1779 portrait by Charles Willson Peale. Courtesy of the Pennsylvania Academy of the Fine Arts, Philadelphia. Gift of Maria McKean Allen.

Thomas Mifflin, portrait in oil by Charles Willson Peale, from life, 1783-84. Independence National Historical Park.

Benjamin Lincoln, portrait by Charles Willson Peale, from life, ca. 1781-1783.

Image Credits

Independence National Historical Park.
Nicholas Herkimer, courtesy of Oneida County (N.Y.) Historical Society, Utica, New York.
Oriskany Battlefield Monument, courtesy of Oneida County (N.Y.) Historical Society, Utica, New York.
John Sullivan, portrait by A. Tenney, after portrait by Ulysses Dow Tenney, developed from 1790 pencil sketch by John Trumbull. Collections of the State of New Hampshire, Division of Historical Resources.
Washington's Headquarters, Brandywine. *Americana Roads* (2002), by Robert M. Kurtz, Jr. Photo by Robert M. Kurtz, Jr.
Lafayette's Headquarters, Brandywine. *Americana Roads* (2002), by Robert M. Kurtz, Jr. Photo by Robert M. Kurtz, Jr.
Charles Grey, courtesy of U. S. History Organization.
Attack on Paoli, painting of the British Light Infantry and Light Dragoons assaulting the Pennsylvania camp, Sept. 20, 1777. Painting done in London by the Italian artist Xavier della Gatta in 1782, presumably for a British officer. Courtesy of British Battles.com website. This painting, as well as one done by Xavier della Gatta on the battle of Germantown, is in the collections of the Valley Forge Historical Society.
Thomas Musgrave at the Chew House. In 1786 (?) the English artist Lemuel Francis Abbott (1760-1803) produced a portrait of Sir Thomas Musgrave in the uniform of the Fortieth Foot at the Chew House. This painting, oil on canvas and 36 x 28 inches, had been with the Schwarz Gallery in Philadelphia. It is reproduced here through the kindness of its present owner, a private collector. Facilitated by Bryn Mawr College.
Assault on the Chew House, painting (1874) by E. L. Henry. Commissioned as part of the Centennial celebration of the Declaration of Independence. Courtesy of Cliveden, a National Trust Historic Site.
Johann De Kalb, 1781-82 portrait by Charles Willson Peale, from life. Independence National Historical Park.
John Burgoyne, portrait painting (1766) by Sir Joshua Reynolds. Copyright The Frick Collection, New York.
Horatio Gates, Charles Willson Peale portrait from life, 1782. Independence National Historical Park.
Daniel Morgan, portrait by Charles Willson Peale, ca. 1794, from life. Independence National Historical Park.
The huts at Valley Forge. *Americana Roads* (2002), by Robert M. Kurtz, Jr. , Photo by Robert M. Kurtz, Jr.
Nathanael Greene, Charles Willson Peale portrait (1783), from life. Independence National Historical Park.
Friedrich Wilhelm Augustus, Baron von Steuben, portrait by Charles Willson Peale, 1781-82. Independence National Historical Park.
Henry Knox, portrait by Charles Willson Peale, from life, ca. 1784. Independence National Historical Park.
Marie Joseph Paul Yves Roch Gilbert Motier, Marquis de Lafayette, portrait by Charles Willson Peale, 1779-80. Independence National Historical Park.
John Graves Simcoe, portrait, oil on canvas, by George Theodore Berthon, ca. 1881.

Image Credits

Courtesy of Governor Simcoe Branch, United Empire Loyalists Association of Canada.
Sir Henry Clinton, courtesy of Clements Library, University of Michigan.
Anthony Wayne, portrait by James Sharples, Sr., from life, 1796. Independence National Historical Park.
Aaron Burr, portrait attributed to Gilbert Stuart, oil on canvas, ca. 1792-1794. From the Collections of the New Jersey Historical Society, Newark, New Jersey. Gift of David A. Hayes, Esq., for John Chetwood, Esq.
Alexander Hamilton, portrait by Charles Willson Peale, from life, ca. 1790-95. Independence National Historical Park.
Benjamin Rush, finished engraving by David Edwin of Thomas Sully's 1813 portrait of Dr. Benjamin Rush (Pennsylvania Hospital, Philadelphia). Exhibited at the Pennsylvania Academy's annual exhibition in 1814. The engraving was done for a series published as "Delaplaine's Repository of the portraits and lives of the Heroes, Philosophers, and Statesmen of America." Charles Willson Peale produced a "portrait after Sully" in 1818. Courtesy of Archives and Special Collections, Dickinson College, Carlisle, Pa.
John André, courtesy of Clements Library, University of Michigan.
Benedict Arnold, portrait by an unknown engraver, after the artist du Similier. Line engraving for a European magazine. Courtesy of Clements Library, University of Michigan.
Joseph Reed, courtesy of University of Pennsylvania Archives.
Cornplanter (Gyantawanka), portrait by F. Bartoli (1796). Collection of the New-York Historical Society, accession #1867.314.
Joseph Brant (Thayendanegea), portrait by Charles Willson Peale, from life, 1797. Independence National Historical Park.
James Clinton, from Frederick Cook's *Journals of the Military Expedition of Major General John Sullivan Against the Six Nations of Indians in 1789 with Records of Centennial Celebrations* (Auburn, N. Y.: Knapp, Peck & Thompson Printers, 1887).
Mary Jemison monument. Author photo, 1995.
Mary Jemison historical marker. Author photo, 1995.
Daniel Brodhead, courtesy of McClain Printing Company, Parsons, West Virginia.
Allegheny River at Redbank Creek. Photo by Thomas Betts, 2002.
Potomac River at Oldtown. Photo by Thomas Betts, 2005.
Johann De Kalb battlefield marker, courtesy of Kershaw County (S.C.) Historical Society. Photo by John Miller, 2004.
Johann De Kalb Monument, Camden, S. C., courtesy of Joanna Craig and Camden (S.C.) Historical Society.
George Rogers Clark, portrait by Matthew Harris Jouett (1788-1827), the Kentucky portrait painter and a favorite student of Gilbert Stuart. Courtesy of The American Revolution Home Page.
Washington at Yorktown, portrait by Rembrandt Peale, 1848. Independence National Historical Park.
Charles Cornwallis, courtesy of Clements Library, University of Michigan.
William Irvine, portrait from an oil painting by B. Otis, after one by Robert Edge Pine, an eminent English artist who came to America in 1784. The original

was taken in New York City, when Irvine (at age 48) was a member of Congress. Courtesy of Archives and Special Collections, Dickinson College, Carlisle, Pa.

Simon Girty, courtesy of the Ohio Historical Society, Columbus, Ohio.

Stockade at Hannastown. Author collection.

Daniel Boone, by John Filson, author of "The Adventures of Col. Daniel Boon," which is an appendix to his *Discovery, Settlement, and Present State of Kentucke* (1784). Filson, like Boone, was a Pennsylvania-born Kentucky pioneer. The only portrait of Daniel Boone from life is that painted by Charles Harding in 1818-20, when Boone was in his eighties. It now hangs in the State House, Frankfort, Kentucky.

John Harris certificate of discharge. Author collection.

Hancock House, photo by Bruce Bacon, 2005.

Quinton Bridge monument. Author collection.

Hancock House memorial marker. Author collection.

Captain William Smith House, courtesy of Salem (N.J.) Historical Society.

Lydia Smith silhouette. Author collection.

Cornplanter monument. Author photo, 2001.

William Crawford cabin. Author collection.

William Crawford cabin historical marker. Author collection.

Josiah Harmar, portrait by Raphaelle Peale, from an engraving by John Sartain. Courtesy of the Ohio Historical Society, Columbus, Ohio.

Little Turtle (Michikinkna), portrait by an unknown artist at an unknown date. Courtesy of the Ohio Historical Society, Columbus, Ohio.

Arthur St. Clair, portrait by Charles Willson Peale, from life, 1782-84. Independence National Historical Park.

John Harris grave marker. Author photo, 1996.

Molly Pitcher monument. Author photo, 2005.

Lafayette historical marker. Author photo, 2004.

Works Consulted

Primary Materials

Abler, Thomas S., *Chainbreaker: The Revolutionary War Memoirs of Governor Blacksnake As Told to Benjamin Williams* (Lincoln: University of Nebraska Press, 1989).
Baurmeister, Carl, L., "Letters of Major Baurmeister to Colonel von Jungkenn Written During the Philadelphia Campaign, 1777 to 1778," ed. by Bernhard A. Uhlendorf and Edna Vosper, *Pennsylvania Magazine of History and Biography*, LIX (Oct., 1935), 392-419, and LX (January and April, 1936), 34-52 and 161-183.
Baurmeister, Carl L., *Revolution in America, Confidential Letters and Journals, 1776-1784 of Adjutant General Major Baurmeister of the Hessian Forces*, Translated and annotated by Bernhard A. Uhlendorf (New Brunswick, N.J.: Rutgers University Press, 1957).
Butterfield, Consul Willshire, ed. *Washington-Crawford Letters* (Cincinnati: R. Clarke & Co., 1877).
Butterfield, Consul Willshire, ed. *Washington-Irvine Correspondence* (Madison, Wisconsin: David Atwood, 1882).
Cleland, Hugh, *George Washington in the Ohio Valley* (Pittsburgh: University of Pittsburgh Press, 1955). Includes journals of Christopher Gist and George Washington.
Cook, Frederick, *Journals of the Military Expedition of Major General John Sullivan against the Six Nation of Indians in 1779 with Records of Centennial Celebrations* (Auburn, N.Y.: Knapp, Peck, and Thomson, 1887).
Custis, George Washington Parke, *Recollections and Private Memoirs of Washington*, ed. Benjamin Lossing (New York: Derby and Jackson, 1860).
Drake, Francis Samuel, *Life and Correspondence of Henry Knox* (Boston: Drake, 1873).
Draper, Lyman C., *Draper Manuscripts* (Madison, Wisconsin: State Historical Society of Wisconsin). 25 vols.
Fitzpatrick, John C., ed. *The Diaries of George Washington* (Boston: Mt. Vernon Ladies' Association, 1925).
Fitzpatrick, John C., ed. *The Writings of George Washington, 1744-1799* (Washington, D. C.: United States Government Printing Office, 1931-1944). 39 vols.
Ford, Worthington Chauncey, collector and editor, *Defences of Philadelphia in 1777* (Brooklyn: Historical Printing Club, 1897).
Ford, Worthington Chauncey, ed. *The Writings of George Washington* (New York: G. P. Putnam's Sons, 1889-1893). 14 vols.
Hamilton, Alexander, and William Irvine, "The Battle of Monmouth, Letters of

Alexander Hamilton and General William Irvine, Describing the Engagement," *Pennsylvania Magazine of History and Biography*, II (1878), 139-148.

Hammond, Otis G., ed. *The Letters and Papers of Major General John Sullivan* (Concord, N.H.: New Hampshire Historical Society Collections, XIII-XV, 1930-39). 3 vols.

Harris, Benjamin, "History of the Harris Family," unpublished letters (Harrison Smith Morris and Amos Harris), April 21, 1850.

James, James Alton, "George Rogers Clark Papers, 1781-1784," in *Collections of the Illinois State Historical Library* (Vol. XIX, Virginia Series).

Jordan, John W., ed. "Adam Hubley, Jr., Lt Colo. Comdt 11th Penna Regt, His Journal, Commencing at Wyoming, July 30th, 1779," *Pennsylvania Magazine of History and Biography*, XXXIII (1909), 129-146; 279-302; 409-422.

Knight, John, "A Narrative of Dr. Knight," *Pennsylvania Archives*, Series 2, vol. XIV, pp. 708-717.

Larrabee, Don Marshall, editor and compiler, *A Reprint of the Journals of George Washington and His Guide, Christopher Gist, Reciting Their Experiences on the Historic Mission from Governor Dinwiddie of Virginia, to the French Forts in November-December, 1753* (np., npbl., 1950).

Lodge, Henry Cabot, ed. *The Works of Alexander Hamilton* (New York and London: G. P. Putnam's Sons, 1904). 12 vols.

Proctor, Colonel Thomas, "Narrative of the Journey of Col. Thomas Proctor to the Indians of the North-West, 1791," *Pennsylvania Archives*, Series 2, vol. IV (1876), pp. 551-622.

Reed, William B., *Life and Correspondence of Joseph Reed* (Philadelphia: Lindsay and Blakiston, 1847). 2 vols.

Simcoe, John Graves, *History of the Operation of a Partisan Corps Called the Queen's Rangers* (written and printed for private distribution) (Exeter, 1787). Reprinted, with a memoir of the author, New York: 1844.

Sparks, Jared, ed. *Correspondence of the American Revolution: Being Letters of Eminent Men to George Washington* (Boston: Little, Brown and Co., 1853). 4 vols.

Sparks, Jared, ed. *The Writings of George Washington, with a Life of the Author* (Boston: American Stationers Co., et al., 1834-1837). 12 vols.

Secondary Materials

Abrahams, Gerald, *Not Only Chess, A Selection of Chessays* (London: Allen and Unwin, 1974).

Adams, John, *The Works of John Adams, Second President of the United States: with a Life of the Author, Notes and Illustrations by His Grandson Charles Francis Adams* (Boston: Little, Brown and Company, 1856). 10 vols.

Albert, George Dallas, ed. *History of the County of Westmoreland, Pennsylvania, with Biographical Sketches of Many of Its Pioneers and Prominent Men* (Phila.: L. H. Everts and Co., 1882).

Alden, John R., *A History of the American Revolution, 1775-1783* (New York: Alfred A. Knopf, 1969).

Works Consulted 339

Amory, Thomas Coffin, *The Military Services and Public Life of Major-General John Sullivan* (Port Washington, N.Y.: Kennikat Press, 1868; rptd. 1968).

Anderson, Troyer Steele, *The Command of the Howe Brothers During the American Revolution* (New York and London: Oxford University Press, 1936).

Arthur, Robert, *The Sieges of Yorktown, 1781 and 1862* (Fort Monroe, Va.: Coast Artillery School, 1927).

"Battle of Quinton's Bridge," *Today's Sunbeam*, Salem, N. J., April 26, 1990, pp. D-1 and D-3.

Bean, Theodore W., and Henry Armitt Brown, *Valley Forge: Proceedings on the Occasion of the Centennial Celebration of the Occupation of Valley Forge by the Continental Army, under George Washington, June 19, 1878* (Philadelphia: Lippincott, 1879).

Bean, Theodore W., *Washington at Valley Forge* (Norristown, Pa.: Charles P. Schreiner, 1876).

Bell, Herbert C., *History of Northumberland County, Pennsylvania* (Chicago: Brown, Runk & Co., 1891).

Bellamy, Francis Rufus, *The Private Life of George Washington* (New York: Crowell, 1951).

Berg, Fred Anderson, *Encyclopedia of Continental Army Units* (Harrisburg: Stackpole Books, 1972).

Betts, Jane J., "Missing the Point: A Tale of the Revolution," *Pittsburgh* magazine (1989-1990 City Guide), p. 108.

Bill, Alfred Hoyt, *Valley Forge, the Making of an Army* (New York: Harper & Bros., 1952).

Billias, George Athan, *General John Glover and His Marblehead Mariners* (New York: Henry Holt & Co., 1960).

Bishop, Christopher, "War's Fury Was Felt in the Tiny Village of Quinton," *Today's Sunbeam*, Salem, N. J., April 26, 1990, pp. D-1 and D-3.

Bodle, Wayne, *The Valley Forge Winter* (University Park, Pa.: The Pennsylvania State University Press, 2002).

Bolton, Charles Knowles, *The Private Soldier under Washington* (Port Washington, N.Y.: Kennikat Press, 1902; rptd. 1964).

Boucher, John N., *Old and New Westmoreland* (New York: The American Historical Society, 1918). 4 vols.

Boyd, Thomas, *Mad Anthony Wayne* (New York: Charles Scribner's Sons, 1929).

Boyd, Thomas, *Simon Girty and the White Savages* (New York: Minton Balch & Co., 1928).

Brooks, Noah, *Henry Knox, A Soldier of the Revolution* (New York: G. P. Putnam's Sons, 1901).

Brownlow, Donald Grey, *A Documentary History of the Battle of Germantown* (Germantown, Pa.: Germantown Historical Society, 1955).

Burk, W. Hubert, *Valley Forge: What It Is, Where It Is, and What to See There* (North Wales, Pa.: Norman Nuss, 1932).

Butterfield, Consul Willshire, *An Historical Account of the Expedition Against Sandusky under Col. William Crawford in 1782* (Cincinnati: R. Clarke & Co., 1873).

Butterfield, Consul Willshire, *History of the Girtys; Being a Concise Account of the*

Girty Brothers–Thomas, Simon, James and George, and of Their Half-brother John Turner: also of the part taken by them in Lord Dunmore's war, in the western border war of the Revolution, and in the Indian war of 1790-95: with a recital of the principal events in the West during these wars, drawn from authentic sources, largely original (Cincinnati: Robert Clarke and Co., 1890). Rptd. by Long's College Book Co., Columbus, Ohio, 1950.

Canby, Henry Seidel, *The Brandywine* (New York and Toronto: Farrar and Rinehart, 1941).

Carroll, John Alexander, and Mary Wells Southworth, completing the biography by Douglas Southall Freeman, *George Washington* (New York: Charles Scribner's Sons, 1957). 7 vols.

Carter, John H., *Early Events in the Susquehanna Valley* (Northumberland, Pa.: Northumberland County Historical Society, 1981).

Carter, John H., "Indian Incursions in Old Northumberland County During the Revolutionary War, 1777-1782," in Charles F. Snyder, ed. *Northumberland County in the American Revolution* (Sunbury, Pa.: Northumberland Historical Society, 1976), pp. 363-380.

Chalmers, Harvey, *Joseph Brant: Mohawk* (East Lansing, Mich.: Michigan State University Press, 1955).

Chidsey, Donald Barr, *Valley Forge* (New York: Crown Publishers, 1959).

Codman, John, *Arnold's Expedition to Quebec*, 2nd edition (New York: The Macmillan Company, 1902).

Colonial Records of Pennsylvania (Harrisburg: published by the State, 1852-53). 16 vols.

Corner, George W., ed. *The Autobiography of Benjamin Rush* (Westport, Conn.: Greenwood Press, 1948).

Craft, David, *The Sullivan Expedition, An Address Delivered at the Seneca County Centennial Celebration in Waterloo, N.Y., Sept.3, 1879* (Waterloo, N.Y.: Observer Book and Job Printing House, 1880).

Craft, David, *Journals of the Military Expedition of Major General John Sullivan against the Six Nations of Indians in 1779* (Auburn, N.Y.: Knapp, Peck & Thomson, Printers, 1887).

Craig, Neville, *Sketch of the Life and Services of Isaac Craig, Major in the Fourth (Usually called Proctor's) Regiment of Artillery During the Revolutionary War* (Pittsburgh: J. S. Davidson, 1854).

Craig, Neville B.,*The History of Pittsburgh* (Pittsburgh: J. H. Mellor, 1851; new edn. 1917).

Cribbs, George Arthur, "The Frontier Policy of Pennsylvania," *The Historical Society of Western Pennsylvania*, II (1919), 5-35; 72-106; 174-198.

Crumrine, Boyd, *History of Washington County, Pennsylvania* (Philadelphia: L. H. Everts and Co., 1882).

Davis, Andrew McFarland, "Account of the Wyoming Massacre of 1778," *Proceedings of the Massachusetts Historical Society*, XXIII (October 1887), 340-347.

Demarest, Thomas, "The Baylor Massacre–Some Assorted Notes and Information," *Bergen County History, 1971 Annual* (River Edge, N.J.: Bergen County Historical Society, 1971), pp. 28-93.

Works Consulted

De Peyster, General J. Watts,*Anthony Wayne, Third General-in-Chief of the United States Army,* printed from the United Service, 1886.
Division of Archives and History (New York), *The Sullivan-Clinton Campaign in 1779* (Albany: University of the State of New York, 1929).
Donehoo, George P., ed. *A History of the Cumberland Valley of Pennsylvania* (Harrisburg: The Susquehanna History Association, 1930).
Downes, Randolph C., *Council Fires on the Upper Ohio: A Narrative of the Indian Affairs in the Upper Ohio Valley until 1795* (Pittsburgh: University of Pittsburgh Press, 1940).
Drinnon, Richard, *Facing West: The Metaphysics of Indian-Hating and Empire Building* (Minneapolis: University of Minnesota Press, 1980).
Dyer, Thomas G., *Theodore Roosevelt and the Idea of Race* (Baton Rouge: Louisiana State University Press, 1980).
Eckert, Allan W., *That Dark and Bloody River* (New York: Bantam Books, 1995).
Egle, William Henry, *An Illustrated History of the Commonwealth of Pennsylvania, civil, political, and military, from the earliest settlement to the present time, including historical descriptions of each county in the state, their towns, and industrial resources* (Harrisburg: De Witt C. Goodrich & Co., 1876).
Egle, William Henry, *The First Indian Massacre in the Valley of Wyoming, Fifteenth of October, 1763. An Address Delivered at the Wyoming Monument on July 3, 1889* (Harrisburg: Harrisburg Publishing Company, 1890).
Ellis, Joseph J., *His Excellency, George Washington* (New York: Alfred A. Knopf, 2004).
Elting, John Albert, *The Battle of Bunker Hill* (Monmouth Beach, N. J.: Philip Freneau Press, 1975).
Eyres, Lawrence E., *Along the Sullivan Trail: The Story of Sullivan's Indian Expedition of 1779 That Opened Northern Pennsylvania and the Finger Lakes and Genesee Regions of New York for Settlement* (Elmira, N.Y.: Advertiser Job Printing, 1954).
Fischer, David Hackett, *Washington's Crossing* (New York: Oxford University Press, 2004).
Fischer, Joseph, *A Well Executed Failure: The Sullivan Campaign Against the Iroquois, July-September, 1779* (Columbia, S.C.: University of South Carolina Press, 1997).
Flexner, James Thomas, *George Washington in the American Revolution (1775-1783)* (Boston: Little, Brown, 1968).
Flick, Alexander C., "General Henry Knox's Ticonderoga Expedition," *Quarterly Journal of the New York State Historical Association,* IX (April, 1928), 472-473.
Freeman, Douglas S., *George Washington* (New York: Scribner's, 1948-57). 7 vols.
Furthey, J. Smith, and Gilbert Cope, *History of Chester County, Pennsylvania: with Genealogical and Biographical Sketches* (Philadelphia: Louis H. Everts, 1881).
Flood, Charles Bracelen, *Rise and Fight Again: Perilous Times along the Road to Independence* (New York: Dodd, Mead, 1976).
Frantz, John B., and William Pencak, eds. *Beyond Philadelphia: The American Revolution in the Pennsylvania Hinterlands* (University Park, Pa.:

Pennsylvania State University Press, 1998).

Garrison, Webb, *Sidelights on the American Revolution* (New York: Abington Press, 1974).

Gilbert, Stephen R., "An Analysis of the Xavier della Gatta Paintings of the Battles of Paoli and Germantown, 1777," *Military Collector & Historian*: part I, 46 (Fall 1994), 98-108; part II, 47 (Winter 1995), 146-162.

Godcharles, Frederic Antes, "The Battle of Fort Freeland," in Charles F. Snyder, ed., *Northumberland County in the American Revolution* (Sunbury, Pa.: Northumberland County Historical Society, 1976), pp. 131-145.

Godcharles, Frederic Antes, "The First Expedition Against the Indians of the Six Nations," in Charles F. Snyder, ed., *Northumberland County in the American Revolution* (Sunbury, Pa: Northumberland County Historical Society, 1976), pp. 103-128.

Gottschalk, Louis, *Lafayette Joins the American Army* (Chicago: University of Chicago Press, 1937).

Graymont, Barbara, *The Iroquois in the American Revolution* (Syracuse, N.Y.: Syracuse University Press, 1972).

Gruber, Ira D., *The Howe Brothers and the American Revolution* (New York: Atheneum, 1972).

Hassler, Edgar W., *Old Westmoreland, A History of Western Pennsylvania During the Revolution* (Pittsburgh: J. R. Weldin & Co., 1900).

Hayden, Horace Edwin, "Echoes of the Massacre of Wyoming," *Proceedings and Collections of the Wyoming Historical and Genealogical Society*, VII (1902), 78-105; XII (1911-1912), 69-104.

Hazard, Samuel, et al., eds. *Pennsylvania Archives*, Sixth Series (Philadelphia and Harrisburg: 1852-1907).

Headley, P. C., *The Life of General Lafayette, Marquis of France, General in the United States Army* . . . .(Auburn, N.Y.: Derby and Miller, 1851).

Headley, Joel Tyler, *Washington and His Generals* (New York: Scribner, Armstrong & Co., 1875).

History of Cumberland and Adams Counties, Pennsylvania (Chicago: Warner, Beers and Company, 1886).

History of Mercer County, Pennsylvania, Its Past and Present (Chicago: Brown, Runk & Co., Publisher, 1888).

Hulbert, Archer Butler, *The Ohio River, A Course of Empire* (New York and London: The Knickerbocker Press, 1906).

Irving, Washington, *Life of George Washington* (New York: G.P. Putnam's and Sons, 1855-59). 5 vols.

Jackson, John W., *With the British Army in Philadelphia, 1777-1778* (San Rafael, Calif., and London, England: Presidio Press, 1979).

James, James Alton, *The Life of George Rogers Clark* (Chicago: University of Chicago Press, 1928).

Jennings, John, *Boston, Cradle of Liberty* (Garden City, N.Y.: Doubleday & Company, 1947).

Johnson, Henry Phelps, *The Campaign of 1776 Around New York and Brooklyn* (New York: Da Capo Press, 1971).

Jones, Charles Henry, *History of the Campaign for the Conquest of Canada in 1776*

(Philadelphia: Porter & Coates, 1882).
Kapp, Friedrich, *The Life of John Kalb, Major-General in the Revolutionary Army* (New York: Henry Holt and Company, 1884).
Kellogg, Louise Phelps, ed. *Frontier Advance on the Upper Ohio, 1778-79* (Madison, Wisc.: 1916). Vol. XXIII of Wisconsin Historical Collections.
Kellogg, Louise Phelps, ed. *Frontier Retreat on the Upper Ohio, 1779-81* (Madison, Wisc.: 1917). Vol. XXXIV of Wisconsin Historical Collections.
Kelsay, Isabel Thompson, *Joseph Brant, 1743-1807: Man of Two Worlds* (Syracuse, N.Y.: Syracuse University Press, 1984).
Ketchum, Richard M., *The Winter Soldiers* (Garden City, N.Y.: Doubleday & Co., Inc., 1973).
Kirkland, Frederic R., ed. "Journal of a Physician on the Expedition Against Canada, 1776," in *Pennsylvania Magazine of History and Biography*, LIX (Oct., 1935), 321-361.
Laird, R. F., "The Skirmish at Quinton's Bridge," *Quinton's Bridge, '78* (Salem, N.J.: Salem County Cultural and Heritage Commission, 1978), pp. 1-9.
Landers, Howard Lee, *The Battle of Camden, South Carolina, August 16, 1780* (Washington, D.C.: U. S. Government Printing Office, 1929).
Landers, Howard Lee, *The Virginia Campaign and the Blockade and Siege of Yorktown, 1781, including a brief narrative of the French participation in the Revolution prior to the Southern Campaign* (Washington, D.C.: U.S. Government Printing Office, 1931).
Landis, John B., "Investigation into American Tradition of Woman Known as Molly Pitcher," *The Journal of American History*, V (1911), 85-86.
Langguth, A. J., *Patriots, the Men Who Started the American Revolution* (New York: Simon and Schuster, 1988).
Leckie, Robert, *George Washington's War, the Saga of the American Revolution* (New York: HarperCollins Publishers, 1992).
Lengyel, Cornel Adam, *I, Benedict Arnold, The Anatomy of Treason* (New York: Doubleday & Company, 1960).
Lengyel, Cornel Adam, *Presidents of the United States* (New York: Golden Press, Inc., 1964).
Latzko, Andreas, *Lafayette, A Life* (translated from the German) (New York: Doubleday, Doran and Company, Inc., 1936). Lippard, George, *The Battle-day of Germantown* (Philadelphia: Diller, 1843).
Lossing, Benson John, *Our Country, A Household History for All Readers, from the Discovery of America to the Present Time* (New York: Johnson and Bailey, 1894). 3 vols.
Lossing, Benson John, *The Pictorial Field-Book of the Revolution* (New York: Harper & Brothers, 1859. 2 vols. Republished (Rutland, Vt. and Tokyo, Japan, 1972). 2 vols.
Macaltioner, George B., "The Coming of the British Army into Salem County During the American Revolution," *150th Anniversary of the Skirmish at Quinton's Bridge and the Massacre at Hancock's Bridge, Quinton, N.J.* (Official Program, May 19, 1928), pp. 8-16, 33, 35.
MacIntire, Jane Bacon, *Lafayette, the Guest of the Nation, the Tracing of the Route of Lafayette's Tour of the United States in 1824-25* (Newton, Mass.: A. J.

Simone Press, 1967).
Manley, Henry S., *The Treaty of Fort Stanwix, 1784* (Rome, N.Y.: Rome Sentinel Company, 1932).
McCullough, David, *John Adams* (New York, London, and Toronto: Simon and Schuster, 2001).
McCullough, David, *1776* (New York, Toronto, London, and Sydney: Simon and Schuster, 2005).
McDowell, Bart, *The Revolutionary War* (Washington, D.C.: National Geographic Society, 1967).
McGuire, Thomas J., *The Surprise of Germantown, or the Battle of Clivedon: October 4th, 1777* (Philadelphia: Thomas Publications, 1994).
Meginness, John Franklin, *Otzinachson, or A History of the West Branch Valley of the Susquehanna; embracing a full account of its settlement, trials and privations endured by the first pioneers, full accounts of the Indian wars, predatory incursions, abductions, massacres, &c., together with an account of the fair play system; and the trying scenes of the big runaway; interspersed with biographical sketches of some of the leading settlers, families, etc., together with pertinent anecdotes, statistics and much valuable matter entirely new* (Philadelphia: H. B. Ashmead, 1857).
Mickley, Joseph J., *Brief Account of Murders by the Indians and the Cause Thereof, in Northampton County, Pennsylvania* (Philadelphia: Thomas William Stuckey, 1875).
Miner, William Penn, *History of Wyoming* (Philadelphia: J. Crissy, 1845).
Mohawk, John C., "Cornplanter," pp. 135-137 in *Encyclopedia of North American Indians*, ed. Frederick E. Hoxie (Boston and New York: Houghton and Mifflin Co., 1996).
Moore, Frank, *Diary of the American Revolution* (New York: Charles T. Evans, 1863). 2 vols.
Moore, H. N., *Life and Services of General Anthony Wayne* (Philadelphia: John B. Perry, 1845).
Mordrall, James C., *The United States Manual of Biography and History* (Philadelphia: James B. Smith & Co., 1856).
Murray, Elsie, "Hartley's and Sullivan's Expedition Against the Iroquois," in Charles F. Snyder, ed. *Northumberland County in the American Revolution* (Sunbury, Pa.: Northumberland County Historical Society, 1976), pp. 129-130.
Myers, Wilbur A., ed. *The Book of the Sesqui-Centennial Celebration of the Battle of Wyoming, July 1st-4th* (Wyoming Valley: A Wyoming Valley Publication, 1928; Wilkes Barre, Pa.: Smith-Bennett Corp., 1928).
Nead, Benjamin N., "A Sketch of General Thomas Proctor, with Some Account of the First Pennsylvania Artillery in the Revolution," *Pennsylvania Magazine of History and Biography*, IV (1880), 454-470.
Nelson, David Paul, *General Horatio Gates* (Baton Rouge: Louisiana State University Press, 1976).
Norris, Major, "Journal of Sullivan's Expedition," *Buffalo Historical Society Publications*, I (1879), 217-252.
Norton, A. Tiffany, *History of Sullivan's Campaign Against the Iroquois* (Lima, N.Y: privately published, 1879).

150th Anniversary of the Skirmish at Quinton's Bridge and the Massacre at Hancock's Bridge (Quinton, N.J.: May 19, 1928).
Palmer, Frederick, *Clark of the Ohio* (New York: Dodd, Mead & Company, 1920).
Parker, Arthur C., "The Indian Interpretation of the Sullivan-Clinton Campaign," *Rochester (NY) Historical Society Publication Fund Series*, VII (1929).
Partridge, Bellamy, *Sir Billy Howe* (London, New York, and Toronto: Longmans, Green and Company, 1932).
Patterson, D. Williams, "Mrs. Skinner and the Massacre at Wyoming," *New England Historical and Genealogical Register*, XIV (July, 1860), 265-266.
Peck, George, *Wyoming: Its History, Stirring Incidents, and Romantic Adventures* (New York: Harper & Bros., 1858).
Peterson, Harold L., *The Book of the Continental Soldier* (Harrisburg: Stackpole Books, 1968).
Pinkowski, Edward, *Chester County Place Names* (Philadelphia: Sunshine Press, 1962).
Pleasants, Henry J., "The Battle of Paoli," *Pennsylvania Magazine of History and Biography*, LXXII (1948), 44-53.
Porter, William A., "A Sketch of the Life of General Andrew Porter," *Pennsylvania Magazine of History and Biography*, IV (1880), 261-301.
Proceedings on the occasion of the dedication of the monument on the one hundreth anniversary of the Paoli Massacre in Chester County, Pa., September 20, 1877 (West Chester, Pa.: F. S. Hickman, printer, 1877).
Public Ledger (Salem, N.J., January, 1932).
Quinton's Bridge, '78 (Salem, N.J.: Salem County Cultural and Heritage Commission, 1978).
Rankin, Hugh F., *The American Revolution* (New York: G. P. Putnam's Sons, 1964).
Reed, John Frederick, *Campaign to Valley Forge, July 1, 1777-December 19, 1777* (Philadelphia: University of Pennsylvania Press, 1965).
Reed, John Frederick, *Crucible of Victory* (Monmouth Beach, N.J.: Philip Freneau Press, 1969).
Ridner, Judith, "William Irvine and the Complexities of Manhood and Fatherhood in the Pennsylvania Backcountry," *The Pennsylvania Magazine of History and Biography*, LXXV (Jan./April, 2001), 5-34.
Roberts, Cokie, *Founding Mothers* (New York: HarperCollins Publishers, Inc., 2004).
Roberts, Octavia, *With Lafayette in America* (Boston and New York: Houghton Mifflin Company, 1919).
Ross, Howard D., "The British Expedition Against Philadelphia and the Battle of Brandywine During the Campaign of 1777," *Picket Post,* No. 22 (1949), pp. 30-34.
Royal Pennsylvania Gazette, Philadelphia, Pa., 1778.
Seaver, James E., *A Narrative of the Life of Mrs. Mary Jemison* (Canandaigna, N. Y.: J. D. Bemis, 1824; Rptd. New York: Corinth, 1961).
Sedgwick, Henry Dwight, *La Fayette* (Indianapolis: The Bobbs-Merrill Company, 1928).
Shaara, Jeff, *Rise to Rebellion* (New York: Ballantine Books, 2001).
Shaara, Jeff, *The Glorious Cause* (New York: Ballantine Books, 2002).
Sickler, Joseph Sheppard., *History of Salem County, New Jersey; being the story of*

John Fenwick's colony, the oldest English speaking settlement on the Delaware River (Salem, N.J.: Sunbeam Publishing Company, 1937).
Sipe, Chester Hale, "General Sullivan's Expedition Against the Six Nations," in Charles F. Snyder, ed. *Northumberland County in the American Revolution* (Sunbury, Pa.: Northumberland County Historical Society, 1976), pp. 191-199.
Sipe, Chester Hale, *The Indian Chiefs of Pennsylvania* (Butler, Pa.: The Zeigler Printing Company, 1927).
Sipe, Chester Hale, *The Indian Wars of Pennsylvania: An Account of the Indian Events in Pennsylvania, of the French and Indian Wars, Pontiac's War, Lord Dunmore's War, the Revolutionary War and the Indian Uprisings from 1787 to 1795* (Harrisburg: The Telegraph Press, 1931).
Smith, Samuel Robert, *The Story of Wyoming Valley* (Kingston, Pa.: S. R. Smith, 1906).
Smith, Samuel Stelle, *The Battle of Monmouth* (Monmouth Beach, N.J.: Philip Freneau Press, 1964).
Smith, Samuel Stelle, *The Battle of Princeton* (Monmouth Beach, N.J.: Philip Freneau Press, 1965).
Smith, Samuel Stelle, *The Battle of Trenton* (Monmouth Beach, N.J.: Philip Freneau Press, 1965).
Snyder, Charles F., ed. *Northumberland County in the American Revolution* (Sunbury, Pa.: Northumberland County Historical Society, 1976).
Sohl, Charles E., "Some Phases of the Battle of Germantown," *Old York Road Historical Society Bulletin,* III (1939), 23-46.
Stevenson, Augusta, *Molly Pitcher, Young Patriot* (New York: Macmillan Publishing Company, 1960).
Stewart, Frank H., "Foraging for Valley Forge, by General Anthony Wayne, in Salem and Gloucester Counties," pamphlet printed in 1964.
Stewart, Frank H., *Salem County in the Revolution* (Salem, N.J.: Salem County Historical Society, 1967).
Stone, Rufus B., "Brodhead's Raid on the Senecas," *Western Pennsylvania Historical Magazine,* VII (1924), 88-101.
Stone, William Leete, *Life and Times of Red-Jacket, or Sa-go-ye-wat-ha, being the Sequel to the history of the Six Nations* (New York and London: Wiley and Putnam, 1841).
Stone, William Leete, *Life of Joseph Brant, Thayendanegea,* (1838) 2 vols. Rptd. St. Clair Shores, Minn: Scholarly Press, 1970.
Stone, William Leete, *The Poetry and History of Wyoming* (Albany: T. Marshall, 1864).
Stoudt, John Joseph, *Ordeal at Valley Forge. A Day-by-Day Chronicle from December 17, 1777 to June 18, 1778,* Compiled from the sources (Philadelphia: University of Pennsylvania Press, 1963).
Stryker, William Scudder, *Official Register of the Officers and Men of New Jersey in the Revolutionary War* (Trenton, N.J.: Wm. T. Nicholson & Co., Printers, 1872; rptd. 1967).
Stryker, William Scudder, *The Battle of Monmouth,* ed. and completed by William Starr Meyers (Princeton: Princeton University Press, 1927; 1963).

Works Consulted

Swiggett, Howard, *War Out of Niagara, Walter Butler and the Tory Rangers*, Empire State Historical Publication XX (Port Washington, N.Y.: Ira J. Friedman, 1963).
Tatum, Edward H., Jr., ed. *The American Journal of Ambrose Serle* (San Marino, Ca.:Huntingdon Library, 1940).
Taylor, Frank H., *Valley Forge, A Chronicle of American Heroism* (Philadelphia: W. S. Slack, 1920).
Thayer, Theodore, *Nathanael Greene, Strategist of the American Revolution* (New York: Twayne Publishers, 1960).
Thomas, Lowell, *The Hero of Vincennes, the Story of George Rogers Clark* (Boston and New York: Houghton Mifflin, 1929).
Thompson, Ray, *Washington at Germantown* (Fort Washington, Pa.: Bicentennial Press, 1970).
Timmins, W. D., "The Affair at Hancock House," *Quinton's Bridge, '78* (Salem, N.J: Salem County Cultural and Heritage Commission, 1978), pp. 11-17.
Trussell, John B. B., Jr., *Birthplace of an Army: A Study of the Valley Forge Encampment* (Harrisburg: Historical and Museum Commission, 1976).
Trussell, John B. B., Jr., *Epic on the Schuylkill: The Valley Forge Encampment, 1777-1778* (Harrisburg: Pennsylvania Historical and Museum Commission, 1974).
Trussell, John B. B., Jr., *The Battle of Brandywine* (Harrisburg: Pennsylvania Historical and Museum Commission, 1974).
Trussell, John B. B., Jr., *The Battle of Germantown* (Harrisburg: Pennsylvania Historical and Museum Commission, 1974).
Trussell, John B. B., Jr., *The Pennsylvania Line. Regimental Organizations and Operations, 1776-1783* (Harrisburg: Pennsylvania Historical and Museum Commission, 1977).
Two Hundred Years in Cumberland County, ed. by committee, D. W. Thompson, chairman (Carlisle, Pa.: The Hamilton Library and Historical Association of Cumberland County, 1951).
Van Every, Dale, *A Company of Heroes* (New York: William Morrow and Company, 1962).
Wallace, Anthony F. C., *The Death and Rebirth of the Senecas* (New York: Knopf, 1970).
Wallace, Willard M., *Traitorous Hero, The Life and Fortunes of Benedict Arnold* (New York: Harper & Brothers, 1954).
Ward, Christopher, *The War of the Revolution*, ed. John Richard Alden (New York: Macmillan Company, 1952). 2 vols.
Weedon, General George, *Valley Forge Orderly Book* (New York: Dodd, Mead & Company, 1902).
Westcott, Thompson, *Names of Persons Who Took the Oath of Allegiance to the State of Pennsylvania Between the Years 1777 and 1789* (Baltimore: 1992).
Whittemore, Charles Park, *A General of the Revolution, John Sullivan of New Hampshire* (New York: Columbia University Press, 1961).
Wilbur, C. Keith, *Picture Book of the Continental Soldier* (Harrisburg: Stackpole Books, 1969, 1980).
Wildes, Harry Emerson, *Valley Forge* (New York: Macmillan, 1938).
Williamson, James R., "Westmoreland County, Connecticut: Bloodiest Battle of the

Revolution," *Connecticut Historical Society Bulletin,* XLVI (July, 1981), 86-96.

Wolfinger, John F., "Northumberland County," in William Henry Egle, *An Illustrated History of the Commonwealth of Pennsylvania, Civil, Political, and Military, from Its Earliest Settlement to the Present Time* (Harrisburg: De Witt C. Goodrich & Co., 1876), pp. 997-1005.

Woodward, W. E., *Tom Paine: America's Godfather, 1737-1809* (New York: E. P. Dutton & Company, 1945).

Wright, Albert H., *The Sullivan Expedition of 1779* (Ithaca, New York: A. H. Wright, 1943).

Zucker, Adolf Eduard, *General De Kalb, Lafayette's Mentor* (Chapel Hill: University of North Carolina Press, 1966).

Notes

Chapter I

1. For the Harris genealogy consult the Salem Historical Society, Salem, N. J.
2. Macaltioner, pp. 9-10.
3. Stewart, *Salem County in the Revolution,* p. 7.
4. Idem.
5. The twenty-year-old John Knox had tried in vain to keep the crowd away from the soldiers. Three of the protesters were killed outright, two died later. Naturally the funeral inspired a heated demonstration. The British officer who had been in charge, and the Redcoats who did the firing, were tried for murder. Robert Treat Paine served as prosecutor. John Adams and Josiah Quincy won an acquittal for six of the defendants. Two were pronounced guilty of manslaughter, but were released after having their thumbs branded.
6. Some historians regard as the first engagement of the Revolution the battle fought on October 10, 1774, at Point Pleasant, Virginia, at the point where the Kanawha and Ohio Rivers come together. Here clashed a force of Virginia militiamen under Andrew Lewis with warriors from a number of Indian tribes, mostly Shawnees, under the Shawnee war-chief Cornstalk. The Indians had been tricked into an ambush by the governor of Virginia, Lord John Dunmore, who had led them to believe that the militiamen were coming to sign a peace treaty. Apparently Dunmore, who was a British Loyalist, had hoped in this way to distract the Virginia colonists from the determination for independence. While this battle of Point Pleasant, because it involved the British, might be considered the first military engagement of the Revolution, it is conventional to regard the Lexington-Concord action as the actual beginning. On September 21, 1959, the Minute Man National Historic Park was authorized. Here are preserved many of the principal features of the war's beginning at Lexington and Concord: the North Bridge, the Minute Man Statue, and the Battle Road.
7. Warner was born in Woodbury (now Roxbury), Ct., in 1743. He was Captain, later Lt. Colonel, of the local regiment (Bennington, Vt.) during the ill-fated 1775 invasion of Canada. In an heroic action, the 300 men under Warner's command repulsed General Guy Carleton's force of 800 when it tried to join McLean to break the siege of Montreal. In July of 1777, Warner was ordered to abandon Ticonderoga. He commanded the rear guard forces, which fought a splendid battle at Hubbardton. He aided John Stark in planning the battle of Bennington and participated courageously. Later, at Lake George Landing, he captured the vessels in which General Burgoyne would have escaped. He died shortly after the war's end, on December 26, 1784.

8. Most of the battle was actually fought on Breed's Hill. Both hills overlook Boston and the harbor. Breed's Hill is not so high as Bunker Hill, and is a little to the southeast. On the second day, June 17, the Americans regrouped on Bunker Hill.
9. Sometimes Colonel William Prescott, who with Putnam shared command of the militia, is credited with this instruction. It was doubtless a cry that echoed throughout the lines.
10. Moore, Frank, *Diary of the American Revolution*, I, 185.
11. Lossing, *Our Country*, II, 816-817.
12. Arnold's expedition, with results in mind, is sometimes derisively referred to as "Colonel Arnold's birch bark canoe invasion."
13. Jones, p. 41.
14. Kirkland, p. 323. Quoted from Jones, pp. 17-18.
15. James, p. 54.
16. Ibid., p. 55.
17. Adams, IX, 407-408.
18. Kirkland, p. 341. The diary kept by Dr. Beebe is *very* interesting, especially for impressions of Benedict Arnold and Generals Enoch Poor and John Sullivan; and for an account of the pitiful dying of General Thomas.
19. James, p. 55. Colonel Bedel, whom Arnold had blamed, was later reinstated.
20. Thompson, a native of Ireland, had served as a captain in the Seven Years' War. As Colonel he had raised six companies of Pennsylvania riflemen and with them had joined Wayne's army at Cambridge. He had been made Brigadier General on March 1 of this year. (Jones, p. 67n.)
21. Sullivan had served with Washington during the siege of Boston, October 1775 through March 1776.
22. Dr. Irvine had been an early and energetic protester of the indignities delivered by King George. He entered the military rebellion on January 9, 1776, as Colonel of the Sixth Pennsylvania Line; he was promoted to Brigadier General on May 12, 1779.
23. Jones, p. 76.
24. *Pennsylvania Archives* (hereinafter *P. A.*), Series 5, II, 195-197.
25. Lt. Colonel Thomas Hartley reported of Wayne that the Colonel "behaved extremely well, and showed himself the man of courage and the soldier." (Jones, p. 77)
26. Codman, p. 308.
27. Boucher, p. 342. The parole of General William Thompson likewise did not end until this time.
28. Jones, p. 77.
29. General Richard Montgomery was the first of six patriot generals to be killed in action during the war. In 1787, shortly after the war's end, the Congress authorized a memorial marker for Montgomery to be erected at Saint Paul's Church in New York City, at that time the nation's capital. Some years later, in 1818, the General's body was moved from its first resting place in Quebec to a position close to the memorial.
30. The Congress had appointed a committee (composed of Benjamin Franklin, of Pennsylvania; Benjamin Harrison, of Virginia; and Thomas Lynch of South

Notes 351

Carolina) to produce a flag for the rebellious colonies. The flag, which was designed by Francis Hopkinson, who later signed the Declaration of Independence, was soon known as the Cambridge flag, and sometimes called the "Continental Colors" (although Washington always preferred the appellation Grand Union Flag). It was the first flag of the country that was being born through revolution, and it served for almost a year following the Declaration of Independence, remaining the national flag until June 14, 1777. But of course it did, in its blue canton, acknowledge a relationship to Great Britain (the red cross of St. George representing England, and the white cross of St. Andrew representing Scotland); so after the proclamation of independence the need for a different flag was obvious. Although features of the story are now discredited, and it is not known just how much Betsy Ross had to do with the actual design of the flag, the traditional view is this: In response to an appeal from Washington, and the very wealthy Robert Morris, and Colonel George Ross, who was the uncle of her first husband, a year later the seamstress Elizabeth Griscom Ross (Betsy Ross) produced a new flag for the nation that was being born. She had it completed by the end of May, and on June 14, 1777, the Continental Congress officially adopted a national flag: "Resolved that the flag of the United States be thirteen stripes, alternate red and white, that the union be thirteen stars, white in a blue field, representing a new constellation." The flag was first officially flown over Fort Stanwix in the State of New York later that year, although some believe that it was first flown at Washington's headquarters at Middlebrook, N. J. In battle it made its first appearance at the Brandywine in September, although some historians insist it had been flown earlier, on July 8, 1777, at the Battle of Fort Ann in New York. It received its first formal salute from a foreign power when John Paul Jones had it flying from his mast when he sailed into a French port. (Colcomb, pp. 345-347) Sadly, the devoted and gallant Betsy Ross paid a heavy price for the freedoms it represented, losing two husbands to the war.

31. For very good accounts of the gun-toting expedition of Henry Knox and of the Dorchester Heights, see McCullough, *1776*, pp. 82-106.
32. Abraham's will, dated Jan. 30, 1776, left to his wife Esther one-third of the profits of the land, and one-third of the moveables. "To my 6 sons, Abraham, Isaac, Jacob, John, Nicholas and Parmanus, my lands." To his daughter Zerviah (Sophia) he left "high drawers." The inventory showed a value of 285 pounds, eight shillings, and four pence. Abraham was interred in the Mill Hollow Baptist Churchyard, but the gravestone marker was later removed to the Clinton Baptist Churchyard.

Chapter II

1. See Troyer Anderson, *The Command of the Howe Brothers During the American Revolution*, passim.
2. Putnam had also been one of a very few survivors of a shipwreck off the coast of Cuba.
3. Drake, p. 28.

4. Lengyel, *Presidents of the United States,* p. 13.
5. Drake, p. 28.
6. In 1872, William S. Stryker, Adjutant General of the State of New Jersey, was commissioned by the state's governor, Theodore Randolph, to produce a register of those officers and men of New Jersey who had served in the Revolution, either in the militia or in the Continental Army. On the militia list appear the names of two of John Harris's brothers, Isaac and Jacob (both identified with Salem County), but not the name of John's brother Abraham, who had served with Captain William Smith's New Jersey company of militia. The name John Harris appears three times on the militia list. One soldier is from Sussex County, in northern New Jersey; another is from Cumberland County; and the third is from Somerset County. The only John Harris listed for the Continental Army is clearly the militia veteran from Sussex County.
7. For details of this action, see Ketchum, p. 139 and Trussell, *The Pennsylvania Line*, p. 202.
8. Even before the end of the war the Commonwealth of Pennsylvania recognized her service. On June 29, 1779, an order was drawn on the Commonwealth Treasury (Joseph Reed, Esq., President of Pennsylvania) . . . "in favour of Margaret Corbin, for Thirty Dollars, to relieve her present necessities, she having been wounded and utterly disabled by three Grape shott, while she filled the post of her Husband, who was killed by her side, serving a piece of artillery at Fort Washington." (*Colonial Records,* XII, 34)
9. Garrison, p. 92, and Trussell, *The Pennsylvania Line,* p. 203.
10. Sometimes rendered Sterling.
11. Drake, p. 29.
12. Described vividly by Jeff Shaara in his recent historical novel *The Glorious Cause.* See also McCullough, *1776,* pp. 186-191.
13. Magaw, who had been born in Philadelphia, was the first attorney to be admitted to the Bedford County courts. After more than four years, on October 25, 1780, he was finally set free from the British prison ships. Before long, as Colonel, he was given command of the 6th Pennsylvania Battalion. After the war, he joined other principal figures of the Revolution, General William Irvine and General John Armstrong, as well as the celebrated Molly Pitcher, in Carlisle, Pa., where he returned to the practice of law.
14. Stewart, *Salem County in the Revolution,* pp. 16-17.
15. Bolton, p. 187.
16. See, for a fine, very readable impression, the recent full account of the Battle of New York, in David McCullough's *1776,* pp. 115-251.

Chapter III

1. Corner, p. 140; quoted by McCullough, *Adams,* p. 154.
2. Tatum, p. 101; quoted by McCullough, *Adams,* p. 158. For a vivid account of the whole business, see McCullough, *Adams,* pp. 154-158.
3. Sullivan had been exchanged by the British for their General Richard Prescott.
4. Historians have suggested that Colonel Rall was not sufficiently alert to the

possibility of an attack. One legend emerging from the affair, one that is not always credited, is that Rall had been sent (via a youngster) a message from a colonial, presumably a Tory, warning that Washington with his forces was preparing to cross the Delaware River. As the story goes, the Colonel, not about to be distracted from the chess game in which he was absorbed, simply placed the note, unread, in his pocket, where it was found after his death at the close of the battle. (See Gerald Abrahams, *Not Only Chess*, 1974) Other accounts have Rall, who loved to play cards and to gamble, and who was a hard drinker, have him absorbed in such pastimes both afternoon and evening on Christmas Day.

5. The very young James Monroe had fought at Harlem Heights and at White Plains. Here, on December 26, when his captain was wounded, he recalled that "the command fell on me," and it was shortly after that that he was wounded. He was made aide-de-camp to Major General Lord Stirling. He participated in the fighting at Brandywine and at Germantown, endured the winter at Valley Forge, and fought at Monmouth. After the war's end he became Governor of Virginia (twice), a United States Senator, was appointed Minister to France, and served as Secretary of State and Secretary of War before becoming the fifth president of the young nation.

6. Trussell, *The Pennsylvania Line*, p. 203. See also David Fischer, p. 244. For the artillery action at Trenton see Fischer, pp. 243-248.

7. Nead, pp. 456-457; Trussell, *The Pennsylvania Line*, p. 203.

8. *P. A.*, Series 1, vol. V, pp. 141-142; Trussell, *The Pennsylvania Line*, p. 203; Nead, p. 457.

9. *P. A.*, Series 1, vol. V, p. 142; Trussell, *The Pennsylvania Line*, p. 203.

10. *P. A.*, Series 5, vol. III, p. 943; Trussell, *The Pennsylvania Line*, p. 203.

11. The Ireland-born Edward Hand was, like William Irvine and Hugh Mercer and Benjamin Rush, a physician. He participated in the siege of Boston, and fought at the Battle of Long Island, and was made Brigadier General in 1777. He would be a major figure in the Sullivan Expedition against the Indians. Known as a very fine horseman, and very daring in battle, he was always very popular with the men under his command. For a fine account of Hand's role, as well as the entire battle of Assunpink, see David Fischer, pp. 280-307.

12. Nassau Hall had been named to honor the memory of the Glorious Revolution King of England William the Third, who had descended in the Netherlands through the House of Nassau, and was in fact the last of the direct male line of the house of Orange-Nassau. During the fighting in Princeton, legend has it, one cannonball launched by the American artillery, very likely Proctor's, or Hamilton's, crashed through a window of the prayer hall portion of the building, and effectively destroyed a portrait of the father of King George III. And Nassau Hall has another claim to distinction. The capital of the new nation was moved eight times during the Revolution. For the months of July through October in the last year of the war, 1783, the capital of the United States was Nassau Hall in Princeton, New Jersey, the Continental Congress meeting in the library! The first post-war capital of the country was New York City. Philadelphia served the nation as capital from 1791 to 1800; and Washington City, on the Potomac River in the District of Columbia, was made

the capital on the first Monday of December, 1800.

13. Although Colonel Cadwalader was late to the battle of Trenton, he did figure in the capture of the Hessians. He had held the rank of general in the Pennsylvania militia, and though in command of a brigade, and always thought of as a brigadier general, he twice declined promotion to that rank in the Continental Army. He would participate a little later in the battles of the Brandywine, Germantown, and Monmouth. Following the war he moved from Philadelphia to Maryland, where he became a state legislator. He died at age forty-three, shortly after the war's end, in 1786.

14. Samuel Stelle Smith, *The Battle of Princeton,* pp. 28-29; Trussell, *The Pennsylvania Line*, p. 204.

15. Hugh Mercer had been born in Scotland. He came to America in March of 1747 as a fugitive from his turbulent homeland, and arrived in Philadelphia in May. He was the first physician to practice medicine in what is today Franklin County, Pennsylvania. As a captain of the Pennsylvania Regiment he shared with Colonel John Armstrong the leadership of the successful Kittanning (Pa.) expedition against the Delawares during the French and Indian Wars. During the action there he was shot in the right arm. He rose to the rank of Colonel and was, at one time or another, in command of the garrisons at Fort Pitt, Fort Augusta, and Venango. During the years 1761-1775 he practiced medicine in Fredericksburg, Virginia (Washington's boyhood home), where one of his patients was Mary Washington, mother of George Washington. He had the command of the Third Virginia Regiment of the Continental Line from the time of its formation (December, 1775) until the time of his promotion to Brigadier General (June, 1776). He had been commissioned by Washington as Surgeon General of the Continental Army. Before being wounded at Princeton, he was right in the middle of the action known as the Second Battle of Trenton, January 2. The oak tree under which the mortally wounded General is thought to have rested was for a long time known as the Mercer Oak, a living memorial to the courageous martyrdom of General Hugh Mercer until it was felled by high winds on March 3, 2000. The Clarke House, to which the wounded General was borne, is to this day preserved on the grounds of the Princeton Battlefield. And the General's sword is today one of the most precious of historical items belonging to the Saint Andrew's Society of Philadelphia. It is carried always in the procession of the Society's Annual Dinner. Four states, besides New Jersey, have honored the General by giving his name to a county. The community of Mercersburg, in Pennsylvania, which is the birthplace of the country's fifteenth President, James Buchanan, bears his name. And so, of course, does The Mercersburg Academy, a private, secondary, co-educational boarding school. In Fredericksburg, Virginia, there was erected to his memory, in 1906, a bronze statue. It stands on Washington Avenue, at Fauquier Street. Two streets in that town are named for Mercer, as well as the apothecary shop and an elementary school. A second memorial statue, on October 25, 1970, was erected at Red Bank, New Jersey, on the Delaware River, south of Camden, and very near to the site of the Revolutionary War fort that was named for the General.

16. Proctor is also spelled Procter. Washington spelled it both ways.

17. Very little is known of this Samuel Blackwood. He is thought to be the son of Samuel Blackwood, Sr., and Abigail Clement of Gloucester County, N. J. Samuel Sr. was born May 31, 1734, and died young, in 1765 (?). Samuel Sr. is the second son of Hugh Blackwood (born ca. 1718 and died 1773), a clothier of Upper Alloways Creek Township, Salem County. Hugh married, in 1739-40, Karenhappuck Sheppard, daughter of the Reverend Job Sheppard and Catherine Bowen. John Harris's friend and war-time companion is thought to be the Samuel Blackwood, II, who was born ca. 1754 and was married in 1774. He had two sons, one born in 1775, before his enlistment, and one after his return from the war, in 1796, when Samuel was forty-two years old.
18. Trussell, *The Pennsylvania Line,* p. 190.
19. Ibid., p. 191.
20. Wilbur, p. 44.
21. Dr. Benjamin Rush, one of the most distinguished of the Revolutionary War patriots, was born in 1745 in Byberry, Pa.. He graduated from the College of New Jersey (now Princeton University) at the age of fifteen. He was a member of the Continental Congress 1776-77, and was for a time Surgeon General of the Continental Army. After the war, from 1797 until 1813, he served as Treasurer of the United States Mint at Philadelphia. After Yorktown, but before the Treaty of Paris, he urged a warning on the new nation: "The Revolutionary War may be over, but the battle of independence has just begun." His achievements in medicine and in the teaching of medicine are most impressive. He produced a great number of influential treatises on medicine and philosophy. He was a principal figure in the formation of the first active anti-slavery society, and one of the founders of Dickinson College, of Carlisle, Pa., the first college (September 9, 1783), to be chartered in the United States. Rush had the college named for his good friend and fellow patriot John Dickinson, who had been a delegate to the First Continental Congress, and who, though declining to sign the Declaration of Independence (still hoping for reconciliation), had helped to draft the Articles of Confederation (1781), and would later serve Pennsylvania (1782-85) as President of the Supreme Executive Council, that is, Governor, and sign (1787) the Constitution of the United States. Honored by the distinction in the name of the College, John Dickinson happily served as the first head of the Board of Trustees, which included Dr. William Irvine. Benjamin Rush, likewise, had a college named in his honor. This is the Rush Medical College of Chicago. Dr. Benjamin Rush died during a typhus epidemic in 1813.
22. Another of the most distinguished figures of the American Revolution, Thomas Mifflin, though a Quaker, became an energetic and ardent patriot, and was appointed Quartermaster General of the Army in August of 1775. He had the command of the Pennsylvania brigades at Brooklyn, and was appointed by Washington to protect the perilous evacuation over the East River. For accepting duty with the Continental Army, Mifflin was read out of the Society of Quakers. He was a member of the First Continental Congress, and, as the war was winding down, he succeeded Franklin, in October, 1780, as President of the Supreme Executive Council of Pennsylvania. He was an early President

of the United States, as he was elected, on November 3, 1783, "President of the United States in Congress Assembled." He served as President for six months, until Congress adjourned on June 3, 1784. (Mifflin was not, however, the first President of the United States, for on November 5, 1781, Maryland's representative at the Continental Congress, John Hanson, had been unanimously elected for a term of one year. Hanson, who had lost two sons in the war, served as President under the Articles of Confederation until November 3, 1782. Mifflin was the third president, and General Arthur St. Clair the sixth.) Later Thomas Mifflin served as a member of the convention which in 1787 framed the Constitution, and of course he was one of the early signers of the document (See Mordrall, pp. 177-178). Considered the first Governor of Pennsylvania, Thomas Mifflin has been honored by the Commonwealth in the names of many city streets and avenues, in the name of one of her sixty-seven counties, and in the names of three communities, none of which is in Mifflin County: Mifflintown (Juniata County), Mifflinburg (Union County), and Mifflinville (Columbia County).

23. Fitzpatrick, *The Writings of George Washington,* VII, 55.
24. Ibid., p. 82.
25. Trussell, *The Pennsylvania Line,* p. 194.
26. Ibid., pp. 194-195.
27. Berg, p. 26.
28. Fitzpatrick, *The Writings of George Washington,* VII, 263.
29. Ibid., VII, 289.
30. Trussell, *The Pennsylvania Line,* pp. 195 and 204.
31. Benjamin Lincoln, though not so conspicuous in history as many of Washington's officers, was in fact a prominent and most important figure in the Revolution. The Massachusetts soldier as Brigadier General commanded the right wing of Washington's beleaguered forces at White Plains. By the time of the Southern Campaign he had been promoted to Major General and given the command of the Southern Department. Unable to save Savannah, he made a valiant attempt to salvage Charleston, finally, after a six weeks' siege, surrendering it on May 12 of 1780. He returned to the army through prisoner exchange in time to participate in the siege of Yorktown. He died, long after the war's end, in 1810.
32. Nead, pp. 458-459.
33. Idem, and Fitzpatrick, *The Writings of George Washington,* VII, 41.
34. At Bound Brook, the oldest community in Somerset County, the battle was re-enacted May 1, 2004.
35. The Betsy Ross flag now flies twenty-four hours a day at the Middlebrook campgrounds; and the Declaration of Independence is read here every July 4. Some believe that the flag was first flown at Fort Stanwix in New York State. The flag's first appearance in battle would come in September with the Battle of Brandywine. For the birth of the Betsy Ross flag see note 30, Chapter 1.
36. Fitzpatrick, *The Writings of George Washington,* VIII, 315-416.
37. Herkimer had served in the French and Indian Wars. He had been appointed Brigadier General in the New York militia. The county and the village of Herkimer, as well as the "Herkimer diamonds" of the region bear his name.

Notes

38. A monument, erected in 1880, marks the site of the battlegrounds, which is now a public park.
39. Trussell, *The Pennsylvania Line,* p. 205; see also Nead, p. 460.
40. Amory, p. 38. For a detailed account of the inquiry, see Amory, pp. 38-39. For accounts of the expedition, see, besides Amory, Whittemore, pp. 54-56, 64, 75.
41. Fitzpatrick, *The Writings of George Washington,* IX, 116.
42. Idem.
43. There are four different spellings currently in use: (1) Chads Ford, which is the correct spelling, inasmuch as the crossing is named for the ferryman and tavern owner John Chads, whose property extended to both sides of the stream. John had changed his name from that of his father, Francis Chadsey, to Chads, which is the spelling that is used today for the family home which was built about 1725. (2) Chad's Ford, which is simply a misspelling (The apostrophe was as troublesome 200 years ago as it is today.). Chads' Ford of course would be correct, but it is not much used. (3) Chadds Ford, which, though an unexplained corruption, is the most popular current spelling. And (4) Chadd's Ford, which compounds the confusion by preserving the double *d* corruption and introducing an errant apostrophe. (See Pinkowski; and see Furthey, Smith and Cope, *History of Chester County.*). As Chadds Ford is the most prevalent spelling nowadays, it will be used in the text of *Bombardier John Harris.*
44. Drake, p.47.
45. Fitzpatrick, *The Writings of George Washington,* IX, 170.
46. For the origin of the name Brandywine there are at least four distinct theories. See Pinkowski; and see Furthey.
47. Nead, p. 460.
48. Idem.
49. Ward, I, 343-344, quoting Baurmeister, p. 13.
50. Ward, I, 353.
51. Trussell, *The Pennsylvania Line,* 205.
52. Ibid., p. 206.
53. Proctor received pay for this horse in the settlement of his accounts with the State of Pennsylvania in 1793. (Nead, p. 461)
54. Trussell, *The Pennsylvania Line,* p. 206.
55. One report of the battle notes that the Americans lost one howitzer and ten field pieces, among which were two brass guns that had been captured at Trenton (Ward, I, 354).
56. Trussell, *The Pennsylvania Line,* p. 206.
57. Ward, I, 468, note 38.
58. In 1780, and again in 1785 and 1825, Lafayette returned to the site of his wounding. A memorial shaft is erected there.
59. For accounts of the battle, see Ward, volume I; and Canby; and Trussell, *The Continental Line.*
60. Drake, p. 49.
61. The Liberty Bell suffered its famous crack while it was being tolled during the funeral services for Chief Justice John Marshall in 1835.
62. Coulomb, p. 345. Today, of course, adorned with its famous motto "Proclaim

liberty throughout all the land and to all the inhabitants thereof," it is housed in Independence Hall on Chestnut Street in Philadelphia. The bell, which was rung on July 8, 1776, to summon the citizens of the city to the first public reading of the Declaration of Independence, actually has its name "Liberty" not from the spirit of the rebellion but from the later 19th century anti-slavery activity.

63. Pleasants, p. 51.
64. Pleasants, p. 44.
65. Historians do not like the term "massacre" for this engagement, pointing out that the assault by the British was strictly a military operation, and that no civilians or innocents were involved. But long before war's end, General Charles Grey acquired a reputation for (1) love of the bayonet, and (2) merciless slaughter of the helpless. Called "No Flint Grey," he was responsible for the Tappan Massacre (often called Baylor Massacre), which occurred on September 28, 1778, one year and one week after Paoli. Near the village of Tappan, along the Overkill Road, in what is now River Vale, near the Hackensack River, the rebellion experienced one of its most grisly moments. Grey's "bayonet-butchers" in another midnight assault on sleeping soldiers put to death by the cold steel of the bayonet the cavalry of Colonel George Baylor, who were quartered in six different barns. How many were killed (30-90?) is not known, but what is known is that many of those slaughtered were soldiers who had surrendered. Grey, quite unlike British General Guy Carleton, was very much of the "kill every man" persuasion.
66. Pleasants, p. 46.
67. Pleasants, p. 45.
68. This journal account is with the Historical Society of Pennsylvania. Pleasants, p. 45. Today the site of the tragedy, on a slight elevation, is preserved pretty much in its original form, and an impressive monument has been erected.
69. Pleasants., p. 52.
70. Ward, I, 361; Baurmeister, p. 21.
71. Trussell, *Birthplace of an Army,* p. 9; and, for an account of first fighting, see Ward, I, 365.
72. Ward, I, 365; Baurmeister, p. 31.
73. The Chew mansion, known as Clivedon, had been built in 1763 on eleven acres by Judge Benjamin Chew, later to be Pennsylvania's Supreme Court Chief Justice. The judge, having been held in New Jersey, was not home on this day. The building is located at 6401 Germantown Avenue, and today houses a museum. For some two decades now, on October 4, the battle of Germantown, which features the Chew mansion, has been re-enacted.
74. Some historians believe it was a mistake for Washington to address the Chew House, for he thus had only the divisions of Wayne and Sullivan to pursue the British down the road.
75. Trussell, *The Pennsylvania Line,* p. 206, and *P. A.,* Series 5, III, 961.
76. Trussell, *The Pennsylvania Line,* p. 206; Nead, p. 461.
77. Ward, I, 366.
78. Trussell, *Birthplace of an Army,* p. 10.
79. Idem.

Notes

80. Ward, I, 371.
81. Drake, p. 53, and Jackson, p. 50.
82. Porter, p. 264. After the war Andrew Porter retired to his farm, declining the invitation by the University of Pennsylvania to head the Department of Mathematics, and noting that since he had commanded men, he would not take up the flogging of boys. He was made Brigadier General in the Pennsylvania Militia in 1801 and later advanced to Major General. In 1809 he was appointed to the post of Surveyor General for the Commonwealth, and trekked across the state to determine the western limits of Pennsylvania. In 1813 he was offered the Cabinet post of Secretary of War in the administration of President James Monroe, but declined. He had thirteen children, five by his first wife, and eight by his second. One of his sons, David Rittenhouse Porter, became Governor of Pennsylvania, and another, George Bryan Porter, became Governor of the Territory of Michigan. A third, James Madison Porter, was a highly esteemed jurist.
83. Drake, pp. 52, 53.
84. Kapp, p. 127; Zucker, p. 154.
85. Drake, p. 53.
86. Fitzpatrick, *The Writings of George Washington*, IX, 390-391; quoted by Ward, I, 378.
87. Jackson, pp. 81-82.
88. Zucker, p. 153; Ward, I, 379.
89. Ward, I, 379.
90. James Irvine (1735-1819) should not be confused with William Irvine. Both were Pennsylvanians, although William was born in Ireland, and James in Philadelphia, the son of the Irish immigrant George Irvine. Both were in command of Pennsylvania units. Both were captured and served long terms as prisoners of war, James not released until 1781! Both attained the rank of Brigadier General. Both served as trustees of educational institutions, William of Dickinson College, and James of the university now known as the University of Pennsylvania. But they are two different men. Besides, there is an Andrew Irvine, a captain in the Seventh Pennsylvania Regiment at the time it was commanded by Colonel William Irvine.
91. Reed had been offered the rank of Brigadier General but declined. He was soon to be President of the Supreme Executive Council in Pennsylvania and a very prominent figure in the political field.
92. Reed, I, 351n.
93. Jackson, p. 115.
94. Irvine was taken to Philadelphia, and, at the time of the British evacuation in the spring, to New York City, and then to Long Island, where he remained until exchanged, June 1, 1781.
95. Ward, I, 381, note 44.

Chapter IV

1. Today, regrettably, the park is threatened by inadequate funding. But a Revolutionary War Museum has been proposed for the park.
2. The army was at Gulph Mill December 14-17. See Bean and Brown, p. 38.
3. Kapp, p. 137, and Ward, p. 385.
4. Bean and Brown, p. 38.
5. Ibid., pp. 38-40.
6. Trussell, *Birthplace of an Army,* p.18.
7. Trussell, *Epic on the Schuylkill,* p. 18.
8. Kapp, p. 127; Zucker, pp. 154-155.
9. Henry Laurens, from South Carolina, was the second President of the Continental Congress. He served from November 1, 1777, to December 9, 1778. He was a signer of the Articles of Confederation.
10. Kapp, p. 145; Zucker, p. 155.
11. Reed, *Crucible of Victory,* p. 25.
12. Trussell, *Epic on the Schuylkill,* p. 7.
13. Gottschalk, p. 104. See whole letter below.
14. Bean and Brown, p. 42.
15. Chidsey, p. 26.
16. Greene, from Rhode Island, was an iron founder by occupation. He had missed some of the Battle of Long Island because of illness.
17. Trussell, *Birthplace of an Army,* p. 76; and note Brooks, p. 115.
18. Trussell, *Epic on the Schuylkill,* p. 11. Valley Forge dramatized the pathetic war-time condition of the rebel army, but it was not only at Valley Forge that the Continental Army found itself tragically impoverished. Throughout most of the rebellion the army was short of food (especially during winter encampments and at garrisoned frontier forts) and clothing (many of the men much of the time not in uniform at all); and, as lead was extremely scarce, many battles, beginning with Breed's Hill, were lost or imperiled by shortages of ammunition.
19. Taylor, p. 14.
20. Trussell, *Epic on the Schuylkill,* p. 15.
21. Fitzpatrick, *The Writings of George Washington,* XI, 487-488; XII, 50, 76.
22. Trussell, *Birthplace of an Army,* p. 65.
23. Trussell, *The Pennsylvania Line,* p. 207.
24. Fitzpatrick, *The Writings of George Washington,* XI, 263-264.
25. Trussell, *Epic on the Schuylkill,* p. 27.
26. Bolton, p. 174.
27. Trussell, *Birthplace of an Army,* pp. 44-45.
28. Reed, *Crucible of Victory,* p. 25.
29. Captain Porter was married twice. His first wife, whom he married March 10, 1767, was Elizabeth McDowell. Some four years after her death, on May 20, 1777, in the spring before Brandywine and Germantown and Valley Forge, Porter married Elizabeth Parker.
30. The core of this story can be found in Porter, p. 293.
31. Drake, p. 18.

Notes 361

32. Trussell, *Epic on the Schuylkill,* p. 18.
33. Trussell, *The Pennsylvania Line,* pp. 195-196, and *Birthplace of an Army,* pp. 71-72; Fitzpatrick, *The Writings of George Washington,* X, 258, and XI, 19-20.
34. Kapp, p. 141; Zucker, p. 166.
35. Whittemore, p. 79, quoting Hammond, I, 603.
36. Wildes, as quoted by McPhee, p. 151.
37. Chidsey, as quoted by McPhee, p. 179.
38. McPhee, p. 176. For an account of the varying views of the shad run in the spring of 1778, see McPhee, Chapter Eight, esp. pp. 170-182, and Bodle, *The Valley Forge Winter.*
39. General John Peter Gabriel Muhlenberg (1746-1807) had been a Lutheran minister and was ordained an Anglican priest. He was in the war from the beginning. In 1775, responding to a plea from Washington, he raised a German company (300 men) for the Continental Army and became Colonel of the 8th Virginia Regiment. At Valley Forge he held the rank of Brigadier General, and he was made a Major General in 1783. Highly esteemed for his valor and for his administrative skills, he participated in a number of major engagements, and fought most effectively at Yorktown. After the war he served as Benjamin Franklin's Vice President on the Supreme Executive Council of Pennsylvania. He represented Pennsylvania in the U. S. House of Representatives for three terms, and in 1801 was elected to the U. S. Senate. In Statuary Hall in Washington, D.C., there stands a statue of him. And a Brigade Marker installed at Valley Forge commemorates the Muhlenberg Brigade, which belonged to General Nathanael Greene's Division. After being on loan for several years to the Library of Congress for its traveling exhibition of *Religion and the Founding of the American Republic, 1607-1835,* the portrait of General Muhlenberg now hangs in the Haas College Center on the Muhlenberg College campus. And an impressive statue of the General has been placed at the front of that building. But the College itself is named for his father, Henry M. Muhlenberg, a principal founder of the Lutheran Church in America.
40. Latzko, p. 60.
41. Sedgwick, pp. 54-55.
42. Among Washington's most severe critics, those who desired to see him replaced by General Horatio Gates, who had won the great victory over Burgoyne, were Dr. Benjamin Rush (his very good friend), Thomas Mifflin, Gates of course, and even John Adams, who had secured the appointment of Washington in 1775. When Conway's plot petered out, and he failed to win his desired promotion, he resigned from the Army. But as he continued to cast aspersions on General Washington he was challenged to a duel by one of Washington's staunchest supporters, Colonel John Cadwalader. In the duel, which took place on July 4, Cadwalader "stopped his lying mouth" by shooting Conway, naturally right in the mouth, a wound which did not prove fatal. After the war the Ireland-born Conway, who had been educated in France and who had served in the French army before coming to the colonies (1777), served as governor of the French colonies in India. He died in exile

in 1800.
43. Abercrombie, eight years younger than Washington, was a veteran of the French and Indian Wars. As Lieutenant Colonel of the 37th Regiment of Foot, he had commanded forces at Long Island, at the Brandywine, at Germantown. He would participate later at Monmouth.
44. Jackson, p. 224.
45. Ibid., pp. 224-225.
46. The *Royal Pennsylvania Gazette*, May 5, 1778. The *Gazette* was published by John Robertson from March 3 through May 26, 1778. Some issues (March 24, May 5, 8, 12, 15) are available in the Library of Congress.
47. Jackson, p. 225. The "massacre" at Hancock's Bridge, which is near John Harris's boyhood home in Salem County, N.J., and which also involved Simcoe's Rangers, is discussed below.
48. Jackson, pp. 224-225.
49. Simcoe, p. 60.
50. Jackson, p. 225.
51. *Royal Pennsylvania Gazette*, May 5, 1778.
52. A monument to the battle has been erected at the Crooked Billet Elementary School, Penn and Meadowbrook Avenues, Hatboro, Pa. The battle has been re-enacted, most recently in 2003.
53. Trussell, *Epic on the Schuylkill*, p. 43.
54. See Jackson, chapter XIV.
55. General Henry Clinton had been a member of the British Parliament. He was field commander for the fighting at Breed's Hill. Like Howe, he had been, in 1777, knighted by the King.
56. Lafayette, whose whole name goes on forever (Marie Joseph Paul Yves Roch Gilbert du Motier, Marquis de Lafayette), many times referred to himself as Washington's adopted son. He had arrived in America at Charleston, S.C., June 13, 1777, and immediately made his way to Philadelphia. Congress on July 21 appointed him a major general. He served throughout the war without pay. In the winter of 1779-80 he returned briefly to France, where he negotiated for French aid. One year after the war's end he returned to the United States at the invitation of Washington. In 1824, he revisited the United States and toured the several states. Everywhere he was welcomed with great enthusiasm. In July of 2002 the United States Congress voted to make Lafayette an honorary citizen of the United States. He had earlier been made a citizen of New York City (1784) and of Maryland (1785). (See Appendix B).
57. Zucker, p. 166.

Chapter V

1. Trussell, *The Pennsylvania Line*, pp. 207 and 213.
2. Stryker, *The Battle of Monmouth*, p. 74.
3. According to the *Pennsylvania Archives,* Series 5, Vol. III, p. 961, detachments of Proctor's Artillery served at Monmouth, but apparently only

Notes

one or two pieces with their crews were involved. Stryker, in his exhaustive account of Monmouth makes no mention of Proctor; nor does John Harris in his recollections of the war ever mention Monmouth. Trussell, while allowing that "some of its cannoneers seem to have been on hand" at Monmouth, declares the 4th Continental Artillery was not present. (*The Pennsylvania Line*, p.13)

4. Drake, p. 57.
5. Stryker, *The Battle of Monmouth*, p. 104.
6. Hamilton and Irvine, p. 147.
7. Drake, p. 58.
8. Fitzpatrick, *The Writings of George Washington*, XII, 142.
9. Curtis, p. 413; Hamilton and Irvine, p. 143; McDowell, p. 136. Washington has been charged with another enraged outburst of profanity, this at the Kips Bay fiasco in New York City. See McCullough,*1776*, p. 212.
10. Hamilton and Irvine, p. 140.
11. Ibid., p. 146.
12. Ibid., p. 148.
13. Fitzpatrick, *The Writings of George Washington*, XII, 142-143.
14. Ibid., XII, 145.
15. Drake, pp. 57-59.
16. Ibid., p. 59.
17. By the end of the war Wayne was one of the most celebrated of Washington's generals, in large measure because of his capture of the British stronghold at Stony Point in a surprise nighttime raid. In the winter of 1776-77 he had been in command at Fort Ticonderoga, and in the summer, by then commissioned a brigadier general, he joined Washington's army at Morristown. He commanded a division at Chadds Ford in the Battle of the Brandywine, which was fought near Wayne's boyhood home in Chester County, Pennsylvania; and at Germantown he had fought bravely. While at Valley Forge he made a number of successful raids on British supplies for the beleaguered encampment. After the war his reputation was further enhanced by his victory over the Ohio Indian forces in the Battle of Fallen Timbers.
18. For the saga of Molly Pitcher, see Appendix A.
19. Fitzpatrick, *The Writings of George Washington*, XII, 144.
20. Washington's mount was a magnificent white stallion which had been presented him as a gift from the Governor of New Jersey, William Livingston, a good friend of Alexander Hamilton. At the end of the day, the animal, terribly spent, fell dead. (McDowell, p. 136)
21. Headley, *Life of General Lafayette*, p. 94.
22. Custis, p. 220; quoted by Stryker, p. 185, and by McDowell, p. 136.
23. Stryker, *The Battle of Monmouth*, p. 225.
24. Stryker, *The Battle of Monmouth*, p. 225, and McDowell, p. 135.
25. Stryker, *The Battle of Monmouth*, p. 258.
26. For the names of the patriots killed, wounded, and missing, or dead because of the heat (or exhaustion), see Stryker, *The Battle of Monmouth*, pp. 288-295.
27. Jackson, p. 266.
28. Idem.

29. On Dr. Rush, see note # 21, Chapter 3.
30. Jackson, p. 267. Some twenty years later, after Philadelphia had returned to a semblance of health, Thomas Jefferson wrote to congratulate Dr. Rush on its recovery, while yet lamenting the life of the city. Rush replied: "I agree with you in your opinion of cities. Cowper the poet very happily expresses our ideas of them compared with the country. 'God made the country–man made the cities.' I consider them in the same light that I do abscesses on the human body, viz., as reservoirs of all the impurities of a community."
31. Drake, p. 57; Stryker, *The Battle of Monmouth,* p. 270.
32. Jackson, pp. 266-267.
33. Ibid., p. 267.
34. André is best known as the British spy who with Benedict Arnold arranged for the capture of West Point. Before the plot could be accomplished, on September 23, 1780, he was captured, by John Paulding, David Williams, and Isaac Van Wert, near Tarrytown, New York. At Washington's headquarters at Tappan, despite the vehement protests of General Henry Clinton, he was tried, found guilty, and condemned to execution as a spy. He had been captured earlier, at St. Johns during the ill-fated Quebec campaign in 1775, by General Richard Montgomery, but had been returned to the British army through prisoner exchange, and made adjutant general under Sir Henry Clinton. While he was still a prisoner of the Patriot forces, he shared a cabin on a very stormy night with the young man destined to head up the Continental artillery, Henry Knox. Indeed they shared a bed.
35. Jackson, p. 268.
36. Besides at Brandywine, Knyphausen, who had served in the army of Frederick the Great, had fought well at White Plains and at Germantown. He would be a principal figure in the action at Monmouth. In the absence of Sir Henry Clinton (1779-80) he commanded the British occupation of New York City.
37. Jackson, pp. 265-268. Arnold was in 1780 made commander of West Point, intending to betray the post for a British commission and a sum of money. Soon after his appointment to the command of West Point, he began his treasonable correspondence with Sir Henry Clinton, who was occupying New York City. When the plot was discovered and the go-between André was arrested and promptly hanged as a spy, Arnold escaped. He then served with the British, leading two savage raids – one against Richmond, Virginia (January, 1781), in which his British troops destroyed warehouses and public buildings, and the other against New London, Connecticut, which he burned, before massacring the surrendered garrison at Fort Griswold. Later that year, 1781, the Arnolds sailed for England, the General having determined upon exile in England and Canada, but eventually falling out of favor with the British. He died in England in June of 1801.
38. Dearborn, like William Irvine, and Hugh Mercer, had studied medicine and had become a physician. But with Lexington-Concord he promptly joined the militia, served as a captain at Breed's Hill, and marched to Quebec with Arnold. Made a major in the Continental Army in 1777 with the 3rd New Hampshire Regiment, he fought at Arnold's side at Saratoga and participated with him in the action at Bemis Heights. After the war, for four years he

served in the Congress, and later as Secretary of War in the Cabinet of Thomas Jefferson. In the War of 1812 he served as a Major General of the U. S. Army. In 1813 he was appointed Commander of New York City, and from 1822 until 1824 he served the country as Minister to Portugal.

39. Willard Wallace, p. 162.
40. Fitzpatrick, *The Writings of George Washington,* X, 324-325.
41. Willard Wallace, p. 162.
42. Ward, I, 355.
43. Willard Wallace, p. 164.
44. Fitzpatrick, *The Writings of George Washington,* XII, 94-95; Willard Wallace, p. 63.
45. Lengyel, p. 33. Joseph Reed graduated from the College of New Jersey (now Princeton University) at age sixteen and later studied law in London. He had been Secretary (Aide-de-Camp) to Washington and later the Army's Adjutant General, rising to the rank of colonel. He had served at Long Island, at Trenton and Princeton, at the Brandywine, Germantown, and Monmouth. He was Governor of Pennsylvania 1778-81, and a signer of Pennsylvania's Articles of Confederation. Shortly after the War's end, in 1785, he died at age forty-four.
46. Drake, p. 60.
47. Idem.
48. Ibid., p. 61.
49. Willard Wallace, p. 190.
50. For a record of the reprimand, see Fitzpatrick, *The Writings of George Washington,* XIII, 479; XIV, 91, 143, 309-311, 322, 328.
51. Lengyel, p. 72.
52. Ibid., p. 80.
53. Ibid., p. 82.
54. Trussell, *The Pennsylvania Line,* p. 207.

Chapter VI

1. Brant is sometimes spelled Brandt.
2. Although the common view is that Joseph was born to Indian parents, there continues to be a difference of opinion on Brant's paternity: "Some people think that Sir William Johnson, the father of a hundred, or hundreds, of children was his sire; others insist that Nickus ["Nicholas"]Brant, the second husband of Joseph's mother, and a steady Mohawk of the solid-citizen type, was his father." From remarks made by Brant from time to time, it would seem that *he* assumed Johnson was his father. (Chalmers, p. 3) Johnson's second wife, his Indian mistress, known as Molly, was Joseph Brant's sister.
3. Graymont, p. 120.
4. Ibid., p. 123.
5. Idem.
6. Abler, pp. 59-63.
7. Ibid., p. 75.

8. Ibid., pp. 76-78. For accounts of the council at Oswego see Stone, *Life of Joseph Brant*, I, 186-188; Anthony Wallace, pp. 132-134; Graymont, pp. 120-124.
9. Myers, p. 13.
10. Idem.
11. Egle, *The First Indian Massacre*, p. 22.
12. Peck, p. 29.
13. "Blacksnake Conversations," Draper MSS 4S27-28, HSW.
14. Samuel Robert Smith, *The Story of Wyoming Valley*, p. 34.
15. Graymont, pp. 168-169.
16. Ibid., pp. 169-171, but see Graymont's note # 29.
17. Samuel Robert Smith, *The Story of Wyoming Valley*, p. 40.
18. Idem.
19. Idem.
20. Samuel Robert Smith, *The Story of Wyoming Valley*, p. 41.
21. Ibid., p. 45.
22. Abler, p. 101.
23. Samuel Robert Smith, *The Story of Wyoming Valley*, p. 45.
24. Swiggett, p. 127.
25. Carter, p. 367.
26. Idem.
27. Mohawk, p. 136.
28. Near present-day Selinsgrove, Pennsylvania, a resident German "did in violation of the public faith and in defiance of all that is human . . . ." (See John Franklin Meginnes, *A History of the West Branch of the Susquehanna*)
29. Graymont, pp. 245, 253-254.
30. Godcharles, "The First Expedition Against the Indians of the Six Nations," p. iv.
31. *P.A.*, VI, 773, and VII, 7-8.
32. Fitzpatrick, *The Writings of George Washington*, XIII, 168n.
33. Ibid., XIV, 198-201.
34. Craft, p. 10.
35. Ibid., p. 9.
36. Trussell, *The Pennsylvania Line*, pp. 207-208; and Nead, p. 462.
37. Graymont, p. 202.
38. Godcharles, "The Battle of Fort Freeland," p. 132.
39. Idem.
40. Ibid., p. 134.
41. See Wolfinger, in Egle's *An Illustrated History of the Commonwealth of Pennsylvania;* and Meginness in *Otzinachson.*
42. Seaver, p. 107.
43. Godcharles, "The Battle of Fort Freeland," p. 136.
44. Seaver, p. 107.
45. Godcharles, "The Battle of Fort Freeland," p. 137.
46. Ibid., p. 136.
47. *P.A.*, VII, 597; Sipe, p. 502.
48. Seaver, p. 107.

Notes

49. Cartwright, p. 37.
50. *P.A.*, VII, 610.
51. Anthony Wallace, p. 141.
52. Godcharles, "The Battle of Fort Freeland," p. 145.
53. Rogers in the year previous had been made Brigade Chaplain in the Pennsylvania Line. Born at Newport, Rhode Island, July 22, 1751, he became Pastor of the Baptist Church in Philadelphia. When the war broke out he was appointed Chaplain of the Pennsylvania Rifle Regiment (Colonel Samuel Miles commanding). He held the position of Brigade Chaplain until 1781, when he retired from military service. In 1789 he was appointed a Professor of English and Belles Lettres at the University of Pennsylvania. In 1816-17 he served in the Pennsylvania Legislature. He died in Philadelphia, April 7, 1824. His journal, with notes and biography, was published as No. 7 of the *Rhode Island Historical Tracts* by Sidney B. Rider, Providence, Rhode Island, 1879. It was reprinted in the *Pennsylvania Archives,* Second Series, XV, 257-288; and in Cook, pp. 247 ff. Some portions were printed in Vols. 1 and 2 of the *Universal Magazine,* 1797. (See Cook, p. 246)
54. *P.A.,* Second Series, XV, 257-258.
55. Idem.
56. Ibid., pp. 258-259.
57. Idem.
58. Ibid., p. 260.
59. Idem.
60. Ibid., pp. 262-263.
61. Idem.
62. Ibid., pp. 264-265.
63. Ibid., pp. 265-266.
64. Idem.
65. These twenty-nine deserters were given varying degrees of sentence, including execution, but all, having been led into repentance by the Reverend Rogers, were eventually pardoned.
66. There is some confusion over the number of boats, some historians reporting numbers as low as 120, but Proctor, writing on March 23, 1791, in his Journal, recollects, "I had the command of 214 vessels on the Susquehanna, taking with me the provisions and stores of 6000 men." (*P.A.,* Second Series, IV, 557)
67. Craft, p. 20.
68. Idem.
69. *P.A.*, Second Series, XV, 268-269.
70. Craft, pp. 20-21.
71. *P.A.,* Second Series, XV, 272.
72. Craft, p. 21.
73. Headley's journal, in Cook, pp. 193-194.
74. Actually, a number of young men from Salem County were members of the expedition. One of these was Lawrence Carney, who had joined the Continental Army on June 2 the summer before. He was two years younger than John Harris.
75. Cook, p. 155.

76. Lt. Dearborn's journal, in Cook, p. 67.
77. Cook, p. 7.
78. *P.A.*, Second Series, XV, 276. A beautiful map of the whole expedition is provided by Captain William Gray of the 4th Pennsylvania Regiment, *P.A.*, Second Series, XV, 289.
79. One of the chief functions of the boats, especially after the artillery was taken ashore, was the transport of the sick, of whom there were regularly many.
80. Joseph Fischer, p. 77.
81. Trussell, *The Continental Line*, p. 207.
82. James Clinton, elder brother of George Clinton, "the father of New York State," had fought in the French and Indian Wars, and had heroically defended Fort Clinton (near Kingston, N.Y.) against the British forces of Sir Henry Clinton who were moving up the Hudson River Valley in 1777. There is a General Clinton Park at Bainbridge, New York, and on each Memorial Day weekend the Sullivan-Clinton Campaign is commemorated with a Canoe Regatta here.
83. Porter, who had been with Proctor's artillery through Brandywine, Germantown, Whitemarsh, and Valley Forge, was detached, with his company, and ordered to Albany to join Clinton's brigade, which was there preparing to participate in the Sullivan Expedition. He left the Artillery Park at Pluckemin on the 6th of May, and joined Clinton on the 13th at Albany. With Clinton his company proceeded to Canajoharie on the Mohawk River, and it was from this point that the troops were marched to the head of Otsego Lake. After the Sullivan Expedition, Porter's company was returned to Washington's main army and wintered at Morristown. (Porter, p. 265)
84. Headley's journal, in Cook, p. 194.
85. "Tioga" is the name which derives from the Iroquois "Teyaogen" (an interval or anything between two other things) or "Teiohoen" (the forks of a river). (Cook, p. 124)
86. Colonel Proctor had declared that he was carrying provisions for 6000 men.
87. Journal of Lt. Colonel Adam Hubley, in Cook, p. 156.
88. Cook, p. 94; Joseph Fischer, p. 89.
89. Joseph Fischer, p. 89.
90. McNeill was born in Montgomery County, Pa., on August 29, 1753. As a volunteer in Captain Longstreth's company, he was wounded at Princeton. Afterwards he was made Brigade Quartermaster to General Edward Hand's Brigade. Late in life he suffered severely from his wounds and died from their effects, May 8, 1817. (*P.A.*, Second Series, XV, 754) McNeill's "Orderly Book" is printed in *P.A.*, Second Series, Vol. XV, pp. 755-759.
91. *P.A.*, Second Series, XV, 755-756; quoted by Joseph Fischer, pp. 90-91. For a full account of the battle, see Fischer, pp. 89-95.
92. Trussell, *The Pennsylvania Line*, pp. 207-208, and Craig, pp. 20-21.
93. *P.A.*, Second Series, XV, 756.
94. Dearborn had been in command of the Third New Hampshire (Scammel's).
95. Cook, pp. 127-128. See also, for a full account of the Battle of Newtown, Craft, pp. 29-40.
96. Trussell, *The Pennsylvania Line*, p. 208.

Notes 369

97. Cook, p. 128.
98. Ibid., pp. 127-128.
99. Cook, p. 199.
100. Ibid., p. 183.
101. Ibid., p. 128.
102. Trussell, *The Pennsylvania Line*, p. 208, and *P.A.*, Series 5, III, p. 1027.
103. Trussell, *The Pennsylvania Line*, p. 208 and 208n.
104. Cook, p. 183.
105. Ibid., p. 199.
106. Ibid., p. 197.
107. Draper MSS, 4 S 36-37; see also Abler, p. 109.
108. *P.A.*, Second Series, IV, 557. While on this mission Proctor saw a lot of the Seneca chiefs Cornplanter and Little Beard. (See his 1791 journal, in *P.A.*, Second Series, IV, 465-594.)
109. Cook, p. 199.
110. Ibid., p. 130.
111. The Reverend John Breckenridge, as quoted by Stone in *The Life and Times of Red-Jacket*, p. 22.
112. Graymont, p. 216.
113. Ibid., p. 217.
114. Idem.
115. Mary Jemison reports that it was a small body of Indians who had been in pursuit of an escaped Oneida warrior (See Seaver, p. 72) under the command of the celebrated Brant, and the same number of Rangers, commanded by the infamous Butler, who had secreted themselves in a ravine of considerable extent, which lay across the track that Lieutenant Boyd had pursued.
116. Seaver, pp. 152-156.
117. Cook, p. 32.
118. Mary Jemison would live seventy-five years with the Senecas, marry two different warriors, and die at age ninety.
119. Seaver, pp. 72-73.
120. Cook, p. 365; Codman, p. 304. Washingtonville is today in Montour County. Boyd's birthplace has been given as Derry, Pa., but that seems to be in error. Boyd was a nephew of the Captain Ebenezer Boyd who was a good friend of Washington and who as Captain of the Third Regiment of Westchester County Militia, had stopped Major André on the day before his arrest as a spy. Thomas Boyd had two older brothers who served the Continental Army. His brother John had a distinguished career. The other brother, William, of the Twelfth Regiment, was slain in the battle of the Brandywine. (See Sipe, "General Sullivan's Expedition Against the Six Nations," p. 199) Lieutenant Thomas Boyd, who was taken prisoner during the fighting at Quebec City, October 31, 1775, was returned to the Army through prisoner exchange in time for the battle of the Stillwater Hills in New York, when Gates defeated the British. He viewed the surrender of General Burgoyne to Gates, and he participated in the battle of Monmouth. There has been erected a Boyd-Parker Memorial. It is located a little to the east of the hamlet of Cuylerville in Livingston County, New York, in the Genesee State Park.

121. Cook, p. 369.
122. Ibid., p. 205.
123. *P.A.,* XII, 105. The excerpts which follow may all be found in *P.A.,* XII, pp. 105-106.
124. Brodhead's very long letter to Washington, dated September 16, 1779, which details the expedition, is printed in Cook, pp. 307-309. The detailed report of his mission can be found in P.A., XII, 155, and in *The Magazine of American History and Biography,* III, 649.
125. Cook, pp. 307-309.
126. Hassler, p. 101.
127. Graymont, p. 192; Joseph Fischer, p. 7.
128. Abler, p. 112; and thirty is the total, with villages named, in Craft, pp. 70-71.
129. Anthony Wallace, p. 144.
130. Craft, p. 70.
131. Joseph Fischer, pp. 100-101. Passage reprinted with the kind permission of the University of South Carolina Press.
132. *P.A.,* Second Series, XV, 757.
133. A. C. Flick, New York State Historian, in Cook, p. 16.
134. Idem.
135. Idem. But see journals of Sullivan's officers in Cook, p. 13 and passim; and Abler, p. 113.
136. The routes followed by the two armies of Clinton and Sullivan are today well defined by thirty-five historical markers.
137. See Graymont, p. 236.
138. William Leete Stone, *Life and Times of Red-Jacket,* p. 127.
139. The scene is variously reported as Canajoharie and, more generally the Schoharie. See Seaver, pp. 77-78; William Leete Stone, *Life and Times of Red-Jacket,* pp. 425-426; Anthony Wallace, p. 145; Graymont, p. 236; *Draper Manuscripts,* 4 S 44-45.
140. Anthony Wallace, p. 145.
141. Ibid., pp. 145-146.

Chapter VII

1. Trussell, *The Pennsylvania Line,* p. 202.
2. The Morristown region, which accommodated two of Washington's major wintertime encampments, was authorized a National Historic Park in 1933, and dedicated March 2, 1993.
3. Craig, pp. 26-27.
4. Idem.
5. Drake, pp. 60-61.
6. *P.A.*, Series 5, III, 963.
7. Butterfield, *Washington-Irvine Correspondence,* p. 406; for a sketch of Captain Isaac Craig, see Neville B. Craig, *Sketch of the Life and Services of Isaac Craig, Major in the Fourth (Usually Called Proctor's) Regiment of Artillery During the Revolutionary War* (Pittsburgh: J. S. Davidson, 1854).

Notes 371

8. Pickering had been elected to the newly organized Board of War of the Continental Congress in the fall of 1777. He would later serve, from August of 1780 through July of 1785, as the fourth Quartermaster General, and after that as Postmaster General and as Secretary of State in Washington's cabinet.
9. *P.A.,* Series 5, III, 966-967.
10. Idem.
11. Idem.
12. *P.A.,* Series 1, XII, 223, and Series 5, III, 969.
13. *P.A.,* Series 5, III, 968.
14. Ibid., p. 969.
15. A road from Shippensburg to the summit of the Allegheny Ridge had been opened in 1755, under the supervision of James Burd. In 1758 British General John Forbes, on a mission to take Fort Duquesne from the French, elected not to follow the calamitous course taken by General Edward Braddock three years earlier, and instead cut his own path. For his army (some 7,000 foot soldiers) he cleared a wagon road across the formidable Alleghenies to present-day Bedford, and from there, following the Indians' Raystown Path, some ten miles beyond the fort at Ligonier. This road became the principal route for western emigration.
16. Located today along present-day U.S. Route 11 (Governor Ritner Highway), just south of Carlisle at the junction with McCallister's Church Road.
17. Oldtown, Maryland, is today on the American Discovery Trail, which follows the towpath along the Chesapeake and Ohio Canal from Washington, D.C., west. The canal, portions of which still exist, was closed in 1924. The Chesapeake and Ohio National Park, which was dedicated in 1971, is 184 miles long. It includes many of the original features, locks, lock houses, and aqueducts. Oldtown is near its western end. Oldtown, today a scattering of homes along the river, features the Low-water Bridge (very often totally immersed), a one-lane plank crossing that was built in 1937. A toll house accommodates a fee collector, who politely accepts fifty cents for passage.
18. Washington and Gist set out on November 15, 1753. Gist had inscribed in his journal for Wednesday, the 14th: "Then Major George Washington came to my house at Will's Creek, and delivered me a letter from the council in Virginia, requesting me to attend him up to the commandant of the French fort on the Ohio River." The mission, of course, turned out to be futile. Washington and Gist both kept journal accounts of the trip; both can be found in Cleland. Both, though they vary a little in some details, include descriptions of their narrow escape (near Murdering Town, on December 27, 1754) from the villainous and treacherous Indian who, while serving as their "friendly" guide, turned on them and fired point blank, fortunately missing.
19. Lengyel, *Presidents of the United States*, p. 12.
20. The fort was built in 1754-55, at a site selected by Washington, on a prominent height overlooking the river. It was 400 feet long and 120 feet wide. The fort no longer exists, and almost nothing in the way of remnants remains, but evidence of its location is still apparent underneath the Emmanuel Episcopal Church, which was built between 1848 and 1851 on the exact site of the fort, in Cumberland, Maryland. Tours of the "tunnels," the underground regions

of the church, are conducted during the city's festive Heritage Days, early in June of each year. These tours give the tourist some idea of the structure of the original fort, of egress and ingress, of the magazines and storage cellars.

21. See Albert, pp. 104-105. Christopher Walthour's brother George was a Continental Army soldier. An historical marker designates the site: "Fort Walthour. Erected about 1774 near this place. This stockade enclosing a blockhouse and several buildings was built by the pioneers of the Brush Creek community on the plantation of Christopher Walthour. It was the chief place of refuge and defense of the early settlers for more than a decade against the frequent Indian raids made in this section and throughout western Pennsylvania."
22. *P.A.,* Series 5, III, 969.
23. Boucher, Vol. I, Chapter XVIII, pp. 324-327.
24. Ibid., vol. I, Chapter XI, 354-357.
25. Laurens was the only Revolutionary War fort in what is now Ohio.
26. Downes, p. 259.
27. Ibid., p. 258.
28. *P.A.,* First Series, XII, 216; Downes, p. 258.
29. Downes, p. 259.
30. Idem.
31. Washington had selected General Nathanael Greene for the command of the Southern Department, but Congress had appointed Gates. General De Kalb was second in command.
32. De Kalb was the highest ranking officer of the Continental Army to be killed in action during the Revolution. Washington, who had come to know the General well at Valley Forge and had always much respected him, said of De Kalb, "The manner in which he died fully justified the opinion which I ever entertained of him, and will endear his memory to the country." Congress promptly passed a resolution, October 14, 1780: "*Resolved,* That a monument be erected to the memory of the late Major General the Baron De Kalb, in the city of Annapolis, in the State of Maryland with the following inscription:

SACRED TO THE MEMORY OF THE BARON DE KALB
KNIGHT OF THE ROYAL ORDER OF
MILITARY MERIT
BRIGADIER OF THE ARMY OF FRANCE
AND MAJOR GENERAL IN THE SERVICE
OF THE UNITED STATES OF AMERICA
HAVING SERVED WITH HONOR AND REPUTATION
FOR THREE YEARS
HE GAVE A LAST & GLORIOUS PROOF OF HIS ATTACHMENT
TO THE LIBERTIES OF MANKIND
A ND THE CAUSE OF AMERICA
IN THE ACTION NEAR CAMDEN IN THE STATE OF SO. CAROLINA
ON THE 16th OF AUGUST 1780
WHEN LEADING ON THE TROOPS OF
THE DELAWARE & MARYLAND LINES AGAINST

SUPERIOR NUMBERS
AND ANIMATING THEM BY HIS EXAMPLE
TO DEEDS OF VALOUR
HE WAS PIERCED WITH MANY WOUNDS
AND ON THE 19 FOLLOWING EXPIRED
IN THE 48 YEAR OF HIS AGE,
THE CONGRESS OF THE UNITED STATES OF AMERICA
IN GRATITUDE TO HIS ZEAL, SERVICES AND MERIT
HAVE ERECTED THIS MONUMENT.

More than a century later, on February 19, 1883, Congress *finally* appropriated the necessary funds, and on August 16, 1886, a statue of the General, fashioned in Rome by the sculptor Ephraim Keyser, was dedicated in Annapolis, Maryland. It stands before the courthouse in the state's capital. Long before that, in 1825, a monument was erected at Camden by the citizens of the community. The cornerstone was laid by his student and dear friend Lafayette when he visited the United States that same year. The silver trowel which Lafayette used is now in the possession of the Grand Lodge of Masons of South Carolina. On one side of the marker is carved: "His love of liberty induced him to leave the old world to aid the citizens of the new in their struggle for independence." Six counties in the United States are named for the much revered General. For an account of the action at Camden, see H. L. Landers, *The Battle of Camden.*

33. *P.A.,* First Series, XII, 265; Downes, p. 263.
34. Downes, p. 263.
35. Ibid., p. 265.
36. Idem.
37. Idem.
38. Sparks, *The Writings of George Washington,* VII, 341; quoted by James, p. 231.
39. Idem.
40. Washington to Brodheaad, in Sparks, *The Writings of George Washington,* VII, 343; James, p. 234.
41. Thomas, p. 88.
42. Clark had already acquired a reputation as an inspirational leader. He was tall and ruggedly handsome, with red hair, and carried himself with great confidence. He had been a prisoner of war for three months, March 8 until June 16, 1779. He led the military action in the northwest until the end of the war.
43. Downes, p. 269.
44. Louisville was a portage place around the Falls until a canal was built in 1830. It was laid out in 1773. George Rogers Clark built a fort here in 1778.
45. Fitzpatrick, *The Writings of George Washington,* XXI, 449-450.
46. Ibid., XXI, 502-503.
47. Ibid., XXII, 184-185.
48. Ephraim Douglass to General James Irvine, August 29, 1781, in "Notes and

Queries," *Pennsylvania Magazine of History and Biography*, IV (1880), 248; see also Butterfield, *Washington-Irvine Correspondence*, p. 55.

49. There are a number of accounts of this expedition. The details do not always correspond. See Downes, pp. 268-269; Boucher's *History of Westmoreland County*, vol. I, Chapter XIX, pp. 338-339; and Albert, pp. 124 ff.
50. Downes, p. 270.
51. Albert, p. 125.
52. For the names of those who eventually returned to their homes in Westmoreland County, see *P.A.*, First Series, IX, 574, 733; *P.A.*, Second Series, XIV; *Colonial Records of Pennsylvania*, XIII 325, 473; and Hassler, p. 144. On the Lochry massacre see Albert, Vol. I, Chapter IX, pp. 338-339. See also "The Haldimand Papers," in *Michigan Pioneer and Historical Collections*, XIX, 655; and Downes, p. 270.
53. Craig was actually a major at this time, as his promotion, which would not be official until March 13, 1782, was back-dated to rank from October 7, 1781.
54. James, "George Rogers Clark Papers, 1781-84," in *Collections of the Illinois State Historical Library,* Vol. XVIII (Virginia Series), p. 608 (Oct. 1, 1781); and James, *The Life of George Rogers Clark*, p. 253.
55. Butterfield, *Washington-Irvine Correspondence*, p. 231.
56. Craig, p. 37.
57. *P.A.,,* First Series, IX, 458.
58. Boucher, I, 362.
59. Francois Joseph Paul de Grasse.
60. Jean Baptiste Donatien de Vimeur comte de Rochambeau.
61. Butterfield, *Washington-Irvine Correspondence,* preface.
62. "Mingo" is the term that the Senecas who had settled in the Ohio River country (as distinct from those of western New York State) were known by.
63. Van Every, p. 285.
64. Idem.
65. Boucher, Vol. I, Chapter XIX, pp. 333-345. See also Albert, p. 133; and Van Every, pp. 285-286.
66. Figures vary slightly in reports, but ninety is now the agreed upon number.
67. Albert, p. 133.
68. Sipe, p. 464.
69. Washington County had been formed March 28, 1781, out of Westmoreland County. For accounts of the massacre, see Boucher, Vol. I, Chapter XIX, pp. 342-345; and Hassler, Chapter XXIII, pp. 152-161. A State Memorial Park marks the site of the massacre.
70. Boucher, I, 346.
71. William Crawford was born in Virginia, but becoming enamored of the mountains and rivers of western Pennsylvania, decided to move his family into that country. In the summer of 1765 he found the spot. It was at a place known then as "Stewart's Crossings," on the Youghiogheny River, present-day Connellsville. He built a home there and next spring moved his family (wife and three children) into the cabin. Washington, with whom he was in partnership in land acquisition and with whom he was in correspondence for sixteen years, visited in the Crawford home. Crawford County, north of

Pittsburgh, was named for Colonel William Crawford on March 12, 1800, when the region was sectioned off from Allegheny County by act of the Pennsylvania legislature. Later, this vast territory was further divided into the counties of Erie, Mercer, Venango, and Warren, besides Crawford.

72. John Rose was known at Fort Pitt as "Major Rose." But he was really a Russian nobleman, and his actual name was Henri Gustave Rosenthal. He had been forced to flee Russia because he had killed a man in a duel. He had served in the Patriot army as a surgeon in the 7th Pennsylvania Regiment. He had been a prisoner of war, but after he was exchanged he was made ensign in the 4th Pennsylvania Regiment, and later, on April 1, 1781, a lieutenant. He had accompanied Irvine to Fort Pitt, and served as Irvine's aide. Irvine was very fond of the young lieutenant Rose, who was the same age as bombardier John Harris, and very respectful of his abilities. (Butterfield, *Washington-Irvine Correspondence*, pp. 114-115; and Boucher, I, 346).
73. Butterfield, *Washington-Irvine Correspondence,* pp. 114-117.
74. Ibid., p. 118; and Downes, p. 273.
75. Butterfield, *Washington-Irvine Correspondence,* pp. 114-115.
76. For full, richly detailed accounts of the battle, see Boucher, I, Chapter XIX; Hassler, pp. 162-168; and Butterfield, *An Historical Account of the Expedition Against Sandusky.*
77. His nephew and his son-in-law, together with a number of other captives, were murdered. Crawford's son John, "after perilous trials," reached home in safety. (Hassler, p. 168)
78. Albert, p. 135.
79. Boucher, I, 347.
80. Knight, p. 711.
81. Albert, p. 135.
82. Simon Girty had been adopted by the Wyandots in 1778, and because he could speak as many as eleven of the Indian dialects and "seemed like an Indian," he enjoyed great influence over the warriors of the various tribes. He was able to save the frontiersman Simon Kenton, as well as other captives, from death at their hands. For a time he served as a spy and as a guide to General Edward Hand, when the General was commanding the Western Department from Fort Pitt. And indeed he once a close friend to Colonel William Crawford. According to the Girty lore, Simon Girty had at one time proposed to the Crawfords' daughter, and had been rejected. But he is generally thought of as "a wretch who enjoyed torture." The common view is that "No other country or age ever produced so brutal, depraved or wicked a wretch." He was surely the most hated man in Revolutionary America. The patriots placed an $800 bounty on his head, but he was never captured, and died in Canada, half-blind and rheumatic, on February 18, 1818. In recent years the popular view of Girty has been much disputed, some accounts insisting that he was helpless at Crawford's torture, and could have interfered only at the risk of his own life. The Commonwealth of Pennsylvania installed an historical marker to him in June of 2001. It stands at Fort Hunter, near Harrisburg, and near the site of Girty's birthplace. The dedication was attended by Ken Girty, a great, great, great, great, great nephew, and other descendants. Girty's Notch, an

impressive outcropping of rock on the western bank of the Susquehanna River, some twenty miles south of Selinsgrove, Pennsylvania, between Liverpool and Montgomery Ferry, is named for Simon Girty.

83. Knight, pp. 714-715.
84. Albert, p. 135.
85. Knight, p. 715.
86. Knight stayed on at Fort Pitt with his Seventh Virginia, and continued to serve until the end of the war. On October 14, 1784, he married Polly Stephenson, daughter of Richard Stephenson, who was Colonel Crawford's half-brother. He later moved to Shelby, Kentucky, and was the father of ten children. He died March 12, 1838. Accounts of the torture of Crawford and the miraculous escape of Dr. Knight appear in Albert's *History of Westmoreland County,* Boucher's *Old and New Westmoreland,* Hassler's *Old Westmoreland,* Crumrine's *History of Washington County,* and Butterfield's *An Historical Account of the Expedition Against Sandusky,* but all derive in great measure from Dr. John Knight's narrative, which appears in *P.A.,* Series 2, XIV, 708-717. For a gripping dramatization of the Battle of Sandusky, as well as the torture-death of Colonel William Crawford, see Allan Eckert, *That Dark and Bloody River,* pp. 335-396.
87. Simon Girty, who was born in 1741, had an older brother, Tom, and two younger brothers, Jim (born 1743) and George (born 1745). He also had a half-brother, John Turner. There is a Girty Run in Pittsburgh, the site of the family home at the time Mary Girty was married to her second husband, the father of John Turner, who died here. A tiny community in Armstrong County in western Pennsylvania is named Girty.
88. *P.A.,* Series 2, XIV, 17-25.
89. There was no printing done in Pittsburgh until the appearance of the *Pittsburg Gazette* in July of 1786. (Butterfield, *Washington-Irvine Correspondence,* pp. 127-128)
90. Downes, p. 272.
91. Butterfield, *Washington-Irvine Correspondence,* p. 132.
92. Ibid., p. 127.
93. Ibid., p. 131.
94. Ibid., pp. 131-132.
95. Ibid., pp. 113-118.
96. In a muster sworn to by General Irvine for February, 1782, and March, 1783, fifty officers and men are still listed. Harris is the only "bombardier." (*P.A.,* Series 5, III, 978-979)
97. Butterfield, *Washington-Irvine Correspondence,* p. 351.
98. Ibid., p. 112.
99. Ibid., p. 174.
100. Craig, pp. 37-38.
101. If Craig's artillery company constitutes the whole work force, the number can be supposed to be fewer than fifty.
102. Butterfield, *Washington-Irvine Correspondence,* pp. 139-140.
103. For a full and trustworthy account of the Indian assault on Hannastown, see Albert, pp. 138-148; see also Hassler, p. 176. A restoration of the stockade is

Notes 377

in place at the site. And a number of cabins as well. Tours of Old Hanna's Town are provided May through October, by guides in colonial garb. Present-day Hannastown, a tiny community of some 500 people, lies about one mile to the west of Old Hanna's Town.

104. Albert, p. 144.
105. Guyasuta, as a young hunter, had accompanied George Washington and two older chiefs on Washington's mission to the French commandant of the forts on the Ohio in 1753. It is thought that it was he who directed the siege of Fort Pitt in 1763, during the time of Pontiac's War; and he was among the Indians at the Battle of Bushy Run. Simon Girty for a time served as his "bodyguard." He was Cornplanter's uncle, brother of Cornplanter's mother.
106. Butterfield, *Washington-Irvine Correspondence*, p. 133.
107. Craig, pp. 38-39.
108. Ibid., p. 39.
109. Albert, p. 147.
110. The Blue Licks Battlefield State Park is located between the communities of Mt. Olivet and Carlisle, some fifty miles north of Lexington in Kentucky.
111. Craig, pp. 40-44.
112. Lieutenant ("Major") John Rose, Irvine's aide, who had been with Craig on the Cuyahoga mission, and who delivered this letter in four days to Craig at Fort Pitt.
113. Butterfield, *Washington-Irvine Correspondence*, pp. 406-407.
114. Ibid., pp. 410-411.
115. From April of 1782 until May of 1783, Washington could be found in an old fieldstone farmhouse in Newburgh, New York. In this house, which belonged to the Hasbrouck family, he established his headquarters. Just twelve miles from the forts at West Point, it seemed to him a good location for keeping an eye on the British in New York City, and from which to keep his army ever at the ready.
116. The treaty was ratified by Congress on January 14, 1784; a proclamation to that effect was published on January 22.

Chapter VIII

1. Irvine had married Ann Callander, eldest daughter of the Seven Years' War militia captain Robert Callander, and by her was the father of ten children. At war's end he did not retire from public life, far from it. After the war he served as a member of Pennsylvania's Constitutional Convention; he was elected to the 3rd Congress of the United States as a representative from Pennsylvania's Cumberland County; he helped to lay out the towns of Waterford, Erie, Franklin and Warren; he commanded Pennsylvania's forces in the suppression of the Whiskey Rebellion, and he was a member of the founding Board of Trustees of Dickinson College (in Carlisle, Pa.), the first college to be chartered in the United States of America, and served until his death, in Philadelphia, July 29, 1804. By the editor of his communications with Washington (see Butterfield, *Washington-Irvine Correspondence*, preface) he

has been described as a man of "incorruptible integrity," a "zealous patriot," a "judicious statesman," and an "able military commander."
2. Butterfield, *Washington-Irvine Correspondence*, pp. 151-152.
3. Irvine's aide, Lieutenant Rose, paid off the troops for the last time.
4. *Pittsburgh Post-Gazette*, Second Section, Jan. 31, 1952.
5. Jane J. Betts, "Missing the Point: A Tale of the Revolution," in *Pittsburgh Magazine* (the 1989-1990 City Guide), p. 108.
6. History of Mercer County, pp. 140-145.
7. The depreciation certificate accounts are on file, in labeled boxes in the office of the Comptroller General in Harrisburg.
8. *History of Mercer County*, p. 145. Mercer County, originally defined by Act of General Assembly, separated theoretically from Allegheny County on March 12, 1800, but was not organized until 1803.
9. Ibid., pp. 143-145.
10. On the tax rolls for 1800-01 John Harris is not listed for any of the defined townships in Mercer County.
11. *Public Ledger*, Salem, New Jersey, Jan., 1932.
12. Idem.
13. Idem.
14. Idem.
15. Stewart, *Salem County in the Revolution*, pp. 36-37. The letter appears in Sparks, *The Writings of George Washington*.
16. Stewart, *Salem County in the Revolution*, p. 37; see also pp. 41-43, 44-45. On Wayne's expeditions into New Jersey, see Stewart, "Foraging for Valley Forge, by General Anthony Wayne in Salem and Gloucester Counties," pamphlet printed in 1964.
17. Simcoe had been placed in command of the Queen's Rangers in 1777. He served in that post until the end of the war. His post-war career is most distinguished. He became the first Lieutenant-Governor of Upper Canada. Lake Simcoe, near Barrie, Ontario, is named for him; so is a small town in southwestern Ontario, north across Lake Erie and south of Brantford, Ontario; and so is Simcoe County, to the west of Lake Simcoe. Several communities in Ontario have their Simcoe streets, and there are the Simcoe roads. Simcoe directed the first drafting of the plans for the city of Toronto. Each of three streets in the city was given one of his names, John Street, Graves Street (later changed), and Simcoe Street. An elegant hotel, named the Lord (!) Simcoe Hotel (later razed), honored him in its name. A provincial holiday held on the first Monday in August is known as Simcoe Day in Toronto.
18. Laird, p. 3.
19. Stewart, *Salem County in the Revolution*, p. 39.
20. Ibid., p. 55.
21. Ibid., pp. 53-56.
22. The Battle of Quinton's Bridge has been described many times. There occurs in these accounts a considerable variance in the details and in the order of events. See Stewart, *Salem County in the Revolution*, pp. 38-102, especially pp. 45-59; Salem's *Public Ledger* of Jan., 1932; *150th Anniversary of the Skirmish at Quinton's Bridge and the Massacre at Hancock's Bridge,* Official

Notes 379

Program of the proceedings at Quinton, New Jersey, May 19th, 1928; and R. F. Laird's account in *Quinton Bridge '78,* Salem, New Jersey, Salem County Cultural & Heritage Commission, 1978, pp. 1-9. See also Christopher Bishop, "War's Fury Was Felt in the Tiny Village of Quinton," *Today's Sunbeam,* Salem, N.J., April 26, 1980, pp. D-1 and D-3.

23. Jacob Harris, who was a very small but wiry man, had been appointed Surgeon's Mate on Feb. 26, 1777, in the New Jersey Continental Line. According to the payroll for killed and wounded, he had served in Captain Smith's company for fifty days, and was awarded four pounds, three shillings and some pence for his time; for his lost gun he was reimbursed three pounds, ten shillings. He was confined to the hospital for fifty-one days, and was still recovering from his wounds more than two months later. (Stewart, *Salem County in the Revolution,* p. 58)

24. Stewart, *Salem County in the Revolution,* p. 58. Isaac had been appointed Surgeon's Mate on November 28, 1776, and Surgeon November 16, 1782. He served with the militia forces until the end of the war. He also served a term as Justice (1777) in Salem County, and was a member of the Standing Committee of Correspondence for Salem County.

25. According to some accounts there were more than one sentry. Major Simcoe's journal account of the expedition (in an awkward grammar) reads: "On approaching the place, two sentries were discovered; two men of the light infantry followed them, and, as they turned about, bayoneted them." Other versions have a sentry at each door, front and rear, both surprised and bayoneted.

26. According to some accounts, not a single shot was fired; others allow that there was "some gunfire." For a straightforward account of the whole affair see Major John Simcoe's journal description (in Stewart, *Salem County in the Revolution,* pp. 61-63. See also Timmins, "The Affair at Hancock House," pp. 11-17.

27. Jackson, pp. 182-183.

28. Colonel Hand's letter has been printed many times.

29. Including much of the original furnishings, the house, four miles south of Salem, is open to the public.

30. Stewart, *Salem County in the Revolution,*, pp. 90 and 92.

31. The John Harris family bible was a gift from Amos Harris's daughter Catherine (Kate) of Salem to her cousin Mrs. Mabel Jackson Ohl of Germantown, Pa. It is presently in the possession of Jane Jackson Betts of Indiana, Pa.

32. For the geology of Ragged and Round Islands and speculation on the life there, see William Vanneman, the "Golden Days" columns appearing in *Today's Sunbeam,* Salem, N.J., March 21, March 28, and April 11, 1975.

33. John's own daughter, the next-to-last-born of his eleven children, Clarissa, with her husband, David S. Ellett, after living their married life in Salem for seven years, moved to Ohio in 1834. In a two-horse wagon they made the journey from Salem, N.J., to Bunker Hill in Goshen Township, near Salem, Ohio, in two weeks.

34. One year after their marriage, Rebecca and Stretch had a new house built for

them on Round Island. In June of that year they went there to live, and stayed on until 1827. Stretch died a wealthy man.

35. It is known now that Cornplanter was not born in the same year as Washington, and that he did not live 100 years. It seems that he lived a mere eighty-four or eighty-five years.

36. Brant's death date is reported variously as August 24, as November 2, and as November 24. The latter would seem to be correct. He died in his home on the Grand River and was interred close to the Episcopal church he had built there. Almost a half century after his death his tomb was restored by the Freemasons. In 1886 at Brantford there was unveiled a bronze statue of the Mohawk chieftain. It has been recorded that the last words spoken by Joseph Brant were addressed to his nephew: "Have pity on the poor Indians; if you can get any influence with the great, endeavor to do them all the good you can."

37. Brant sent two of his sons to Dartmouth College. Another son, Isaac, who had assaulted him in a drunken rage, he killed in self-defense.

38. Fallen Timbers, so named for the many trees that had been felled by tornadoes, is just southwest of present-day Toledo, Ohio.

39. This attitude toward the first Americans, firmly fixed by the colonials, and continuing throughout the westward movement, persisted through the administrations of Andrew Jackson and continued clear through the administration of Theodore Roosevelt. Roosevelt actually applauded the infamous Sand Creek, Colorado (1869), cowardly slaughter of 150 Indian boys and girls and squaws and old men (while the braves were absent on hunting missions). It was, Roosevelt insisted, one of the moments in American history most to be cherished: "In spite of certain most objectionable details ... it was on the whole as righteous and beneficial a deed as ever took place on the frontier." (Dyer, p. 79) And it was Roosevelt whose unbridled arrogance perpetuated the popular view: "I don't go so far as to think that the only good Indians are dead Indians, but I believe nine out of ten are, and I shouldn't like to inquire too closely into the case of the tenth." (Dyer, p. 86) Roosevelt's historical view was intended to justify the exploitation of the Indians: "The conquest and settlement by the whites of the Indians was necessary to the greatness of the race and to the well-being of civilized mankind. Such conquests are commonly undertaken by ... a masterful people, still in its new barbarian prime, which finds itself face to face with the weaker and wholly alien race which holds a coveted prize in its feeble grasp." (Dyer, p. 78)

40. Ellis, p. 56.
41. This is the same Crawford who was later tortured by the Delawares.
42. Bellamy, pp. 144-145.
43. Hulbert, p. 86.
44. Idem.
45. Cleland, p. 239.
46. Armstrong, born in Ireland, was fifteen years older than Washington, and, like Washington, had fought in the French and Indian Wars. Colonel Armstrong had led the successful attack on the Delaware Indian stronghold at Kittanning on the Allegheny River north of Pittsburgh, September 8, 1756, and in that

Notes   381

battle was seriously wounded. He was very active during the Revolution, with an important command at Germantown. He was made Brigadier General on March 1, 1776, and was promoted to Major General in 1777. He was always a warm supporter of Washington, and strongly urged his election as President. He had made his home in Carlisle, Pennsylvania, which town he had helped to map out in 1750-51. He was known as "the first citizen of Carlisle." He was a member of the Second Continental Congress. He had served as a trustee of the Carlisle Grammar School, and when Dr. Benjamin Rush proposed a college for the community, he presented a vigorous opposition. When Rush won out, Armstrong, persuaded of its rightness, agreed to serve, together with General William Irvine, as a trustee of Dickinson College. He died on March 9, 1795. He should not be confused with his most distinguished son, who was born in Carlisle and also named John, and who also participated in the American Revolution, serving as a twenty-year-old on the staff of General Horatio Gates. The younger Armstrong served as a U. S. Senator, 1800-04, as Ambassador to France, 1804-10, and as Secretary of War in the administration of President Madison. He was the author of *Notices of the War of 1812* and of biographies of Generals Richard Montgomery and Anthony Wayne. Armstrong County, in western Pennsylvania, is named for him.

47. Bellamy, p. 154.
48. Cleland, p. 238.
49. Ibid., pp. 342-343. Crawford's log cabin was located on the banks of the Youghiogheny River, at what is called Braddock's Crossing. The tiny structure, only eighteen square feet in size, with a stone chimney, has been preserved and was reconstructed in 1976. It may be viewed today, at the Yough Park of Connellsville, Pennsylvania, and is a principal feature on the Youghiogheny River Trail.
50. Ibid., pp. 288-289.
51. Bellamy, p. 152, and Cleland, p. 302.
52. Bellamy, pp. 152-153.
53. Ibid., pp. 146-147.
54. Ellis, p. 212.
55. Ibid., p. 213.
56. General Harmar, who had been born in Philadelphia, exactly two months after John Harris was born in nearby Salem (1753), was at this time forty-seven years old. It was he who had carried to Paris (with greatly detailed instructions and the blessing of President Thomas Mifflin), after it had been ratified by Congress, the treaty ending the Revolutionary War. In October of 1785 he built Fort Harmar, at the point where the Muskingum River enters the Ohio, in order to discourage settlement in the Ohio Valley. Ironically, because it seemed to afford protection, the fort only invited settlement. His conduct during the Indian wars in Ohio came under investigation, and he was accused of wrongdoing during the campaign, including being drunk on duty. The court-martial that was convened in 1791 to try Harmar, finally exonerated him of all charges. But he shortly thereafter, on January 1, 1792, retired from the Army. When he returned to his native state, he soon became the Adjutant-General of Pennsylvania, serving until 1799. He was dismissed from the

Jefferson administration for his opposition to statehood for Ohio. He died August 20, 1813. He had had his portrait painted by Raphael Peale, the artist son of Charles Willson Peale.

57. The Miami war-chief Michikinikwa, known as Little Turtle, was born in 1752 (some historians give the date as early as 1747) on the Eel River (Kenapocomoco). He was a most courageous and able warrior. After the Treaty of Greenville, he led his people, as Cornplanter was doing for his Senecas, toward peaceful living with the white settlers. He urged them away from alcohol and into farming. Little Turtle met with Washington in Philadelphia in the last year of the President's second term. He had his portrait painted by Gilbert Stuart. He died in Fort Wayne on July 14, 1812. It was in this same year that the village in which he was born and reared, on the Eel River, was destroyed by American troops. Most members of the tribe had been removed from Indiana by 1845.

58. St. Clair, who was born in Scotland, had served under General James Wolfe during the siege of Quebec in 1759. He had crossed the Delaware with Washington to attack Trenton, and he was encamped with Washington during the terrible winter at Morristown. St. Clair was in command when Fort Ticonderoga was lost back to the British in 1777, an event which caused Washington much distress, as the news came to him as a shock. The Commander-in-Chief had the report early in July, and on the 10th he wrote to General Philip Schuyler that while he was happy that General St. Clair was not in the hands of the enemy, the evacuation of Ticonderoga and Mount Independence was not "within the compass of my reasoning." And on the 18th, again in a dispatch to Schuyler, he declared, "I will not condemn or even press censure upon any officer unheard, but I think it is a duty which General St. Clair owes to his own character, to insist upon an opportunity of giving his reasons for his sudden evacuation of a post, which but a few days before, he, by his own letters, thought tenable, at least for a while." (Irving, III, 104-105) St. Clair, while the country was governed by the Articles of Confederation, served as the sixth President of the United States. The General in 1812 published a defense of his conduct in the Indian wars. His last years were lived out in poverty. He died August 31, 1818, and is interred in the General Arthur St. Clair Cemetery in Greensburg, Pa., the western Pennsylvania community which was named for the General's fellow officer, General Nathanael Greene. Upper St. Clair Township, a suburb to the south of Pittsburgh, is named for General St. Clair.

59. Irving, vol. 5, pp. 108-109.
60. H. N. Moore, p. 170.
61. Carroll, pp. 14-15.
62. H. N. Moore, p. 189.
63. Typhus was very prevalent at this time, in the Philadelphia region and in New Jersey. The disease is spread by rats and mice, by the fleas which they carry. One form is carried by lice. The symptoms, besides the fever, are intense headache, frequent chills and general aches and pains, followed by a rash which can cover most of the body.
64. Peter, youngest son of John and Lydia Harris, would never see the Mercer

Notes 383

County land in Pennsylvania. He died within the year from the same typhus fever, which he had contracted while sleeping in a tent, on the ground, while serving in the militia at Billingsport during the war of 1812. John's brother Isaac also died of the typhus fever at very nearly this same time, April 5, 1814.

65. Among the effects surviving was the epaulet worn by Bombardier John Harris. This was exhibited at the World's Columbian Exposition held in Chicago from May through November, 1893. It had been preserved initially by John's daughter Elizabeth, and was presented in 1945 to Mrs. Richard P. Williamson, another descendant.

Appendix A

1. Editor's note in Landis, p. 83.
2. Landis, p. 85.
3. Roberts, p. 78.
4. Stryker, p.192

Appendix B

1. Benjamin Franklin, the "wisest American," in whose person was embodied most impressively the soul of the Revolution, was laid to a well-deserved rest in the Christ Church Burial Ground at Fifth and Arch Streets in his beloved Philadelphia. In his company repose the remains of four other signers of the Declaration of Independence and a number of other prominent Revolutionary War figures.
2. For accounts of the tour see Octavia Roberts, *With Lafayette in America*, and Jane Bacon McIntire, *Lafayette, the Guest of the Nation; the tracing of the route of Lafayette's tour of the United States in 1824-25.*

INDEX

Abeel, John, 141, 203-204
Abercrombie, Robert, 109, 362
Adams, John, 7, 13, 21, 23, 36, 37, 133, 271, 273, 329, 349, 361
Adams, Samuel, 5
Adventure, the, 170, 175
Akron, 141
Albany, N.Y., 19, 59, 60, 92, 107, 131, 140, 141, 156, 195, 203, 330, 368
Alden, Ichabod, 156
Alexander, John, 322
Alexander, William (Lord Stirling), 28-29, 30, 62, 83, 104, 118, 120, 121, 209, 245, 353
Aliquipiso, 141
Allegheny River, 158, 195, 196, 197, 198, 202, 224, 227, 228, 229, 231, 233, 249, 267, 280, 281, 300, 301, 380
Allen, Ethan, 6, 10
Allentown, Pa., 70
Alliance with France, 104, 111
Alloway's Creek, 3, 284, 286, 287, 289, 293
André, John, 69, 112, 130, 135, 364, 369
Armstrong, John, Jr., 381
Armstrong, John ("Jack"), 75, 78-79, 80, 196, 306, 352, 354, 380, 381
Arnold, Benedict, 6, 7, 9, 10-11, 13, 19, 60, 121, 122, 124; in command of Philadelphia, 130-137; 193, 328, 350, 364
Assunpink, 42-43, 46, 53, 56, 174, 353

Bacon, Andrew, 286, 287, 288, 294
Baldwin, Isaac, 186
Baltimore, 64, 70, 126
Barker, Joseph, 77

Barton, William, 173, 175, 183
Battle Hill, 28
Baurmeister, Carl L., 66, 69
Baylor, George, 358
Beatty, Reverend Charles Clinton, 221
Beatty, Erkuries, 191, 194
Bedel, Timothy, 13
Beebe, Lewis, 13, 350
Bemis Heights, 131, 364
Bethlehem, Pa., 70
Bilderback, Charles, 248
Billingsport Fort, 211, 285, 383
Billopp House, 37
Blacksnake (Dahgayadoh), 143-145, 148, 151, 155, 157, 185, 186, 187, 188, 202, 203, 205
Blackwood, Herenhappuch, 299
Blackwood, Samuel, 4, 47, 51-52, 55-56, 100, 127, 172, 191, 209, 210, 214, 216, 217, 241, 244, 249, 262, 275, 282, 355
Blaire, John, 31-32
Blake, Thomas, 194
Blue Jacket, 312, 316
Blue Licks, battle of, 268-269, 377
bombardier, 51
Boone, Daniel, 162, 268-269
Boone, Hawkins, 162
Boone, Israel, 269
Boonesborough, 268
Borre, Prudhomme, 61
Boston, 2, 3-4, 6, 7, 8, 12, 20-24, 27, 93, 99, 126, 157, 267, 330, 331, 350, 352, 353
Boston Massacre, 5
Boston Tea Party, 6
Boudinot, Elins, 120, 122
Bound Brook, battle of, 56-58, 356
Bowman's Creek, 148
Boyd, Thomas, 188-193, 253, 369
Boylan, John and Eleanor, 210

385

Brackenridge, Hugh Henry, 256, 258, 308
Braddock, Edward, 7, 159, 220, 371
Braddock's Road, 306
Brandywine, 19, 21, 62; battle of, 63-71; 72, 74, 79, 80, 93, 95, 99, 100, 101, 102, 113, 123, 127, 130, 157, 158, 211, 235, 250, 280, 296, 331, 350, 351, 353, 354, 356, 357, 360, 362-365, 368, 369
Brandywine, the frigate, 332
Brant, Joseph, 14, 140-145, 147, 148, 156, 164, 178, 180, 183, 188, 202, 203, 235-236, 268, 302, 329, 362, 365, 369, 380
Brant's Ford (Brantford), 302
Breed's Hill, 7, 23, 28, 331, 350, 360, 362, 364
Brinton's Ford, 68, 102
Briscoe, Dr. John, 308-309
Brodhead, Daniel, 158; Allegheny expedition, 195-202; 211, 213, 214, 221, 222; at Fort Pitt, 223-245; 246, 250, 370
Brokenstraw Creek, 197
Brown, Christian, 147
Brown, Jacob, 10
Brown, John, 93
Brownlee, John ("Jack"), 265
Brunswick (New Brunswick), 37, 57-58, 120
Brush Creek, 224-225, 372
Buchloons (Buckaloons), 198
Bucks County, Pa., 61, 62
Bullock Pens, 221
Bunker Hill, 7, 8, 11, 21, 26, 299, 350, 379
Bunner, Rudolph, 125
Burgoyne, John, 18, 46, 58-59, 60, 81-82, 116, 131, 173, 328, 349, 361, 369
Burlington and Burlington Bay, Ontario, 302, 329
Burr, Aaron, 11, 26, 41, 118, 122, 123, 328, 329
Butler, John, 140-141, 143, 147-150, 152, 155, 156, 164, 178, 180, 183, 184, 188, 190, 196, 329, 369
Butler, Walter, 156, 180
Butler's Rangers, 140, 147-153, 155, 174, 188, 196, 228
Butler, Zebulon, 149, 152, 157, 167, 168
Butterfield, Isaac, 13
Byberry, 129, 355

Cadmus, the, 330
Cadwalader, John, 39, 40, 43, 44, 85, 88, 130, 134, 354, 361
Cahokia, 231
Callander, Ann, 377
Cambridge, Massachusetts, 8, 10, 20, 21, 24, 26, 350, 351
Camden, S. C., battle of, 225-227; 327, 330, 354, 372, 373
Camilla, the frigate, 285
Campbell, Thomas, 139
Camp Fatigue, 165
Canajoharie, 141, 203, 368, 370
Canawagus, 141, 202
Canon, John, 249
Carleton, Guy, 11, 13, 19, 271, 349, 358
Carlisle, Pa., 14, 15, 48, 118, 127, 207, 211-212, 214, 216, 221, 245, 248, 260, 261, 263, 270, 271, 272, 275, 278, 280, 307, 321-325, 352, 354, 355, 371, 374, 377, 381
Carney, Lawrence, 367
Carroll, Charles, 12
Cartwright, Richard, 152
Cat Gut, 297
Catherine's Town, 183, 187, 195, 199, 201
Cayuga Indians, 148, 159, 203
Cayuga Lake, 201
Cedars, see The Cedars
Certificates of Depreciation, 281
Chadds Ford, 63, 64-66, 68-69, 100, 357, 363
Chambers, James, 67-68, 71
Chamblee, 10
Chandler, John, 3
Charlemagne, 2

Index

Charleston, S.C., 21, 225, 243, 356, 362
Charlestown, 7
Chartiers Creek, 229, 306, 308
Chase, Samuel, 12
Chatterton's Hill, 31
Chautauqua (Jadaque), 267
Chemung village, 178, 180, 187, 200
Chemung River, 173, 176-177, 178, 180, 197, 202
Cherry Tree, 145
Cherry Valley, 156, 163, 203, 291, 303
Chester, Pa., 63, 68, 69
Chestnut Hill, 76, 84
Chew, Judge Benjamin, 77, 358
Chew Mansion, 77-80, 83, 95, 331, 358
Chillicothe, 269
Chippewa Indians, 303, 315, 316
Christina River, 64
Clark, George Rogers, 196, 224, 229-239, 240, 260, 266, 269, 280, 303, 329, 373
Clark, John, battle of Newtown, 179-188
Clarke, Thomas, 43, 44, 45, 354
Clinton, George, 96, 284, 368
Clinton, Henry, 38, 112, 116-119, 125-127, 129, 130, 132, 242-243, 329, 362, 364, 368
Clinton, James, 158, 174, 177-178, 181-182, 184, 202, 368
Cobleskill, 147
Cohansey, 2, 286
Compston, John, 121
Conawango, 198
Connellsville, Pa., 221, 229, 306, 307, 374, 381
Connisius Lake, 188
Conway, Thomas, 76, 106-107, 361
Cook, David, 121
Cooperstown, 177
Corbin, Margaret ("Molly"), 28, 321, 352
Cornelius Eoff Farm, 210
Cornplanter (Gyantawanka), Council at Oswego, 140-148; at Wyoming, 148-151; 156, 159, 162, 164, 178, 185,187, 188, 194, 197, 198, 199, 202, 203, 204-205, 246, 249, 282, 300-302, 305, 314-317, 329, 369, 377, 380, 382,
Cornplanter Grant, 300
Cornplanter Town, 300
Cornstalk, 349
Cornwallis, Charles, 32, 38, 42-44, 57; at Brandywine, 64-71; 74, 191, 225, 241-244, 269, 329
Coshocton, 228-229, 250
Courteney, Hercules, 52, 56, 58, 60, 100-101
Craig, Isaac, 69, 127, 179, 209-225, 228, 230-244, 249, 250, 260-262, 269-272, 368, 374, 376, 377
Crane, John, 48, 121
Crawford, John, 253
Crawford, William, 229, 230; the Sandusky expedition, 250-260; 306-308, 330, 374, 375, 376, 380, 381
Crawford, William (nephew to William), 253, 257
Cresap, Thomas, 218
Croghan, George, 308
Croghan, William, 235
Crooked Billet, 109-111, 289, 362
Cumberland, Md., 219-220, 371
Custis, George Washington Parke, 89
Cuyahoga ("the Crooked River"), 270

Danbury (East Stroudsburg), 195
Dartmouth College, 142, 380
Dauphin Jail, 18
Davis, John, 118
Dearborn, Henry, 131, 182, 201, 364
Declaration of Independence, 12, 22, 37, 38, 88, 129, 304, 329, 351, 355, 356, 358, 383
Dehguswaygahent, 198
Delaware Indians, 146, 157, 196, 197, 224, 227, 228-229, 230, 231, 248, 250, 253-255, 281, 303, 305, 316, 354, 380

Delaware River, 36, 39, 47, 52, 55, 56, 58, 60, 63, 64, 108, 132, 168, 171, 211, 289, 296, 297, 309, 352, 353, 354, 382
Denison, Nathan, 149, 152
Detroit, 198, 202, 224, 227, 229, 230, 232, 238, 240, 268, 272, 317
Dickinson College, 355, 359, 377, 388
Dickinson, Edmund B., 125
Dickinson, John, 5, 39, 355
Dinwiddie, Robert, 219
Dorchester Heights, 12, 20, 99, 351
Douglass, Ephraim, 233-234, 373
Downingtown, Pa., 64
Du Bois, Jacob, 31
Dubuysson, Charles, 227
Duffy, Patrick, 41-42, 52, 127
Duncan, King of Scots, 3
Dunmore, Lord John, 349

Earl, William, 179
Easton, Pa., 155, 158-159, 164, 168, 169, 195
East River, 29, 355
Eaton, Joshua, 296
Eleventh Pennsylvania Regiment, 155, 169
Elizabethtown (Elizabeth), 61, 209
Ellett, David, 299, 379
Elsinboro, 289
Emerson, Ralph Waldo, 1
Emes, Worley, 41
English Graveyard of Carlisle, 323-324
Englishtown, 117, 119
Erwin, Joseph, 265
Ewald, Johann, 57
Ewing, James, 39, 40

Fallen Timbers, 303; battle of, 316-317, 328, 363, 380
Farmer's Brother, 148, 159, 203, 266
Fennel, Daniel, 63
Finley, John, 261
Finn's Point, 285
First Continental Congress, 6, 355
Fish Carrier, 148, 188, 203

Fishing Creek, 154, 297
Fitzpatrick, John, 157
flogging, 95-96, 359
Flying Camp, 4, 22, 27, 274
Fogg, Elijah, 298
Fogg, Jeremiah, 178
Forbes, John, 221, 371
Ford, Jacob, 209
Forrest, Thomas, 41-42, 52, 55, 56, 174, 177, 179
Forts: Ann, 351; Armstrong, 197, 223; Augusta, 160, 161, 354; Boone, 162; Constitution, 33; Crawford, 197, 223; Crown Point, 6, 11, 20; Cumberland, 219-220; Duquesne, 220, 221, 371; Freeland, 159-164; Griswold, 364; Harmar, 381; Henry, 205, 228, 234, 238, 241, 246, 258, 266, 310; Island (Mud Island), 42, 47, 60, 285; Jefferson, 312; Jenkins, 148, 149, 152; Lee, 25, 32-33; Laurens, 223, 245, 372; Le Boeuf, 219; McIntosh, 197, 223, 245, 256, 261, 282; Muncy, 155, 160; Nelson, 238; Niagara, 163, 224, 317; Nonsense, 208; Pitt, 140, 157, 196, 197, 202, 205, 207, 211-215, 220-225, 227, 228, 230, 231, 232, 233, 235, 238, 240, 241, 244, 245, 248-250, 252, 256, 259-263, 265, 267-272, 274, 277-280, 282, 289, 295, 303, 354, 375-377; Recovery, 311; Stanwix, 59-60, 274, 281-282, 305, 351, 356; Sullivan, 176; Ticonderoga, 6, 7, 9, 10, 13, 19, 20, 59, 60, 99, 121, 134, 349, 363, 382; Washington, 25, 27, 30, 32-33, 39, 60, 66, 291, 321, 352; Wintermoot, 148-153, 167, 168; Forty Fort, 148, 150, 152, 164, 167
4th Continental Artillery, 41, 47, 56, 60, 77, 100, 116, 127, 137, 138, 147, 153, 164, 207, 208, 209, 214, 215, 235, 245, 250, 329, 364
Fox Indians, 315, 316
Franklin, Benjamin, 5, 12, 25, 35-37,

Index

74, 80, 93, 111, 115, 128, 130, 163, 271, 273, 304, 327-328, 350, 354, 355, 361, 383
Franklin, John, 151
Frederick the Great, 92, 99, 364
Freehold Village (Monmouth Court House), 117, 322
French Alliance, see Alliance with France
French and Indian War (Seven Years' War), 8, 15, 25, 39, 142, 221, 245, 304-305, 306, 310, 350, 354, 356, 362, 368, 377, 380
French Canadians, 12
French Creek, 198

Gage, Thomas, 3, 6, 7, 8, 21, 23
Gates, Horatio, 60, 79-80, 81-84, 107, 131, 157, 173, 208, 225-226, 328, 361, 369, 372, 381
Genesee Castle (Genishau), 188, 191, 193-194
Genesee River, 140-141, 155, 188, 190, 198, 200, 202
Gerard, Conrad Alexander, 128
German Flats, 140
Germantown, 19, 72, 74; battle of, 75-82; 83, 88, 93, 95, 99, 100, 101, 106, 111, 127, 157, 158, 177, 211, 235, 280, 331, 334, 353, 354, 358, 360, 362, 363, 364, 365, 368, 379, 380
Gettysburg, 159, 214, 222
Gibson, John, 230, 259
Gilpin, Gideon, 65
Girty, George, 257, 376
Girty, James, 236, 376
Girty, Simon, 254, 266, 268, 375, 377
Girty, Thomas, 376
Gist, Christopher, 219-220, 221, 371
Glover, John, 29, 40, 104
Gnadenhuetten, massacre, 246-252; 258, 291
Gore, Obadiah, 183-184
Grand Alliance Ball, 210
Grand River, 270, 302, 380
Grand Union Flag, 20, 21, 351

Grasse, Francois Joseph Paul, comte de, 241-242
Graymont, Barbara, 149
Great Egg Harbor, 156
Great Falls (Louisville), 230, 231, 234, 238, 239, 244, 262
Great Island, 163
Great Meadows, 306
Great Road (Forbes Road), 214, 221
Great Runaway, 155, 163
Great Swamp, 165
Great Tree, 187, 282
Greene, Nathanael, 28, 30, 33, 40, 43, 69, 75, 78-79, 80, 83, 88, 93-94, 96, 102, 104, 118, 121, 208, 230, 287, 327, 360, 361, 372, 382
Grey, Charles, 71, 76, 85, 358
Greyhound, the, 4
Gridley, Richard, 48
Griffin, Edmund D., 146
Groveland, N.Y., 188, 190
Guilford Courthouse, 243
Gulph Mill, 88-89, 360
Guyasuta, see Kyashota

Haldimand, Sir Frederick, 302
Half-Town, 148, 282
Halifax, 10
Hamilton, Alexander, 40, 101, 118, 120, 122-125, 136, 300, 315, 328, 353, 363
Hancock House, 283, 284; massacre, 289-291; 294, 362-379
Hancock, Judge William, 290
Hancock's Bridge, 109, 284, 286, 289, 292, 362
Hancock's Village, 290
Hand, Edward, 43, 157, 164, 169, 174, 176, 178; at Newtown, 179-185; 223, 353, 368, 375, 379
Hand, Elijah, 286, 288, 291-293, 294
Handsome Lake, 148, 159, 203
Hannastown, 234, 244; the burning of, 263-267; 376-377
Hanover, 61
Hanson, John, 356
Harding, John, 148

Harding massacre, 148
Harlem Heights, 25, 30, 41, 96, 353
Harlem River, 27
Harmar, Josiah, 311, 316, 381
Harris: Abraham, Jr., 4, 22, 283, 288, 289, 299, 352, 353; Abraham, Sr., 3, 22, 351; Amos, 296, 380; Benjamin, 15, 296, 297, 318; Beulah, 299; Clarissa, 299, 318, 380; Elizabeth, 318, 382; Isaac, 283, 284, 288, 289, 299, 352, 353, 379, 380, 383; Jacob, 4, 283, 284, 288, 289, 298, 299, 352, 353, 380; John, 1, 3, 4, 14, 21-22, 27, 28, 29, 30, 31, 36, 38, 41, 47, 49, 51, 52, 55, 56, 58, 63, 64; at Brandywine, 65-71; 73; at Germantown, 77-79; 82, 83; at Valley Forge, 87-114; 127, 130, 153, 154, 164, 165, 167, 171; on Sullivan expedition, 172-191; 200, 203, 207, 209, 211-214; journey to Fort Pitt, 214-225; 226, 228; with George Rogers Clark, 233-241; 242, 244, 249, 250, 262, 270, 274-275; discharged at Fort Pitt, 278-282; in Salem after the war, 283-318; 319, 330, 350, 353, 356, 363, 364, 368, 377, 379, 380-384; Lydia Smith, 296-299, 318, 337, 383; Margaret, 299, 318; Nicholas, 283, 289, 295, 300, 352; Parmenas, 283, 298; Peter, 282, 318, 383; Samuel, 3; Sarah, 295; Stretch, 296, 297, 299, 318, 380-381; Thomas, 2; Zerviah (Sophia), 1-2, 112, 283, 299, 351
Harrison, Benjamin, 350
Harrison, Charles, 48
Harrison, William, 253
Hartley, Thomas, 155-156, 187, 216, 350
Hartsville, 62
Havard, Samuel, 93
Hays, John Casper, 48, 322
Hays, John Ludwig, 323
Hays, Molly Ludwig (Molly Pitcher), 19, 123, 321-325, 352, 363
Headley, Joel Tyler, 171-173
Head of Elk, 62-64
Heckewelder, John, 246
Hector, Edward, 68
Heister, Leopold Philipp, von, 29
Henry, Patrick, 5, 106, 230, 328
Herkimer, Nicholas, 59-60, 356
Heth, Henry, 233
Hiester, Joseph, 323
Hiokatoo, 148, 159, 161, 162, 193
Hobson's Choice, 314
Holme, Benjamin, 283, 286, 288, 291, 294
Holme, John, 287
Hood, Rachel, 3
Hood, Robert, 3
Hood, Thomas, 277
Hope Creek, 297
Hopkinson, Francis, 351
Hovendon, Richard, 109
Howe, Sir Richard, 24-25, 36-37, 57
Howe, Sir William, 7, 8, 9, 21; battle of New York, 23-36; 38, 53, 60, 62-63; at Brandywine, 64-70; 71, 74, 75, 76, 80, 82, 84, 85, 86, 102, 107, 108, 109, 111-113, 126-128, 133, 135, 329, 362
Hubbardton, 349
Hubley, Adam, 169, 173
Hudson River, 23, 25-26, 32-33, 58, 137, 333, 368
Huffnagle, Michael, 263
Hunt, John, 117
Hunter, Samuel, 160
Huzzars, 286

Intolerable Acts, 6
Iroquois League (Six Nations), 139-140, 141-144, 160, 166, 196-202, 281, 302, 305, 314-315
Irvine, James, 84, 86, 134, 233, 360
Irvine, William, in Quebec, 14-18; 19, 61; at Monmouth, 118-120; at Fort Pitt, 240-275; 277, 278-280, 323, 351, 353, 354, 356, 360, 364, 365, 376, 377, 378, 382

Index 391

"Irvine's Reserve," 278
Irving, Washington, 312
Isaac Potts House, 93, 112

Jack, Captain Matthew, 263
Jacquese's Furnace, 218
Jay, John, 196, 271, 273
Jefferson, Thomas, 196, 227-233, 304, 315, 329, 364, 365, 381
Jemison, Mary, 159, 161-162, 192, 204, 369
Jenkins, John, 157
Jersey, the, 32-33, 287
Jockey Hollow, 208
Johnson, Nicholas, 3
Johnson, Sarah, 3
Johnson, Sir John, 204
Johnson, Sir William, 140, 142, 305, 365
Jones, John Paul, 351
Joseph Brant Memorial Hospital, 302

Kalb, Johann (Baron De Kalb), 19, 80-83, 88, 90-92, 96, 101, 113, 208; at Camden, 225-226; 327, 330, 372
Kanadaseaga, 187
Kanawha River, 234, 236, 310, 349
Kaskaskia, 231
Kendaia, 187
Kennebec River, 10
King George III, 2, 12, 21, 34, 41, 74, 126, 132, 139, 141, 142, 167, 269, 270, 302, 304, 329, 333, 350, 353
King George Proclamation of 1763, 304, 306, 310
King Henry I, 3
King John, 3
Kings Mountain, 243
Kinzua Dam, 301
Kips Bay, 30, 363
Kiskiminetas River, 266
Kittanning, 75, 196, 197, 354, 380
Knight, Dr. John, his miraculous escape 252-259; 376
Knox, Henry, 20, 26-27, 29, 40, 43, 46, 48, 54, 55-56, 58, 62, 63, 70, 79, 80, 81, 83, 93, 94, 99-101, 102, 111, 114, 116-119, 121, 125, 129, 133, 135, 136, 209-211, 243, 300, 311, 313, 314, 315, 328, 349, 351, 364
Knox, Lucy, 29, 63, 70, 81, 99, 118, 129, 135, 210
Knox, William, 20, 116, 129
Knyphausen, Wilhelm, 32, 65-68, 130, 364
Kyashota (Guyasuta), 140, 143, 266

Lacy, John Jr., 108-110
Lafayette, Marquis de, 19, 64, 66, 69, 80; at Valley Forge, 88-114; 118, 123, 124, 226, 241, 243, 244, 304; Lafayette's return, 327-332; 357, 362, 373
Lake Champlain, 6, 12, 19, 21, 28
Lake Ontario, 59
Lake Otsego, 177, 368
Lake Seneca, 187, 188
Lamb, John, 48
Lancaster, Pa., 70, 74, 146, 207
Langdon, Samuel, 8
Langley, Esther, 3
Laurel Hill, 27, 214
Laurens, Henry, 91, 119, 223, 360
Laurens, John, 78, 83, 120, 304
Lear, Tobias, 312
Learned, Ebenezer, 131
Lee, Charles, 12, 25, 33, 56, 118-124
Legion Ville, 314
Lenape, 64
Leslie, William, 53-54
Lewis, Andrew, 349
Lexington and Concord, 2, 3, 4, 6, 20, 26, 115, 136, 139, 200, 245, 272, 349, 364
Liberty Bell, 70, 357
Lichtenau, 228
Licking Creek, 218
Licking River, 268-269
Lincoln, Benjamin, 56-57, 131, 262, 266, 356
Little Beard, 148, 159, 164, 188, 191-194, 197, 203, 369

Little Conococheague Creek, 215
Little Egg Harbor, 156
Little Turtle (Michikinkna), 303, 311-316, 382
Little Tymochtee Creek, 253
Livingston, James, 10
Livingston, William, 363
Lochry, Archibald, massacre on the Ohio, 229-240; 260
Lock Haven, Pa., 163
Longfellow, Henry Wadsworth, 6
Long Island, battle of, 25-43; 104, 122, 135, 157, 196, 235, 280, 283, 287, 353, 359, 360, 362, 365
Ludwig, John George, 321
Lycoming Creek, 154-156, 160
Lynch, Thomas, 350-351
Lyndell, 64

Macbeth, 3
Macdonald, Peter, 54
Maclay, William, 160, 163
Madison, James, 41, 44
Magaw, Robert, 30, 32, 33, 288, 291, 352
Mahoning, 197, 299
Malcolm, King of Scots, 3
Manatawney (Ridge) Road, 84
Marcus Hook, 285
Marshall, John, 41, 357
matross, 28, 50, 51, 78, 95, 234
Maumee River, 303
Mawhood, Charles, 285; occupation of Salem, 286-293; 333
Maxwell, William, 16, 17, 65, 67, 69, 70, 71, 76, 164, 167, 170, 174, 181
McAllister's, 214
McCauley, George, 323
McCleester, Polly, 324
McConkey's Ferry Inn, 39
McDonald, John, 159, 161, 162, 163, 178
McGary, Hugh, 268
McIntosh, Lachlan, 223, 245
McKee, Alexander, 268
McKnight, James, 160

McLane, Allen, 84, 85
McMullen, William, 78
McNeill, Samuel, 179, 201, 368
McPherson, Captain J., 11
Meadville, Pa., 330
Mercer County, Pa., 281
Mercer, Hugh, 43, 44, 46, 54, 353, 354, 364
Mercer Oak, 354
Metuchen Hill, 75
Miami Indians, 304, 305, 311, 312, 313, 315, 316, 382
Miami River, 235, 236, 237, 240
Michikinkna, see Little Turtle
Middlebrook, 56, 58, 351, 356
Mifflin, Thomas, 54, 106, 355-356, 361, 381
Miller's Fort (Miller's Station), 265
Miller's Run, 308
Mill Hollow, 287, 351
Mingo Bottom, 246, 251, 252
Mingo Indians, 256, 303, 374
Mogulbughtiton Creek, 281
Mohawk, John, 152
Mohawk River, 59, 141, 158, 203, 204, 302, 368
Mohawk Valley, 140, 203, 205, 310
Monckton, Robert, 125
Monmouth, 19, 21, 48, 116; battle of, 117-126; 127, 129, 147, 245, 321-325, 329, 331, 353, 354, 360, 361, 362-365, 369
Monongahela River, 220, 224, 233, 280-281, 306
Monroe, James, 41, 327, 329, 353, 359
Montgomery, Richard, 9-12, 14, 19, 69, 122, 350, 364, 381
Montour, Catherine, 187
Montreal, 10, 13, 14, 58, 60, 237, 349
Moore, William, 240, 249, 259, 262
Moor's Charity School, 142
Morgan, Daniel, 11, 84, 85, 86, 181
Morris, Robert, 351
Morristown, 45, 46, 52, 54-56, 136, 156, 191, 208-212, 363, 368, 370, 382
Moultrie, William, 21

Mount Airy, 76
Mount Pleasant, 220
Mount Vernon, 303, 310, 327
Mount Washington, 32
Muhlenberg, Henry M., 361
Muhlenberg, John Peter Gabriel, 104, 361
Muncy Indians, 198, 199, 263
Muse, George, 309
Musgrave, Thomas, 76, 77, 334
Muskingum River, 228, 270, 381

Nash, Francis, 58, 60, 62, 63, 76, 79
Nassau Hall, 44, 353
Nelson, Thomas, 238
Nesbitt, John Maxwell, 129
Neshamini, 62
Newburgh, N.Y., 260, 272, 377
Newtown, battle of, 178-188; 200, 280
New York City, battle of, 23-34
Nicollet (Nicolet), 15
"night of darkness," 260
North Castle, 31
Northumberland County, Pa., 145, 154, 155, 188, 193, 202
Nova Scotia, 21, 25, 27

Ogden, Matthias, 61-62, 182
Ohio Company, 218-219
Ohio River, 141, 142, 207-241, 245, 251-252, 256, 258, 269, 274, 280-281, 297, 303, 304-305, 308, 310, 311, 313, 314, 315, 349, 371, 374, 377, 381
Old Flint's, 218
Old Smoke (Sayenqueraghta), 143, 145, 154, 164, 178, 188, 203, 205, 246
Old Town (Oldtown), 218-219, 371
Olentangy, 252
Oneida Indians, 59, 142, 145, 158, 369
Onondaga Indians, 148, 178
Oriskany, 59-60, 147, 205
Oswald, Eleazer, 121
Oswego (Ontario), 140; council at, 142-143; 147, 317
Ottawa Indians, 303, 315, 316
Oxford University, 37

Padgett, Rebecca, 299
Paine, Robert Treat, 349
Paine, Thomas, 23, 30, 93, 112, 328
Paoli Massacre, 71-74, 76, 111, 122, 313, 334, 342, 358
Parker, Michael, 188-195
Parker, Robert, 183, 185, 186, 195
Passaic River, 52
Paulding, John, 364
Paulin (Pacelin), William, 299
Pauling's Settlement, 215, 218
Pearl, the frigate, 18, 27, 285
Pelham Manor, 76
Penn House, 133
Pennsylvania Council of Safety, 47, 55, 56, 58, 88
Pennsylvania Gazette, 146
Pennypacker's Mill, 74, 79
Pensell, Henry, 168
Pensell, John, 168
Pentecost, Dorsey, 229
Perkiomen, 74, 103
Perth Amboy, 58
Peters, Richard, 129
Peterson, Reverend Peter, 296
Philadelphia, 2, 6, 13, 22, 30, 36, 39, 40, 47, 52, 53, 54, 56, 60, 62, 63, 64, 68, 70, 71, 72, 74, 75, 80, 82, 83, 84, 85, 86, 88, 91, 95, 102, 107, 108, 109, 112, 115, 116, 117, 120, 126; restoration of, 127-140; 147, 155, 160, 211, 230, 233, 235, 259, 280, 282, 285, 287, 300, 312, 314, 317, 322, 324, 327, 330, 331, 334, 352, 353, 354, 355, 358, 359, 362, 364, 367, 377, 381, 382, 383
Philips, John, 261
Pickering, Timothy, 146, 212, 371
Pimoacan (Chief Pipe), 253
Pitcher, Molly, see Hays, Molly
Pittsburg(h), 158, 179, 195, 197, 207, 213, 221, 224, 225, 227, 228, 229, 231, 233, 234, 235, 239, 241, 246,

247, 256, 258, 260, 261, 274, 277, 278, 280, 281, 308, 313, 314, 330, 375, 376, 380, 382
Plainfield, 57
Plains of Abraham, 8, 9
Pluckemin, 52, 53, 54, 211, 368
Pointe du Lac, 15
Point-no-Point Road, 120
Point Pleasant, Va., 310, 349
Pontiac's Rebellion, 142
Poor, Enoch, 119, 164, 174; at Newtown, 179-185, 350
Porter, Andrew, 79, 83, 97, 177, 359, 360, 368
Porter, Lady Elizabeth, 97, 98
Potomac River, 215, 216, 217, 218, 219, 220, 353
Potawatami Indians, 315, 316
Pott's Grove, 74
Prescott, Richard, 352
Prescott, Robert, 10
Prescott, William, 8, 26, 350
Prince of Wales, the, 18
Princeton, 19, 37, 42; battle of, 43-47; 52, 53, 54, 56, 80, 99, 127, 157, 211, 285, 353, 354, 355, 365, 368
Proclamation of Cessation of Hostilities, 271
Proctor, Francis, 47
Proctor, Thomas, 41, 42, 44, 47, 48, 52, 55-58, 60; at Brandywine, 62-79; 95, 97, 100, 107, 113, 115, 116, 127, 137, 156, 158, 159, 164; on Sullivan expedition, 166-200; 208, 209, 211, 212, 214, 225, 245, 260, 274, 314, 323, 354, 355, 358, 363-364, 368, 369, 370
Prospect Hill, 20
Providence, R.I., 24, 273, 330, 367
Putnam, Israel, 7, 8, 25, 350, 351

Quebec, 8, 9, 10, 11, 12, 13, 14, 15, 20, 22, 69, 121, 122, 131, 134, 155, 193, 245, 350, 364, 382
Quebec Act of 1774, 12
Quebec City, 10; battle of, 11, 19; 131, 134, 369

Queen Esther, 150, 151, 153, 155, 166, 187
Queen's Rangers, 67, 70, 84, 109, 127, 268, 285-287, 378
Quincy, Josiah, 349
Quinton, N.J., 293, 294
Quinton's Bridge, 3, 214, 283-291, 293, 294, 296, 300, 378

Ragged Island, 298-300
Rall (Rahl), Johann Gottlieb, 39-41, 352, 353
Randolph, Edmund, 315
Raritan River, 56, 58
Red Jacket, 143, 144, 148, 149, 186, 187, 203
Reed, Joseph, 39, 85, 88, 134, 160, 197, 224, 352, 359, 365
Reedy Island, 285
Revere, Paul, 5, 6
Ring, Benjamin, 64
Ritter, William, 77, 95
Roberts, Cokie, 322
Rochambeau, Jean Baptiste, comte de, 242, 243
Roebuck, the, 285, 333
Rogers, Reverend William, 164-167, 175, 367
Roosevelt, Theodore, 380
Rose, John (Henri Gustave Rosenthal), 251, 252, 270, 271, 375
Ross, Elizabeth ("Betsy") Griscom, 20, 30, 58, 351, 356
Ross, George, 351
Round Island, 296-300, 380
Royal Pennsylvania Gazette, 109, 111, 362
Rush, Dr. Benjamin, 36, 53-54, 106, 128-129, 328, 335, 353, 355, 361, 364, 381
Rush Meadow Creek, 175
Rutledge, Edward, 37

Sac Indians, 315, 316
Sagwarithra, 148, 188, 203
St. Clair, Arthur, 15, 16, 43, 208, 232, 311-312, 316, 356, 382

Index 395

St. John's, 10
St. Lawrence River, 9, 13, 14, 15, 19
St. Leger, Barry, 46, 59-60
St. Maurice River, 14
Salem Creek, 285, 289
Salem, Indian village, 246
Salem, N.J., 2, 3, 4, 21, 31, 38, 47, 55, 77, 104, 112, 175, 214, 275, 278, 280, 282-300, 309, 318, 333, 352, 355, 362, 367, 378-379, 381
Salem Sunbeam, 286
Salmon, John, 188-191
Salter, Annie, 3
Sandusky Campaign, 231, 250-253, 260
Sandy Hook, 18, 119
Saratoga Springs, 60, 81, 82, 83, 131, 173, 364
Savannah, 225, 243, 356
Schoenbrun, 246
Schoharie Expedition, 147, 204
Schoharie Valley, 147
Schuyler, Philip, 9, 12, 382
Schuylkill River, 47, 71, 82, 88, 89, 102-103, 108, 132
Schweitzer, Otto J., 324
Scioto River, 231
Scott, Charles, 119-120
Scovell, Elisha, 148
Seaver, James, 188, 369
Second Continental Congress, 6, 20, 22, 381
Second Pennsylvania Brigade, 245
Seneca Indians, 140-148, 152, 156, 158, 159, 178, 186, 187, 192, 195, 197, 199, 202-205, 227, 249, 266, 267, 282, 300, 305, 314-316, 369, 374, 382
Seneca Lake, 188
Seventh Pennsylvania Regiment, 19, 322, 359
Seven Years' War, see French and Indian War
Seward, Thomas, 121
"Shades of Death," 165
Shaw, Margaret ("Peggy"), 265
Shawnee (Shawanese) Indians, 154, 159, 224, 231, 236, 254, 268, 269, 303, 304, 305, 312, 315-316, 349
Sheppard, Sarah, 300
Shippen, Judge Edward, 136
Shippen, Margaret ("Peggy"), 135-136
Shippensburg, Pa., 215, 371
Shirley, William, 220
Shreve, Israel, 167, 176
Sideling Hill Creek, 218
Simcoe, John Graves, 70, 84, 86, 109, 110, 127, 285; at Hancock House, 289-290; 378, 379
Simpson, Michael, 188, 193
Sixth Pennsylvania Regiment, 15
Skippack Road, 75, 84
Slocum, Giles, 168
Slover, John, his miraculous escape, 256-259, 308
Smallwood, William, 61, 73
Smith, Hannah, 296
Smith, Matthew, 160, 193
Smith, Peter, 294
Smith, William, 283; at Quinton's Bridge, 286-294; 295, 296, 352, 379
Smith's Clove, 58
Smith, Washington, 294
Somerset, 36, 46
Sons of Liberty, 5
Sorel, 15
Spahr, Peter, 324
Spotswood, 119
Stacy Potts House, 39
Stamp Act, 4, 5, 12
Standing Stone, 154, 175, 176
Stark, John, 349
Staten Island, 18, 24, 27, 37, 58, 61, 62, 101, 102, 158, 209
Steed, Thomas, 261
Stephen, Adam, 78
Steuben, Friedrich Wilhelm, Baron von, 92, 94, 98, 99, 114, 117, 118, 241, 327
Stewart, Frank, 293, 378
Stirn, Johann, 67
Stony Point, 169, 363
Storey, Samuel, 211

Strobagh, John, 42, 52
Stryker, William Scudder, 124, 325, 352, 363
Stump the Indian Killer, 154
Sullivan Expedition, 155-203, 204, 205, 207, 211-212, 216, 217, 223, 224, 229, 253, 280, 303, 354, 369, 370, 371
Sullivan Island, 21
Sullivan, John, 13, 14, 28, 29, 36, 37, 39, 40, 43, 54, 55, 61, 62, 68, 73, 75, 76, 78, 83; at Valley Forge, 101-104; 155; on Susquehanna Expedition, 156-203, 215, 245, 328, 351, 353, 359
Sullivan, Thomas, 73
Supreme Executive Council of Pennsylvania, 110, 133-134, 155, 160,, 212, 355, 359, 361
Susquehanna River, 139, 145, 152, 154, 155, 156, 158, 159, 163, 167, 168, 171, 173, 176, 177, 178, 191, 195, 199, 229, 231, 235, 297, 305, 367, 376
Swamp Fox (Francis Marion), 225

Tappan (Baylor) massacre, 358, 364
Telenemut (Thomas Hudson), 187
Ten Crucial Days, 46
The Cedars, battle of, 12-14; 19
Thomas, John, 12, 14, 19, 350
Thompson, Andrew, 235
Thompson's Bridge, 284
Thompson, William, 14-19, 61, 350
Three Rivers (Trois Rivieres), battle of, 14, 15, 19, 43, 61, 155
Tioga (Tioga Point), 150, 155, 172, 176, 177, 178, 186, 191, 195, 197, 200, 201, 368
Todd, John, 268
Towamencin, 79
Townshend Acts, 5, 6
Townshend, Charles, 5
Treaty of Alliance with France, see Alliance with France
Treaty of Greenville, 316, 317, 328, 382

Treaty of Paris, 269, 271-274, 304
Tredyffrin, 71
Trenton, 19, 21, 37; battle of, 39-43; 44, 45, 46, 47, 52, 53, 58, 60, 70, 80, 93, 104, 127, 177, 209, 211, 250, 321, 322, 354, 365, 382
Trigg, Stephen, 268
Tuscarawas River, 223, 228, 244, 246, 256
Tuscarora Indians, 142, 145, 203
Tutelu, 254-257
Tweedy, Thomas, 183-184

Utica, N.Y., 59

Valley Creek, 93
Valley Forge, 19, 51, 87-113, 115, 116, 118, 122, 127, 131-135, 196, 208, 225, 227, 235, 241, 280, 283, 284, 285, 289, 296, 300, 322, 327, 328, 329, 331, 353, 360, 361, 363, 368, 372, 378
Van Horne House, 57
Van Wert, Isaac, 364
Varnum, James Mitchell, 96
Vincennes, 231, 328

Wabash River, 238, 311
Wachatomakak, 256
Wadsworth House, 8
Wait, Jason, 178
Walker, Reverend J. G., 87
Walthour's, 221, 372
Warner, Seth, 7, 349
Warren, Joseph, 7-8
Warrior's Run, 159, 162
Warriors' Trail, 218
Washington, George, named Commander-in-Chief, 7; 8, 9, 12, 13, 19, 20, 21; battle of New York, 23-34; battle of Trenton and Princeton, 35-46; 47, 48, 50; at Morristown, 52-62; battle of Brandywine, 63-70, 71, 74; at Germantown, 75-80; 81-83; at Whitemarsh, 84-86; at Valley Forge, 87-114; at Monmouth, 115-

126; 127, 132, 133-137, 141, 145-147, 155-158, 167, 177, 181, 186, 193, 196, 197, 199, 207, 208-215, 219-224, 227-233, 241; at Yorktown, 242-244; 245, 246, 249, 250-252, 259-262, 266, 267, 270, 272, 274, 279, 282, 284, 285, 289, 291, 294, 296, 300; on slavery, 303-304; attitude toward Indians, 304; passion for land, 305-310; Ohio Indians, 310-317; 318, 323, 328, 329-331, 352, 354, 355, 357, 359, 362, 363, 364, 366, 369, 372, 373, 375, 378, 381, 382, 383
Washington, John, 307
Washington, Martha, 97, 99
Washington, Mary, 354
Washington, Samuel, 307
Washington, William, 41
Washington's Run, 306
Washingtonville, Pa., 193, 369
Wayne, Anthony, 14, 15, 18, 51, 63, 65; at Brandywine, 67-71; at Paoli, 71-74; 76; at Germantown, 78-80; 83, 88, 104, 108, 111, 118; at Monmouth, 122; 169, 241, 283, 284; at Fallen Timbers, 303, 313-316; 317, 329, 359, 364, 379, 382
Weatherby, Benjamin, 287-289
Weehawken, N.J., 328
West Chester, Pa., 64, 331
Westmoreland County, Pa., 196, 197, 221, 223, 224, 230, 231, 233, 236, 237, 240, 249, 250, 252, 260, 263, 272, 374
West Point, 137, 364, 377
Wheeling, Va., 205, 234, 239, 246, 272, 310
White Horse, 73
Whitemarsh, 83; battle of, 86-88; 126, 280, 368
White Plains, 25, 30-31, 39, 41, 66, 96, 156, 280, 283, 287, 318, 353, 356, 364
Wick Farm, 208
Widow Meyers' Wayside Inn, 221

Wigenund, 253
Williams, Ben, 144
Williams, David, 364
Williams, Otho, 215
Williamson, David, 246-251, 252
Williamsport, Pa., 145, 163
Wills Creek, 219
Wilmington, Del., 62, 63, 64, 88
Wolfe, James, 8, 9, 382
Woodhull, Nathaniel, 29
Wyalusing, 155, 163, 175
Wyandot Indians, 224, 250, 272, 281, 303, 304, 315, 316, 375
Wyoming, 139, 145; massacre, 146-153; 154, 155, 156, 157, 159, 161, 163, 164, 165, 166, 168, 169, 171, 173, 181, 187, 191, 195, 196, 199, 200, 201, 203, 205, 250, 291

Yahrungwago, 198
York, Pa., 70, 107
Yorktown, 21, 34, 48, 121, 241; battle of, 242-244; 269, 273, 284, 328, 331, 355, 356, 361
Youghiogeny River, 220, 229, 230, 306, 307, 374, 381
Young, Mary, 299

Zion Reformed Church, Allentown, 70

www.ingramcontent.com/pod-product-compliance
Lightning Source LLC
Chambersburg PA
CBHW070058020526
44112CB00034B/1437